There are few leaders who have the integ
years of experience shaping leaders as Dr.
student, his writings were already helping to shape my understanding of a biblical church. Once again, utilizing the lenses of Scripture, History, and Culture, Gene carefully examines the unique mission and focus of the church as Jesus intended it to be. I highly recommend this completely updated *Sharpening the Focus of the Church*. It may revolutionize your understanding of the most powerful organism God designed to accomplish His purposes on earth.

MARK JOBE, President, Moody Bible Institute

Gene Getz has given his life to serve the church and has poured that rich experience into this book, filled with examples, wisdom, and, above all, biblical roots. Distinguishing form from function is a key focus, but even more than that is sorting out what is cultural from what is transcultural. *Sharpening the Focus* sorts out those differences well and illustrates them repeatedly. After fifty years of serving churches, the author has given this important book new life in this reworked form.

DARRELL L. BOCK, Executive Director for Cultural Engagement at the Hendricks Center and Senior Research Professor of New Testament Studies at Dallas Theological Seminary

The original *Sharpening* launched many of us on a movement of doing church biblically and effectively for an always changing culture. In a full rewrite, Gene once again serves as a reliable and much needed guide for the challenges and opportunities facing the church today. You will find the new *Sharpening* to be biblically rich, historically insightful, culturally astute, and surprisingly comprehensive. As Gene's pastoral successor, I'm excited about helping our current leaders to take a fresh look at the enduring truths that should guide us in doing church.

JEFF JONES, Lead Pastor, Chase Oaks Church

For over forty years, BEE World has provided a course based on Dr. Gene Getz's original book *Sharpening the Focus of the Church*. This outreach began behind the Iron Curtain and eventually expanded to over sixty other countries. Over 100,000 pastors and church leaders have used this text. And now Gene has completely updated this book! I unreservedly endorse its timeless and cross-cultural truths.

JOSEPH DILLOW, Th.D., Founder of BEE World

As a young pastor in an unreached area of Romania, I was invited to study a course using *Sharpening the Focus of the Church*. This experience laid the foundation for a biblical philosophy of ministry for almost thirty years. Since then, I have taught these biblical principles in my local church, shared them with fellow pastors locally and nationally, and with my students from the Baptist Theological Institute of Bucharest.

This new and expanded edition will continue to impact churches throughout Romania and other European countries.

DANIEL FODOREAN, Associate Professor and Academic Dean at Baptist Theological Institute of Bucharest, Romania

It's no secret that the world has dramatically changed since 1974, when my seminary professor, Gene Getz, published his impactful first edition of *Sharpening the Focus of the Church.* The cultural issues are different now, but the fundamental principles of a biblical view of the church and its strategic role in society have not changed. Our challenge is to adjust the application of these principles to be empowered as church leaders to effectively impact a changed world while staying in the lane of biblical truth. When I think of this new edition of *Sharpening the Focus of the Church,* words like wise, intune, relevant, insightful, practical, and stimulating come to mind.

JOE STOWELL, former president of Moody Bible Institute and Cornerstone University

Reading and watching Gene Getz is always a fresh exposure to the Word of God and the profound wisdom that comes from a lifetime and commitment to ministry shaped by the Scriptures. This book shows how timeless are the biblical principles and how relevant they are for contemporary application. I had the unique privilege to pastor one of the churches Gene helped plant, and the foundation laid proved to be a great blessing. May this completely updated edition further sharpen the focus of the church as Jesus Christ meant it to be.

MARK L. BAILEY, Chancellor and Sr. Professor of Bible Exposition, Dallas Theological Seminary

The original edition of this book transformed a generation of pastors. I was one of them, sent out by Gene Getz and the elders at Fellowship Bible Church North to plant a new church. Now enriched with fifty years of hard-won practical wisdom, Gene's complete rewrite of *Sharpening the Focus of the Church* will open your eyes to enduring biblical truth applied to current issues, including racism and sexuality. When he shares what he would do differently, he proves inspiring and surprising. Read this book with your leadership team.

BRUCE B. MILLER, Senior Pastor, Christ Fellowship

When I became a student at Dallas Theological Seminary, three encounters shaped my future life and ministry. First, Gene Getz became an amazing teacher, mentor, pastor and friend. Second, I read his *Sharpening the Focus of the Church,* and it changed my distorted view of the church. And finally, I saw the application of biblical principles in real time when I became a part of the ministry team at the first Fellowship Bible Church. This new version is filled with more biblical insights, lessons learned, and practical applications. I urge you to read *Sharpening the Focus of the Church* and use the QR codes to listen to Gene as he teaches and shares insights from his pastoral journey.

DAVE KRUEGER, Former VP Search Ministries, Former PGA Tour Chaplain

The initial edition of *Sharpening the Focus of the Church* had a profound influence on my life and caused a veritable paradigm shift in the way I approached ministry in Japan. Taking God at His Word and letting culture have its proper place and influence without letting it change the biblical focus of the church seeped into my mind and heart and helped me to differentiate between essential and nonessential elements as I led teams in successful church planting and renewal. This new and updated edition of *Sharpening the Focus of the Church* is a must-read for worldwide church leaders, just as a level or a plumb line is indispensable in the tool chest of a carpenter.

JON JUNKER, second generation TEAM missionary in Japan

I remember well those days in the early '70s as I sat in the classes Gene Getz describes in the introductory chapters in this new edition of *Sharpening the Focus of the Church*. They were life-changing hours spent searching Scripture, considering our mission in life, and making significant decisions that altered the course of our service for God. The simple concept of evaluating life and ministry through the lenses of Scripture, History, and Culture has been profound. It has impacted what my wife and I have done over the past fifty years across eastern Europe and now worldwide with Global Church Movements.

EDWARD MURRAY, Emeritus Professor, Global Academy for Transformational Leadership

In my early twenties (fifty years ago!) I read *Sharpening the Focus of the Church*. That book had a foundational, profound, transformative impact on my thinking about the nature of the church and how it should function. The churches I have helped to plant and the church that I served as pastor for fifteen years—Fellowship Bible Church, Roswell, GA—have been shaped by the biblical principles and insights found in this treasured resource. That's why I am thrilled that Gene Getz has done this new and updated version of *Sharpening the Focus of the Church*. What a strategic, encouraging gift this is to the body of Christ!

CRAWFORD W. LORITTS JR., author, speaker, radio host, president, Beyond Our Generation

It was like living in the book of Acts! The most fruitful years ever of evangelizing our neighbors occurred when we joined the staff at the original Fellowship Bible Church. We saw believers living out the principles in the first edition of *Sharpening the Focus of the Church*. We had freedom and motivation to win our neighbors to Christ as never before! Whole families became believers and formed the foundation for another Fellowship Church in our own neighborhood! We can only imagine the impact this new and fresh edition will have on local churches worldwide! Read it! Experience it!

NORM AND BECKY WRETLIND, cofounders of NeighborHope Ministries, International

When your professor walks into class halfway through the semester and tells you to trash the syllabus, you know something is happening. Students were asking penetrating questions about the relevancy of the church and Gene Getz felt he needed to take us back to the New Testament story to address these questions. The result was *Sharpening the Focus of the Church*. Subsequently, my wife and I started Midlothian Bible Church, where for forty years I served as pastor and saw the effectiveness of these biblical principles. In this brand-new edition, Gene has sharpened his focus even more clearly, and now challenges another generation of church leaders to be bold, to get serious about discovering a New Testament perspective.

DAVID WYRTZEN, Founding Pastor, Midlothian Bible Church

As a young pastor seeking answers for navigating the radical cultural transformations of the 1970s, *Sharpening the Focus of the Church* proved invaluable. Filled with rich insights, big-picture biblical perspectives, and practical real-world engagements, it quickly became one of my go-to lifelines for establishing a path forward in leading my church. Now, the issues that were first bubbling up in the '70s are today boiling over, unleashing not just greater evils into our culture, but intimidating, undermining, and dividing the church itself. That's why after fifty years, this totally new edition is so needed. You'll see the timeless, but expanded, blueprint of God's church but you'll also witness that blueprint attached to fifty years of honest reflection, evaluation, and practical updating.

ROBERT LEWIS, pastor at Fellowship Bible Church Little Rock; founder, Men's Fraternity/BetterMan

In the 1960s and 1970s leadership distrust was high. Established systems, including churches and church leaders, were viewed with suspicion and contempt. At that moment, Dr. Gene Getz stepped into the mix with *Sharpening the Focus of the Church*. In this major update, Gene does what he always does. He transparently explains what he has learned and would do differently. He's one of the most teachable and humble men I've ever known. And that's even more compelling as he takes us back to Scripture. And while our cultural context has changed, pastors, elders, and church leaders need to be reminded of what never changes. And again, Gene will take us by the hand and sharpen our focus.

MICHAEL EASLEY, pastor and former president of Moody Bible Institute

SHARPENING
THE
FOCUS
OF THE
CHURCH

—

a **BIBLICAL**
FRAMEWORK
for **RENEWAL**

GENE A. GETZ

Moody Publishers
CHICAGO

First edition published as *Sharpening the Focus of the Church* (Moody Publishers, 1974); second edition published by Victor Books (1984); third edition published by Wipf and Stock Publishers (2012).

Unless otherwise noted, Scripture quotations are taken from the Christian Standard Bible®, Copyright ©2017 by Holman Bible Publishers. Used by permission. Christian Standard Bible® and CSB® are federally registered trademarks of Holman Bible Publishers.

Scripture quotations marked (ESV) are from the ESV® Bible (The Holy Bible, English Standard Version®), © 2001 by Crossway, a publishing ministry of Good News Publishers. Used by permission. All rights reserved. The ESV text may not be quoted in any publication made available to the public by a Creative Commons license. The ESV may not be translated in whole or in part into any other language.

Scripture quotations marked NASB taken from the (NASB®) New American Standard Bible®, Copyright © 1960, 1971, 1977, 1995, 2020 by The Lockman Foundation. Used by permission. All rights reserved. lockman.org

Scripture quotations with words in **bold** reflect the author's added emphasis.

Edited by Kevin Mungons
Interior design: Ragont Design
Cover design: Brittany Schrock

Library of Congress Cataloging-in-Publication Data

Names: Getz, Gene A., author.
Title: Sharpening the focus of the church : a biblical framework for
renewal / Gene Getz.
Description: Fourth edition. | Chicago : Moody Publishers, 2024. | Includes
bibliographical references. | Summary: "A timeless classic for solid
grounding and renewal. Is your church adrift? Many churches are
struggling to stay focused-to stay on point and hold fast to gospel
essentials. Competing voices threaten to divide rather than unite and
grow the church. In Sharpening the Focus of the Church, Dr. Gene Getz
has written a classic, insightful, biblical treatise on church renewal.
Getz focuses on New Testament principles as applied to the unique needs
of contemporary culture and roots readers in the perspective of the
history of the church. Discover how to sharpen your church's focus
through the lenses of Scripture, church history, and present-day needs.
As you embark on this in-depth study of New Testament teaching, you will
experience the power of the Word and the power of the Spirit
transforming your church from the inside out. You'll find positive,
biblical solutions to the problems facing the church today, with
practical advice for finding solutions to contemporary questions"--
Provided by publisher.
Identifiers: LCCN 2024019422 (print) | LCCN 2024019423 (ebook) | ISBN
9780802431448 (paperback) | ISBN 9780802473233 (ebook)
Subjects: LCSH: Church. | Church renewal. | Theology, Practical. | BISAC:
RELIGION / Christian Church / Growth | RELIGION / Christian Church /
General
Classification: LCC BV600.2 .G44 2024 (print) | LCC BV600.2 (ebook) | DDC
262.001/7--dc23/eng/20240607
LC record available at https://lccn.loc.gov/2024019422
LC ebook record available at https://lccn.loc.gov/2024019423

Originally delivered by fleets of horse-drawn wagons, the affordable paperbacks from D. L. Moody's publishing house resourced the church and served everyday people. Now, after more than 125 years of publishing and ministry, Moody Publishers' mission remains the same—even if our delivery systems have changed a bit. For more information on other books (and resources) created from a biblical perspective, go to www.moodypublishers.com or write to:

Moody Publishers
820 N. LaSalle Boulevard
Chicago, IL 60610

1 3 5 7 9 10 8 6 4 2

Printed in the United States of America

Contents

Introduction

"I Will Build My Church": Jesus Christ in Matthew 16:18

Without question, the "church"—as this term is often used—is facing some unusual challenges and criticism. Perhaps the most critical and startling comment goes something like this—"I love Jesus, but I hate the church."

Though perhaps hyperbole, this comment reflects serious disenchantment with what God designed to be attractive and beautiful. It also reflects an attitude that is seriously out of sync with Paul's statement that "Christ **loved** the church and gave himself for her" (Eph. 5:25).

Regardless of the way the church has often failed to be what God intended, Jesus' passionate words to the church in Laodicea in the first century are still true today: "See! I stand at the door and knock. If anyone hears my voice and opens the door, I will come in to him and eat with him, and he with me" (Rev. 3:20).

Those metaphorical words are often used to refer to the "door" of an unbeliever's heart. But clearly, the context reveals that Jesus is addressing believers in a local church who were seriously flawed and living out of the will of God!

Applied to any community of faith today, these words from Jesus mean that He "loved the church"—those for whom He "gave himself" as "a sacrificial and fragrant offering to God" (Eph. 5:2). This has also been true for nearly two thousand years!

"Who Needs the Church?"

As I've reflected on negative attitudes toward the church today, my mind goes back to the seminary classroom of fifty years ago. I was teaching a course on various ministries of the church, when, to my surprise, one student blurted out—"Who needs the church? Maybe God is going to bypass the church."

I must add that most of the students at that time certainly believed that Jesus would "build" His "church, and the gates of Hades" would "not overpower it"—the Savior's very words. But they also were concerned that the church was failing to be what God intended it to be.

As I'll explain in detail in the following chapters, these concerns impacted my life as a professor, resulting in the first edition of this book, and then led me to leave the sacred halls of learning to become a church planting pastor. Though I've had my share of challenges, I consider these experiences the most rewarding and encouraging years in my ministry life.

And now, nearly half a century later, Moody Publishers has invited me to update this book. In many respects, we're facing challenges today that are similar to those that resulted in the first edition. Many who claim to follow Christ are seriously disenchanted with the church. As we'll see in the section "Lens of Culture," the issues are much more intense and universal. But I'm firmly convinced the foundational steps in renewing the church at any moment in history and in any culture of the world are the same and always will be. We need to continually look through the lens of Scripture in order to sharpen our focus on God's plan for the church. And, if we do, as pastors and leaders, we can lead our churches to continue "growing into maturity with a stature measured by Christ's fullness" (Eph. 4:13).

Serving in the Trenches

I'm honored and deeply grateful for the invitation to "update" my original publication, *Sharpening the Focus of the Church*. Though "update" is certainly a legitimate word, I quickly determined that "rewrite" is a better description. Nearly fifty years have passed since the original publication came off the press. I've since spent much of that time attempting to apply what I wrote as I became involved in planting and pastoring churches. Furthermore, and unexpectedly, our efforts here in Dallas led to a multitude of other church plants in the US and in some foreign countries identified as the Fellowship Bible Church movement.

Needless to say, serving "in the trenches" has been filled with significant learning experiences. It's one thing to explore biblical truths regarding God's plan for the church in an academic setting. It's quite another thing to apply these truths at "the grassroots level." Whichever metaphor we use, serving as a pastor is uniquely different than being a professor.

Please don't misunderstand. Teaching at the academic level—first at Moody Bible Institute and then at Dallas Theological Seminary—represented some of the most exciting and significant learning experiences in my life. I've been greatly challenged and rewarded. But serving as a pastor took my learning experiences to a whole new level. As a professor I often attempted to get beyond "theory" and "principles," but planting and pastoring local churches left no questions in terms of reality and application.

Back to Basics

In this rewrite, I've attempted to do several things. *First,* I've carefully reviewed the biblical story of the church, again finding it exhilarating and a renewed learning experience as I took a fresh look at how the followers of Jesus Christ carried out the Great Commission and planted churches throughout the Roman world. This is not surprising since the Source has been the inspired Scriptures that provide us with a depth of knowledge and wisdom that is incomparable and enduring (Rom. 11:33). Consequently, I've included a number of new chapters in this edition.

Second, I've refined what I believe are supracultural principles that emerge from the biblical story. Even though I've defined principles as enduring truths in the original publication, there will always be a reflection of human effort—even though I've sincerely desired to interpret the Word of God accurately and to rely on divine guidance from the Holy Spirit. Nevertheless, I believe we should periodically review our interpretations and conclusions by taking a fresh look at Scripture.

Third, as I've refined and restated what I believe are supracultural principles that can be applied at any moment in history and in any culture of the world, I've relied on my years of pastoral and teaching experience. This has also involved gaining many helpful insights from many fellow pastoral leaders as well as dedicated mission leaders as I've had the opportunity to minister in many countries in the world.

Fourth, in the section that I've called "The Lens of History," I've included what for me are some new insights, particularly in the area of leadership. I've also included what I could not have included fifty years ago—some things I've learned from my own church planting experiences, focusing primarily on what I would do differently or better.

Fifth, in the section I've called "The Lens of Culture," I've addressed issues that were not even on the horizon in the 1970s. As spiritual leaders, we have no choice but to consider the reoccurring racial tensions, the pervasive emphasis on gender identification, the tragic sin that continues to be associated with abortion, as well as other moral and spiritual issues. I've included biblical guidance as to how believers should relate to political issues and the overall direction of our society.

Sixth, and foundational in this rewrite, I've included an introductory section in which I describe the challenging questions I faced as a professor and the subsequent research design and process that precipitated my writing the first edition. As you'll see, I'm convinced this research design is just as relevant, necessary, and applicable in all cultures of the world today as it was then. I've also encouraged everyone who is seriously interested in renewing the church to join me in using this design and process to take a fresh look at the unfolding biblical story and the way New Testament leaders and communities of faith carried out the Great Commission throughout the Roman world in the first century. The first three chapters are designed to help facilitate this process.

Seventh, to assist in both studying the biblical story of the church and applying the principles, I've included QR codes at the beginning of each chapter. These codes enable all readers to access videos I've designed to motivate and aid in the learning process, particularly with group interaction and application.

This fresh biblical study of the church Jesus loved and died for has ignited in me a new flame of heartfelt motivation to help all churches become what God intended them to be! Though all of us as pastoral leaders are facing challenges that are intense and deep, and in many cases divisive, I'm confident we can be light in this world as never before—if indeed we follow the Spirit's voice that has spoken so specifically and dramatically through the authors of Scripture. Most importantly, we need to be greatly encouraged by the words of Jesus Himself, when He said— "I will build my church, and the gates of Hades will not overpower it" (Matt. 16:18).

—Gene A. Getz

Section 1

A LIFE-CHANGING MINISTRY EXPERIENCE

Video Intro from Gene

3lenses.org/sc1

My original *Sharpening the Focus of the Church* grew out of a dynamic teaching-learning opportunity as a professor at Dallas Theological Seminary. Little did I realize what would happen when I embarked on a productive and rewarding academic journey with my students, taking a fresh look at how the apostles and other New Testament leaders carried out the Great Commission and planted churches throughout the Roman world. This life-changing experience, in turn, literally propelled me out of the academic world into a church planting ministry.

The process I engaged in with my students in itself was personally revolutionary in terms of doing biblical research. I've chosen to introduce this "rewrite" by sharing what happened when my students began to raise some straightforward but relevant questions about the church. Hopefully what I share in the next three chapters will help you—and all readers—take a fresh and exciting look at what God intended the church to be. Perhaps it will be revolutionary for you as well. Please join me as I re-create this experience and, hopefully, you'll become an active participant!

1

From Professor to Pastor

Video Intro from Gene

3lenses.org/c01

In society generally, we were living through some rather turbulent years in the late 1960s and early 1970s. Challenged by questions and comments from my students, I abruptly shifted gears midsemester to once again see how the apostles and subsequently all believers carried out the Great Commission. Ultimately, this led me to author the first edition of this book.

As a result of this dynamic classroom experience, and writing *Sharpening the Focus of the Church*, I became a church planting pastor after nearly twenty years in the academic world. Frankly, it's been a great adventure with numerous hills, curves, bumps in the road—and some fairly deep valleys—but always ultimately upward. It's been a tremendous learning experience. It's my prayer that you'll be challenged by some of these insights and personal lessons reflected in this new edition.

A Decision That Changed My Ministry Life

Several families in Dallas kept abreast of the stimulating discussions we were having on the seminary campus. They asked me to meet with them in a home meeting to share the results of several years of biblical research and interaction.

I had just completed the original manuscript for *Sharpening the Focus of the Church*, so I shared the essence of this forthcoming book with this small group. Excited by what they heard, these eight couples asked me if I would help them start a new church and become their founding pastor.

They were particularly intrigued with the thesis of this book—that the Holy Spirit has inspired the authors of Scripture to give us absolute functions and supracultural principles to enable us to plant and produce mature churches at any moment in history and in any given culture of the world. These biblical writers, again under the inspiration of the Holy Spirit, have given us freedom to apply these principles by developing cultural forms and structures that will enable us to carry out the Great Commission—also at any moment in history and in any culture in the world. In essence, functions and principles (correctly stated) are enduring and never changing, but forms are non-absolutes. Structures are simply a cultural means for applying biblical absolutes.[1]

A Very Encouraging Response

As the evening progressed, I couldn't ignore the enthusiasm these concepts generated. Neither could I ignore the invitation to help them start a new church. To add to the encouraging and positive response from these couples, some of my most enthusiastic students at the seminary were encouraging me to do the same thing—particularly to put into practice what we were discovering from Scripture. I was challenged, along with my wife, Elaine. After praying specifically about this opportunity, we helped start the first Fellowship Bible Church and I served as the lead pastor.

From the beginning, all of us agreed not to do things differently just to be different. But neither were we going to do things the same way because they had been done that way before. Rather, we decided to focus on what we believed were normative, supracultural, and enduring principles. We would then allow the forms and structures to emerge that would help us apply these principles in our particular cultural context.

Little did we anticipate the explosion of interest among both believers and nonbelievers. Within a year, I knew I could not continue to be a full-time professor and a full-time pastor. Frankly, I was overwhelmed. Initially all of us as elders attempted to find someone who would replace me as lead pastor—so I could once again devote all my efforts ministering to students at the seminary. Frankly this was my personal desire. But at the last minute, a viable pastoral prospect decided not to accept our invitation.

I was initially disappointed. But a short time later both my wife and I sensed we needed to accept the elders' invitation for me to become their first full-time lead pastor. I soon discovered that in spite of our unusual church planting success, there was much more for me—and my fellow elders—to learn in this relatively new approach to church life. Little did I realize how much that was true—which is reflected in this "rewrite."

God continued to bless our efforts, and by the end of the first five years, we had four identical weekend services in the original church building and helped launch six other Fellowship Bible Churches in other areas of the Dallas Metroplex, including Oak Cliff Bible Fellowship pastored by Dr. Tony Evans. Unexpectedly, we also began to see a number of other Fellowship Bible Churches spontaneously come into existence beyond the Dallas area. What was particularly rewarding and encouraging was that many of these church planters used the principles outlined in the original edition of this book.

Three Perspectives

The metaphorical structure for this book emerged over a process of time as I engaged in this fresh ecclesiological research with my students. I was also greatly encouraged that several other faculty members joined us in this exciting adventure. And as the process unfolded, I also shared our observations and conclusions with a number of fellow pastors and missionaries, seeking their wisdom. From the beginning I was committed to engaging in this theological research in community.

A Biblical Perspective

I make no apologies regarding what was and still is my view of Scripture. I believe the Bible is God's inspired document as He used authors in a supernatural way to record His divine message for all humanity. Consequently, to answer my students' questions regarding the relevancy of the church, I was convinced that we needed to take a fresh look at the biblical story. What does the Bible actually say about the church? And in what ways do the functions of the church in the New Testament apply to us today?

Early on in this process I also determined to focus, first and foremost, on what God says—not what others say God says! With my students I wanted to take a careful look at the biblical story apart from previous perspectives. I wanted all of us to discover more specifically God's plan for the church as recorded in Scripture without being influenced by our previous knowledge and experiences.

An Historical Perspective

Taking a fresh look at the biblical story of the church did not mean that we were going to ignore the vast number of ecclesiological perspectives that have come down to us from the church fathers, biblical exegetes and interpreters, current theologians, as well as practitioners—and even social historians. Beyond looking at biblical perspectives, I wanted my students to understand that we need to learn lessons from history to help us evaluate what we've done well, what we've not done well, and what we could do better.

As stated, I wanted this to be the secondary goal. First and foremost, I wanted to look carefully at the way the apostles, other New Testament leaders, and all believers carried out the Great Commission as recorded in Scripture. In other words, divinely inspired church history [the Bible] flows naturally into extrabiblical church history, which can help us understand and evaluate what happened to local churches following the New Testament era. What should we emulate and what should we discard? And when we emulate what others have done, how can we do it better?

A Cultural Perspective

Cultural perspectives and historical perspectives certainly overlap. We cannot understand the biblical story of the church effectively without understanding New Testament cultures. This is an important part of accurate biblical exegesis and hermeneutics. But to apply scriptural truth effectively, we also need insights regarding the multitude of cultures in the world. And we certainly need to understand our own cultures when we're attempting to carry out the Great Commission of our Lord Jesus Christ.[2]

A Three-Lens Metaphor

At some point during this research with my students and fellow professors, I began using what I called the Lens of Scripture, the Lens of History, and the Lens of Culture to communicate how to gain biblical, historical, and cultural insights. This not only resonated with my students, but I quickly discovered it helped both local church leaders and congregants, as well as church planting missionaries, to understand God's plan for the church at any moment in history and in every culture of the world. And since I found it to be helpful in my own ongoing biblical research and teaching, I've continued to use this research design.[3]

Please understand that it's possible to use these three lenses separately in doing ecclesiological research, but ultimately they must be used in an integrated way. In fact, the more you study ecclesiology using these three lenses, the more you will interact with all three perspectives in an interrelated fashion. But to be true to a high view of Scripture, both history and culture must be secondary. Though absolutely necessary in developing an adequate philosophy of ministry, the Word of God provides us with the only sure foundation for our thoughts and actions.

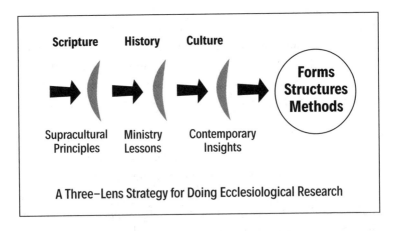

A Three-Lens Strategy for Doing Ecclesiological Research

Personally, I believe that using the three-lens process in our ecclesiological studies enables us to develop an approach to local church ministry that is in harmony with God's revealed will in Scripture. This research model guides us in developing forms, structures, and methods that are culturally relevant and also in harmony with biblical functions and principles. In summary, this is what *Sharpening the Focus of the Church* is all about.

A Question for Thought and Discussion

What can happen when church leaders develop forms and structures by looking through the lens of culture and neglecting the lens of Scripture?

2

Challenging Questions and a New Direction

Video Intro from Gene

3lenses.org/c02

The story behind the first edition of *Sharpening the Focus of the Church* correlates with what was happening in the American culture at large and how it impacted my own ministry career. After serving on the faculty of Moody Bible Institute (from 1956–1968), I was invited by the late Howard Hendricks to become his associate at Dallas Theological Seminary. As excited and challenged as I was teaching undergraduate students at Moody and directing the evening school, I felt I should consider this new opportunity to teach at the graduate level. Since I had just finished my PhD at New York University, my wife and I felt this was God's timing. Little did we realize what would happen in my own life as both a professor and subsequently as a church planting pastor.

A New Challenge

I arrived on the Dallas Seminary campus in the fall of 1968. Most of my students felt called to some form of full-time ministry. A small group were relatively new believers who had recently been converted on the college campus through parachurch ministries. Some of them raised questions that changed my ministry life, such as the student who blurted out in the middle of the class session, "Who needs the church? Perhaps God is going to bypass the church."

It was obvious this student had recently come to Christ and had little biblical background. After all, Jesus said, "I will build my church, and the gates of Hades will not overpower it" (Matt. 16:18). Unfortunately, this student not only had limited biblical knowledge, but he had enough disappointing experiences in various local churches to conclude they didn't measure up—at least to his expectations.

It didn't take many class sessions to discover that other students had similar thoughts and questions. The majority were committed to the biblical concept of the church. But at the same time, they had serious doubts about the way it was functioning—particularly in the current culture. A few, however, even felt the church was totally ineffective and they wanted to move in another direction.

A Unique Opportunity

I was taken aback by these reactions. To be honest, it initially felt threatening, but I soon discovered that crisis experiences can become our greatest opportunities to expand our horizons and make necessary changes.

Cultural Changes

Without question, a decade of cultural changes had impacted these students. We were still in the middle of the Vietnam War, which many students on the university campus opposed. Some were marching in Washington, DC, carrying placards that read "Make love not war." The free speech movement was in full force. Many opposed the structures and demands on the university campus—and in the government generally. A number felt they had become depersonalized by the advancements in technology. And it was obvious all these cultural changes had also impacted these seminary students, often precipitating their challenging questions.

Institutionalism

At that time much of what was happening in our culture at large was identified as "institutionalism." Both secular and Christian authors were addressing the issue. From a secular perspective, John W. Gardner, past president of the Carnegie Corporation, was a key spokesman. He wrote, "Like people and plants, organizations have a life cycle. They have a green and supple youth, a time of flourishing strength, and a gnarled old age."[1] However, Gardner went on to add this positive note: "Organizations need not stagnate. They often do, to be sure, but that is because the arts of organizational renewal are not yet widely understood. Organizations can renew themselves continuously."[2]

From a Christian point of view, several prominent authors addressed the problem of institutionalism.[3] Perhaps the most strategic voice was that of Dr. Francis Schaeffer, embodied in *The Church at the End of the 20th Century*. Writing out of a comprehensive understanding of Scripture, history, and culture, he spoke directly to the problem of differentiating absolutes from non-absolutes in Scripture. He wrote—"In a rapidly changing age like ours, an age of total upheaval like ours, to make non-absolutes absolutes guarantees both isolation and the death of the institutional, organized church."[4]

A Midcourse Correction

As this cultural phenomenon gripped my thoughts, I knew I had to address my students' questions head-on. While some of their comments were over-reactionary and even superficial, I could not ignore the reality that prompted their questions.

After seriously reflecting on what was happening, I came to the class about midway through the semester and asked the students to tear up the course syllabus—which, of course, included all assignments. "Trash it," I said—and then admitted that I obviously had not prepared the objectives and content for this course to address the questions they were asking. I told them we were going back to *the* Syllabus—namely, the New Testament, beginning with the Great Commission as stated by Jesus—"Go, therefore, and make disciples of all nations . . . teaching them to observe everything I have commanded you" (Matt. 28:19–20). I made it clear that together we were going to take a fresh look at what Jesus meant and how the apostles and other New Testament believers carried out this command.

Everyone was in shock. In some respects, so was I. My announcement happened on a Thursday and the next class session was on the coming Tuesday. This gave me only four days to restructure the course for the second half of the semester and to face what was predictably significant anticipation on the part of my students—more than I'd ever seen in my entire teaching career.

The Great Commission

Following the resurrection of Jesus Christ, the apostles met Jesus in the Galilean region—home country for most of them. Matthew has recorded:

> The **eleven disciples** traveled to Galilee, to the mountain where Jesus had directed them. When they saw him, they worshiped, but some doubted. Jesus came near and said to them, "All authority has been given to me in heaven and on earth. Go, therefore, and **make disciples** of all nations, **baptizing them** in the name of the Father and of the Son and of the Holy Spirit, **teaching them** to observe everything I have commanded you. And remember, I am with you always, to the end of the age." (Matt. 28:16–20)

I vividly remember going to my office early on Saturday morning and prayerfully opening my Bible to this challenging command. With Jesus' words in mind, I was determined to spend the next two days taking a new and fresh look at the book of Acts and the rest of the New Testament. How did the apostles and others make disciples and start New Testament churches—beginning with the church in Jerusalem? Needless to say, I was highly motivated! Time was of the essence!

Two Basic Commands

There is some discussion regarding what Jesus meant when He said to "make disciples." But practically speaking, it's an imperative. The word *go* (going) is a participle in the original text, along with two additional participles in verses 19–20—"baptizing" and "teaching." However, regardless of the grammar, Jesus gave two basic commands. First, they were to share the gospel so people could put their faith in Christ for salvation and become disciples. Second, they were "to teach" these disciples to become mature followers of Christ.

A Specific Illustration

This two-fold imperative is visibly and dramatically illustrated on Paul's first missionary journey. Paul had been stoned in Lystra and left outside the city for dead (Acts 14:19). However, God miraculously healed him, and he and Barnabas left for Derbe. When Luke recorded what happened next, he illustrated in a specific way what Jesus meant when He gave the Great Commission. We read—

> After they had **preached the gospel** in that town [Derbe] and **made many disciples**, they returned to Lystra, to Iconium, and to Antioch, **strengthening the disciples** by **encouraging them** to continue in the faith. (Acts 14:21–22)

Initially, Jesus commissioned the apostles to **make disciples** and then to teach them. Clearly, that's what Paul and Barnabas had done in Antioch, Iconium, and Lystra. They made disciples but then returned to these cities and carried out the second part of the Great Commission—**to teach these disciples**. The basic words "strengthening" and "encouraging" are functions that expand on the concept of what it means to "teach" believers so they'll grow in their Christian faith (for an elaboration on these concepts, see chapter 11: "Teaching Authentic Disciples").

A Research Design

When I began my research that Saturday morning, I created the following "Research Design" based on Jesus' two directives in the Great Commission.[5]

Making Disciples (Evangelism)	Equipping Disciples (Edification)[6]
Book of Acts *(Functions and Results)*	Book of Acts *(Functions and Results)*
Making Disciples (Evangelism)	Equipping Disciples (Edification)
New Testament Letters *(Directives and Objectives)*	New Testament Letters *(Directives and Objectives)*

With this design guiding my thoughts, I began reading the book of Acts, recording relevant scriptural content that related specifically to "making disciples" and "equipping disciples." However, as I read about the founding of particular churches in Acts, I immediately read the letters written to these churches, also noting examples and instructions regarding "making disciples" and "equipping disciples." For example, during Paul's first missionary journey I read the epistle of James, which was probably written during this period of time. I also read Galatians, which was evidently written after Paul and Barnabas returned to Antioch and prior to the council meeting in Jerusalem. In other words, as much as possible, I read the New Testament letters as they coincided with the planting of churches in the book of Acts.[7]

An Inductive Study

To brief you on the end result of my weekend journey through Scripture, following are biblical references related to carrying out the Great Commission. From these references, I printed out the complete texts of Scripture, which I then placed in the hands of the students in my next class session on Tuesday morning. (Throughout this design you'll note that some references blend both evangelism and edification. These passages flow from column 1 to column 2.)

Making Disciples (Evangelism)	Equipping Disciples (Edification)
Act 1:8	
Acts 2:14	
Acts 2:41–47[8]	
Acts 4:1–2, 4	
Acts 4:31	Acts 4:32
Acts 5:12–14	
Acts 5:19–21	
Acts 5:25	
Acts 5:27–28	
Acts 5:42	
Acts 6:4, 7	
Acts 8:1b, 4	

James

During this period of time, it appears that James, the Lord's half-brother, became the lead elder-pastor in Jerusalem. Subsequently, he wrote a letter to the Jewish believers who were dispersed abroad. Following are selected directives and objectives for carrying out the Great Commission.

	James 1:2–4
	James 1:5
James 1:16–18	
	James 1:19
	James 1:22
	James 1:27
	James 2:1
	James 2:26
	James 3:1

Making Disciples (Evangelism)	Equipping Disciples (Edification)
	James 3:13
	James 4:7–8a
	James 4:11
	James 5:9
	James 5:14
Continuation of Luke's narrative in Acts	
Acts 8:5	
	Acts 8:12
Acts 8:25	
Acts 8:35	Acts 8:36, 38
	Acts 9:18
Acts 9:20	
Acts 9:31	
Acts 10:42–43	
Acts 11:19–21	
Acts 11:22–26	
	Acts 11:27–30
Acts 12:21–24	
	Acts 13:1–3
Acts 13:5	
Acts 13:12	
Acts 13:13–16	
Acts 13:42–44	
Acts 13:45–49	
Acts 14:1	

Making Disciples (Evangelism)	Equipping Disciples (Edification)
Acts 14:5–7	
Acts 14:19–21a	Acts 14:21b–23
Acts 14:25–28	

Galatians

When Paul and Barnabas returned to Antioch of Syria, they evidently heard that false teachers had confused the believers in the churches in Pisidia, Iconium, Lystra, and Derbe by teaching works for salvation. Some believe that Paul wrote to these Galatian believers to correct this problem. It appears this happened before the Jerusalem council. If he had written it following the council, he certainly would have mentioned this significant event where the law/grace issue was settled and which he addressed in Galatians. Following are selected directives and objectives for carrying out the Great Commission.

Gal. 2:7–9	
Gal. 3:23–26	Gal. 3:27–29
	Gal. 5:1
	Gal. 5:13–14
	Gal. 5:16
	Gal. 5:19–21
	Gal. 5:22–23
	Gal. 5:25–26
	Gal. 6:1–2
	Gal. 6:6
	Gal. 6:10
Continuation of Luke's narrative in Acts	
	Acts 15:1–4
	Acts 15:22–23a, 30–32
Acts 15:35	
	Acts 15:36, 40–41

Making Disciples (Evangelism)	Equipping Disciples (Edification)
	Acts 16:1–4
Acts 16:5	
Acts 16:9–10	
Acts 16:13–14	Acts 16:15
Acts 16:29–32	Acts 16:33–34, 40
Acts 17:1–4	

1 and 2 Thessalonians

During this time frame in Luke's narrative, Paul wrote two letters to the Thessalonian believers. Following are selected directives and objectives for carrying out the Great Commission.

1 Thess. 1:4–10	
	1 Thess. 2:7–12
	1 Thess. 3:1–5
	1 Thess. 3:9–13
	1 Thess. 5:11
	1 Thess. 5:14–15
	2 Thess. 1:3
	2 Thess. 1:5
	2 Thess. 2:15–17
2 Thess. 3:1–2	

Continuation of Luke's narrative in Acts

Acts 17:10–12	
Acts 17:16–18	
Acts 17:22–34	
Acts 18:4–5	

Acts 18:8–11

Making Disciples (Evangelism)	Equipping Disciples (Edification)

The Corinthian Letters

Paul actually wrote four letters to the Corinthians. Two are included in the New Testament. He wrote 1 Corinthians when he returned to Ephesus and it seems he wrote 2 Corinthians while traveling through Macedonia. Following are selected directives and objectives for carrying out the Great Commission.

Making Disciples (Evangelism)	Equipping Disciples (Edification)
	1 Cor. 1:4–7
	1 Cor. 1:10
1 Cor. 1:17	
1 Cor. 1:21–24	
1 Cor. 2:1–5	
	1 Cor. 4:17
	1 Cor. 5:9–10
	1 Cor. 6:9–10
1 Cor. 9:16	
1 Cor. 11:26	
	1 Cor. 13:11–13
1 Cor. 14:23–25	
	1 Cor. 15:58
2 Cor. 1:19	
2 Cor. 3:2–3	
2 Cor. 4:5	
2 Cor. 5:18–20	

Continuation of Luke's narrative in Acts

Making Disciples (Evangelism)	Equipping Disciples (Edification)
Acts 18:19–21	Acts 18:22–23
Acts 18:24–28	
	Acts 19:1–7

Making Disciples (Evangelism)	Equipping Disciples (Edification)
Acts 19:8	
Acts 19:9–10, 20	
	Acts 19:23; 20:1–2

Romans

During this time frame, Paul wrote a letter to the believers in Rome, which was probably delivered by Phoebe, a deacon in the church in Cenchreae (Rom. 16:1–2). Following are selected directives and objectives for carrying out the Great Commission.

Rom. 1:8–9	Rom. 1:10–13
Rom. 1:14–15	
Rom. 3:23	
Rom. 5:1	
	Rom. 6:1–2
	Rom. 12:1–2
	Rom. 12:4–5
	Rom. 12:10
	Rom. 12:16
	Rom. 13:8–10
	Rom. 14:19
	Rom. 15:5
	Rom. 15:7
	Rom. 15:14
Rom. 16:25–27	

Continuation of Luke's narrative in Acts

	Acts 20:5–7
	Acts 20:17–20

Making Disciples (Evangelism)	Equipping Disciples (Edification)
Acts 20:21	
Acts 20:22–25	Acts 20:28–32

Read the following chapters and note Paul's witness.

Acts 22	
Acts 23	
Acts 24	
Acts 25	
Acts 26	
Acts 27	
Acts 28:23–24	
Acts 28:30–31	

During Paul's two years in prison in Rome, he wrote four letters:

A Letter to Philemon in Colossae

	Philem. 9–10
	Philem. 15–16a

A Circular Letter to the Ephesians

	Eph. 1:3
	Eph. 1:15–19
	Eph. 2:19–22
Eph. 3:8–9	
	Eph. 3:14–19
	Eph. 4:1–3
	Eph. 4:11–16
	Eph. 4:17
	Eph. 5:1–2

Making Disciples (Evangelism)	Equipping Disciples (Edification)
	Eph. 5:8
	Eph. 5:15–16
	Eph. 5:22
	Eph. 5:25
	Eph. 6:1–4
	Eph. 6:10–18
Eph. 6:19–20	
A Letter to the Colossians	
	Col. 1:3–5a
	Col. 1:9–12
Col. 1:25–27	
Col. 1:28	
	Col. 2:2–5
	Col. 3:16
	Col. 3:18–23
Col. 4:5–6	
A Letter to the Philippians	
Phil. 1:3–5	
Phil. 1:12–14	
Phil. 1:27–28	
	Phil. 2:1–4
	Phil. 2:5–8
	Phil. 2:19–24
	Phil. 4:9

Making Disciples (Evangelism)	Equipping Disciples (Edification)

After Paul was released from prison, he wrote three pastoral epistles. His first letter was to Timothy, followed by a letter to Titus. He then wrote a second letter to Timothy, which is his final letter before his execution. Following are selected directives and objectives for carrying out the Great Commission.

Paul's First Letter to Timothy

Making Disciples (Evangelism)	Equipping Disciples (Edification)
	1 Tim. 1:3–7
1 Tim. 2:1–4	
	1 Tim. 3:1–7
	1 Tim. 4:11–16
	1 Tim. 5:17
1 Tim. 6:1–2	

Paul's Letter to Titus

Making Disciples (Evangelism)	Equipping Disciples (Edification)
	Titus 1:5–9
	Titus 2:1–7
Titus 2:8	
	Titus 2:11–14

Paul's Final Letter to Timothy

Making Disciples (Evangelism)	Equipping Disciples (Edification)
2 Tim. 1:6–8	
2 Tim. 1:11–12	
	2 Tim. 2:2
	2 Tim. 3:14–17
	2 Tim. 4:1–2
2 Tim. 4:4–5	

Additional Letters
Hebrews

Making Disciples (Evangelism)	Equipping Disciples (Edification)
	Heb 3:12–14
	Heb 5:12–14

Making Disciples (Evangelism)	Equipping Disciples (Edification)
	Heb 6:1
	Heb 10:24–25
1 and 2 Peter	
	1 Peter 2:1–5
1 Peter 2:12	
1 Peter 2:18	
1 Peter 3:1–2	
1 Peter 3:15	
	1 Peter 4:10–11
	1 Peter 5:1–3
	2 Peter 1:3–7
2 Peter 3:8–9	
	2 Peter 3:14
	2 Peter 3:17–18
1, 2, and 3 John	
1 John 1:1–2	
	1 John 1:3–4
1 John 1:5–6	
	1 John 1:7
	1 John 2:1
	1 John 2:3
	1 John 2:10
	1 John 2:15–16
	1 John 3:11
	1 John 3:14

Making Disciples (Evangelism)	Equipping Disciples (Edification)
	1 John 3:16
	1 John 3:18
1 John 3:23	
	1 John 4:7
	1 John 4:11
	1 John 4:12
1 John 4:14	
	1 John 4:19
	1 John 4:21
	2 John 6
	2 John 10
	3 John 5–7
Jude	
	Jude 12
	Jude 22–23

An Exciting Marathon

In retrospect, I am indeed thankful for the questions I faced from my students in the late 60s and early 70s. Ultimately, they resulted in a new and fresh perspective on the great mystery that was revealed to the apostles and to Paul particularly—the church of our Lord Jesus Christ (Eph. 3:3–6).

A Question for Thought and Discussion

What are some limitations in interpretation and comprehension
when we fail to study and understand events as they unfold
chronologically in the biblical story?

3

A Dynamic Classroom Adventure

Video Intro from Gene

3lenses.org/c03

'll never forget the first session with my students following my decision to trash the syllabus midsemester. I began the class by sharing my marathon experience reading through the book of Acts and the New Testament letters and documenting how the apostles and all believers carried out the Great Commission. I then handed out the results of my biblical research, which included a printout of all the complete biblical texts referenced in the previous chapter. Needless to say, you could sense an atmosphere of surprise and anticipation.

At this point, I want to invite you to join in the same inductive process as my students, remembering that the biblical story is forever relevant.
To do so, please turn to Appendix A where you can scan a QR code or use a link to access all the references in chapter 2, plus the full biblical texts that I put in the hands of my students. You can then print out this material which also includes the following assignments I gave the students.

An Introductory Assignment

After putting this biblical data in the hands of the students, I asked them to carefully read all the full biblical texts referenced in Appendix A, by using suggested color codes to highlight the following:

1. MAKING DISCIPLES (**evangelism functions**) in column one in the book of Acts.
2. EQUIPPING DISCIPLES (**edification functions**) in column two in the book of Acts.
3. MAKING DISCIPLES (**evangelism directives**) in the New Testament letters.
4. EQUIPPING DISCIPLES (**edification objectives**) in the New Testament letters.

Stimulating Interaction

As a result of this assignment, I asked the students in our next class session to begin to share some of their observations and insights—and their questions. I say "begin to share" since this first assignment laid the foundation for the rest of the semester. Some of the students reported that they had spent eight to ten hours highlighting observations—which indicated their intense interest and motivation.

As I've reflected on this experience and those to follow, I must admit that now—many years later—I've had some of the same feelings of excitement. The class sessions were electric. Though we had two-hour discussions, time flew by as we interacted with Scripture in a new and fresh way—looking at the way New Testament leaders and all believers carried out the Great Commission. It was obvious that the Holy Spirit was giving all of us some new insights regarding God's plan for His church.

To go more deeply into the results of this first assignment and in sessions to follow, I used the following questions to prod our thinking:

1. To "**make disciples,**" what kind of evangelism FUNCTIONS did the apostles and other key leaders engage in as recorded in the book of Acts?

2. To "**equip disciples,**" what kind of edification FUNCTIONS did the apostles and other key leaders engage in as recorded in the book of Acts?
3. To "**make disciples,**" what evangelism DIRECTIVES are given to all believers by the writers of the New Testament letters?
4. To "**equip disciples,**" what edification DIRECTIVES are given to all believers by the writers of the New Testament letters?

Digging Deeper

The students' enthusiastic response to this initial assignment set the stage for the next one. Again, using the scriptural data in the printout from Appendix A, I once again suggested using color codes:

1. In the book of Acts, highlight the **results** in column 1 of MAKING DISCIPLES (evangelism functions).
2. In the book of Acts, highlight the **results** in column 2 of EQUIPPING DISCIPLES (edification functions).
3. In the New Testament letters, highlight the **results/objectives** in column 1 **expected from** MAKING DISCIPLES.
4. In the New Testament letters, highlight the **results/objectives** in column 2 **expected from** EQUIPPING DISCIPLES.

Follow-Up Discussions

When we met together in sessions to follow, we used the preceding exercise for class discussions. After highlighting each of the four sections above, we discussed the results and objectives of each section.

An Applicational Assignment

In this assignment, we intentionally moved from making and discussing observations from the biblical story to the way spiritual leaders today should use these insights to make a difference in their local church ministries. This actually began to happen naturally during our discussions as a result of the first two assignments.

Principles from Scripture

At this point, I defined what I believe is a supracultural principle based on normative biblical functions and directives:

> A supracultural principle is an **absolute** and **enduring** biblical truth that can and should be applied **in all cultures** of the world and **at any moment in history**.

Based on this definition, I asked the students to carefully review their observations from the biblical story and then to answer the following questions:

1. As a result of the two previous assignments, what are the supracultural, enduring, and universal principles for MAKING DISCIPLES (evangelism) and how can we apply them in our churches today?
2. As a result of the two previous assignments, what are the supracultural, enduring, and universal principles for EQUIP-PING DISCIPLES (edification) and how can we apply them in our churches today?

An Ongoing Process

These three major assignments provided basic content for dynamic interaction and discussion for many class sessions—and for several full semesters thereafter. Since we began the first experience halfway through the semester, we only touched the tip of the iceberg in looking at biblical ecclesiology and how our insights apply to us today. This initial experience was multiplied many times over in semesters to follow.

Clearly, what happened in these class sessions continued to be life-changing. To this day I meet former students, many who are pastors and missionaries, who share how this experience impacted their ministry lives. And, for me, this experience led me to become a church planting pastor.

An Inductive Process

If you are a pastor, please consider engaging in the same process outlined in this chapter, particularly with others who are sincerely interested in refining their thinking on what God intended the church to be. Based on Paul's statement to Timothy regarding the penetrating power of God's word, I'm confident it will be a life-changing experience:

> All Scripture is inspired by God and is profitable for teaching, for rebuking, for correcting, for training in righteousness, so that the man [and woman] of God may be complete, equipped for every good work. (2 Tim. 3:16–17)

If you engage in the inductive study outlined in Appendix A, I'm confident you'll discover that reading the following chapters will be much more meaningful.

Doing Theology in Community

Fellow Professors

Engaging in this process with my students also opened the door to invite several professors from other departments to share their own insights and to interact with the students. My first invitation went to the late Dr. Phil Hook who taught in the Theology Department. Phil had heard about our dynamic class discussions and took a keen interest in what was happening. He accepted my invitation to visit the class to join in our discussions. He became so interested he voluntarily attended every class session for several semesters. His input was invaluable.

As a result, I prepared new and fresh lectures. And since this was a two-hour class, I proposed to Phil that I deliver these lectures during the first hour and that he evaluate my presentations during the second hour. He accepted my invitation, and you can imagine what happened!

The students were captivated, and Phil let the students know he was also gaining fresh insights—which was also affirming to me personally.

After all, he was a reputable and experienced theologian. I'm deeply indebted to Phil—and told him so before he entered heaven's gates. In fact, he encouraged me to write the first edition of this book.

I'm also indebted to the late Dr. George Peters and the late Dr. Zane Hodges. Dr. Peters taught in the Missions Department and Dr. Hodges taught in the New Testament Department. Both of these men accepted my invitation to stage a debate on the subject of local church "function" and "form." Hodges developed the thesis that the New Testament prescribes both "functions" and "forms" that are universal and absolute. Peters, on the other hand, took the position that only biblical "functions" are absolute and supracultural, whereas "forms" are cultural and not prescribed in Scripture.

Both men staged these debates for several semesters. As a result, it was basically unanimous among the students that Dr. Peters won these debates—that we have freedom in form. Before Dr. Hodges also entered heaven's gates, he thanked me for the opportunity to participate and stated that it was a personal learning experience for him. This, again, was encouraging and affirming since I deeply respected Zane as a New Testament scholar. Koine Greek was his second language.

Pastors and Missionaries

While preparing this material for publication, I also shared the results of our classroom experiences in a number of leadership conferences, both in the United States and abroad. This gave me feedback and perspective from those who were ministering at the local church level in a variety of cultures. Again, I am deeply indebted to a number of pastors and missionaries I'll never meet again until we see each other in heaven. They helped me move from theory to practice.

A Half-Century Later

Without question, this half-century has been one of the most exciting and fulfilling periods of my life—and my greatest learning experience in ministry. And now, the challenging opportunity to once again review the biblical story of the church and share how I've attempted to apply supracultural principles has added to my excitement and ongoing learning experience. I trust that what I share in this completely rewritten edition will enhance your own appreciation and love for one of God's greatest gifts to humanity. Following the immeasurable gift of His Son, I'm referring to the church of Jesus Christ.

A Question for Thought and Discussion

When looking for enduring truths in Scripture (supracultural principles), why is it important to consult fellow believers and seek their wisdom?

Section 2

THE LENS OF SCRIPTURE

Video Intro from Gene

3lenses.org/sc2

To become the church God intended us to be, we must consult the only reliable Source—the New Testament. Jesus came to lay the foundation for the church, which includes a body of authentic disciples who represent "every tribe and language and people and nation" (Rev. 5:9).

As the apostles and other key leaders carried out the Great Commission, Luke recorded the birth and growth of the church in the book of Acts. Local communities of faith came into existence throughout the Roman world. As these churches were planted, a majority of the New Testament letters were written to these churches to help them continue to grow "into maturity with a stature measured by Christ's fullness" (Eph. 4:13).

By design, the largest section of this book unfolds this remarkable, overwhelming story. As Paul stated in his letter sent first to the Ephesians, the church was a profound "mystery of Christ . . . revealed to his holy apostles and prophets by the Spirit" (Eph. 3:4–5).

Please join me in this study and hopefully you'll have—as I have had—and even deeper appreciation of the great reality shared by Paul:

> For he [God the Father] chose us in him [Christ], before the foundation of the world, to be holy and blameless in love before him. (Eph. 1:4)

4

Authentic Disciples

"Go, therefore, and make disciples of all nations."
(MATT. 28:19)

Video Intro from Gene

3lenses.org/c04

Before we look at the way the apostles, key leaders, and subsequently all believers carried out Jesus' commission to make disciples, we need to understand what Jesus actually meant. In general, the term "disciple" (*mathetes*) refers to a follower or student of a teacher. For example,

- Matthew referred to the "disciples" of John the Baptist (Matt. 9:14).
- Mark referred to the "Pharisees' disciples" (Mark 2:18).
- John referred to "Moses's disciples" (John 9:28).

However, the vast majority of references in the Gospels describe the "disciples of Jesus." Matthew and John each used the term this way over seventy times. But, when Jesus commissioned the apostles to "go make disciples," He was referring to far more than enlisting people to follow Him as a teacher or philosopher. To distinguish between the way "disciples" is used generally in the Gospels and what Jesus had in mind in the Great Commission, I've used "authentic disciples."

Disciple in "Name Only"

This distinction becomes clear following the magnificent miracle when Jesus multiplied the loaves and fish and fed five thousand men and their families. Following this amazing event, many of the people followed Jesus to Capernaum, clearly with materialistic motives. If he would become their king, they would have plenty of food (John 6:15, 26).

At that moment, Jesus knew the thoughts of their hearts and challenged them to "work for food" that lasts for eternal life. Clearly, Jesus was *not* saying they could earn salvation through good works. Rather He was asking them to experience "the work of God," to "**believe in the one he has sent**" (John 6:29). And, to expose their motives even further, Jesus stated that He is "the bread of life" and "that everyone who sees the Son and **believes in him will have eternal life**" (6:40).

Note two more references in this discourse that demonstrate clearly that Jesus was referring to saving faith:

> "I am the bread of life . . . No one who comes to me will ever be hungry, and no one who **believes in me** will ever be thirsty again." (John 6:35)

> "Truly I tell you, anyone who **believes** has eternal life." (John 6:47)

At some point the crowd dispersed and a smaller group gathered in the synagogue in Capernaum to hear more (6:59). To test their motives even further, Jesus used a graphic metaphor to reveal their unbelief (6:64)—"Truly I tell you, unless you **eat the flesh** of the Son of Man and **drink his blood**, you do not have life in yourselves" (6:53).

When many in this group heard this statement, they bristled. Rather than asking for clarification from the one who had performed an incredible miracle, they rejected Jesus as their teacher. John recorded—"Therefore, when many of **his disciples** heard this, they said, 'This **teaching** is hard. Who can accept it?'" (6:60).

Since Jesus knew what was in their hearts and minds, He was not surprised at their response. They did not understand and believe that He is the Son of God and one with the Father. We see their true motives when John recorded—"From that moment **many of his disciples** turned back and no longer accompanied him" (6:66). From Jesus' point of view, they were not authentic disciples.

Peter's Confession

It was then Jesus turned to the Twelve who were, of course, also called disciples and asked, "You don't want to go away too, do you?" Simon Peter's response at that moment certainly helps clarify what Jesus had in mind when He commissioned the apostles to "**go make disciples**." Peter responded—"Lord, to whom will **we** go? You have the words of eternal life. **We have come to believe and know that you are the Holy One of God**" (6:67–69). Though at this point Peter probably didn't understand fully what he was confessing, he was in essence defining an "authentic disciple"—one who believes that Jesus Christ is the "Son of God, and that by believing" has eternal life (John 20:31).

The unfolding biblical story demonstrates that becoming an authentic disciple is based on sincerely and genuinely believing in the Lord Jesus Christ—who He is and what He has done for us through His death and resurrection. Though the apostle John wrote decades later following Peter's confession, he certainly verified what happened in the book of Acts. After recording seven significant miracles to demonstrate that Jesus was the "word" who "became flesh," he concluded his gospel with these descriptive words: "Jesus performed many other signs in the presence of his disciples that are not written in this book. But these are written so that you may **believe** that Jesus is the Messiah, the Son of God, and that by **believing** you may have life in his name" (20:30–31).

"Go Make Disciples"

These observations set the stage for the Great Commission, which Jesus gave initially to those He had chosen as apostles. Judas had defected and so Matthew has recorded that "the **eleven disciples** traveled to Galilee, to the mountain where Jesus had directed them" (Matt. 28:16). It was on this mountain that Jesus commissioned them to "go, therefore, and **make disciples** of all nations." Though they were still immature, they were authentic in their belief.

The term *disciple* is used five times in the book of Acts to refer to individuals who had an authentic belief in the Lord Jesus Christ. The plural term "disciples" is used twenty-five times—also referring to authentic believers. Furthermore, you'll note that in each case where Luke used the plural term "disciples," he was referring to communities of believers or churches located throughout the Roman world. This is especially clear in the following references:

Disciples as Authentic Believers

6:1	"The **disciples** were increasing in number [in Jerusalem]"
6:2	"The Twelve summoned the whole company of the **disciples**"
6:7	"The **disciples** in Jerusalem increased greatly in number"
9:1	"Now Saul was still breathing threats and murder against the **disciples** of the Lord"
9:10	"There was a **disciple** in Damascus named Ananias"
9:19	"Saul was with the **disciples** in Damascus for some time"
9:25	Saul's "**disciples** took him by night and lowered him in a large basket"
9:26a	"He [Paul] tried to join the **disciples** [in Jerusalem]"
9:26b	"They [the **disciples** in Jerusalem] did not believe he [Saul] was a **disciple**"
9:36	"In Joppa there was a **disciple** named Tabitha"
9:38	"The **disciples** [in Joppa] heard that Peter was there [in Lydda]"
11:26	"The **disciples** were first called Christians at Antioch"
11:29	"Each of the **disciples** [in Antioch], according to his ability, determined to send relief"
13:52	"And the **disciples** [in Pisidia Antioch] were filled with joy and the Holy Spirit"

14:20	"After the **disciples** [in Lystra] gathered around him [Paul]"
14:21	"After they had preached the gospel in that town [Derbe] and made many **disciples**"
14:22	Paul and Barnabas "returned to Lystra, to Iconium, and to Antioch, strengthening the **disciples**"
14:28	"And they spent a considerable time with the **disciples** [in Antioch]"
15:10	"Why are you testing God by putting a yoke on the [Gentile] **disciples'** necks?"
16:1	"Paul went on to Derbe and Lystra, where there was a **disciple** named Timothy"
18:23	"He [Paul] set out, traveling through one place after another in the region of Galatia and Phrygia, strengthening all the **disciples**"
18:27	"The brothers and sisters [in Ephesus] wrote to the **disciples** [in Achaia] to welcome him [Apollos]"
19:1	Paul "found some **disciples** [in Ephesus]"
19:9	He [Paul] withdrew from them [unbelievers], taking the **disciples**"
19:30	"The **disciples** [in Ephesus] did not let him" go into the amphitheater
20:1	"Paul sent for the **disciples** [in Ephesus]"
20:30	"Men will rise up [in Ephesus] . . . to lure the **disciples** into following them"
21:4	Paul and his traveling companions "sought out the **disciples** [in Tyre] and stayed there seven days"
21:16a	"Some of the **disciples** from Caesarea also went with us [to Jerusalem]"
21:16b	"Some . . . brought us to Mnason of Cyprus, an early **disciple**, with whom we were to stay"

The Church

A relatively short time before Jesus' death and resurrection, He referred to "authentic disciples" as the church. Speaking particularly to Peter, He said—"I will build **my church** (*ekklesia*), and the gates of Hades will not overpower it" (Matt. 16:18b). Significantly, Jesus identified believers as His church, which is in contrast to those "disciples" who "turned back and no longer accompanied him" (John 6:66).

Ekklesia in its most basic meaning refers to "an assembly of people." For example, when the riot took place in Ephesus, Luke used this term three times to refer to those who had gathered to protest Paul's ministry. In most literal translations of the New Testament, *ekklesia* here is translated "assembly" (see Acts 19:32, 39, 41). When Jesus used the term, He was referring to a **group of authentic disciples** who had been born again because of their saving faith in who He is (John 3:3, 16).

Interestingly, a local community of believers is first identified as the church in the book of Acts after the shocking experience involving Ananias and Sapphira (Acts 5:1–10). As a result of their sudden death, Luke recorded, "Then great fear came on the **whole church** [authentic disciples] in Jerusalem" (Acts 5:11).

From this point forward, Luke used the terms *church* and *disciples* interchangeably. This is clear in Paul's ministry when he left on his second missionary journey. We read that "he traveled through Syria and Cilicia, **strengthening the churches**" (Acts 15:41). Later, when he left on his third journey, Luke recorded that Paul "set out, traveling through one place after another in the region of Galatia and Phrygia, **strengthening all the disciples**" (18:23).

Throughout the book of Acts, Luke used the terms *church* or *churches* eighteen times to refer to local communities of authentic disciples:

- Eight times to refer to the church in Jerusalem
- Four times to refer to the church in Antioch of Syria
- Two times to refer to the church in Ephesus
- Four times to refer to churches in various geographical areas

The following are the specific references:

The *Ekklesia* in Acts

5:11	"Then great fear came on the whole **church** [in Jerusalem]"
8:1	"A severe persecution broke out against the **church** in Jerusalem"

9:31	"So, the **church** throughout all Judea, Galilee, and Samaria had peace and was strengthened"
11:22	"News about them [believers in Antioch] reached the **church** in Jerusalem"
11:26	"For a whole year they [Barnabas and Paul] met with the **church** [in Antioch]"
12:1	"King Herod violently attacked some who belonged to the **church** [in Jerusalem]"
12:5	"The **church** [in Jerusalem] was praying fervently to God for him [Peter]"
13:1	"Now in the **church** at Antioch there were prophets and teachers"
14:23	"When they [Paul and Barnabas] had appointed elders for them in every **church** [in Lystra, Iconium, and Antioch in Pisidia]"
14:27	"After they arrived and gathered the **church** [in Antioch] together"
15:3	"When they had been sent on their way by the **church** [in Antioch of Syria]"
15:4	"They [Paul and Barnabas] were welcomed by the **church** [in Jerusalem]"
15:22	"Then the apostles and the elders, with the whole **church** [in Jerusalem]"
15:41	"He [Paul] traveled through Syria and Cilicia, strengthening the **churches**"
16:5	"So the **churches** [in various towns] were strengthened in the faith and grew daily in numbers"
18:22	"He [Paul] went up to Jerusalem and greeted the **church**"
20:17	"Now from Miletus, he [Paul] sent to Ephesus and summoned the elders of the **church**"
20:28	"Shepherd the **church** of God [in Ephesus], which he purchased with his own blood"

Following the book of Acts, the term *disciples* is never used again to refer to a community of believers. Neither is *disciple* used to refer to an individual believer. However, this is not true of "church" or "churches," which are used approximately one hundred times in the New Testament. Of these references, *ekklesia* refers to the universal church, approximately twenty times. The remaining references (about 80 percent of the time) refer to local churches or geographical communities of faith.

Note: For a complete listing of the terms *church* or *churches*, see the link in Appendix B. You'll also be able to see how these two terms compare with Luke's use of "disciple" or "disciples" in the book of Acts.[1]

Brothers and Sisters

Adelphoi is the most common word used to describe authentic disciples and those who comprise New Testament churches. Unfortunately, translating this Greek word into English is a problem since "brothers" is a literal translation of *adelphoi* and when translated in this way, it appears to be "masculine." However, in the Greek text the word can mean "brothers" or both "brothers and sisters"—depending on the contextual meaning. The following is a list of the times *adelphoi* is used in the book of Acts to mean both "brothers and sisters":

Adelphoi in the Book of Acts[2]

1:15	"Peter stood up among the **brothers and sisters**"
6:3	"**Brothers and sisters**, select from among you seven men"
11:1	"The **brothers and sisters** who were throughout Judea"
11:29	"Each of the disciples . . . determined to send relief to the **brothers and sisters** who lived in Judea"
15:3	"They [Paul and Barnabas and others] brought great joy to all the **brothers and sisters**" in Phoenicia and Samaria.
15:32	"Both Judas and Silas . . . encouraged the **brothers and sisters**" in Antioch.
15:33	"They were sent back in peace by the **brothers and sisters**" in Antioch.
15:36	"Let's go back and visit the **brothers and sisters** in every town" in Galatia.
15:40	"But Paul chose Silas and departed [on the second missionary journey], after being commended by the **brothers and sisters**"
16:2	"The **brothers and sisters** at Lystra and Iconium spoke highly of him [Timothy]"[3]
16:40	"They [Paul and Barnabas] saw and encouraged the **brothers and sisters**" at Lydia's house.

17:10	"The **brothers and sisters** [in Thessalonica] sent Paul and Silas away to Berea"
17:14	"The **brothers and sisters** [in Berea] immediately sent Paul away to go to the coast"
18:18	"Paul said farewell to the **brothers and sisters** [in Corinth]"
18:27	"The **brothers and sisters** wrote to the disciples to welcome him [Apollos]"
21:7	"We [Paul and his team] greeted the **brothers and sisters**" in Ptolemais.
28:14	"There [in Puteoli] we found **brothers and sisters**"
28:15	"Now the **brothers and sisters** from there [Rome] . . . had come to meet us"

It's significant that *adelphoi* (meaning both "brothers and sisters") is used more frequently than any other description of believers in the New Testament—nearly two hundred times. In other words, God designed the local church to be much more than just a *group* of true believers who, as authentic disciples, have put their faith in the Lord Jesus Christ for salvation. They are to be people growing in relationship with one another. (To see how the term *adelphoi* is translated throughout the New Testament and how it compares with "disciples" and "church," see Appendix B).

Saints

The word *hagios*, translated "saints," is another word used by New Testament authors to describe all authentic disciples. It actually means "holy ones," and regardless of their level of maturity, these New Testament believers are identified as "saints." This is obvious from Paul's letter to the Corinthians. Though Luke identified them as disciples, they were an immature and carnal group of believers (Acts 18:27; 1 Cor. 3:1–3).[4] Paul also greeted them as "those **sanctified** in Christ Jesus, called as **saints**, with all those in every place who call on the name of Jesus Christ our Lord—both their Lord and ours" (1 Cor. 1:2; see also 2 Cor. 1:1).[5]

Hagios appears four times in Acts. Luke referred to:

- The "**saints** in Jerusalem" (9:13)
- The "**saints** who lived in Lydda" (9:32)
- The "**saints**" in Joppa (9:41)
- The "**saints**" in prison (26:10)

When we look at the rest of the New Testament, the term is used more than forty times (to see all instances when the term *saints* is used in the book of Acts and the rest of the New Testament letters, see Appendix B).

Clearly, the word *saints* is used to refer to all believers. Because of their faith in the death and resurrection of the Lord Jesus Christ, God sees all authentic disciples as perfectly holy. In fact, because of His sovereign elective grace, God sees all true believers in Christ as already seated "with him in the heavens" (Eph. 1:4; 2:6).

The Scriptures make it clear, however, that all who are identified as saints were to experience **progressive sanctification**—that is, to grow more and more "into maturity with a stature measured by Christ's fullness" (Eph. 4:13). This process is to continue until Christ returns and all believers are transformed into His image. As John wrote, "Dear friends, we are God's children **now**, and what we **will be** has not yet been revealed. We know that when he appears, **we will be like him** because **we will see him as he is**" (1 John 3:2).

The Body

The Greek word *soma* that is translated "body" is also an important and descriptive concept in describing authentic disciples. It's a metaphor used only by the apostle Paul. He inscribed the word *soma* fifteen times in 1 Corinthians 12 to refer to the human body. He then made the application four times to refer to the church as the **body** of Christ. More specifically he wrote—"Now you are the **body of Christ**, and individual members of it" (1 Cor. 12:27).

When Paul wrote to the Romans, he used the same metaphor, succinctly summarizing what he wrote to the Corinthians: "Now as we have many parts in **one body**, and all the **parts** do not have the same function, in the same way we who are many are **one body** in Christ and

individually members of one another" (Rom. 12:4–5). (To see how the term *body* is used in the letters Paul wrote, see Appendix B.)

The significance of this metaphor becomes obvious in the New Testament letters. All believers need one another and are to minister to one another in order to become more and more like Christ. In fact, a functioning body (meaning "church") is an important way for all "saints" who have been "saved by grace through faith" to become mature, demonstrating "we are his workmanship, created in Christ Jesus for good works, which God prepared ahead of time for us to do" (Eph. 2:8–10). Paul went on in his letter to the Ephesians to make this clear: "From him the **whole body**, fitted and knit together by **every supporting ligament**, promotes the growth of the body for building itself up in love by the proper working of **each individual part**" (Eph. 4:16).

Temple or Building

The terms *temple* or *building* are also used exclusively by the apostle Paul. Writing to the Corinthians, he stated, "Don't you yourselves know that you are **God's temple** and that the Spirit of God lives in you? If anyone destroys **God's temple**, God will destroy him; for **God's temple** is holy, and that is what you are" (1 Cor. 3:16–17).

Ironically, Paul identified these carnal believers in Corinth as a "holy temple" even though the majority were woefully immature and living in an unholy way. However, when Paul used this term, it indeed correlates with his instructions to grow spiritually and as "saints" (holy ones) to more and more measure up to their true identity in Christ.

Paul underscores this important truth when he wrote to the Romans:

> What shall we say then [since they had been justified by faith (Rom. 5:1)]? Should we continue in sin so that grace may multiply? Absolutely not! How can we who died to sin still live in it? (Rom. 6:1–2)

Paul continued this emphasis in his second letter to the Corinthians, emphasizing that as believers they were not to continue in any way to worship idols in **pagan temples** and engage in any form of unrighteousness—which certainly involved sexual immorality. Paul then stated why they should not be in fellowship or partnership with unbelievers in Corinth. As authentic disciples they were "the **temple** of the living God" (2 Cor. 6:16).

Paul also addressed this same spiritual reality in his letter to the Ephesians. In this instance, he used the term *building*, a metaphor emphasizing that all believers are to build their lives "on the **foundation** of the apostles and prophets, with Christ Jesus himself as the **cornerstone**" (Eph. 2:20).

Note here the correlation with Paul's reference to God's temple when he wrote to the Corinthians: "In him the **whole building**, being put together, grows into a **holy temple** in the Lord. In him you are also being built together for God's dwelling in the Spirit" (Eph. 2:21–22).

Clearly, Paul was contrasting God's spiritual temple—the church—with the Old Testament temple, which began with the tabernacle at Mount Sinai. Because Christ sacrificed His life on the cross as the perfect Lamb of God, all believers can enter God's presence. We are positionally sanctified. Since as believers we are God's spiritual, holy temple, indwelt by the Holy Spirit, we are to more and more reflect God's holiness in our relationships with God and with one another.

The apostle Peter utilized a similar metaphor to describe the church. He wrote, "You yourselves, as **living stones**, a **spiritual house**, are being built to be a holy priesthood to offer spiritual sacrifices acceptable to God through Jesus Christ" (1 Peter 2:5; see Rom. 12:1–2).

God's Household

There is another significant term used to describe who believers are once they become authentic disciples. As Christ's church, we are God's **household** or **family**. Paul described this reality in his letter to the Ephesians: "So, then, you are no longer foreigners and strangers, but fellow citizens with the saints, and members of God's **household**" (Eph. 2:19).

Though this term is used only a few times to describe authentic disciples, it correlates beautifully with that pervasive concept—that all believers are "brothers and sisters" in Christ. As we've noted, this is a term used nearly two hundred times to describe our relationship with one another as believers. As "brothers and sisters" we are members of **God's household** or **family**.

As the biblical story of the church continued to unfold, the "household" concept is important in understanding God's plan for leadership in the church—the "household of God." Paul wrote that every spiritual leader should be able to "manage **his own household competently**." If this is not true, how will he be able to "take care of God's church?"— namely, **God's household** (1 Tim. 3:4–5).

Concluding Thoughts

All of these terms and concepts introduce us to what Jesus had in mind when He told the apostles to "go make disciples." In a later chapter we'll look at the supracultural principles that emerge from these observations and conclusions.

1. When Jesus said go "make disciples," He was in essence commissioning these men and all believers thereafter to make "authentic disciples"—people who sincerely believe in the Lord Jesus Christ, not just as a great teacher—but as the Son of God who is one with God the Father.
2. When Jesus said go "make disciples," He was referring to establishing groups of people called churches. These churches were in turn to become maturing communities of faith located throughout the world, communicating to unbelievers who the Lord Jesus Christ is—the one who came from the Father to be the Savior of the world.
3. When Jesus said go "make disciples," He was referring to establishing churches where all members function as brothers and sisters, developing deeper and deeper relationships with one another, and also demonstrating to the world who the Lord Jesus Christ is.
4. When Jesus said go "make disciples," He was referring to helping all believers understand they are "saints" or "holy ones" in God's sight. Positionally, they are "perfectly holy" in God's redemptive

plan. They are all to reflect their authentic relationship with Jesus Christ by developing Christ's holiness until He returns, and are transformed fully into His image (Eph. 2:8–10).

5. When Jesus said go "make disciples," He was referring to establishing local communities of faith where each functions as a local "body" of believers where "all members" of that "body" participate in building up one another.

6. When Jesus said go "make disciples," He was referring to communities of believers who are spiritual "temples" or "buildings" where all believers are "living stones" indwelt by the Holy Spirit. They are "to present" their "bodies as a living sacrifice, holy and pleasing to God" which is their "true worship" (Rom. 12:1).

7. When Jesus said go "make disciples," He was referring to functioning as God's household. As God's adopted children through Jesus Christ, all believers become brothers and sisters in Christ who are to love one another as Christ has loved them (Eph. 1:5; Rom. 12:10).

A Question for Thought and Discussion

How do the various terms and concepts that describe believers help us understand the way God designed the church to function?

5

Making Disciples in Acts

Video Intro from Gene

3lenses.org/c05

After Jesus ascended to heaven and the Holy Spirit came on the day of Pentecost, the apostles began immediately to carry out the Great Commission—to make disciples. They began in Jerusalem as Jesus had directed and then carried the good news to "all Judea and Samaria, and to the ends of the earth" (Acts 1:8).[1]

As we've seen from Paul's first missionary journey, "making disciples" simply meant to lead people to put their faith in Jesus Christ as the Messiah and Son of God. As Luke recorded, "After they had preached the gospel in that town [Derbe] and **made many disciples**, they returned to Lystra, to Iconium, and to Antioch, **strengthening the disciples** by encouraging them to continue in the faith" (Acts 14:21–22a).

Luke used a number of words in the book of Acts to describe this evangelistic activity and function (see chart on the following page). However, there are several basic words that appear frequently, and each contributes to our understanding of how the unsaved world was reached with the gospel of Christ in the first century. And, as multitudes "became disciples," they were instructed to join the apostles and other key leaders in carrying out this initial step in the Great Commission—to multiply themselves by also "making disciples."

Evangelistic Functions: Words Luke Used to Describe "Making Disciples" in the Book of Acts

• Declared	• Testified	• Refuted
• Spoke	• Witnessed	• Explained
• Taught	• Exhorted	• Demonstrated
• Proclaimed	• Praised	• Gave evidence
• Preached	• Reasoned	• Persuaded

They Spoke

One of the most common words is the one translated "speaking" or "spoke." The verb *laleo* simply means "to talk" or "to tell," although it is often associated with "teaching" and "preaching." It describes both natural and formal communication. For example, we read that Peter and John were in the temple "**speaking** to the people" (Acts 4:1). This communication is later described as "**teaching** the people and **proclaiming** in Jesus the resurrection of the dead" (4:2).

One of the most informal settings happened when Paul and his missionary companions went "outside the city gate" while in Philippi. They discovered a group of women by the riverside. Luke—who was with Paul—has recorded: "We sat down and **spoke** to the women gathered there" (Acts 16:13). Obviously, this was evangelistic communication that was more natural and intimate. As a result, Lydia, a well-to-do businesswoman, became a believer, along with her household.

Though this word (*laleo*) is the most common one used in describing the way the message of Christianity was presented, we can learn several lessons from the context in which the word was used.

They "**spoke** the **word**" (their message; Acts 16:32).

They **spoke** "in the **name of Jesus**" (their authority; Acts 3:6; 4:10, 18; 5:40; 9:27; 10:48; 16:18; 19:5, 13, 17).

They **spoke** with "**boldness**" (their manner; Acts 4:31; 28:31).

They were to **speak** "and **tell** the people all about **this life**" (the life of Jesus; Acts 5:20).

They "**spoke** in such a way that a great number of both Jews and Greeks **believed**" (their objectives, Acts 14:1).

They Evangelized

This basic Greek word (*euangelidzo*) is frequently translated "proclaimed the good news" or they were "preaching the gospel" (Acts 8:12, 25; 16:10). Clearly, it is a word that implies "content." It refers to the message that was being spoken as well as the way it was being communicated. In Acts 5:42, Luke recorded this evangelistic activity by the apostles: "Every day in the temple, and in various homes, they continued teaching and **proclaiming the good news** that Jesus is the Messiah."

This communication involved more than just a natural conversation. It was more deliberate and intentional and often accompanied with miraculous manifestations. In this sense, it was a process carried on primarily by the apostles and key men like Stephen and Philip and the others who were selected to care for the widows in Jerusalem. Note how the basic word *euangelidzo* is used as the redemptive story unfolds in the book of Acts. Note, too, that translators have used several words in English to translate this Greek word and to describe this process.

Philip in Samaria:

> Philip went down to a city in Samaria and **proclaimed the Messiah** to them. (Acts 8:5)

Peter and John in Samaritan villages:

> So, after they had testified and spoken the word of the Lord, they traveled back to Jerusalem, **preaching the gospel** in many villages of the Samaritans. (Acts 8:25)

Philip and the Ethiopian eunuch:

> Philip proceeded to **tell him the good news** about Jesus, beginning with that Scripture. (Acts 8:35)

Men from Cyprus and Syria in Antioch:

> But there were some of them ["those who had been scattered as a result of persecution"], men from Cyprus and Cyrene, who came to Antioch and began speaking to the Greeks also, **proclaiming the good news** about the Lord Jesus. (Acts 11:20)[2]

Paul and Barnabas in Lystra and Derbe:

> There they continued **preaching the gospel**. (Acts 14:7)

Paul and Barnabas in Derbe:

> After they had **preached the gospel** in that town and **made many disciples**, they returned to Lystra, to Iconium, and to Antioch. (Acts 14:21)

Paul's vision to go to Macedonia:

> After he had seen the vision, we immediately made efforts to set out for Macedonia, concluding that God had called us to **preach the gospel** to them. (Acts 16:10)

They Taught

Though *didasko,* meaning "to teach," is one of the most common words in the New Testament used to help believers become mature in Christ, it is also used frequently to describe communicating the gospel to the unsaved. In this sense, the word appears most frequently in the opening chapters of the book of Acts, particularly in chapters 4 and 5. The focus is on the apostles, particularly Peter and John. Their evangelistic teaching ministry became a great frustration to the religious leaders. In fact, the terms *preaching* and *teaching* unfold the narrative.

In the opening verses of chapter 4, "the Sadducees confronted" the apostles "because they were annoyed that they were **teaching** the people and **proclaiming** in Jesus the resurrection of the dead" (Acts 4:1–2). The Sadducees then "took them into custody" (Acts 4:3).

The other factor involved the beggar whom Peter and John had healed. The religious leaders could not deny the miracle so they simply "ordered them not to **speak** or **teach** at all in the name of Jesus" (4:18).

The apostles responded by saying they had no choice but to continue. They were once again arrested and jailed—but were miraculously delivered by an angel who told them to continue their ministry. "They entered the temple at daybreak and began to **teach**" (5:21), and "someone" then rushed off to tell the chief priests that the men they had locked in prison the day before were "standing in the temple and **teaching** the people" (5:25). Again, the apostles were taken into custody. In consternation, the high priest said, "Didn't we strictly order you not to **teach** in this name? Look, you have filled Jerusalem with your **teaching**" (5:28).[3]

The most significant observation regarding this **teaching** process in the early days of the church is that it was used primarily by the apostles and others who were empowered by the Holy Spirit in a special way. This implies that it was a more sophisticated process than just "speaking" or sharing the gospel—calling for greater skill and knowledge. Clearly, it involved more than just presenting the gospel message regarding the death and resurrection of Jesus Christ. Rather, it included the presentation of the total redemptive message throughout the Scriptures. For example, after the apostles were arrested and jailed for their powerful healing ministry, they were miraculously delivered by an angel of the Lord, who then said—"Go and stand in the temple, and **tell the people all about this life**" (Acts 5:20).

This is indeed a comprehensive statement that is later illustrated in the life of Stephen, who stood before the Jewish ruling body (the Sanhedrin) and delivered a powerful message summarizing the redemptive message in the Old Testament—beginning with Abraham's special calling. The overall content of his message pointed to the coming of Jesus Christ, whom the religious leaders had rejected (Acts 7:51–53).

The apostles, of course, were in a unique position to communicate the total redemptive message, having spent nearly three years being trained by the greatest teacher who ever lived. When the rulers and scribes "observed the boldness of Peter and John and realized that they were uneducated and untrained men, they were amazed and recognized that **they had been with Jesus**" (Acts 4:13).

This ability to teach was also directly related to Jesus' promise to the eleven in the upper room. Knowing they were nervous and insecure with His statement that He was "going to prepare a place for" them, Jesus promised to send the Spirit of truth to "guide" them "into all the truth," to "remind" them of everything He had taught them during His three years of ministry (John 14:2, 26; 16:13). We also see this happening in the book of Acts. First, the apostles **spoke** and then they **wrote**, giving us significant portions of the New Testament.

At this point, it's also helpful to note the close relationship between "speaking" (telling), "proclaiming," and "teaching." In addition to referring to more natural and intimate communication, "speaking" often included "proclaiming," which is usually more intentional and formal communication. This is illustrated in the following references:

Peter and John in the temple court:

> While they were **speaking** to the people, the priests, the captain of the temple police, and the Sadducees confronted them, because they were annoyed that they were **teaching** the people and **proclaiming** in Jesus the resurrection of the dead. (Acts 4:1–2)

The apostles' communication:

> But an angel of the Lord opened the doors of the jail during the night, brought them [**the apostles**] out, and said, "Go and stand in the temple, and **tell the people** all about this life." Hearing this, they entered the temple at daybreak and began to **teach**. (Acts 5:19–20)

> After they called in **the apostles** and had them flogged, they ordered them not **to speak** in the name of Jesus and released them. . . . Every day in the temple, and in various homes, they continued **teaching** and **proclaiming the good news** that Jesus is the Messiah. (Acts 5:40, 42)

Men from Cyprus and Cyrene:

> But there were some of them, men from Cyprus and Cyrene, who came to Antioch and began **speaking** to the Greeks also, **proclaiming the good news** about the Lord Jesus. (Acts 11:20)

They Proclaimed or Preached

The word *kerusso* means "to cry" or "proclaim as a herald." In this sense, the meaning is similar to *euangelidzo*—though seemingly more intense communication. Again, like teaching, this evangelistic activity among unbelievers seemed to be the responsibility of certain gifted individuals who had been chosen and empowered by God to proclaim in a special way the gospel of Christ.

This is illustrated in the life of Philip, who "went down to a city in Samaria and **proclaimed** the Messiah to them." Consequently, "the crowds were all paying attention to what Philip said, as they listened and **saw the signs** he was performing" (Acts 8:5–6).

Peter also illustrates *euangelidzo* when he was sent by the Holy Spirit to witness to the Gentile, Cornelius. Thus, he testified:

He commanded us **to preach** to the people and **to testify** that he is the one appointed by God to be the judge of the living and the dead. All the prophets testify about him that through his name everyone who believes in him receives forgiveness of sins. (Acts 10:43)

Paul, too, illustrates that proclaiming the gospel message in this way (*kerusso*) was done by those who had a unique calling or gifts. Consider these references:

After Paul's conversion:

And after taking some food, he regained his strength. Saul was with the disciples in Damascus for some time. Immediately he began **proclaiming** Jesus in the synagogues: "He is the Son of God." (Acts 9:19–20)

Paul and the Ephesian elders:

And now I know that none of you, among whom I went about **preaching** the kingdom, will ever see me again. Therefore I declare to you this day that I am innocent of the blood of all of you, because I did not avoid **declaring** to you **the whole plan of God**. (Acts 20:25–27)

Paul while in prison:

> Paul stayed two whole years in his own rented house. And he welcomed all who visited him, **proclaiming** the kingdom of God and **teaching** about the Lord Jesus Christ with all boldness and without hindrance. (Acts 28:30–31)

They Announced

A word closely related to *kerusso* is the word *katangello*, meaning "to announce publicly," or "to proclaim and tell thoroughly." In most instances, it is used to describe Paul's evangelistic ministry in the various Jewish synagogues. Here in these religious centers of learning and worship Paul thoroughly announced and proclaimed the Word of God.

Paul and Barnabas in Cyprus:

> So being sent out by the Holy Spirit, they went down to Seleucia, and from there they sailed to Cyprus. Arriving in Salamis, they **proclaimed** the word of God in the **Jewish synagogues**. (Acts 13:4–5)

Paul in the Synagogue in Pisidia Antioch:

> Therefore, let it be known to you, brothers and sisters, that through this man forgiveness of sins is being **proclaimed to you**. Everyone who believes is justified through him from everything that you could not be justified from through the law of Moses. (Acts 13:38–39)

Paul and Barnabas' ministry on the first journey:

> After some time had passed, Paul said to Barnabas, "Let's go back and visit the brothers and sisters in every town where we have **preached** the word of the Lord and see how they're doing." (Acts 15:36)

Paul in the synagogue in Thessalonica:

> As usual, Paul went into the **synagogue**, and on three Sabbath days reasoned with them from the Scriptures, explaining and proving that it was necessary for the Messiah to suffer and rise from the dead: "This Jesus I am **proclaiming** to you is the Messiah." (Acts 17:2–3)

They Solemnly Testified

A common word for testify is *martureo*, meaning "to bear witness" (Acts 1:8). However, in the book of Acts, Luke used the verb *diamarturomai* to describe the evangelistic process that is translated "solemnly testified." It means to "earnestly charge and attest," and has both strong intellectual and emotional overtones. The Word of God was being presented seriously, carefully, and with determination. If *martureo* means "to bear witness," *diamarturomai* means "to bear a **thorough witness**."

This concept first appeared at the beginning of Acts in Peter's sermon on the day of Pentecost: "With many other words he **solemnly testified** and kept on urging them, saying, 'Be saved from this perverse generation!'" (Acts 2:40 NASB). It appeared finally in the last chapter of Acts, where we find Paul in Rome. He was given a degree of freedom but with a "soldier who guarded him" (28:16).

Within just three days, Paul called together the Jewish leaders and rehearsed the events from Jerusalem onward. They were interested and set aside a day for Paul to present his total case. And on that day, many came as Paul explained his mission "by **solemnly testifying** about the kingdom of God and trying to persuade them concerning Jesus, from both the Law of Moses and from the Prophets, from morning until evening" (Acts 28:23 NASB).

As you trace this word through the book of Acts, it takes on a strong "apologetic" tone and meaning. Both Peter and Paul were attempting to convince their hearers that Jesus Christ was truly the Messiah. They were not simply presenting the gospel but were attesting and giving evidence from the Old Testament as well as from their own personal experience that Jesus was and is the Christ.

Note these additional references:

Peter with Cornelius:

> And He ordered us to preach to the people, and to **testify solemnly** that this is the One who has been appointed by God as Judge of the living and the dead. All the prophets testify of Him, that through His name everyone who believes in Him receives forgiveness of sins. (Acts 10:42–43 NASB)

Paul before the Ephesian elders:

> But I do not consider my life of any account as dear to myself, so that I may finish my course and the ministry which I received from the Lord Jesus, to **testify solemnly** of the gospel of God's grace. (Acts 20:24 NASB)

Paul in Corinth:

> But when Silas and Timothy came down from Macedonia, Paul began devoting himself completely to the word, **testifying** to the Jews that Jesus was the Christ. (Acts 18:5 NASB)

The Lord's words to Paul in Jerusalem:

> But on the following night, the Lord stood near him and said, "Be courageous! For as you have **testified** to the *truth* about Me in Jerusalem, so you must **testify** in Rome also." (Acts 23:11 NASB)

They Reasoned

The word *dialegomai*, meaning "to reason, to discourse with, or to discuss," is used only of Paul's communication with the non-Christian world. The word does not appear in Acts until Paul arrived in Thessalonica on his second journey. Here we find him going "into the synagogue, and on three Sabbath days **reasoned** with them from the Scriptures, explaining and proving that it was necessary for the Messiah to suffer and rise from the dead" (Acts 17:2–3). Luke's use of "explaining" and "proving" certainly reinforce the meaning of the word *dialegomai*.

When Paul and Silas left Thessalonica and arrived in Berea they obviously engaged in the same process (*dialegomai*), since the Jews particularly "received the word with eagerness and **examined the Scriptures daily** to see if" the message regarding Jesus Christ was indeed accurate and true (Acts 17:10–11). As a result, "many of them believed" (17:12).

Luke also used this word to describe Paul's communication in Athens. When he arrived, he was "deeply distressed when he saw that the city was full of idols. So he **reasoned** in the synagogue with the Jews and with those who worshiped God, as well as in the marketplace every day with those [both Jews and Gentiles] who happened to be there" (Acts 17:16–17).

As you look at this communication process (*dialegomai*), which involves extensive dialogue and interaction, note that Paul's ministry was increasingly taking him into a pagan environment permeated with Greek and Roman thought and culture. Both Jews and Greeks were ignorant of what had really transpired in the land of Palestine over the last several years. To the religious Jews, the promised Messiah was not a new concept, but they probably knew little about Jesus of Nazareth. And what they *had* heard was no doubt distorted. The Greeks, of course, would have known little if anything, since their primary source of information was what they heard from the Jewish community.

Notice, too, that Luke began recording time factors in the context where this word *dialegomai* is used. For example, Paul stayed on in Corinth for a **year and a half** (Acts 18:11) and in Ephesus for **three years**.

Taking into consideration the mentality of these people, their cultural backgrounds, their total ignorance regarding Christianity, as well as the method of communication they were used to, the implication is obvious. Paul used a means of communication that could more effectively reach these people with the gospel. He knew he had no foundation on which to build, so he settled into these strategic communities, got to know the thinking of these people, and taught the Scriptures in-depth on their mental and emotional wavelengths.

This is dramatically illustrated in Paul's extended ministry in Ephesus. He first entered the synagogue and Luke used several words to describe his communication—including the basic word *dialegomai*: "And he entered the synagogue and continued speaking out boldly for three months, **having discussions** and persuading them about the kingdom of God." (Acts 19:8 NASB)

When some of the Jews rejected Paul's efforts, and verbally attacked those who put their faith in Jesus Christ, Paul left the synagogue and went to the "school of Tyrannus," and for two years he devoted his time to "**[have] discussions daily**" with those who would listen (Acts 19:9 NASB). Many from all over Asia put their faith in Christ and probably returned to their respective cities and started churches—seven of which are mentioned in the book of Revelation: the churches in Ephesus, Smyrna, Pergamum, Thyatira, Sardis, Philadelphia, and Laodicea (Rev. 1:11).

Note additional references to this "reasoning" process as Paul communicated the gospel:

Paul in Corinth:

He **reasoned** in the synagogue every Sabbath and tried to persuade both Jews and Greeks. (Acts 18:4)

Paul's first experience in Ephesus:

They came to Ephesus, and he left them there. Now he himself entered the synagogue and **reasoned** with the Jews.
(Acts 18:19 NASB)

Paul before Felix:

And **as he reasoned about** righteousness and self-control and the coming judgment, Felix was alarmed and said, "Go away for the present. When I get an opportunity I will summon you." (Acts 24:25 ESV)

Concluding Thoughts

As stated at the beginning of this chapter, there are a number of words used to describe the evangelistic process in the book of Acts. These words certainly clarify and support the six key concepts outlined and described in this chapter. As demonstrated, these words in the Greek text provide nuances that are difficult to capture in English but are helpful in understanding the overall process of "making disciples."

It's also clear from this study that God initially launched the church through the men Jesus chose as apostles as well as other key individuals such as Philip, Stephen, Barnabas, Silas, Timothy, Titus, and others. They became traveling evangelists and teachers.

Clearly, they were supernaturally and uniquely equipped to carry out the Great Commission. This is directly related to Jesus' promise to the apostles just before He ascended back to heaven (Acts 1:2, 4, 6):

He said to them [the eleven apostles], "It is not for you to know times or periods that the Father has set by his own authority. But you will receive **power** when the Holy Spirit has come on you, and you will be my witnesses in Jerusalem, in all Judea and Samaria, and to the ends of the earth." (Acts 1:7–8)

As the story unfolds in the book of Acts, it's obvious this "power" Jesus initially referred to related directly to the **supernatural ability to verify the gospel with signs, wonders, and miracles.** This is clear from the following observations:

- The apostles spoke living languages they had never learned. "When this sound occurred, a crowd came together and was confused because each one heard them **speaking in his own language.** They were astounded and amazed, saying, 'Look, aren't all these who are speaking Galileans [the eleven apostles]? How is it that each of us can hear them **in our own native language?**'" (Acts 2:6–8).
- Peter spoke of God's **power** that **enabled** the apostles to be witnesses of the resurrection of Christ. "When Peter saw this, he addressed the people: 'Fellow Israelites, why are you amazed at this? Why do you stare at us, as though we had made him walk by our own **power** or **godliness?**'" (Acts 3:12).
- After Peter and John were arrested, the Jewish leaders asked them "by **what power** or in **what name**" they had healed this lame man (Acts 4:7).
- After Peter and John were released, we read that "with **great power** the **apostles** were giving testimony [witness] to the resurrection of the Lord Jesus, and great **grace** was on all of them"— namely, all the apostles (Acts 4:33).
- Following the dreadful event involving the death of Ananias and Sapphira, "many **signs** and **wonders** were being done among the people through the hands of **the apostles.**" Consequently, "believers were added to the Lord in increasing numbers—multitudes of both men and women" (Acts 5:12, 14).
- The power of the Spirit was so obvious in Peter's ministry that people "would carry the sick out into the streets and lay them

on cots and mats so that when Peter came by, at least his shadow might fall on some of them" (Acts 5:15).

- Stephen, one of the Grecian Jews chosen to minister to the neglected widows, was among those who experienced God's supernatural anointing. We read—"Now Stephen, full of **grace** and **power**, was performing **great wonders** and **signs** among the people" (Acts 6:8)—which led to his sermon before the Sanhedrin and his martyrdom (7:1–60).

- Philip, like Stephen, experienced an unusual anointing. He went to minister to the Samaritans, who witnessed "the **signs** he was performing" (Acts 8:6). Many who were **demon possessed**, **paralyzed**, and **crippled** were healed (8:6–8).

- When the apostle Paul arrived in Cyprus, he **struck a sorcerer blind**, which caused the proconsul, Sergius Paulus, to believe in the message about Christ (Acts 13:12).

- When Paul and Barnabas arrived in Iconium, "they stayed there a long time and spoke boldly for the Lord, **who testified to the message of his grace** by enabling **them** [both Paul and Barnabas] to do **signs** and **wonders**" (Acts 14:3). Many people believed, and a church was born.

- When Paul arrived in Lystra, he healed a man who "had never walked" (Acts 14:8). This led to his being stoned and left for dead. But Paul survived, and we read that the "**disciples** gathered around" him—indicating people in Lystra responded to the gospel that was verified by this miracle (14:20).

- When the Jerusalem council met with the apostles and elders, "the whole assembly became silent and listened to Barnabas and Paul describe all the **signs** and **wonders** God had done through them among the Gentiles" on this first missionary journey (Acts 15:12). As a result, churches were born, particularly in Pisidian Antioch, Iconium, Lystra, and Derbe.

- When Paul spent three years in Ephesus, we read that "God was performing **extraordinary miracles** by Paul's hands, so that even **facecloths** or **aprons** that had touched his skin were brought to the sick, and the **diseases left them**, and the **evil spirits came out of them**" (Acts 19:11–12). Many became believers (19:18).

Since God is God, He can certainly work signs, wonders, and miracles anytime He wishes in order to convince unbelievers to put their faith in Jesus Christ. There are reports of miraculous events today that seem to be validated—particularly in parts of the world that are virtually pagan and dominated by false religions. However, there has never been an authenticated, inspired record of the specific kinds of signs and wonders like those described in the book of Acts and the New Testament letters. These miracles were so verifiable that no one, including those hostile to the gospel, could deny there were supernatural events, as illustrated by those in Sanhedrin: "What should we do with these men [Peter and John]? For an **obvious sign** has been done through them, **clear to everyone** living in Jerusalem, and **we cannot deny it**" (Acts 4:16).

All this sets the stage for the way churches throughout the centuries are to continue to carry out the Great Commission. As we'll see, Jesus spoke of and prayed for another supernatural and supracultural way to verify who He is and that through faith in Him we can have eternal life.

A Question for Thought and Discussion

How do the functional terms used to describe evangelism in the unfolding story in the book of Acts help us develop appropriate forms and effective methods of communication?

6

Making Disciples in the New Testament Letters

Video Intro from Gene

3lenses.org/c06

As we trace evangelistic communication in the book of Acts, the focus is clearly on the activities and functions of the apostles and other prominent leaders like Stephen, Philip, Paul, Barnabas, Silas, Timothy, and Titus. They spoke about Christ, told the good news, taught, proclaimed, testified, and reasoned with unbelievers. When we continue to study the New Testament letters, evangelistic activities and functions become directives and exhortations. However, we also see an added dimension and emphasis that takes us back to the upper room when Jesus met with the apostles. Jesus gave them a command that fully sets the stage for carrying out the Great Commission in communities where local churches were located.

Love One Another

Without question, this command provides continuity for making disciples as it is described in the New Testament letters.

The Setting

Jesus was in Jerusalem with the Twelve celebrating the Passover. Knowing His time was short, He sent Peter and John to prepare the Passover meal. But when all of them entered the room, it was obvious that Peter and John had not secured a servant to wash their feet—a custom that was not only practical but had deep meaning. Pragmatically, these men had just come in off the dirty, contaminated streets of Jerusalem. But spiritually the Passover meal was considered a holy remembrance.

The basin was there with water for washing feet. The towel was also there for drying. But the missing servant was a stark reminder that Peter and John had failed to secure this important person. However, they began the meal without engaging in this Jewish ritual and custom.

Jesus' Example

Once the meal had begun, it appears Jesus was waiting to see if Peter or John—or any of the other men—would volunteer to be the servant. No one made a move, so Jesus proceeded to wash their feet. It's understandable why Peter was so embarrassed, refusing to allow Jesus to wash his feet (John 13:6–10). He knew he and John had failed to secure a servant and he should have taken on this role.

Following this embarrassing time for all the apostles, Jesus made His point. Returning to His place at the table, He may have quietly looked each one in the eye—beginning with Peter and then John who reclined next to him—and asked this practical and convicting question:

> "Do you know what I have done for you? You call me Teacher and Lord—and you are speaking rightly, since that is what I am. So if I, your Lord and Teacher, have washed your feet, you also ought to wash one another's feet." (John 13:12b–14)

This was just the beginning of Jesus' lesson—a lesson in how to carry out the Great Commission.

Jesus' New Command

Jesus reiterated that it was time for His departure from the earth. In this context, He gave them a foundational commission prior to the Great Commission: "I give you a new command: **Love one another.** Just as I have loved you, you are also to **love one another.** By this everyone will know that you are my disciples, if you **love one another**" (John 13:34–35).

Jesus' three-fold command to "love one another" to demonstrate they were His disciples was indeed a prelude to His commission to make disciples. Clearly, Jesus told these men that as they carried out this commission, He wanted people everywhere to know what characterized authentic disciples—love for one another as Jesus loved them. They were to model what Jesus had just taught them.

Lessons Learned

Shortly after the church was born, John learned what Jesus really meant in the upper room when He charged them to love one another as He loved them. John saw this meaning literally fulfilled when his brother James paid the ultimate price—martyrdom (Acts 12:1–2). This was indeed the meaning of the foot washing experience—to follow Jesus' example, even if it meant death.

Years later—probably when John was ministering in Ephesus in his nineties—he picked up a scroll and penned these words, which reveal that he understood the true meaning of the foot washing experience. "This is how we have come to know love: **He laid down his life for us.** We should also **lay down our lives for our brothers and sisters**" (1 John 3:16).

Throughout this letter, John used the phrase to "love one another" five times (1 John 3:11, 23; 4:7, 11, 12). As he penned these words, it's obvious he had not forgotten Jesus' three-fold command decades earlier.

Producing Much Fruit

After Jesus and the eleven disciples left the upper room, they passed a vineyard that had been freshly pruned. As often happened in His ministry, Jesus used this opportunity to expand on what He had just shared in the upper room—namely, "By this everyone will know that you are my disciples, if you love one another" (John 13:35).

Perhaps pointing to the freshly pruned branches, Jesus made a statement that is basically identical to His command in the upper room: "My Father is glorified by this: that you produce **much fruit** and **prove to be my disciples**" (John 15:8).

The correlation is obvious, particularly when we compare the following statements with the "new command" Jesus had just given them at the Passover meal:

> This is my command: **Love one another as I have loved you**. . . .
> This is what I command you: **Love one another**.
> (John 15:12, 17; compare with 13:34)
>
> As the Father has loved me, I have also loved you. **Remain in my love**.
> (John 15:9)
>
> If you keep **my commands** you will **remain in my love**.
> (John 15:10)

A Deeper Dimension of Love

When Jesus stated it was to the Father's glory that they "produce much fruit," He was clearly elaborating on the concept of "loving one another." It also seems evident that He was referring to a deeper dimension of love than serving one another—as He had modeled with His own life in the upper room. Rather, Jesus was referring to the "fruit of righteousness" that is also a reflection of Christ's love when we keep His commandments. In other words, love as Jesus defined it refers not only to relationships but to character.

Paul captured this definition of love in his prayer for the Philippians:

> And I pray this: that **your love** will keep on growing in knowledge and every kind of discernment, so that you may **approve the things that are superior** and may be **pure and blameless** in the day of Christ, filled with the **fruit of righteousness** that comes through Jesus Christ to the **glory and praise of God**. (Phil. 1:9–11)

A Definite Correlation

When we compare Paul's prayer with Jesus' statements, we see a direct correlation:

1. Jesus wanted these men to produce **fruit**. Paul in turn prayed that the Philippians would be filled with the **fruit** of righteousness.
2. Jesus wanted them to not only produce **fruit,** but **more fruit** and **much fruit** (John 15:2–3, 5). In the same way, Paul prayed that the Philippians' **love** would abound **more** and **more**.
3. Jesus said that His "**Father is glorified**" by this kind of fruit bearing (John 15:8). Paul later wrote that the "**fruit of righteousness**" would be to the "**glory and praise of God** (Phil. 1:11)."

Clearly then, there is a dimension of love that goes beyond serving one another. It involves righteousness and holiness.

Jesus' Prayer for Oneness

Leaving the vicinity of the vineyard and continuing toward the Kidron Valley, Jesus made another significant point which was an extension of the foot washing lesson to love one another as He had love them. He did it in the form of a powerful and convicting prayer for these men—and for all of us who have put our faith in Christ. Addressing the heavenly Father, Jesus said:

> As you sent me **into the world**, I also have sent them **into the world**. I sanctify myself for **them**, so that **they** also may be sanctified by the truth. I pray not only for **these** [**the apostles**], but also for **those** who believe in me through their word [**believers of all time**]. May they **all be one**, as you, Father, are in me and I am in you. May they also be in us, **so that the world may believe you sent me.** I have given them the glory you have given me, **so that they may be one as we are one.** I am in them and you are in me, **so that they may be made**

completely one, that the world may know you have sent me and have loved them as you have loved me. (John 17:18–23)

Jesus' prayer clearly relates to communicating with unsaved people that He truly became the God-man. In a miraculous way, when we love one another as Jesus has loved us, it creates a powerful unity that demonstrates to the world that Jesus Christ is truly the Son of God and is one with the Father.

This is the message of the incarnation—"That is, in Christ, God was reconciling the world to himself, not counting their trespasses against them." God "has committed the message of reconciliation to us" and "we are ambassadors for Christ, since God is making his appeal through us" (2 Cor. 5:19–20a).

As I was researching this concept with my students at Dallas Theological Seminary, I was deeply moved by Francis Schaeffer's book *The Church at the End of the 20th Century*. Dr. Schaeffer included a powerful chapter called "The Final Apologetic," which is just as applicable today as when he wrote it. When local churches demonstrate the love and unity Jesus prayed for, it serves as a powerful bridge to the world—demonstrating that Jesus Christ is who He claimed to be—the incarnate Son of God.[1] This is an enduring truth that is applicable at any moment in history and in every culture of the world.

New Testament Correspondence

As we continue to follow this theme in the letters written to the churches, the correlation is obvious. We see consistent exhortations to "love one another" and to reflect this divine love in righteous and holy relationships. We also see a constant emphasis on what Jesus prayed for—oneness and unity. This is abundantly clear from the following references:

Christ's Command to "Love One Another"

The command to "love one another" is illustrated throughout the New Testament letters. (For a more exhaustive list, see chapter 17.)

Indeed, if you fulfill the royal law prescribed in the Scripture, **Love your neighbor as yourself**, you are doing well. (James 2:8)

And may the Lord cause you to increase and overflow with **love for one another** and **for everyone**, just as we do for you. (1 Thess. 3:12)

Love never ends. . . . Now these three remain: faith, hope, and **love**—but the greatest of these is **love**. (1 Cor. 13:8a, 13)

Walk worthy of the calling you have received . . . **bearing with one another in love**. (Eph. 4:1–2)

And I pray this: that **your love will keep on growing** in knowledge and every kind of discernment. (Phil. 1:9)

I want their hearts to be encouraged and **joined together in love**. (Col. 2:2a)

Above all, maintain constant **love for one another**, since **love** covers a multitude of sins. (1 Peter 4:8)

Let brotherly **love** continue. (Heb. 13:1)

Dear friends, if God **loved** us in this way, we also must **love one another**. (1 John 4:11)

Christ's Command to "Bear Much Fruit"

Perhaps the most direct references to a deeper dimension of love is what Paul wrote to the Ephesians:

Therefore, be imitators of God, as dearly loved children, and **walk in love**, as Christ also loved us and gave himself for us, a sacrificial and fragrant offering to God. But **sexual immorality** and **any impurity** or **greed** should not even be heard of among you, as is proper for saints. (Eph. 5:1–3)

For you were once darkness, but now you are light in the Lord. **Walk as children of light**—for the **fruit of the light** consists of all goodness, righteousness, and truth—testing what is pleasing to the Lord.

Don't participate in the **fruitless works of darkness**, but instead expose them. (Eph. 5:8–11)

Christ's Prayer to "Be One"

We also see a strong emphasis in the New Testament letters regarding what Jesus prayed for. In the following examples, note the emphasis on harmony, peace, being like-minded, and being one.

Now I urge you, brothers and sisters, in the name of our Lord Jesus Christ, that all of you **agree** in what you say, that there be **no divisions** among you, and that you **be united** with the same understanding and the same conviction. (1 Cor. 1:10)

Live in **harmony with one another**. (Rom. 12:16)

So then, let us pursue what **promotes peace** and what builds up one another. (Rom. 14:19)

Note: Paul's prayer is nearly identical to Jesus' prayer in John 17:21–23.

Now may the God who gives endurance and encouragement grant you to **live in harmony** with one another, according to Christ Jesus, so that you may glorify the God and Father of our Lord Jesus Christ with **one mind and one voice**. (Rom. 15:5–6)

Therefore I, the prisoner of the Lord, urge you to walk worthy of the calling you have received . . . making every effort to keep the **unity of the Spirit** through the **bond of peace**. (Eph. 4:1, 3)

Make my joy complete by thinking the same way, having the same love, **united in spirit**, **intent on one purpose**. (Phil. 2:2)

Community Evangelism

What Jesus said in conversation with His disciples sets the stage for the way all believers are to "make disciples" in their local communities. This is obvious in the letters that were written to these New Testament churches.

Business Life

Paul admonished the Thessalonians particularly to conduct their business affairs in a proper manner. Some of them were using the doctrine of the second coming of Christ as an excuse for being lazy. Paul exhorted them "to seek to lead a quiet life, to mind [their] own business, and to work with [their] own hands" (1 Thess. 4:11). He then gave the reason why: "So that you may behave properly in the presence of **outsiders** and not be dependent on anyone" (4:12). These believers were to live responsible and respectful lives so they, in turn, could effectively communicate the gospel to their unsaved neighbors.

Both Paul and Peter were also concerned that Christian slaves and masters should maintain a good testimony for others to see. Speaking of slaves, Paul said, "All who are under the yoke as slaves should regard their own masters as worthy of all respect, so that **God's name** and **his teaching** will not be blasphemed" (1 Tim. 6:1). In other words, it was God's will that unbelievers have a positive response to the way the gospel impacted those under the yoke of slavery.

Peter was even more specific when he said, "Household slaves, submit to your masters with all reverence not only to the **good** and **gentle** ones but also to the **cruel**. . . . But when you do what is good and suffer, if you endure it, this brings favor with God" (1 Peter 2:18, 20b).

In many instances slaves won their unsaved masters to Christ as well as winning their freedom. It happened because of their submissive attitudes and actions. Doing the opposite in those days could have brought instant persecution and even death. This was an amazing display of character to further the cause of Christ and played a vital role in eliminating slavery in the church.[2]

Regarding Paul's approach to the problem of slavery, Merrill Tenney has succinctly observed: "Nowhere in its pages is the institution [of slavery] attacked, nor is it defended. According to Paul's letters to the Asian churches, there were both slaves and slaveholders who were Christians. The slaves were enjoined to obey their masters and the masters were commanded not to be cruel to them. Such was the power of Christian fellowship, however, that the institution of slavery gradually weakened under its impact and finally disappeared."[3]

Social Life

Many of the believers in the New Testament world were converted out of a culture that involved a lifestyle seriously unbecoming to a follower of Jesus Christ. With their unsaved friends in view, Paul admonished these believers to "give no offense to Jews or Greeks" in their social life. "So, whether you eat or drink, or whatever you do, do everything for the glory of God" in order, said Paul, "that they may be **saved**" (1 Cor. 10:31–33).

Paul wrote these words to the Corinthian church. Many of these believers were living carnal lives, so much so that Paul stated they were living like the pagans they once were (1 Cor. 3:2). In essence, Paul was telling the Corinthians that the way to win people to Christ was not to claim to be followers of Jesus Christ and then to participate in their immoral and anti-Christian activities either within the church or outside in the community. To do so would only create a stumbling block for unbelievers and create disillusionment with the true message of Christianity.

Peter addressed this same issue: "Dear friends, I urge you as strangers and exiles to abstain from sinful desires that wage war against the soul. Conduct yourselves **honorably among the Gentiles**, so that when they slander you as evildoers, they will **observe your good works and will glorify God** on the day he visits" (1 Peter 2:11–12).

Peter was not saying that all would respond to the gospel. But he was saying that when the Holy Spirit begins His work in someone's heart, that person needs the backdrop of godly lifestyles to be able to evaluate objectively the claims of Christ's followers. Peter stated that those who respond negatively will be "put to shame" (1 Peter 3:16).

Home Life

Predictably, there were those in New Testament days who responded to the gospel, but their marital partners did not. Peter addressed believing wives and told them their unbelieving husbands "may be **won over** without a word by the way" they lived, demonstrating purity and reverence (1 Peter 3:1–2). Unsaved husbands would see "the imperishable quality of a gentle and quiet spirit" (3:4).[4]

Peter then turned to husbands and said, "Live with your wives in an understanding way" (3:7). Here Peter was addressing believing husbands and how they were to live with both believing and unbelieving wives. Once they became followers of Christ, they should no longer behave like pagan men who had little sensitivity toward women generally and their wives particularly.

Paul underscored this message to believing husbands when he told them to love their "wives, just as Christ loved the church and gave himself for it" (Eph. 5:25). Though he was obviously referring to believing wives, what he wrote applied to their unsaved spouses and correlates with Peter's words to live with their wives "in an understanding way, as with a weaker partner, showing them honor as coheirs of the grace of life, so that your prayers will not be hindered" (1 Peter 3:7).[5]

Peter and Paul were both stating a profound truth! It's not the words per se that convince unsaved spouses—or anyone—that they need Christ, but rather the impact of a continuous Christlike lifestyle that reflects the fruit of the Holy Spirit (Gal. 5:22–23a).

Church Life

Paul's letter to local churches especially demonstrates the effectiveness of their witness, both to believers and unbelievers.

The Church in Thessalonica—"And you yourselves became imitators of us and of the Lord when, in spite of severe persecution, you welcomed the message with joy from the Holy Spirit. As a result, you became an example to all the believers in Macedonia and Achaia. For the **word of the Lord rang out from you**, not only in Macedonia and Achaia, but in **every place that your faith in God has gone out**. Therefore, we don't need to say anything, for they themselves report what kind of reception we had from you: how you **turned to God from idols to serve the living and true God** and to wait for his Son from heaven, whom he raised from the dead—Jesus, who rescues us from the coming wrath" (1 Thess. 1:6–10).

The Church in Rome—We see this same dynamic in Paul's prayer for the Roman believers: "First, I thank my God through Jesus Christ for all of you because **the news of your faith is being reported in all the world**" (Rom. 1:8).

Here Paul was obviously referring to the witness of the numerous household communities of faith in Rome that met in the homes of a number of key believers. At the end of his letter to these believers, he referred to the church that met in the home of Priscilla and Aquila (Rom. 16:3–9) and in the household of Aristobulus (Rom. 16:10). He also mentioned the household of Narcissus (16:11). It appears that churches also met in the homes of Asyncritus, Phlegon, Hermes, Patrobas, and Hermas, since Paul referred to the "brothers and sisters who are with them" (Rom. 16:14). The same was true of Philologues and Julia, Nereus and his sister, and Olympas, since Paul referred to "all the saints who were with them" (Rom. 16:15).

Again, as Paul was praying for these believers in their household churches, he was grateful for their witness for Christ that was known far beyond the city of Rome—"in all the [known] world."

The Church in Corinth—It's important to note that the Corinthian church stands out as a negative example. Their meetings were chaotic. Paul then asked a pointed question: "If . . . **unbelievers** come in, will they not say that you are out of your minds?" (1 Cor. 14:23).

Paul later reminded the Corinthians that "God is not a God of disorder but of peace" (14:33). They were to communicate the Word of God to one another in an orderly and understandable fashion. Then, Paul said, when "**some unbeliever or outsider comes in**," he will be convicted by all and "the secrets of his heart will be revealed, and as a result he will **fall facedown and worship God**, proclaiming, '**God is really among you**'" (1 Cor. 14:24–25).

The Church in Ephesus—Churches were also to engage in another important evangelistic ministry—prayer. Paul addressed this issue when he wrote to Timothy, who was helping establish the church in Ephesus: "First of all, then, I urge that **petitions**, **prayers**, **intercessions**, and **thanksgivings** be made for everyone, for **kings** and **all those who are in authority**, so that we may lead a **tranquil and quiet life** in all godliness and dignity. This is good, and it pleases God our Savior, who **wants everyone to be saved** and to come **to the knowledge of the truth**" (1 Tim. 2:1–4).

Think for a moment about what Paul was asking. He had just been released from prison and was exhorting Timothy and the believers in Ephesus to pray for evil leaders like Nero, who was eventually responsible for Paul's martyrdom. He was asking prayer for wicked governors like

Felix and Festus and a pagan king like Herod—men who were indirectly responsible for his imprisonment (Acts 24–26).

Paul then stated why believers are to pray for these government leaders —that Christ followers everywhere "may lead a tranquil and quiet life in all godliness and dignity. This is good," wrote Paul, "and it pleases God our Savior, **who wants everyone to be saved** and **to come to the knowledge of the truth**" (1 Tim. 2:2–4). Paul was saying that more people will become believers in a peaceful environment than in one that is hostile and opposed to the gospel.

Believers are also to pray for those who are called in a special way to preach the gospel that reaches beyond their own communities. On several occasions Paul requested prayers for his own evangelistic ministry. For example, after exhorting believers in Ephesus and other Asian cities to pray for one another, he asked for personal prayer: "Pray also for me, that the message may be given to me when I open my mouth to **make known with boldness the mystery of the gospel**. For this I am an ambassador in chains. Pray that I might **be bold enough to speak about it as I should**" (Eph. 6:19–20).

Life in General

Though the New Testament letters pinpoint special situations and environments in which Christians were to maintain a good testimony, they also speak to life in general.

> You yourselves are our letter, written on our hearts, known and read by **everyone**. (2 Cor. 3:2)

> Act wisely toward **outsiders**, making the most of the time. Let your speech always be gracious, seasoned with salt, so that you may know how you should answer **each person**. (Col. 4:5–6)

> But in your hearts regard Christ the Lord as holy, ready at any time to give a defense to **anyone** who asks you for a reason for the hope that is in you. (1 Peter 3:15)

Concluding Thoughts

In terms of an emphasis on "making disciples" in the New Testament letters, we see the results of an unfolding story that began in the upper room just prior to Jesus' death on the cross. Though the apostles and other New Testament leaders were able to confirm the message of salvation with "signs and wonders and various miracles," the enduring verification of Christ's deity was to be love and oneness among all believers. This was to be the background against which a verbal witness was to be shared with unsaved people. It's God's will that this supernatural dynamic be evident in all aspects of our lives as believers.

A Question for Thought and Discussion

Why is it important to understand the difference between the apostolic ministry of evangelism and church planting described primarily in the book of Acts and the approach described for local communities of faith in the New Testament letters?

7

Household Conversions

Video Intro from Gene

3lenses.org/c07

When my students at Dallas Theological Seminary were asking challenging questions about the relevancy of the church, the late Dr. George Peters became a great resource in exploring the answers. A theologian in his own right, he served as chairman of the Missions Department. I often invited him to be a special guest in my class, giving the students opportunity to ask questions and interact with his comments. His depth of knowledge—biblically, historically, and culturally—was obvious. I sensed he enjoyed the experience since he was at his best in the dialectic atmosphere that had developed in these classes.

One of the biblical subjects Peters had carefully explored in his book *Saturation Evangelism* was the subtopic household evangelism. Laying the foundation for this subject, he wrote:

> The family did not just happen. It is God-ordained and instituted. Household is a fundamental biblical concept. God willed the family and the home. It is the original, divinely-instituted, natural, social and specific unit; it is essential to the well-being of the human race.[1]

Peters went on to explore biblically how the God-ordained family unit became a strategic means of household evangelism. Initially, I incorporated some of these concepts in the first edition of this book. However, in this revision nearly fifty years later—and after spending the same amount of time in church planting—I concluded I needed to devote an entire chapter documenting what the Bible really teaches about this subject and how we can reach families for Christ in our own respective cultural settings.

The Family in God's Plan

The family came into existence when God created Adam and Eve. Though their sin impacted this divine social unit, Israel's history demonstrates its importance nationally and in society generally. Fathers and mothers were responsible to lead their families and teach their children the laws of God. Moses reiterated and summarized this responsibility just prior to Israel's entrance into the land of Canaan:

> "These words that I am giving you today are to be in your heart. Repeat them to your children. Talk about them when you sit in your house and when you walk along the road, when you lie down and when you get up. Bind them as a sign on your hand and let them be a symbol on your forehead. Write them on the doorposts of your house and on your city gates." (Deut. 6:6–9)

As the children of Israel settled into the promised land, it's abundantly clear that when parents failed to carry out Moses' instructions, family life deteriorated and affected the whole nation. Consequently, Joshua—just before he passed to his eternal reward—gathered the children of Israel together to give them a final exhortation:

> "Therefore, fear the LORD and worship him in sincerity and truth. Get rid of the gods your ancestors worshiped beyond the Euphrates River and in Egypt, and worship the LORD. But if it doesn't please you to worship the LORD, choose for yourselves today: Which will

you worship—the gods your ancestors worshiped beyond the Euphrates River or the gods of the Amorites in whose land you are living? As for **me and my family, we will worship the LORD.**" (Josh. 24:14–15)

With this farewell message, Joshua demonstrated how important family units are in God's divine plan. He also modeled how important fathers are in teaching children to live in the will of God. When parents failed to follow Joshua's example, the family disintegrated and the whole nation collapsed. This happened repeatedly as illustrated in the book of Judges.

Jesus' Ministry to Families

During the centuries described in the Old Testament, the children of Israel were to be a witness to Gentile nations (Isa. 43:10). However, they failed miserably. But when Jesus Christ came, the specific redemptive promise to Abraham became clear—that "all the peoples on earth will be blessed through you" (Gen. 12:3). Here God was referring to the seed of Abraham that began to be fulfilled as the Savior was born and "increased in wisdom and stature, and in favor with God and with people" (Luke 2:52).

Even before the church was born on the day of Pentecost, Jesus engaged in family evangelism. Note His ministry to Zacchaeus. This unscrupulous tax collector put his faith in Jesus and demonstrated true repentance in being willing to right his wrongs. Jesus' response clearly illustrates family evangelism: **"Today salvation has come to this house"** (Luke 19:9). Jesus was saying that Zacchaeus was now able to lead his whole family to also put their faith in the Savior.

Household evangelism is also illustrated in the life of the royal official described in John's gospel. He lived in Capernaum and his son became deathly ill. He had heard of Jesus' miraculous powers and when the Savior returned to Cana, this nobleman hurriedly went to see Jesus and asked Him to come and heal his son. Seeing this man's earnestness, Jesus told him his son would live.

As he was rushing back to Capernaum, this royal official met a servant who informed him that his son was no longer ill. Realizing it was at the very time Jesus had told him his son would live, John recorded that "he [the nobleman] himself **believed**, **along with his whole household**" (John 4:53). Again, we see the results of family evangelism.

The Apostles' Ministry to Families in Jerusalem

As a result of the apostle Peter's message on the day of Pentecost, three thousand people became believers (Acts 2:41). These conversions certainly involved a multitude of parents who in turn would have shared the gospel with the rest of their extended families who in turn responded in faith.

Household evangelism is also implied in the next reference to those who believed. After hearing Peter and John sharing the gospel, "**many** of those who heard the message **believed**, **and the number of the men came to about five thousand**" (Acts 4:4).

In view of the cultural dynamics that existed in the Jewish community and described in both in the Old and New Testaments, this reference to "men" represented **thousands of households**. Again, these fathers in turn would have shared the salvation message with their extended family members. Because "fathers" in the Jewish community greatly influenced all aspects of family life, whole households would have become followers of Christ.

As the apostles continued their preaching ministry in Jerusalem, "**believers** were added to the Lord in **increasing numbers**—multitudes of **both men and women**"—another reference to whole family units that had become believers (Acts 5:14).

We also read that a "large group of priests became obedient to the faith" (Acts 6:7). This reference is also significant in terms of "households." For example, when an angel appeared to Zechariah, a Jewish priest, there were approximately twenty thousand of these men in Israel (Luke 15:25). Though childless at the time, Zechariah and his wife, Elizabeth, would have potentially represented some **twenty thousand households** in Israel. Many of these priests would have been in Jerusalem for this annual celebration. We can only imagine the number of family units that became believers when these men responded to the gospel.

Peter's Ministry to Families Beyond Jerusalem

The next significant illustration regarding household evangelism involved a Gentile named Cornelius. He was a high-powered centurion in the Roman army. Though not Jewish, "he was a devout man and feared God **along with his whole household**" (Acts 10:2).

As a result of a vision, the apostle Peter visited Caesarea, entered Cornelius's household, and proclaimed the gospel. Cornelius's **whole extended family then became believers**—which also included relatives and close friends (Acts 10:24, 44). This implies that on this occasion more than one household responded to the salvation message.

Paul's Missionary Journeys

Household Conversions in Philippi

The next specific reference in Acts to family evangelism involved Lydia. Paul, Silas, and Timothy were in Philippi on their second missionary journey. Luke has recorded that "a God-fearing woman named Lydia, a dealer in purple cloth from the city of Thyatira," became a believer (Acts 16:14). After responding to the gospel, we read that "she and **her household** were baptized" (16:15).

Lydia may have been divorced or perhaps widowed, since many women lost their husbands in the Roman wars. But whatever her circumstances, she was a successful businesswoman and the leader in her household, and when she came to faith in Christ, her family followed.

The next convert in this city was "a slave girl" (Acts 16:16–23). Her conversion landed Paul and Silas in prison since their owners could no longer use her clairvoyant abilities. However, a violent earthquake shook the foundations of the prison. The doors were thrown open and the prisoners' chains fell off.

The Philippian jailor was horrified, believing the prisoners had escaped—which would have led to his own death. Rather than face the Roman hierarchy, he decided to take his own life. But Paul and Silas immediately alerted him that no prisoners had escaped. As a result, he asked Paul and Barnabas what he must do to be saved (Acts 16:30).

Their response is significant in terms of family evangelism. Paul and Silas responded—"Believe in the Lord Jesus, and you will be saved—**you and your household**" (16:31).

The jailor responded in faith and invited this missionary team to share the good news with the rest of his family. These men then "spoke the word of the Lord **to him** along with **everyone in his house**" (Acts 16:32). The jailor's **whole family** responded to the gospel and "right away he and **all his family** were baptized" (Acts 16:33). Luke further reinforced this "household conversion" when he wrote that the jailor "set a meal before them, and rejoiced because **he had come to believe in God with his entire household**" (16:34).

At this point, it's important to share more specifically what household evangelism entails. Because the Philippian jailor believed in Jesus Christ and was saved does not mean his family members were automatically saved. Salvation has always been a personal experience in Scripture. This is why Paul and Silas explained the gospel message to "**everyone in his house**." As a result, each family member—obviously of understandable age—believed in the Lord Jesus Christ and inherited salvation. We can assume this was also true of Lydia's children, if she had any.

Household Conversions in Corinth

Luke once again referenced household conversions when Paul came to Corinth. Here he met Aquila and Priscilla who had left the city of Rome because of an antisemitic movement. They settled in Corinth and continued their profession as tentmakers. Initially, Paul stayed with them and cared for his personal needs by participating in their tentmaking business (Acts 18:1–3).

Though we are not told specifically when this couple became believers, it no doubt happened in Corinth. Though this conversion involved only a man and his wife, Aquila and Priscilla became a dynamic ministry couple, assisting Paul not only in making disciples but also helping these disciples to mature. Since this couple appears to have had no children, this gave them the opportunity to travel and minister with Paul in establishing a number of churches, particularly among the Gentiles.

This ministry is verified when Aquila and Priscilla were able to return to Rome. They opened their home to minister to other couples, families, and individuals as Paul had ministered to them. In fact, Paul greeted them in his letter to the Romans: "Give my greetings to Prisca and Aquila, my coworkers in Christ Jesus, who risked their own necks for my life. Not only do I thank them, but **so do all the Gentile churches. Greet also the church that meets in their home**" (Rom. 16:3–5a).

The next significant family conversion in Corinth happened in the life of Crispus. He was "the leader of the synagogue," and as a result of Paul's ministry, he "believed in the Lord, along with his **whole household**" (Acts 18:8a). This was a startling development. Since Crispus had such a significant role as a leader in the Jewish community, "many of the Corinthians, when they heard, believed and were baptized" (18:8b).

Contextually, we can conclude that this prominent "family response" to the gospel impacted other entire households. One of those families may have been "the **household of Stephanas**" that Paul himself baptized (1 Cor. 1:16). The **household of Chloe** may have been another family since Paul mentioned them in his first letter to the Corinthians. It was "members of **Chloe's people**" (1:11) who had informed him of some of the problems in the church. It would appear that these "people" were members of Chloe's extended household.

A Household Conversion in Colossae

Needless to say, the Corinthian church was primarily established on households—just as the other New Testament churches. At times one individual family unit became the beginning of a larger church community. This no doubt is what happened in Colossae. Philemon was a well-to-do businessman in this city. He may have become a believer when he visited Ephesus and heard Paul teaching in the school of Tyrannus.

Eventually his whole household became believers, including his slaves, who in this culture were considered a part of the extended family. However, one of the slaves named Onesimus rejected the gospel and fled—eventually ending up in Rome.

Providentially, Paul—who was in prison—met Onesimus and led him to believe in Christ. He then sent him back to Philemon as a brother in

Christ and a restored member in his extended household. Here is what Paul shared in his letter to Philemon:

> For perhaps this is why he was separated from you for a brief time, so that you might get him back permanently, no longer as a slave, but more than a slave—as a dearly loved brother . . . So if you consider me a partner, welcome him as you would me. (Philem. 1:15–16a, 17)

Once again Paul's experience with Philemon illustrates the power of household evangelism, particularly when a father becomes a believer. And when both father and mother respond to the gospel—which was the norm in the New Testament world—the power of family evangelism becomes even more effective.[2]

It also appears that Philemon's household became the first believers in this city. In this case, he, as a father, may have become the first elder/pastor as more and more households came to Christ and became the official church in Colossae.

Concluding Thoughts

In summary, household evangelism was the norm in making disciples during the first century and following. Dr. Harry Boer stated it this way:

> The Church was not built up of so many individual Christians but of *basic social units*, of *organic wholes*, and these units, these wholes, were the fundamental cells of society, namely *families*. . . . It is clearly around this divinely given social unit that the churches founded by the apostolic witness were built. Families entered the Church as units and their integrity was guarded by express apostolic concern.[3]

Dr. George Peters summarized and substantiated this concept as well:

> There were household movements in Jerusalem, in Caesarea, and in Asia and in Greece. We find it among Jews, Romans, Samaritans, Greeks. It was not confined just to one people, one place or one

97

culture. It was as universal as the family is universal. **The opponents of the Gospel worked in a similar manner and were overthrowing whole houses** (Titus 1:11, emphasis added).

Household evangelism and salvation are not exceptional cases in the New Testament. It is the divine ideal throughout the Scriptures and the apostolic norm. It is biblical and social; only to Western individualism does such a phenomena seem strange and peculiar.[4]

A Question for Thought and Discussion

When considering enduring results from various approaches to evangelism, why are household conversions so important and effective?

8

Principles of Evangelism

Video Intro from Gene

3lenses.org/c08

As we look carefully at the way leaders in the New Testament carried out Jesus' commission to make disciples, we can discover supracultural principles that are applicable in every culture of the world and at any moment in history.

Demonstrating Love and Unity

Principle 1: Every community of believers should make every effort to demonstrate love and unity so that "the world may know" and "believe" that the Lord Jesus Christ is one with the Father and came from the Father to be the Savior of all who believe.

Throughout the biblical story, God has initially confirmed His redemptive message with irrefutable signs and wonders. It happened at Mount Sinai when He gave Israel the Ten Commandments and the sacrificial system—a mountain overshadowed with fire, thunder, and smoke.

In the context of this miraculous setting, God revealed His message to the children of Israel and to Moses, who recorded it in the first five books of the Old Testament. In turn, the children of Israel were responsible to teach God's redemptive message to their children and to be a light and witness to the Gentile world (Deut. 6:6–9; Isa. 45:22; Amos 9:11–12; Acts 15:15–17).

The next major event in God's redemptive revelation involved the coming of the promised Messiah. Again, God affirmed the salvation message, not only through Jesus' miracles but through those of the apostles and other key biblical personalities as well as through the gifts of the Holy Spirit. The author of Hebrews affirmed this when he wrote,

> How will we escape if we neglect such a great salvation? This salvation had its beginning when it was **spoken of by the Lord**, and it was **confirmed** to us by **those who heard him** [primarily the apostles]. At the same time, God also **testified** by **signs** and **wonders**, various **miracles**, and **distributions of gifts from the Holy Spirit** according to his will. (Heb. 2:3–4)

The Final Apologetic

In keeping with God's design to affirm the redemptive message, He has established an **ongoing miraculous plan**. It's embodied in what Jesus Christ prayed for on the way to the garden of Gethsemane—love and unity in the body of Christ. This is also the emphasis throughout the New Testament letters and summarized succinctly by Paul and Peter (Eph. 4:1–3; 1 Peter 3:8–15). This potential miracle has existed for nearly two thousand years.

This does not mean that God in His sovereignty has not miraculously affirmed His redemptive message with unusual verification throughout church history. We must not limit the power of the Holy Spirit. In fact, there are some stories today that appear reliable. However, we have no verifiable historical record that compares with what happened at Mount Sinai or in the first century and described in the New Testament.

A Memorable Experience

In terms of this "final apologetic," I'm reminded of a couple who entered our church one Sunday morning. In my message, I emphasized that Jesus Christ was God who came in human flesh. Following our time in the Scriptures, we had an open service where believers shared special needs and we all prayed for one another. It was a warm and caring service. You could sense an unusual love and unity. Even now as I reflect on that experience, I'm reminded of the lyrics of a song we often sang—"There's a sweet, sweet Spirit in this place and I know that it's the Spirit of the Lord."

In a later conversation, this couple told me an amazing story. When they entered the service, they did not believe in Christ's deity. In their minds, Jesus was just a man and a good teacher. However, because they had witnessed our deep love and concern for one another, they became convinced that Jesus Christ was who He claimed to be! Clearly, it was this experience that confirmed my reference to Christ's deity in my message, and they responded by believing that Jesus Christ was more than just a man. He is the eternal Son of God.

I could only thank the Lord for His instructions to love one another as He has loved us and for His prayer that we might be one as He is one with the Father. Over my fifty-plus years as a pastor I could share a number of times where the love and unity in the church body confirmed the gospel message that Jesus Christ is indeed the Son of God.

Satan's Two-Fold Strategy

The potential power in implementing this principle leads to a penetrating question: Where has Satan attacked the church of Jesus Christ the hardest throughout church history? Clearly, this master of evil and deception has a two-fold strategy.

First, Satan attempts to create "love" and "unity" in false cults and religions.

I remember ministering to a young woman who became a part of a "Christian" cult that denied the deity of Jesus Christ. She had been raised in a dysfunctional Christian home and had come in contact with members of this religious group on her college campus. One of our pastors attempted to help her by sharing some clear biblical doctrines regarding Christ's statement that He and the Father are One (John 14:8–11). However, in a later conversation, this young woman shared with me her response. "I know all about the biblical information about Christ's deity," she said, "but these people love and accept me!"

That was the end of our discussion. Doctrinal evidence meant little to her. Satan had used Jesus' "final apologetic" in a distorted and deceptive way to lead this young woman astray.

I remember another startling conversation with a missionary to the Mormons. He had just heard me speak on love and unity as the "final apologetic." He shared that he had met a young man who had graduated from a well-known evangelical Bible college where he had prepared to become a missionary. However, in order to learn more about his vision, he decided to move into a Mormon community to learn about their mission strategy.

This missionary then told me that this young man decided to become a Mormon because he had seen more love and unity in this religious group than in any of the Bible-believing churches he had attended. Clearly, there are a lot of wonderful, sincere, and caring people in the Mormon church. However, they are not taught that Jesus is one with God, which is at the heart of the true gospel message (John 1:1–14).[1]

Second, Satan attempts to destroy love and unity in churches that have a correct view of the deity of Christ.

Think for a moment about what has happened throughout church history. Divisions and splits have happened again and again, not just in denominations but in local churches that have a correct doctrinal view regarding Christ's deity. Consequently, some Bible-believing communities of faith have become objects of ridicule and criticism by the world. "Christians are hypocrites," they say. Young Christians particularly become disillusioned and withdraw from the church.

Satan's strategy accomplishes two things. It attracts people to religious communities that deny the true basis of salvation. At the same time, it drives unbelievers and even believers away from churches that have correct doctrine but are failing to love one another and to become one as Christ is one with the Father. Needless to say, this is a powerful strategy that unfortunately has worked for Satan and his evil cohorts since the first century.

But there is good news. It need not happen! The Scriptures clearly teach us that we can defeat Satan by "making every effort to keep the unity of the Spirit through the bond of peace" (Eph. 4:3). We can defeat our arch enemy when we "put on the full armor of God" in order to "stand against the schemes of the devil" (Eph. 6:11). Here Paul used second person plural pronouns. In other words, as a **community** of believers, we together as one unified body are to "take up the full armor of God" (6:13–17).

Finally, Paul exhorts us to pray together, asking God to help us become one as the Son is one with the Father (Eph. 6:18). Paul underscores this in his prayer for the Roman believers that beautifully and powerfully correlates with Jesus' prayer in John 17.

> Now may the God who gives endurance and encouragement grant you to live in **harmony with one another**, according to Christ Jesus, so that you may glorify the God and Father of our Lord Jesus Christ with **one mind and one voice**. (Rom. 15:5–6)

Teaching the Word of God

Principle 2: As pastors and teachers, we should follow the apostles' and other New Testament leaders' example and clearly teach God's total redemptive message in the Word of God.

Understanding the Redemptive Story

In the book of Acts, there are numerous references to making disciples by teaching the redemptive story. This does not mean that the Holy Spirit cannot use a few selective verses to explain the gospel. However, a more in-depth biblical approach to evangelism helps lead to authentic conversions rather than just "decisions." Personal faith should be based on a substantial and clear understanding of the redemptive story.

We have examples of this in the book of Acts. We have Stephen's comprehensive message before the Sanhedrin (Acts 7:2–53). We have Paul's experience in Berea where unbelievers "received the word with eagerness and **examined the Scriptures daily** to see if these things were so" (Acts 17:11b–12). We have Paul's witness while he was in prison in Rome. Luke has recorded that "from dawn to dusk he **expounded** and **testified** about the kingdom of God. He tried to **persuade** them about Jesus **from both the Law of Moses and the Prophets**" (Acts 28:23b).

This approach to evangelism is also in harmony with a strong emphasis on teaching the Word of God to believers. The disciples in Jerusalem devoted themselves to the "apostles' teaching" (the revealed Word of God), which led to spiritual growth. But it was also a significant factor in "having favor with" unbelievers (Acts 2:42–47).

Following these models, local church pastors and teachers should unfold the total biblical story directly from the Scriptures, sharing this message with both believers and unbelievers. In other words, we must not dilute the Word of God in order to reach unbelievers. When the Scriptures are clearly taught in all their fullness and with love and compassion, I've discovered that the vast majority of unbelievers will respond positively and with respect, even though they may not accept the life-changing message—at least initially. But when they do respond, their faith is based on a significant understanding of the full redemptive message. We must remember there is miraculous power in the biblical message.[2]

Memorable Experiences

One of my significant experiences happened when my wife and I were conducting a Bible study in our home. Our approach was what we called "a walk through the Bible"—unfolding God's redemptive story from Genesis to Revelation. One of our neighbors, an intelligent woman, attended but claimed to be agnostic. After several months and after understanding God's redemptive message, Lois became a believer and began attending our church and grew spiritually in a remarkable way.

This second principle that focuses on "Teaching the Word of God" is also directly related to **the first principle,** "Love and Unity." Lois was not only exposed to the total redemptive message, but she was impacted by the loving relationships she saw in the believing couples who attended, as well as their acceptance of her. These two dynamics worked together in an amazing way.

Here's another dramatic story that illustrates these two principles working together. When I was ministering in Brazil, I met Mario Nietzsche. Years earlier he had been a committed Marxist—a devoted atheist. But on one occasion, a Christian psychologist from America was speaking in a community center. Since Mario was interested in psychology, he attended.

At that time, my good friend Jim Peterson—a missionary with the Navigators—interpreted this psychologist's message in Portuguese. Following the session, Jim engaged Mario in conversation and asked him if he would like to know more about the Bible.

Priding himself on being open-minded, Mario agreed—and they simply began with the book of John, reading together verse by verse. When they came to a reference regarding God, Jesus, or the Holy Spirit, Mario made it clear he didn't believe in these three persons in the Trinity. "That's okay," Jim said. "Let's just insert the letter 'X' whenever we come to those names." Mario was disarmed, and so, they did.

This intelligent atheist became so interested in studying the Bible with Jim that he actually attended various studies off and on for four years. He then became a devoted believer in Jesus Christ.

When I met Mario, he was in charge of a number of fellow missionaries throughout southern Brazil. During his ministry, hundreds of other Brazilians who were Marxists also became believers as a result of studying the Bible with Mario.

As we sat together over breakfast in his home, I asked Mario why he had continued to study the Bible with Jim for four years. He thought for a moment and then said, "I saw sincere love in Jim's marriage and family life, and I knew it had to be related to what they believed in the Bible."

Again, we see a relationship between **Principle 1** and **Principle 2**. Love and unity serves as a verifying miracle that the message of the Word of God regarding the Lord Jesus Christ is true.

Reaching Whole Households

Principle 3: To maximize our efforts in reaching unbelievers, we should target whole households.

As I was updating this book, my wife and I attended a memorial service at Woodcreek Church, one of our church plants from the original Fellowship Bible Church. We were honoring the life of Jerry Ryan, an elder who had passed away. As we sat in that service, Jerry's wife and their extended family members—numbering nearly thirty—entered the sanctuary and took their place. Most were believers, representing all ages.

In some respects, this group of children, grandchildren, and great-grandchildren reflected a "household" in the New Testament culture, not just numerically, but spiritually. And to understand and appreciate the significance of this somber but joyful event, it's important to get a much larger perspective on Jerry's extended family experience.

A Neighborhood Ministry

Norm Wretlind joined our pastoral staff in the mid 1970s at the original Fellowship Bible Church. He and his wife, Becky, settled into a neighborhood in a Dallas suburb and began to build bridges to their neighbors with the goal of sharing the gospel. In turn, they decided to invite couples to attend a Christmas party. Since almost everyone in the American culture enjoys this holiday, many neighbors accepted the invitation regardless of their religious or nonreligious beliefs.

Both the invitation and the event at the party were nonthreatening. There was a natural opportunity to share the true meaning of Christmas and what it means personally. This was just the beginning of a remarkable outreach in household evangelism. Norm and Becky shared this remarkable story:

> During the next three years, we helped neighbors host Christmas parties, a women's Valentine's Day coffee, a couples' pool party, a kids' backyard Bible club, a weekend marriage seminar in the neighborhood clubhouse, and three weekly Bible studies (one for women, one for men, and one for couples). By God's work and His glory alone, we saw more than sixty neighbors come to know Christ, including nine of the twenty-eight who had attended that first open house.[3]

Eventually this core group of families helped launch one of our branch churches, Richland Bible Fellowship—now called Woodcreek Church. It was in this church my wife and I attended Jerry Ryan's funeral service. Going back to his personal experience, here's what Jerry shared in the book *When God Is the Life of the Party*:

After that Christmas party, we did draw closer to many of the people there, but I felt they were just nice folks. What they were doing was fine; it just wasn't for me. After a while, Jeanne and our six kids started attending Fellowship Bible Church. I didn't mind that either. In fact, I liked having Sunday morning to myself to read the paper.

But as time went on, I could see that she and the kids were actually *enjoying* church. Occasionally I went with them, and we made a lot more friends. I began attending fairly regularly, and I heard the message about salvation every week. But I still didn't grasp it. Finally, on a Sunday morning in January 1976, [Pastor Gene Getz] laid it out clearly for me. I accepted Christ that day.

During those months leading up to that Sunday, I *felt* the warmth before I *saw* the light. The warmth came from the people we were meeting and from the Christmas party. Some had been Christians for a long time. Most, however, were new believers.[4]

This remarkable story demonstrates the power of family evangelism. Eventually, Jerry became an elder in this Fellowship Bible Church. He and his wife, Jeanne, were faithful servants for a number of years.

As my wife and I sat in this church participating in Jerry's funeral service, two of his grown sons—now married with families of their own—spoke glowingly of their parents' relationship with Christ. The number of seats reserved for this extended family testified to the effectiveness of family evangelism.

The Graveyard of Christian Missions

There's much more to this wonderful story. Norm and Becky had the opportunity to participate in "Amsterdam 2000," an international conference for evangelists. They set up a booth and shared their family evangelism strategy. An Indian pastor named E. A. Abraham attended the same conference. He had been ministering in an area of India called "the graveyard of Christian missions." He was deeply concerned about a way to reach his unsaved neighbors with the gospel.

When he stopped by the Wretlinds' booth, he was intrigued. After hearing Norm and Becky share their Christmas party story, Pastor Abraham realized this approach to evangelism might work in India, since his people loved Christmas—which was introduced to this culture under British control. Though most Hindus and Muslims didn't understand the true meaning of this holiday, they loved the festivities that were mostly secular.

To make a long story short, Pastor Abraham held his first party during the Christmas season in the year 2000. The attendance was so great they sponsored a party the next year just for VIPs—government officials and the police. Both Hindus and Muslims responded well to this Christmas celebration. Pastor Abraham was able to share a message from the Bible on the real meaning of Christ's birth. He then presented every family with a Christmas gift—a Bible in Hindi.

By 2009, this approach to family evangelism had spread to half the states in India. In his book *Why Die Before Your Time?*, Pastor Abraham shared the results:

> By 2009 Neighborhood Hope India had spread to over half the states in India and had trained more than 6000 pastors in this method of evangelism. As a result, tens of thousands of Hindus and Muslim's all over India heard the Gospel every Christmas season. Many have come to faith and have joined local churches.[5]

Christmas parties, of course, are cultural. But effective household evangelism is supracultural. It happened in the first century, and it can happen in various ways throughout the world today. As Dr. George W. Peters has reminded us, "In view of the fact, however, that the family is not only a universal social institution, but also a divinely-created social unit, and holds a unique place throughout the Bible, household evangelism deserves our closest attention as a biblical priority and ideal."[6]

Local Church Life

Principle 4: We should integrate new believers into the life of the local church as soon as possible.

What it means to be a part of a local church will be discussed in great detail later. However, new believers will not grow into mature disciples of Jesus Christ apart from being involved with other believers. They need three vital experiences that God has designed as absolutely essential for spiritual growth (see chapters 12 and 13).

This raises an important question. How does this principle relate to parachurch ministries? Without question, God has raised up various organizations to supplement the work of the local church. These organizations can do what many churches have failed to do and, in many instances, cannot do. However, these ministries must not ignore biblical examples and principles. Metaphorically speaking, ecclesiology is the glue that holds the New Testament together. Jesus Christ came the first time to give birth to the church. The book of Acts and the Epistles are, in essence, the story of local churches. New believers must be a part of a functioning body of Christ in order to grow spiritually.

Every parachurch organization should seriously consider its relationship to the local church. It must teach this biblical doctrine, promote the church as God's basic unit for Christian nurture, and strive in a loving and tactful way to correct both the church's theological and functional errors. Parachurch organizations must not become a substitute for nor be antagonistic to the local church. They must in every way cooperate in furthering the ministry and outreach of this God-ordained plan.

Again, I'll never forget the wonderful opportunity I had to spend a number of days ministering with the Navigators in Brazil. Jim Peterson had invited me to share biblical principles of church life with a number of believers who met in small groups in various parts of the country. He was concerned that these groups—in reality, "small churches"—practice what the Scriptures teach in terms of ecclesiology. Later, I was actually invited to the Navigators headquarters to meet with the top leaders to discuss the principles I had included in the first edition of this book. They were also concerned that as an organization, they should work more closely with local churches.

Missions Outreach

Principle 5: Every local church should encourage and support those who have a special burden and desire to be directly involved in sharing the gospel with the unsaved.

As we've seen, all believers are to be involved in what I like to call "body evangelism." This is what Jesus prayed for. Love and unity should involve all authentic disciples and, as we've seen, is the enduring apologetic in affirming in a miraculous way that Jesus Christ came from the Father and is one with the Father and is the Son of God and Savior of the world.

However, there are those in the church who feel called to be more directly involved in sharing the gospel with the unsaved, as evangelists "worthy of double honor." Here I've simply used biblical terminology regarding elders who are supported financially and have applied it to those who need financial support for a special ministry in evangelism (1 Tim. 5:17).

Earlier I referenced Norm Wretlind, who joined our full-time Fellowship Bible Church staff. He and his wife both had a desire to reach unbelievers. His job description focused not only on direct evangelism but also on helping all members of the church to be a part of our outreach to the world. This involved training people in how to share the gospel.

This approach is in harmony with what we see in the book of Acts. Many believers "spoke" the message of Christ and were involved "in telling the good news." However, it was the apostles especially who engaged in evangelistic teaching and preaching. It was Peter and particularly Paul who engaged in an evangelistic ministry characterized by "solemnly testifying" and "reasoning" with unbelievers. This called for special giftedness and training.

In summary, the whole local body of believers should be involved in evangelism. All are to be an integral part of the enduring apologetic—demonstrating love and unity and saturating the community with the reality of Christianity and the message of the gospel. Not all may be able to "draw the net" with ease. But in the final analysis, all are to be involved in making disciples—which is what we see modeled in the New Testament story—particularly in the Epistles written to the churches.

As we and many churches have discovered, one way to create a desire for evangelism is to encourage both young people and older adults to participate in mission ministries, particularly on a short-term basis. There are organizations that provide outstanding opportunities for this experience.

For those who cannot finance themselves, the church can support them financially.

We've seen the effects of this opportunity in our own family. When our son was in junior high school, he spent two summers in Sweden and another in Switzerland. Both times he served on a work team but had opportunities to be involved in evangelism. The impact on his life was enormous. And, as I pen these words, our son's son, now in college, is on a similar mission trip!

Local churches are also responsible to pray for those individuals who engage in a part-time or a full-time ministry of evangelism and missionary work. This is certainly modeled for us in the New Testament, particularly in the life of the apostle Paul, who wrote to the Ephesians and said, "Pray also for me, that the message may be given to me when I open my mouth to make known with boldness the mystery of the gospel. For this I am an ambassador in chains. Pray that I might be bold enough to speak about it as I should" (Eph. 6:19–20).

Forms and Methods

Principle 6: Every local church should develop creative forms and utilize contemporary methods to apply the principles of evangelism that are supracultural and enduring.

This principle is clear from the study of the functions of the New Testament church. What they were to believe and teach about the gospel is unchanging and consistent. However, the way they said it and how they went about evangelizing varies from culture to culture. Normative functions, directives, and principles are absolute. But forms and methods are relative and non-absolute and should uniquely serve as the means to accomplish divine ends.

The apostle Paul demonstrated this principle in a remarkable way when he wrote to the Corinthians: "I have become **all things** to **all people**, so that I may by **every possible means** save some" (1 Cor. 9:22b). Paul was certainly committed to never compromising God's eternal, unchanging truth. But he was always open to being creative in the area of form and methodology.

In summary, we must avoid locking into forms and patterns. Every church in every culture and subculture should develop its own unique approaches to evangelism that are in harmony with absolute supracultural biblical principles. In other words, under the creative leadership of the Holy Spirit, and using all of the human resources available, we need to be dynamic twenty-first-century churches that are creating contemporary evangelistic strategies that are built on New Testament principles and guidelines.

A Question for Thought and Discussion

Can you share an event where you have seen Satan's two-fold strategy at work in keeping a church or churches from demonstrating authentic love and unity?

9

Baptizing Authentic Disciples

Video Intro from Gene

3lenses.org/c09

The next clear directive Jesus gave in the Great Commission was to baptize those who responded to the gospel and became authentic disciples. Thus, Jesus said to the eleven apostles on the mountain in Galilee—"Go, therefore, and **make disciples** of all nations, **baptizing them** . . ."—that is, these "disciples" (Matt. 28:19).

Before exploring further what Jesus meant with this command to baptize, it's important to review the concept of saving faith—namely, personally and sincerely believing in the Lord Jesus Christ. It's this kind of faith that causes an individual to become an authentic disciple (Eph. 2:8–9).

As we've noted in chapter 4, the apostle John explained this great truth when he recorded a conversation Jesus had with those who claimed to be disciples but who were not *authentic* disciples. They turned and walked away when Jesus challenged their motives (John 6:15, 26). Several times He told them they must *believe* in Him who is one with the Father, who was sent by the Father and who is the Father's Son (6:26–29, 40). In order to inherit eternal life, they must *believe* these great truths (6:35, 40, 47).

Though John wrote his gospel at least a half century after Christ's death, resurrection, and ascension, his primary purpose was to make sure all people understood that "God loved the world in this way: He gave his one and only Son, so that everyone who **believes in him** will not perish but have **eternal life**" (John 3:16).

But to help his readers respond in faith, believing that Jesus is indeed the Son of God, he recorded seven significant miracles to prove Christ's deity. He then stated his expanded purpose by referencing these miracles at the end of this marvelous document:

> Jesus performed many other signs in the presence of his disciples that are not written in this book. But these [signs] are written so that you may **believe** that Jesus is the **Messiah**, the **Son of God**, and that by **believing** you may have **life in his name**. (John 20:30–31)

Commenting on John's purpose in writing this gospel, the late Dr. Merrill Tenney stated:

> The entire book is an attempt to swing the reader to the side of acceptance, as embodied in the word **believe**. The underlying Greek word, **pisteuo**, is used no less than ninety-eight times in the Gospel and is customarily translated **believe**.[1]

As we follow the unfolding story in the book of Acts, people clearly became authentic disciples by believing in the Lord Jesus Christ. Paul summarized this great doctrinal truth when he wrote, "For you are saved by grace through faith, and this is not from yourselves; it is God's gift —not from works, so that no one can boast" (Eph. 2:8–9).

Following are numerous references throughout Luke's account that refer to belief that resulted in salvation. Note also how this concept of faith and belief relate directly to the geographical references in Jesus' promise to the apostles just before he ascended: "But you will receive **power** when the Holy Spirit has come on you, and you will be my witnesses in **Jerusalem**, in all **Judea** and **Samaria**, and to the **ends of the earth**" (Acts 1:8).

Belief: The Basis of Salvation

2:44	"Now all the **believers** were together and held all things in common"	**Believers in Jerusalem**
4:4	"But many of those who heard the message **believed** . . ."	
4:32	"Now the entire group of those who **believed** were of one heart and mind . . ."	
5:14	"**Believers** were added to the Lord in increasing numbers . . ."	
8:12	"But when they **believed** Philip, as he proclaimed the good news about the kingdom of God and the name of Jesus Christ, both men and women were baptized."	**Believers in Samaria**
9:42	"This [Tabitha's resurrection] became known throughout Joppa, and many **believed** in the Lord."	**Believers in Joppa**
10:43	"All the prophets testify about him [Jesus Christ] that through his name everyone who **believes** in him receives forgiveness of sins."	**Believers in Caesarea**
10:45	"The circumcised **believers** who had come with Peter were amazed because the gift of the Holy Spirit had been poured out even on the Gentiles."	
11:17	"If, then, God gave them [the Gentiles] the same gift that he also gave to us [as Jews] when we **believed** in the Lord Jesus Christ, how could I possibly hinder God?"	
11:21	"The Lord's hand was with them [men from Cyprus and Cyrene], and a large number who **believed** turned to the Lord."	**Believers in Antioch**
13:12	"Then, when he saw what happened, the proconsul **believed**, because he was astonished at the teaching of the Lord."	**A Believer in Cyprus**
13:39	"Everyone who **believes** is justified through him [Jesus Christ] from everything that you could not be justified from through the law of Moses."	**Believers in Pisidia Antioch**
13:48	"When the Gentiles heard this, they rejoiced and honored the word of the Lord, and all who had been appointed to eternal life **believed**."	

14:1	"In Iconium they [Paul and Barnabas] entered the Jewish synagogue, as usual, and spoke in such a way that a great number of both Jews and Greeks **believed**."	**Believers in Iconium**
14:23	"When they had appointed elders for them in every church and prayed with fasting, they committed them to the Lord in whom they had **believed**."	**Believers in Lystra, Iconium, and Antioch**
15:5	"But some of the **believers** who belonged to the party of the Pharisees stood up and said, 'It is necessary to circumcise them and to command them to keep the law of Moses.'"	**Believers in Jerusalem**[2]
15:11	"On the contrary, we **believe** that we are saved through the grace of the Lord Jesus in the same way they are."	**Peter's Message in Jerusalem**
16:1	"Paul went on to Derbe and Lystra, where there was a disciple named Timothy, the son of a **believing** Jewish woman . . ."	**Believers in Lystra**
16:31	"They [Paul and Silas] said, '**Believe** in the Lord Jesus, and you will be saved—you and your household.'"	**Believers in Philippi**
16:34	"He [the Philippian jailer] brought them into his house, set a meal before them, and rejoiced because he had come to **believe** in God with his entire household."	
17:12	"Consequently, many of them [the Bereans] **believed**, including a number of the prominent Greek women as well as men."	**Believers in Berea**
17:34	"However, some people joined him [Paul] and **believed** . . ."	**Believers in Athens**
18:8a	"Crispus, the leader of the synagogue, **believed** in the Lord, along with his whole household."	**Believers in Corinth**
18:8b	"Many of the Corinthians, when they heard, **believed** and were baptized."	
18:27b	"After he [Apollos] arrived, he was a great help to those who by grace had **believed**."	
19:1b-2	"He found some disciples and asked them, 'Did you receive the Holy Spirit when you **believed**?'"	**Believers in Ephesus**

19:4	"Paul said, 'John baptized with a baptism of repentance, telling the people that they should **believe** in the one who would come after him, that is, in Jesus.'"	
19:18	"And many who had become **believers** came confessing and disclosing their practices."	
21:20	"When they heard it, they glorified God and said, 'You see, brother, how many thousands of Jews there are who have **believed**, and they are all zealous for the law.'"	**Believers in Jerusalem**
21:25	"With regard to the Gentiles who have **believed** . . ."	**James' Message in Jerusalem**
22:19	"But I said, 'Lord, they know that in synagogue after synagogue I had those who **believed** in you imprisoned and beaten.'"	**Paul's Message in Jerusalem**
24:14	"But I admit this to you: I worship the God of my ancestors according to the Way, which they call a sect, **believing** everything that is in accordance with the law and written in the prophets."	**Paul's Testimony Before Felix**
26:27	"King Agrippa, do you **believe** the prophets? I know you **believe**."	**Paul's Message to King Agrippa**
28:24	"Some were persuaded by what he said, but others did not **believe**."	**Believers in Rome**

In view of Luke's many references to those who **believed**, we can understand more fully what Jesus meant when He commissioned the eleven apostles to "go, therefore, and **make disciples** of all nations, **baptizing them** . . ." (Matt. 28:19). Clearly, those who were baptized in this biblical story became authentic disciples by putting their faith in the Lord Jesus Christ and receiving eternal life.

Who Baptized the Apostles?

At this point, Jesus' commission to the apostles to baptize believers raises some interesting questions:

- Why is there no reference to the apostles' baptisms?
- Is it possible that these men were never baptized by human hands?

Obviously, we have no definitive answer to these questions. Some believe the apostles were baptized in water since they feel it would be inconsistent for them to require obedience to Jesus' command without being baptized themselves. However, it seems questionable that Luke would have omitted such a significant event.

Here's another possibility. Perhaps they considered their baptism with the Holy Spirit all that was necessary when "tongues like flames of fire" appeared and "rested on each one of them"—which was visible to a number of people who had gathered because of the "violent rushing wind" (Acts 2:2–3, 6). If so, this would be consistent with John the Baptist's statement to Jewish onlookers that he **baptized** "with water for repentance" but Jesus would later "**baptize** . . . with the Holy Spirit and fire" (Matt. 3:11b). Jesus reminded the apostles of this statement just before He ascended:

> While he was with them [the apostles], he commanded them not to leave Jerusalem, but to wait for **the Father's promise.** "Which," he said, "you have heard me speak about; for **John baptized with water**, but **you will be baptized with the Holy Spirit** in a few days." (Acts 1:4–5)[3]

This, of course, is only speculation. But it's abundantly clear that these men understood what Jesus meant when He commissioned them to "make disciples . . . baptizing them" (Matt. 28:19). All who put their faith in Jesus Christ were to be baptized, utilizing water to symbolize that they were personally identifying with the death, burial, and resurrection of Jesus Christ. It's also obvious that other spiritual leaders mentioned in Acts understood Jesus' commission as well. This is verified in the following baptismal events recorded by Luke.

Baptismal Events in Acts

The Day of Pentecost

The apostle Peter demonstrated his understanding of Jesus' commission when a multitude of Jews responded with deep conviction to his message. Luke has recorded:

> When they heard this, they were pierced to the heart and said to **Peter** and **the rest of the apostles**, "Brothers, what should we do?" Peter replied, "**Repent** and be **baptized, each of you**, in the name of Jesus Christ for the forgiveness of your sins, and you will receive the gift of the Holy Spirit. . . . So those who accepted his [Peter's] message were **baptized**, and that day about three thousand people were added to them [the apostles]." (Acts 2:37–38, 41)

This had to be an incredible scene. However, thousands more would have missed this localized phenomenon. They would not have heard these men "speak in different tongues"—namely, their own languages (Acts 2:6). However, they certainly didn't miss seeing whole households being baptized throughout the Jerusalem area. Without question, they would have also heard firsthand explanations as to why these authentic disciples were engaging in this baptismal activity—namely, that Jesus Christ had died, rose again, and ascended into heaven, and was going to come again!

Ceremonial Cleansings

As we reflect on what took place that day in Jerusalem, we need to understand the ceremonial cleansings that were a common practice in Judaism. We know from archeological discoveries that there were many immersion pools called *mikva'ot* in Jerusalem that Jews used for purification before they entered the temple to worship. There were also the huge pools of Bethesda and Siloam.

These three thousand people were probably baptized in these pools. It no doubt involved various forms. Jews were used to doing self-immersions, which was how *mikva'ot* baptisms occurred. Though the apostles perhaps participated in baptizing some of these believers, they were certainly not able to accommodate three thousand people in one day. Many of these believers may have immersed themselves—as they were used to doing as an act of Jewish ceremonial cleansing.[4]

This baptismal experience would have taken on a whole new meaning for these Jewish believers—namely, an act of corporate repentance for rejecting the Messiah (Acts 2:36–38). In this sense, they were repenting and seeking forgiveness as representatives of the Jewish nation for rejecting the promised Messiah—not personal forgiveness for their sins. As Peter later explained to Cornelius and other Gentiles gathered, "all the prophets testify about him that through his name **everyone who believes in him receives forgiveness of sins**" (Acts 10:43).

This would have also been a unique emotional experience for whole Jewish households who had approved of Jesus' crucifixion, but who now believed that He was the resurrected Messiah and the Son of God. Though their faith experiences were personal, in a special way this also represented household conversions. Knowing the parental authority of fathers in Judaism, many of these men would have baptized their wives and their children who were old enough to understand the gospel and respond in faith. This would have included their servants who had also received Jesus Christ.

Consider also the five thousand men who later responded to the gospel (Acts 4:4). It's generally agreed that the majority were fathers representing nearly five thousand extended family units. As these fathers and their family members were baptized throughout the Jerusalem area, thousands more would have witnessed what was happening, which led to more conversions.

Philip's Evangelistic Ministry

Philip, who was one of the seven men appointed to care for the Grecian widows, illustrates that Jesus' statement that the apostles would be "witnesses in Jerusalem, in all Judea and Samaria, and to the ends of the earth" applied to more than these eleven men. We read that Philip "went down to a city in Samaria and proclaimed the Messiah to them." Many "saw the signs he was performing," responded in faith, and "were baptized" (Acts 8:5–6, 12).

It's also important to note that those who were baptized were "both men and women" (8:12). This is an important observation when interpreting other baptismal events in Acts, particularly in the references to whole households believing and being baptized. Though this no doubt included single men and women, the majority were probably fathers and mothers who in turn may have baptized their children who were old enough to believe.

When word got back to the apostles in Jerusalem, they sent Peter and John to evaluate what had happened. When they arrived, they recognized the reality of these conversions. However, "they had only been **baptized in the name of the Lord Jesus**" rather than with a trinitarian blessing. Obviously, Peter and John did not baptize them again but simply "laid their hands on them, and they received the Holy Spirit" (8:16–17). This was obviously a supernatural manifestation similar to what happened in Jerusalem.[5]

In the next baptismal event, Philip met the Ethiopian eunuch who was on his way back to his own city. Probably a wealthy Jewish proselyte, he evidently purchased a scroll of Isaiah while in Jerusalem.[6] And while traveling along in his chariot, he was reading Isaiah's prophesies regarding the suffering and death of Jesus (Acts 8:32–33; Isa. 53:7–8). Since the official did not understand, Philip explained the passage and as a result the eunuch believed that Jesus was the promised Messiah. It was then that Philip baptized this man, giving us the first direct reference to water. They both "**went down into the water**" and "**came up out of the water**" (Acts 8:38–39). This description seems to correlate with the definition of the Greek terms *baptizo* and *baptisma*, which mean "to dip, immerse, sink, plunge." However, this general description regarding the Ethiopian's baptism allows for different "forms" than immersion. Some believe this could have involved pouring or sprinkling.

Also, there's additional variance in this baptismal experience. There's no reference to the coming of the Holy Spirit upon this Ethiopian or his entourage—only that this man believed in Jesus as the Messiah and was baptized in water. Paul later elaborated on what happens in the lives of all believers who put their faith in Christ and become authentic disciples: "For we were all **baptized by one Spirit into one body**—whether Jews or Greeks, whether slaves or free—and we were all given one Spirit to drink" (1 Cor. 12:13).[7]

In other words, all redemptive and born-again experiences are supernatural and involve the Holy Spirit, whether affirmed by miraculous phenomena or a simple faith experience that leads to "peace with God through our Lord Jesus Christ" (John 3:1; Rom. 5:1). Regardless, the Ethiopian's experience demonstrates that all believers should be baptized with water to symbolize our identification with Christ's death and resurrection.

Paul's Baptismal Experience

Paul's conversion on the road to Damascus is one of the most well-known in church history. However, his baptism is only briefly described in two references. After his sight was restored, he "**was baptized**" (Acts 9:18). And, years later, he described this experience to a hostile audience in Jerusalem—Jews who claimed to be believers but were convinced that it was necessary to keep the law of circumcision to be saved. Paul shared his encounter with Jesus, which involved his conversion experience and his calling to be a witness "to all people." In this revelatory experience, Jesus said to Paul, "Get up and be **baptized**, and wash away your sins, calling on his name" (22:16).

It appears that Paul's baptismal experience correlates with what Peter told the Jewish community in Jerusalem when they asked what they must do "for the forgiveness of their sins." In this instant, Paul is back in Jerusalem as Exhibit A in demonstrating with his baptism the need for the Jewish nation to repent for rejecting the Messiah.

Though Paul referred to "the forgiveness of sin" in relationship to his baptism, he later made it clear in his letter to the Ephesians what brings personal forgiveness of sins: "In him [Jesus] we have **redemption through his blood**, the **forgiveness of our trespasses**, according to the riches of his grace" (Eph. 1:7).

The apostle John reinforced this same great truth in his first epistle:

> If we walk in the light as he himself is in the light, we have fellowship with one another, and the **blood of Jesus his Son cleanses us**

from all sin. . . . If we confess our sins, he is faithful and righteous to **forgive us our sins** and to **cleanse us from all unrighteousness**. (1 John 1:7, 9)

The author of Hebrews wrote:

For if the blood of goats and bulls and the ashes of a young cow, sprinkling those who are defiled, sanctify for the purification of the flesh, how much more will **the blood of Christ**, who through the eternal Spirit offered himself without blemish to God, **cleanse our consciences from dead works** so that we can serve the living God? (Heb. 9:13–14)[8]

The author of the great gospel song captured this great truth and reality when he wrote:

What can wash away my sin?
Nothing but the blood of Jesus;
For my cleansing this my plea—
Nothing but the blood of Jesus!
Nothing can for sin atone,
Nothing but the blood of Jesus![9]

Cornelius and His Household

Up to this point in the biblical story, the apostle Peter believed that the gospel was only for the Jews. He confessed this to Cornelius, a God-fearing Gentile after the Lord had spoken to both of them through visions. "Now I truly understand," Peter said, "that God doesn't show favoritism, but in every nation the person who fears him and does what is right is acceptable to him. He sent the message to the Israelites, proclaiming the good news of peace through Jesus Christ—**he is Lord of all**. . . . All the prophets testify about him that through his name **everyone who believes in him receives forgiveness of sins**" (Acts 10:34–36, 43).

Following this redemptive experience in the lives of this large group of Gentiles, Peter said: "'Can anyone withhold **water** and prevent these people from being **baptized**, who have received the Holy Spirit just as we have?' He commanded them to be **baptized** in the name of Jesus Christ" (Acts 10:47). In other words, since the Holy Spirit had visibly come on these believers in a supernatural way, Peter did not use the trinitarian blessing. Also, this is the second reference to "water" in conjunction with baptism as recorded in the book of Acts.

It appears that "the large gathering of people" (10:27)—obviously Gentiles—responded in faith to Peter's message of salvation and were saved. And, once again, we see the miraculous affirming ministry of the Holy Spirit enabling these Gentile believers to speak "in tongues" and to declare "the greatness of God" (10:46).[10]

Lydia and Her Household

Luke recorded two similar baptismal events in Philippi. *First,* because of the ministry of Paul's missionary team, a prominent woman named Lydia became a believer. As a result of her conversion, she shared the gospel with her whole family. Consequently, we read: "After she and her **household were baptized**, she urged us, 'If you consider me a **believer in the Lord**, come and stay at my house.' And she persuaded us" (Acts 16:15).

The Philippian Jailor and His Household

The second baptismal event involved the Philippian jailer and his family. Following the supernatural earthquake, this man feared for his life and asked Paul and Silas what he must do to be saved. These men responded—"**Believe** in the Lord Jesus, and **you will be saved—you and your household**" (Acts 16:31). Consequently, the jailer "took them the same hour of the night and washed their wounds. Right away he and **all his family were baptized**" (Acts 16:33).

Here we have no reference to the coming of the Holy Spirit with signs and wonders as in previous situations. Perhaps the earthquake was affirmation enough in God's redemptive plan. Like the Ethiopian eunuch, there doesn't seem to be any unusual or miraculous event other than their "born again" experience.

Baptismal References in the Epistles

Paul's Letter to the Corinthians

When Paul arrived in Corinth, he first "testified to the Jews that Jesus was the Messiah." However, when his own people rejected the gospel, Paul turned to the Gentiles and "many of the Corinthians, when they heard, **believed** and **were baptized**" (Acts 18:8).[11]

Paul stayed in Corinth "a year and a half, teaching the word of God among them" (18:11). But when he left this city, these believers were still living carnal lives, so much so that Paul in his first letter to these believers accused them of "behaving like mere humans"—namely, **unbelievers** (1 Cor. 3:3). Paul stated in his introductory comments that he thanked God that he had **baptized** none of them "except Crispus and Gaius" as well as "the household of Stephanus." He then stated why. He was glad that no one could say that they were **baptized in Paul's name** (1 Cor. 1:14–16).

Paul then made a significant statement: "For Christ did not send me **to baptize**, but **to preach the gospel**" (1:17). And later in the same letter, he defined what he meant by the gospel he had preached to them by which they were saved—"that Christ **died for our sins** according to the Scriptures, that **he was buried**, that he was **raised on the third day** according to the Scriptures" (1 Cor. 15:1–4).

Paul clearly believed in water baptism, but he wanted everyone to understand that water baptism was not part of the gospel. And he wanted the Corinthians to know that believers were to be baptized in the name of the Father, the Son, and the Holy Spirit and not in his or any other person's name. This is why he was glad that he, in a year and a half of ministry among them, had only baptized a few people.[12] However, he also wanted them to know that all true believers are "baptized by one Spirit into one body—whether Jews or Greeks, whether slaves or free—and we're all given one Spirit to drink" (1 Cor. 12:13).[13]

Here Paul was departing from the usual use of the term *baptism*. As we've seen, the majority of references in the book of Acts refer to water baptism. Here Paul wrote about the Spirit's baptism which relates to a believer's position in Christ. Paul was reminding the Corinthians that they were all members of one body, although some were claiming otherwise because of their particular gifts.

Paul's Letter to the Romans

While Paul was in Corinth, it appears he wrote a letter to the believers in Rome. Perhaps still deeply concerned about the Corinthian carnality, he made specific reference to baptism in chapter 6:

> What should we say then? Should we continue in sin [e.g., like the Corinthians] so that grace may multiply? Absolutely not! How can we who died to sin still live in it? Or are you unaware that all of us who were **baptized** into Christ Jesus were **baptized** into his death? Therefore we were buried with him **by baptism** into death, in order that, just as Christ was raised from the dead by the glory of the Father, so we too may walk in newness of life. (Rom. 6:1–4)

Here, in my opinion, we have the most significant definition and meaning of water baptism. All believers who have by faith both died with Christ and have been given new life are to walk in newness of life, which is illustrated by water baptism. Paul devoted the rest of this chapter explaining why believers should not be slaves to sin but be enslaved to righteousness.

Paul's Prison Epistles

Paul made only brief references to baptism in his prison correspondence. While writing to the Colossians, he compared baptism to the Jewish rite of circumcision. In fact, he identified baptism as "the circumcision of Christ"—when these believers were "buried with him [Christ] **in baptism**, in which [they] were also raised with him through faith in the working of God, who raised him [Christ] from the dead" (Col. 2:12–13). As in Romans, Paul appears to be referring to water baptism.[14]

Writing to the Ephesians, Paul identified baptism in a series of references that focus on both singularity and unity in Christ. He wrote: "There is one body and one Spirit—just as you were called to one hope at your calling—one Lord, one faith, one baptism, one God and Father of all, who is above all and through all and in all" (Eph. 4:4–6). In context,

Paul was stating that there is not a baptism for Jewish believers and one for Gentile believers, but all believers are one in Christ and water baptism illustrates that all who put their faith in Christ for salvation have been buried with Him and raised to a new life.

Peter's First Letter

The apostle Peter compared water baptism with the ark that saved Noah and his family "through water." He stated that "baptism, which corresponds to this, now saves . . . through the resurrection of Jesus Christ" (1 Peter 3:18–21).

Some use this passage to teach that water baptism is essential for salvation. If this is what Peter meant, he would have been contradicting his references in the first chapter of this letter to faith only as the basis of salvation (see 1 Peter 1:1–5; 2:6). This interpretation would also contradict the multitude of references to the fact that we are saved by grace through faith (Eph. 2:8–9). Even Abraham was justified [that is, saved] when he **"believed God**, and it was credited to him for righteousness" (Rom. 4:3). We're told he experienced salvation long before he was circumcised (Rom. 4:9–11) and he was made righteous by faith nearly four hundred years before the law was given at Mount Sinai (Gal. 3:17–18). In other words, salvation has always been by grace through faith.

And let's not forget the thief on the cross who, before his death, acknowledged Jesus' perfect life. Even this man's simple but sincere faith in the Son of God—apart from baptism—resulted in eternal life. Jesus responded to his faith and said—"Truly I tell you, today you will be with me in paradise" (Luke 23:43).

Concluding Thoughts

Without question, Jesus made it clear in the Great Commission that, as believers, we're all to be baptized once we become authentic disciples. Clearly, we become authentic disciples through faith in Jesus Christ and what He has done for us at the cross and through His resurrection. Water baptism in turn illustrates what has happened in our lives and experiences once we "are saved by grace through faith" (Eph. 2:8). We have been spiritually identified with Christ's death, burial, and resurrection. "In Christ," every born-again believer is "a new creation; the old has passed away, and . . . the new has come" (2 Cor. 5:17).

As we'll see in the next chapter, baptismal events are to be personal and corporate worship experiences for believers, as well as personal and corporate witnessing experiences to those who are yet unsaved.

A Question for Thought and Discussion

Since the book of Acts illustrates again and again that baptism happened to those who put their faith in Jesus Christ for salvation, why do some Bible believing Christians teach and practice infant baptism (by sprinkling)?

10

Principles for Baptizing Believers

Video Intro from Gene

3lenses.org/c10

As we've seen in the previous chapter, Jesus made it clear to the apostles in the Great Commission that they were to baptize all those who became authentic disciples. Obviously, they were not able to perform all of these baptisms, but they were to teach those who responded to the gospel to engage in this experience.

The book of Acts and the rest of the New Testament illustrate and teach us how this happened throughout the Roman world. In these baptismal events and additional instructions, God has given us supracultural principles that can and should be applied throughout church history and any place in the world.

A Biblical Directive

Principle 1: We must encourage all believers in Jesus Christ to be baptized, demonstrating and illustrating that they have by faith been "buried with him" and raised to "walk in newness of life" (Rom. 6:4).

As we follow the unfolding story in the book of Acts and the New Testament letters, it's abundantly clear that we become authentic disciples by placing our faith in the Lord Jesus Christ. It's also clear that most references to baptism specifically refer to being baptized as believers. Water is involved and it illustrates our new life and position in Christ—that we have died with Christ, been buried with Him, and raised to new life.

It's also obvious from the biblical story that there is a lot of variances in terms of when this event happened, where it happened, and how it was done. Form is never specifically described, only alluded to—with the exception of the Ethiopian eunuch. Though immersion is not fully described, it appears this happened (Acts 8:36–39).

This lack of specificity seems to be by the Holy Spirit's design, giving some freedom in terms of experiencing and engaging in this God-ordained event. But without question, to be obedient to Jesus' commission, all believers should be baptized—following the examples in the book of Acts. Jesus clearly said, "Go . . . **make disciples . . . baptizing them**"— that is, baptize those who sincerely believed in the Lord Jesus Christ.

This raises an important question. What about infant baptism? Obviously, a newborn is not old enough to experience a personal faith in Christ. However, baptizing infants has been practiced in various groups within Christendom for many centuries.

To justify this practice, sincere Bible interpreters point to the household texts to support baptizing babies (Acts 10:24; 16:15, 31–34; 18:8; 1 Cor. 1:16). However, as pointed out by the late Stanley Grenz, "Careful exegesis . . . has netted the conclusion that the inclusion of infants in such baptisms, while possible, is remote." He then stated that "many scholars now agree that there is no direct evidence of infant baptism in the first century."[1] In fact, most scholars who promote baptizing infants will also agree that their primary evidence comes from theological support—such as the practice of circumcision in Judaism, God's sovereign election, and from church history recorded following the biblical records.

From my own personal study of this subject, my preference is to base my own conclusions and convictions on what is specifically recorded in the New Testament, particularly in terms of the practices described by Luke in the book of Acts. This leads me then full circle back to what I believe is a supracultural principle: **We must encourage all believers in Jesus Christ** to be baptized, demonstrating and illustrating that they have by faith been "buried with him" and raised to "walk in newness of life" (Rom. 6:4).

Choosing the Best Form

Principle 2: We should choose the best form for baptism that demonstrates that believers have, by faith, been "buried with Christ" and raised to "walk in the fullness of life."

During the many discussions with my seminary students prior to becoming a church planting pastor, I'll never forget a statement made by missions professor Dr. George Peters. As explained in chapter 3, he was one of the seminary teachers I invited into my class sessions to interact with the students as we were taking a fresh look at ecclesiology. At one point, this astute theologian and missiologist asked two thought-provoking questions: "When is baptism *baptism*? When you have a certain form or a certain meaning?"

As we were deep in thought regarding these questions, he went on to state that he personally believed that immersion in water is indeed the best form. But he still believed that God honored other forms—such as pouring and sprinkling. In other words, he was saying that the true meaning of baptism—identification with Christ—is the biblical absolute, not specific forms.

I would agree with Dr. Peters's statement regarding "freedom in form." However, when I became involved in church planting I taught and practiced immersion as the best form. But we faced a practical problem when we started the first Fellowship Bible Church in 1972. We began to meet in a church building we acquired from an Episcopal Diocese in Dallas. Since those who initially occupied this facility practiced infant baptism, there was no baptistry for practicing immersion. Consequently, I made a trip to a nearby city where I purchased a cattle tank. We were able to place this tank in our worship center, fill it with water, and baptize believers.

Interestingly, we had many people attending who became or had become believers who had been baptized as infants. Once they understood our preference regarding baptism and observed it modeled, many wanted to be immersed since they became convinced this form was the best in demonstrating that they, too, were believers in the Lord Jesus Christ.

Personally, this brought back many memories for me since I was immersed in a cattle tank as a young believer. Now years later as a pastor, I was encouraging believers to be baptized in the same way—not to be different, but because it was a practical solution.

In terms of others who had been baptized as infants but who felt any additional form was unnecessary, we did not make this an issue in our relationships. However, I continued to teach and model immersion. I must add, however, that many of those believers who had been baptized as infants eventually asked to be rebaptized by immersion. As they continued to witness "believers' baptism," they became convinced that this was the best form to illustrate that they had, by faith, died with Christ, been buried, and resurrected to "walk in newness of life."

Who Can Baptize?

One woman in our church had become a believer after experiencing unusual marital abuse. She eventually experienced wonderful healing, emotionally, spiritually, and even physically, and she became a remarkable witness for Christ.

On one occasion she led a young man to Christ and encouraged him to be baptized. When she shared his story with me, I immediately suggested that she baptize this new believer, as together they shared his conversion experience. As we all met on Sunday morning in our worship center, I simply set the stage for this to happen. Everyone focused on what happened that day and responded with an applause of praise. I'll never forget that remarkable experience!

In responding more specifically to the question regarding who can baptize, I'd like to respond with another question. Where in the biblical story does it say that only spiritual leaders should baptize—and only men? Yes, a commission was given to the apostles, but as we pointed out earlier in this chapter and the previous one, these men would not have been able to baptize three thousand believers in one day. Who helped make this happen? No doubt thousands of fathers and mothers were involved.

In terms of parents, I often use this biblical freedom during family baptisms. For example, I've encouraged husbands to baptize their wives, and then together to baptize their believing children. I can still envision these wonderful events and "hear" the shouts of amen from the congregation.

Unfortunately, traditions have developed following the New Testament story that have been absolutized and interfere with the freedom we have in practicing baptismal experiences. But there's one "tradition" that should have developed. We could even call it another supracultural principle: *Any dedicated believer has the freedom to baptize any other person who has sincerely become an authentic disciple of Jesus Christ.*

What About Church Membership?

Is "water baptism" a requirement for church membership? This is definitely a "form" question which is never answered in the New Testament. However, many churches have used this "freedom in form" to make this a requirement.

For us, this was not an issue since we did not have what would be identified as formal church membership. We, too, used "freedom in form." The closest resemblance to this kind of experience was regular attendance in small groups that we called "mini-churches" (small home meetings now called Life Groups). However, we have never required people to be believers to attend these meetings. In fact, many made personal decisions for Christ because they attended.

A Worship and Witness Experience

Principle 3: We should encourage believers to get baptized in order to engage in a personal worship experience and to be a witness and blessing to others, including both believers and unbelievers.

Witness in the Biblical Story

In terms of baptism being a witness, we certainly see this happening in the biblical story as it unfolds in the book of Acts.

- A multitude of unbelievers certainly witnessed three thousand baptisms that were performed throughout Jerusalem in one day (Acts 2:41).
- Though we're not told definitively who baptized the men and women in Samaria, it was certainly a public event (8:12).
- When Philip baptized the Ethiopian eunuch, this man's whole entourage would have witnessed what had happened (8:36–38).
- When Cornelius and his household were baptized, his invited guests certainly witnessed this event. In fact, it appears that most of them also believed and were baptized (10:24–47).
- When the households of Lydia and the Philippian jailor were baptized, it would naturally have been in the river that flowed through the city. We can only imagine the unsaved people—both Jews and Gentiles—who observed and listened as these baptismal events took place, especially after the earthquake (16:15, 33).
- When the believers in Corinth "believed and were baptized," it's feasible that it was in the immersion pools next to the synagogue. This would have served as a very public witness to the unsaved Corinthians—particularly the Jewish population (18:8).

A Personal Pastoral Experience

As I reflect on these New Testament baptismal events, I'm reminded of an experience participating and practicing this principle of baptism. It happened in Ukraine when it was still a part of the Soviet Union. In fact, all the countries within the Soviet Union were beginning to experience much more freedom, both in church worship and in witnessing to unbelievers. Perestroika and glasnost were gaining momentum under the leadership of Mikhail Gorbachev. Christians particularly were beginning to enjoy this new freedom.[2]

I was invited by several pastors to participate in a baptismal service for a group of new believers. In an open-air meeting next to a small lake, I opened the Scriptures and explained baptism from several biblical texts. A number of people were sitting nearby who had come to spend time at the beach. Most were no doubt unbelievers. It was clear they were watching and listening.

Following this event, I'll never forget meeting the Communist mayor from the nearby village. Since he had given permission for this event, it was obvious perestroika and glasnost had impacted his thinking. He was feeling a new sense of freedom, knowing he wouldn't get into trouble with the Communist hierarchy. He was actually interested in talking about what he was witnessing. Needless to say, this was a marvelous opportunity to share the gospel.

In terms of our own culture, it is certainly a blessing to be able to utilize baptismal facilities within church buildings, but we're often ministering primarily to believers—and in some cases, only to extended family members and close friends. Fortunately, we can baptize in rivers, lakes, and swimming pools, and invite both our Christian and non-Christian neighbors. This is particularly effective when we build relationships with those who are living around us.

The Jordan River Experience

My greatest memories regarding baptism have been when I've conducted trips to Israel. I've had the privilege of baptizing many believers in the Jordan River. In fact, the majority of participants had been baptized previously, but they wanted to be rebaptized in the same river where the Lord Jesus was baptized.

This has always been a remarkable worship experience for everyone involved—but especially for those who are being baptized for the first time. In fact, it was also a witnessing experience since we always had onlookers, some of whom were probably unsaved.

I'll never forget baptizing my own grown daughters. They had become believers and were baptized at an early age. Yet they too wanted to be rebaptized in the Jordan, and this time the experience was obviously more meaningful than before—for them, and certainly for me and their mother.

The River in Philippi

There is another personal and meaningful experience for me and my wife. Both of us as believers had been baptized early in life—through immersion. However, on one occasion we were on a "Journeys of Paul" trip. We revisited Philippi where Lydia and the Philippian jailor were baptized along with their households in the river that flowed near the outskirts of the city.

We stood by that very river where this would have happened. Our leader—who happened to be a Presbyterian minister—invited any one of us in the group to be baptized by being sprinkled. My wife and I stood on a rock on that riverbank, worshiping the Lord through this new experience and being a witness to others who were observing. By the way, the river today is not deep enough for immersion—and it was a very cold day!

I must add that I'm still convinced that immersion is the best form in most cultures of the world to illustrate that we, as believers, have died, been buried, and have risen with Christ. In fact, in God's sight we're already glorified:

> He also raised us up with him and seated us with him in the heavens in Christ Jesus, so that in the coming ages he might display the immeasurable riches of his grace through his kindness to us in Christ Jesus. (Eph. 2:6–7; see also Rom. 8:30)

Water baptism, then, also reminds us of this glorious positional reality! While this has not literally happened yet, it will someday. But in God's sight, we're eternally redeemed!

A Question for Thought and Discussion

*As you reflect on your own baptismal experience,
why was it meaningful?*

11

Teaching Authentic Disciples

Video Intro from Gene

3lenses.org/c11

Jesus' next significant command in the Great Commission moves us from evangelism to edification—equipping those who responded to the gospel. Though the baptismal experience is certainly a means of spiritual growth, the next step relates to the ongoing process of becoming a mature believer. Thus, Jesus said, "Go, therefore, and make disciples . . . baptizing them in the name of the Father and of the Son and of the Holy Spirit, **teaching them to observe everything I have commanded you**" (Matt. 28:19–20a).

In Jerusalem

We see this happening as soon as the church was born in Jerusalem. "Three thousand people" became believers, were baptized, and immediately "devoted themselves to the **apostles' teaching**" (Acts 2:41a, 42a).

The term "teaching" is *didache* in the Greek text, and in this context referred to the truth the Holy Spirit was revealing to the apostles. And, to understand what was actually happening, we once again need to return to the upper room just prior to the crucifixion.

The Spirit of Truth

Jesus informed the apostles that He was "going away to prepare a place for" them. They were obviously nervous and confused, not understanding God's redemptive plan for the whole world.

Jesus then told them He was going to ask the Father to give them "another Counselor" [*parakletos*], namely, "the Spirit of truth" (John 14:16). When He came, He would "teach" them "all things and remind" them "of everything" Jesus had taught them during the three-plus years He was with them (14:16, 26). When Jesus referred to "everything" in this promise, it correlates directly with His commission to teach those who had become authentic disciples "everything" He had taught them.

As these men left the upper room heading toward the garden of Gethsemane, Jesus continued His conversation about the coming of the Holy Spirit:

> "When the Counselor comes . . . he will **testify about me**" (15:26).

> "When the Spirit of truth comes, he will guide you into **all the truth**" (16:13a).

The apostles certainly didn't understand what Jesus was promising them prior to His death, resurrection, and ascension. However, they began to understand these promises when the "Spirit of truth" descended on them on the day of Pentecost. "Peter stood up with the Eleven, raised his voice," and cited Joel's prophecy to explain what was taking place (Acts 2:14).

Oral to Written Revelations

This was just the beginning of the way in which the "Spirit of truth" revealed God's redemptive plan to the apostles. *First,* these men spoke and eventually wrote much of what we have in our New Testament. This was a process that began in a special way on the day of Pentecost as the three thousand "devoted themselves to the **apostles' teaching**" (Acts 2:42a).[1]

In chapter 4, we've already looked at how the apostles and other key spiritual leaders made disciples throughout the Roman world. Clearly, evangelism is a major focus in the book of Acts. However, Luke succinctly recorded the way in which the apostles and other gifted individuals began to carry out Jesus' command to teach these disciples the eternal truth revealed by the Holy Spirit. And again, we can unfold these references geographically, a fulfillment of Jesus' promise in Acts 1:8: "But you will receive power when the Holy Spirit has come on you, and you will be my witnesses in **Jerusalem**, in all **Judea** and **Samaria**, and to the **ends of the earth**" (Acts 1:8).

In Judea, Galilee, and Samaria

Luke chose two basic Greek words to describe the results of teaching what was being revealed by the "Spirit of truth." The term *episterizo* refers to **confirming** or **strengthening** the disciples. The term *parakaleo* refers to **exhorting**, **comforting**, and **encouraging** these new believers. Luke recorded:

> The church throughout all **Judea**, **Galilee**, and **Samaria** had peace and was **strengthened**.[2] Living in the fear of the Lord and **encouraged by the Holy Spirit**, it [the church] increased in numbers. (Acts 9:31)

When Luke explained that the church was "encouraged by the Holy Spirit," it appears to be a direct reference to Jesus' promises to the apostles regarding the coming of the Spirit of truth. Thus, we could paraphrase that these believers were "encouraged and exhorted by the Spirit of truth as He spoke through the apostles and other key individuals, revealing God's Word."

In Antioch of Syria

This church was born when some "men from Cyprus and Cyrene" came to this pagan city and began speaking to the Jews as well as to the Greeks, "preaching the Lord Jesus" (Acts 11:20).[3] A large number became disciples, and when the leaders in Jerusalem learned about these Gentile converts they sent Barnabas to Antioch to teach these new believers. Since Barnabas was also a New Testament prophet (13:1), he was specially anointed by the Holy Spirit and was able to assist the apostles in carrying out this second directive in the Great Commission. Thus, we read:

> When he [Barnabas] arrived [in Antioch] and saw the grace of God, he was glad and **encouraged** all of them [the disciples] to remain true to the Lord with devoted hearts. (Acts 11:23)

Since Barnabas "was a good man, full of the Holy Spirit and of faith," we read that "large numbers of people were added to the Lord" (Acts 11:24). Needing help in teaching these new believers, Barnabas secured the help of Saul (Paul), who came from Tarsus to Antioch and joined Barnabas in a nurturing ministry. Consequently, we read that "for a whole year they met with the church and **taught large numbers**" (12:46).

Again, we have a clear example of doing what Jesus had commissioned them to do. They were teaching these new disciples the truth being revealed by the Holy Spirit. This included what the Holy Spirit had already revealed through the authors of the Old Testament as well as what eventually would become the New Testament.

In Lystra, Iconium, and Antioch of Pisidia

Luke's next specific reference to teaching those who had become disciples happened on the first missionary journey. Paul and Barnabas had started churches in four major cities in the Galatian region. Before returning to Antioch in Syria, Luke recorded their ministry in carrying out the second directive in the Great Commission.

> After they [Paul and Barnabas] had preached the gospel in that town [Derbe] and **made many disciples**, they returned to Lystra, to Iconium, and to Antioch, **strengthening** the disciples by **encouraging** them to **continue in the faith** and by telling them, "It is necessary to go through many hardships to enter the kingdom of God." (Acts 14:21–22)

As we've noted in an earlier chapter, this is the most comprehensive reference in the book of Acts to carrying out the two main directives in the Great Commission. And, as Paul and Barnabas taught these new believers, they emphasized continuing "in the faith" since there was a great deal of persecution in these cities, precipitated primarily by the unbelieving Jews. In fact, these believers had certainly heard about Paul's experience in Lystra when he was stoned and left for dead. On this return trip, they would have no doubt observed the marks of this horrendous experience on Paul's body. Without question, this would have created fear in their hearts. These relatively new believers would have needed a message of strength and encouragement "to continue in the faith."

In Antioch of Syria

After Paul and Barnabas returned from this first missionary journey to Antioch in Syria, they faced an intense encounter from several Jews from Jerusalem who claimed to believe in Jesus Christ, but who also believed Gentile converts needed to be circumcised in order to be saved. This resulted in the Jerusalem Council and a letter written primarily to Gentile converts to reassure them that they were justified by grace through faith, not by keeping this Old Testament law (Acts 15:11). The Council then authorized Paul and Barnabas as well as two prophets, Judas and Silas, to deliver this letter to the Gentile believers and to do additional teaching about how to live the Christian life (15:25–27, 32).

To summarize what happened, Luke recorded:

> So, they [Paul, Barnabas, Judas, Silas] were sent off and went down to Antioch, and after gathering the assembly, they **delivered the letter**. When **they read it**, they rejoiced because of its **encouragement**. Both Judas and Silas, who were also prophets themselves, **encouraged** the brothers and sisters and **strengthened** them with a **long message**. (Acts 15:30–32)

We can assume this "long message" explained more fully God's plan of salvation and what was further discussed and concluded in the Jerusalem Council. These men would certainly have also shared the remarkable story regarding the Gentile Cornelius and his household—which Peter had reported in full. What Peter had personally learned through this experience, namely, that God does not show favoritism, would be reassuring to the Gentile converts in Antioch (Acts 11:1–18).

In Syria and Cilicia

While in Antioch, Paul felt led to return to the cities where he and Barnabas had started churches. He was concerned about their status spiritually (Acts 15:36). However, because of a dispute regarding John Mark, Paul and Barnabas went their separate ways. Paul chose the prophet Silas as his missionary companion, although it appears they didn't travel together until Paul eventually returned to Lystra.

In the meantime, Paul evidently visited a number of churches in Syria and Cilicia—perhaps in close proximity to Antioch. We're not told how and when these churches came into existence. However, it may have happened as a result of the intense one-year ministry Paul and Barnabas had ministering together in Antioch and the surrounding area prior to the first missionary journey (15:25–26).

Luke has recorded:

> But Paul chose Silas and departed, after being commended by the brothers and sisters [in Antioch] to the grace of the Lord. He [Paul] **traveled through Syria and Cilicia, strengthening the churches**. (Acts 15:40–41)[4]

Though specifics are lacking, one thing is clear. Paul's primary ministry in these areas was to carry out the second directive Jesus gave in the Great Commission—to teach and establish these churches.

In the Galatian Region

When Paul arrived in Lystra, he became acquainted with Timothy, who became a believer when Paul and Barnabas came to the city on their first missionary journey. Luke has reported that "the brothers and sisters at Lystra and Iconium spoke highly of him" (Acts 16:2), which encourged Paul to enlist this young man to become his missionary companion. As a result, we read:

> As they [Paul, Silas, and Timothy] traveled through the towns, they **delivered the decisions** reached by the apostles and elders at Jerusalem

for the people to observe. So the churches were **strengthened in the faith** and **grew daily in numbers**. (Acts 16:4–5)

We're not told which towns were involved but it certainly included Iconium and Antioch of Pisidia. And it's clear that this missionary team focused on both directives in the Great Commission since these churches "grew daily in numbers." They continued to "make disciples" and "to teach them."

In Thessalonica

Luke continued to focus on making disciples in the unfolding story in the book of Acts. For example, he reported on what happened when this missionary team responded to the Macedonian call and came to Thessalonica. As usual, Paul took the lead and entered the Jewish synagogue with the goal to make disciples. We're told he reasoned with the Jews on three Sabbath days. Some Jews responded to the gospel, but we read that "a large number of God-fearing Greeks" and "a number of the leading women" also became believers (Acts 17:1–4).

Beyond the reference to three Sabbath days in Luke's account, we're not told how long this missionary team stayed in Thessalonica. But when Paul wrote his first letter to this church, we are given unusual insights as to what happened in this city as these men carried out the second directive in the Great Commission:

> Although we could have been a burden as Christ's apostles, instead we were gentle among you, as a **nurse** [nursing mothers] **nurtures her own children**. . . . As you know, like a **father with his own children**, we **encouraged**, **comforted**, and **implored each one of you** to walk worthy of God, who calls you into his own kingdom and glory. (1 Thess. 2:7, 11–12)

This is indeed a profound paragraph that describes what Jesus meant when He said, "Go . . . make disciples" and "**teach them**." Paul used three words to describe this teaching ministry in the lives of these believers—"to

encourage,"[5] to **comfort**,"[6] to **implore**."[7] To carry out this teaching ministry, they engaged in a personalized approach. They ministered to individuals, not just a group of believers. To make his point clear, Paul utilized the mother and father model, ministering to them as "their children," literally "one by one."[8]

To underscore even more emphatically his concern for helping believers grow in their faith, Paul reminded these believers that his missionary team was so concerned about their spiritual growth that they sent Timothy back to continue to teach them. Thus, Paul wrote:

> And we sent Timothy, our brother and God's coworker in the gospel of Christ, to **strengthen** and **encourage** you concerning your faith. (1 Thess. 3:2)

In Corinth

Paul spent eighteen months in this city on his second missionary journey. Much of his time was devoted to teaching new converts how to live in the will of God. Luke recorded:

> He [Paul] stayed there [in Corinth] a year and a half, **teaching the word of God** among them. (Acts 18:11)

However, this ministry in Corinth was one of his most disappointing experiences. Unfortunately, when he left this city, the majority of these believers were still living sinful lives. He did not give up on teaching them God's truth, however, which is clearly demonstrated in his letters, two of which are included in the New Testament.[9]

In Galatia and Phrygia

Following his return to Antioch in Syria, Paul continued to carry out the Great Commission, once again focusing on the second directive as he began his third journey. Luke has recorded:

> After spending some time there [in Antioch of Syria], he [Paul] set out, traveling through one place after another in the region of Galatia and Phrygia, **strengthening** all the disciples. (Acts 18:23)

As we reflect on Paul's concerns to help disciples mature in the faith, we must not forget what he suffered because of his evangelistic efforts. Writing to the Corinthians, he outlined very specifically his imprisonments, his beatings, and his near-death experiences (2 Cor. 11:23–27). However, one of his greatest concerns related to the spiritual welfare of those who became disciples as a result of his efforts. He wrote, "There is the daily pressure on me: my **concern** for all the churches" (2 Cor. 11:28). This "concern" related to these believers' spiritual status, which in turn motivated Paul to nurture them with the Word of God.

In Macedonia

As Paul continued on this third missionary journey, he spent three years ministering in Ephesus, focusing on both dimensions of the Great Commission. Two of those years were spent in the lecture hall of Tyrannus. Not only did he minister to the brothers and sisters in Ephesus, but he communicated the gospel to residents from all over Asia who came to Ephesus to shop, recreate, worship in the temple of Diana, and engage in other venues in big city life. Many heard Paul teach, and Luke recorded "that all the residents of Asia, both Jews and Greeks, **heard the word of the Lord**" (Acts 19:10).

Paul's teaching ministry was so effective in competing with the idolatrous activities in Ephesus, it led to serious persecution and a dangerous riot. Fortunately, the city clerk calmed the storm, but Paul felt it was time to leave Ephesus. Luke recorded:

> After the uproar was over, Paul sent for the disciples, **encouraged them**,[10] and after saying farewell, departed to go to Macedonia. And when he had passed through those areas and offered them many **words of encouragement**, he came to Greece. (Acts 20:1–2)

Once again, Paul visited the churches in Macedonia—which certainly included disciples in Berea, Thessalonica, and Philippi. And as we read, he "offered them many words of **encouragement**." Paul never stopped teaching believers the Word of God. To him, Jesus' directive to "teach disciples" was just as important as "making disciples."

The New Testament Letters

As stated earlier, the apostles first **spoke** the truth revealed to them by the "Spirit of truth." Eventually, they and other key individuals were inspired to compose the documents that comprise the entire New Testament. Luke, of course, was one of these key individuals.

The primary purpose of the New Testament letters was to carry out Jesus' second directive in the Great Commission—to **strengthen** and **encourage** believers by affirming God's redemptive plan and **teaching** them how to live in the "good, pleasing, and perfect will of God" (Rom. 12:1–2).

Concluding Thoughts

As we once again follow the story in the book of Acts, it's clear that the apostles, along with other key leaders, took Jesus' commission very seriously—to teach those who became disciples. We see this illustrated particularly in the ministry of Paul and his missionary companions. As they visited church after church, they "encouraged" and "strengthened" these new believers by teaching them the Word of God.

As we'll see in the next chapter, learning the Word of God was only foundational in "growing into maturity with a stature measured by Christ's fullness" (Eph. 4:13). This process involved additional experiences which are clearly illustrated when the church was born in Jerusalem.

A Question for Thought and Discussion

What characterizes Bible teaching that results in affirmation, strength, and encouragement?

12

The Jerusalem Model

Video Intro from Gene

3lenses.org/c12

As we've noted in the previous chapter, the apostles and other key leaders faithfully carried out Jesus' directive to teach those who, by faith, became disciples. But it's also clear from Scripture that believers need more than a knowledge of the Word of God to become mature in Christ. They need three vital experiences, which are described and illustrated by Luke in the church in Jerusalem. Though this community of faith eventually faced serious problems because of false teachers, its three functions provide believers with a profound model.

Three Vital Experiences (Acts 2:42–47)

I. Learning the Word of God

"They devoted themselves

    *A. to the **apostles' teaching,***

II. Relating to One Another and to God

    *B. to the **fellowship,***

        *1. to the **breaking of bread,***

        *2. and to **prayer.***

Everyone was filled with awe, and many wonders and signs were being performed through the apostles.

Now all the believers were together and held all things in common.

They sold their possessions and property and

      3. **distributed the proceeds to all, as any had need.**

Every day they devoted themselves to meeting together in the temple, and broke bread from house to house.

They ate their food with joyful and sincere hearts,

      4. **praising God** *and*

III. Witnessing to the Unsaved

    C. *enjoying the favor of **all the people.***

Every day the Lord added to their number those who were being saved.

Vital Learning Experiences with the Word of God (The Apostles' Teaching)

When the apostles began to teach the three thousand who had become believers, it was clearly the beginning of what Jesus promised in the upper room on the way to the garden of Gethsemane. The "Spirit of truth" had come, reminding the eleven apostles not only of what Jesus taught them, but of "all things" (John 14:25). Initially they were marvelously and supernaturally "declaring the magnificent acts of God" to a number of different language groups which came from all over the Roman world. However, these men and other spiritual leaders continued to communicate God's truth, demonstrating that learning God's revealed word is foundational in being able to grow spiritually.

Years later, Peter affirmed this reality when he exhorted: "Like **new-born infants**, desire the **pure milk of the word**, so that by it you may **grow up** into your salvation" (1 Peter 2:2).

Paul expanded on the importance of having a vital learning experience with the Word of God in his final letter to Timothy:

> **All Scripture** is inspired by God and is profitable for teaching, for rebuking, for correcting, for training in righteousness. (2 Tim. 3:16)

And in this final letter Paul also exhorted Timothy to continue to communicate the Word of God:

> Hold on to the pattern of **sound teaching** that you have heard from me, in the faith and love that are in Christ Jesus. Guard the **good deposit** through the Holy Spirit who lives in us. (2 Tim. 1:13–14)

> What you have **heard from me** in the presence of many witnesses, commit to **faithful men** who will be able to **teach others also**. (2:2)

> Be diligent to present yourself to God as one approved, a worker who doesn't need to be ashamed, correctly **teaching the word of truth**. (2:15)

> **Preach the word**; be ready in season and out of season; **correct, rebuke**, and **encourage** with great patience and **teaching**. For the time will come when people will not tolerate **sound doctrine**, but according to their own desires, will multiply teachers for themselves because they have an itch to hear what they want to hear. (4:2–3)

Eventually, the "Spirit of truth" also inspired the authors of Scripture to give us the New Testament—which provides us with the totality of God's written revelation. It's this revelation—and particularly the letters that are written to the churches—that enable us to be able to "discern what is the good, pleasing, and perfect will of God" (Rom. 12:2; Eph 4:1). And the author of Hebrews stated why the Word of God is so significant in our spiritual growth. He wrote,

> For the **word of God** is living and effective and sharper than any double-edged sword, penetrating as far as the separation of soul and spirit, joints and marrow. It is able to judge the thoughts and intentions of the heart. (Heb. 4:12)

Vital Relational Experiences with One Another and with God ("The Fellowship")

As we've just noted, the first vital experience involved **learning the Word of God.** However, as "they devoted themselves to the **apostles' teaching**," they also "devoted themselves . . . to the **fellowship**" (*koinonia*). In itself, this word describes human relationships, but used here in this paragraph, it involves both deep relationships among believers as well as worshipful relationships with God.

The Agape *Meal*

After introducing us to this second vital experience in the lives of the believers in Jerusalem, Luke then listed four human and divine relationships that describe this **fellowship**. *First,* they "devoted themselves . . . to the **breaking of bread**" (Acts 2:42b). Later in the same paragraph we read that these believers "**broke bread** from house to house" and "**ate their food** with joyful and sincere hearts" (2:46).

To understand the human and divine aspects of this fellowship, we need to once again revisit what happened in the upper room during the Passover meal. The apostles indeed ate a meal together. In his gospel, Luke—and later Paul in his letter to the Corinthians—described this experience as a "supper" (Luke 22:20; 1 Cor. 11:24). The bread Jesus broke to illustrate His broken body was a significant part of this supper. However, Jesus proceeded to break the bread before they began the main meal. Then, "after supper," Jesus took "the cup" of wine to illustrate His blood that would be "poured out" at the cross (Luke 22:20; 1 Cor. 11:25).[1]

When the church was born, the apostles not only remembered this experience but now understood what Jesus was teaching them. Perhaps the "Spirit of truth" reminded them of Jesus' very words in the upper room (John 14:26). They in turn must have shared this divine message with the three thousand believers, who then also remembered the Lord's redemptive sacrifice, enabling them to eat "their food with joyful and sincere hearts." In other words, the very sophisticated Passover meal—which all God-fearing Jews understood—became a simple, communal meal. However, with the apostles, these new believers also understood the true meaning of what Jesus did at the Passover meal as they "broke bread from house to house."

Though Luke did not mention drinking from "the cup," it does not mean it was not a part of this fellowship experience. A communal meal in which believers remembered the broken body and shed blood of Christ very quickly became a regular part of the relational experiences in the New Testament churches. It's later called the *agape* meal or "love feast." In fact, Jude referred to unbelievers who ate with believers at their "love feast" but "without reverence" (Jude 12).

This *agape* meal is also illustrated in the Corinthian church, but because these believers were woefully immature, they misused and abused this "supper" in a shameful way. Paul addressed this sinful behavior, saying, "When you come together, then, it is not to eat the **Lord's Supper**. For at the meal, each one eats his **own supper**. So one person is hungry while another gets drunk!" (1 Cor. 11:21).

Prior to their conversion, many of the Corinthians gorged themselves with food and uninhibitedly drank wine in the pagan temples and also engaged in temple prostitution. Now in their carnality as believers, they allowed this behavior to become a part of what was supposed to be a sacred meal. Consequently, Paul reviewed what happened on the night Jesus was betrayed and explained the true meaning. He also warned them that if they continued this behavior, they would experience the Lord's discipline (1 Cor. 11:29–30).

This horrible abuse in no way negates the profound relational experience God intended to be associated with this meal. As the believers in Jerusalem "broke bread from house to house," they experienced deep, Christlike fellowship with one another, and at the same time they had sincere worship and fellowship experiences with God. With "joyful and sincere hearts" they remembered the price Jesus paid for their salvation (Acts 2:46).

Corporate Prayer

The second fellowship and relational experience involved corporate prayer—a totally new experience for these Jewish believers. In fact, there is no evidence that even the apostles ever prayed together prior to Christ's ascension. Even though they asked Jesus on one occasion to teach them to pray, it happened because they had observed Jesus' personal prayer life. Though they may have tried to imitate Jesus in their own personal lives, there's no evidence they ever did. In fact, it's hard to imagine that James and John, who had such self-righteous attitudes and self-centered motives even at the Last Supper, ever spent time in personal prayer, let alone praying together. If they had, it would've been pure ritual.

However, following Jesus' ascension, the apostles were introduced to meaningful corporate prayer—perhaps for the first time. Luke recorded that all these men along with Jesus' brothers, Mary, and some other women met in an upper room and "were **continually united in prayer**" (Acts 1:13–14). Though we're not told, it would follow naturally that an aspect of the "apostles' teaching" involved the importance of corporate prayer. Consequently, the three thousand that responded to Peter's message not only shared their meals together, remembering the Lord's broken body and shed blood, but "**devoted themselves . . . to prayer**" (2:42b).

As the apostles and other key leaders learned more about prayer, it became a significant part of their human and divine relational experiences. This is certainly true in what Paul wrote in his epistles. Note the following exhortations:

- "**Pray** constantly" (1 Thess. 5:17)
- "Be persistent in **prayer**" (Rom. 12:12)
- "Devote yourselves to **prayer**" (Col. 4:2)
- "**Pray** at all times in the Spirit with every **prayer** and **request**, and stay alert with all perseverance and **intercession** for all the saints" (Eph. 6:18)
- "Don't worry about anything, but in everything, through **prayer** and **petition** with **thanksgiving**, present your **requests** to God" (Phil. 4:6)
- "First of all, then, I urge that **petitions**, **prayers**, **intercessions**, and **thanksgivings** be made for everyone" (1 Tim. 2:1)

If we look at these exhortations in context, it's clear they refer primarily to praying with and for one another. Though not obvious in our English Bibles, the authors of Scripture most often used plural pronouns to exhort believers to pray in concert with one another.

These observations certainly do not replace personal prayer as modeled by Jesus. Paul illustrates this in his own life, primarily because he was alone in prison. He had no one to join him in this relational experience (Phil. 4; Eph. 1:15–19; 3:14–21). And so the main emphasis in his epistles is on praying together.

In summary, the brothers and sisters in the Jerusalem church "devoted themselves . . . to prayer." Again, this corporate *koinonia* experience was both **horizontal** and **vertical**. As they prayed for one another and their special needs, they were in communion with their Father in heaven.[2]

Mutual Sharing of Material Possessions

Luke next described the two-fold relational experiences that involved their material possessions:

> Now all the believers were together and held all things in common. They sold their possessions and property and **distributed the proceeds to all, as any had need**. (Acts 2:44–45)

To understand this incredible and generous dynamic, we need to review what had happened in Jerusalem prior to Pentecost. A great multitude of God-fearing Grecian Jews had come to Jerusalem to worship in the temple. This was nearly a two-month event. It ended with "the day of Pentecost"—the final day before these faithful Jews had made plans to return to their respective homes in Mesopotamia, Cappadocia, Pontus, Asia, Phrygia, Pamphylia, Egypt, and Rome (Acts 2:8–11). But it was on this final day that the Holy Spirit came as Jesus had promised. These Jewish foreigners heard the gospel in their own languages as the men of Galilee—the apostles—explained what had just happened (Acts 2:5–8).

It was then that Peter delivered his message and three thousand responded and became believers. A short time later, Luke recorded that "the number of the men" who believed "came to about 5,000," which no doubt referred to the number of whole households (4:5). Consequently, multiplied thousands responded to the gospel and many, if not the majority, were from other parts of the world.

Rather than returning to their homes, they decided to stay in Jerusalem to see what was going to happen next. This is predictable since this was such a phenomenal experience hearing the apostles share the gospel in their various languages and then watching them perform "many wonders and signs" (Acts 2:4, 43). Those who lived in Jerusalem and in the immediate vicinity even decided to provide for those who stayed. This is predictable since the last direct revelatory message the apostles had heard prior to Pentecost came from two angelic beings:

> They said, "Men of Galilee [the apostles], why do you stand looking up into heaven? This same Jesus, who has been taken from you into heaven, will come in the same way that you have seen him going into heaven." (Acts 1:11)

There is no evidence the Holy Spirit at this point revealed to these men any additional eschatological information, so they proceeded to live as if the promise of Christ's return could happen at any moment.

What happened in the days and weeks to follow soon made it clear that staying in Jerusalem was not God's plan. Jesus was not going to return at that time to set up His earthly kingdom. These believers thus returned to their homes in various areas of the empire. However, the relational dynamic of sharing material possessions to meet people's needs and worshiping and honoring God together continued, particularly as believers were encouraged to do so in the New Testament letters.

Ironically, the economic dynamics changed dramatically in the Jerusalem area when the famine hit this area of the world. It became the motivating force that caused Paul to receive offerings from various churches to meet the needs of believers in Jerusalem and Judea. This financial need also motivated Paul to share with the predominantly Gentile churches what have become guidelines for generosity throughout church history.

This is particularly evident in Paul's second letter to the Corinthians. Following are his directives in chapter 9:

- They were to take a step of faith and trust God to enable them to give based on their future income (v. 5a).

- They were to plan their giving so they could give with a positive attitude (v. 5b).
- They were to give generously so that God would bless them generously—often in nonmaterial ways (v. 6).
- They were to be cheerful givers (v. 7).
- God would meet their material needs—not necessarily their wants—if they were generous givers (v. 8).
- If they were generous, God will enable them to continue to be generous, even with what little they may have had (v. 11).
- If they were generous, other believers would praise and glorify God (v. 13).
- If they were generous, other Christians would respect and love them (v. 14).
- Their motivating factor for being generous should be God's generosity in His gift of Jesus Christ (v. 15).

Again, we see two dimensions in the Jerusalem church, this time in corporate sharing—**meeting one another's needs** while also worshiping God with material gifts. As Jesus taught, "Whoever gives even a cup of cold water to one of these little ones because he is a disciple, truly I tell you, he will never lose his reward" (Matt. 10:42). Later, when Jesus responded to those who cared for others' material needs, he said, "Whatever you did for one of the least of these brothers and sisters of mine, **you did for me**" (Matt. 25:40).

Corporate Praise

Luke identified the fourth fellowship experience as "praising God," which is directly related to what happened at the end of the Passover meal. Both Matthew and Mark have recorded: "**After singing a hymn**, they went out to the Mount of Olives" (Matt. 26:30; Mark 14:26). When believers met throughout Jerusalem "with joyful and sincere hearts, praising God," this certainly involved, or at least set the stage for, corporate singing.

In God's plan for the church, music has always been a part of both teaching and worship. This was true in Israel's history, and it took on an even greater significance under the new covenant, as exhorted by the apostle Paul as he wrote to the Ephesians:

> But be filled by the Spirit: **speaking to one another** in psalms, hymns, and spiritual songs, **singing and making music with your heart to the Lord**. (Eph. 5:18b–19)[3]

Paul in essence repeated the same exhortation in his letter to the Colossians: "Let the **word of Christ** dwell richly among you, in all wisdom **teaching and admonishing one another** through psalms, hymns, and spiritual songs, **singing to God with gratitude in your hearts**" (Col. 3:16).

Note three important things. *First,* what Paul stated about "teaching and admonishing one another" with the "word of Christ" related specifically to the "apostles' teaching"—God's revealed message.

Second, the basic content and application of biblical truth is described in three ways: psalms, hymns, and spiritual songs.

Some believe that Paul may have been referring to the Old Testament psalter when he referred to "psalms." If so, nothing can surpass the very "words of God" as a basis for edification.

The term *hymn* refers to "praise songs" based on biblical truth. These hymns were to be used to teach one another and to glorify God.

"Spiritual songs" refers to "spiritual odes." The term *odes* used by itself is broad in meaning and refers to any poetry, sacred or secular. Believers, however, were to make melody in their hearts with spiritual odes—songs that expressed their attitudes and feelings toward the Lord and each other.

Third, music was to be used at both the human and divine level, just as the other *koinonia* experiences. They were to teach one another with the very words of Scripture and with poetic expressions that represented the inspired Word of God. But at the same time they were to make melody in their hearts to the Lord.

It should also be noted that no reference is made in the New Testament to the musical "forms" used to sing these psalms, hymns, and spiritual songs. This is significant, which we'll address later.

In summary, these believers in Jerusalem continued to learn biblical truth from the apostles. However, they also engaged in fellowship in four ways at both the human and divine levels. In this sense, they had vital relational experiences with one another and with God:

- While eating together, they regularly remembered the Lord's sacrifice on the cross.
- While praying for one another, they worshiped and praised God.
- While sharing their material possessions to meet one another's needs, they were expressing their gratitude to God.
- While teaching and admonishing one another with music, they were lifting their voices in praise to the Lord.

Vital Witnessing Experiences with the Unsaved World ("Enjoying the Favor of All the People")

CORPORATE WITNESS

The disciples in Jerusalem had an important third experience. While "they devoted themselves to the apostles' teaching" and engaged in dynamic fellowship with one another and with God, they were "enjoying the favor of **all the people**"—namely, the thousands of unbelievers in Jerusalem. Consequently, "every day the Lord added to their number those who were being saved" (Acts 2:47).

Here we once again see continuity and fulfillment that relates to what Jesus taught the apostles in the upper room and on the way to the garden of Gethsemane:

- The church in Jerusalem was a marvelous example of what happens when believers love one another as Christ had loved them, demonstrating to unbelievers that they were His disciples—not just followers of some religious philosopher (John 13:34–35).
- The believers in Jerusalem demonstrated what should happen when believers allow love for one another to express itself in the "fruit of righteousness"—again, demonstrating to unbelievers they are Christ's disciples who are reflecting His character (John 15:1–8).

- What happened in Jerusalem is also what should happen when Christ's prayer for all believers is answered—that becoming one as He is one with the Father demonstrates to the world that Jesus Christ is indeed the incarnate Son of God (John 17:20–23).[4]

In essence, because of their love for one another, their godly lives, and their oneness in Christ, these believers in Jerusalem were "enjoying the favor" of unbelievers, who in turn responded to the gospel message they saw lived out in this community of faith. Thus, Luke recorded: "Every day the Lord added to their number those who were being saved" (Acts 2:47b).

Concluding Thoughts

To become local communities of faith that are "growing to maturity with a stature measured by Christ's fullness," all believers must have **three vital experiences** on a regular basis:

- Vital learning experiences with the eternal Word of God
- Vital relational experiences with one another and with God
- Vital witnessing experiences with the unsaved world

This also relates to another important question: What kind of "forms" and "structures" does it take to provide believers with these three vital experiences?

The answer to this question is clear in Scripture—we are never told! If the Holy Spirit had inspired "forms" and "structures" that are normative and absolute, it would have made it difficult, if not impossible, to carry out the Great Commission beyond Jerusalem, Judea, Samaria, and the Roman world. God has designed "freedom in form" to keep Christianity from becoming just another world religion that is so closely aligned with its cultural milieu in form and structure that it's difficult to function outside its culture without changing its basic theology. The fact is, Christianity through biblical functions can thrive in any culture of the world, creating its own relevant forms without changing or compromising its enduring and eternal message. In the next chapter we'll look at the supracultural principles that can guide us in developing these forms and structures to provide believers with these three vital experiences anywhere in the world and at any moment in history.

A Question for Thought and Discussion

Why do some churches tend to focus on one of these three experiences rather than all three?

13

Biblical Principles of Edification—Part 1

Video Intro from Gene

3lenses.org/c13

Providing Three Vital Experiences

In its beginning, the church in Jerusalem modeled what God intends the church to be, perhaps more completely than any community of faith throughout church history. Unfortunately, a number of believers of this church were eventually impacted by Judaic legalism. Yet this in no way detracts from what happened as described by Luke following the day of Pentecost.

As noted in the previous chapter, these authentic disciples consistently engaged in three significant experiences:

1. **Vital Learning Experiences with the Word of God**
2. **Vital Relational Experiences**
   With One Another and
   With God
3. **Vital Witnessing Experiences with the Unsaved World**

As also noted, these three experiences are emphasized and illustrated throughout the rest of the biblical story. They are indeed supracultural functions that become supracultural and enduring principles.

Vital Learning Experiences with the Word of God

Principle 1: To equip communities of faith to become the church God intended, we must consistently and clearly teach the Scriptures in such a way that all believers will be able to understand, internalize, and apply God's truth.

In chapter 11, "Teaching Authentic Disciples," we've already looked at the way this principle is illustrated throughout the book of Acts, resulting in believers being encouraged and strengthened. In the Jerusalem church, they "devoted themselves to the apostles' teaching" (Acts 2:42a). And as the gospel spread beyond Jerusalem, resulting in conversions, the teaching process continued. The New Testament letters were then written to provide believers with both Holy Spirit–inspired content and instructions to enable this process to be ongoing, even to this very day.

Freedom in Form

Teaching and preaching the Word of God are supracultural functions. However, the Holy Spirit never inspired the authors of Scripture to give us forms and methods that are normative and absolute. Those that are alluded to are partial and varied, illustrating freedom in methodology. This "freedom" enables spiritual leaders and all members of the body of Christ at any moment in history to be creative and culturally relevant in communicating biblical truth.

The Composition of Scripture

The way the biblical authors composed the documents in both the Old and New Testaments in itself illustrates "freedom in form." Consider the variety in the four gospels and particularly John's record of Jesus' life. Compared with the synoptics, his methodology is unique. He clearly stated his purpose in writing and then used a variety of compositional structures to communicate that purpose (John 20:30–31). And when John wrote his three letters, he used a totally different literary style than in his gospel.

Also consider Paul's letters. When you look carefully at how he composed his letter to the Romans, you can see what is progressive logic. He carefully laid out propositional truth regarding God's unfolding plan of redemption, leading to logical conclusions. And he frequently used the term *therefore* to make his transitions and develop his theological points (Rom. 2:1; 5:1, 12; 6:12; 7:4; 8:1; 12:1; 14:13; 15:7, 17).

To an extent, Paul did the same in his letter to the Ephesians, but many of his other letters have different literary styles. Whether he was writing to various churches or to individuals such as Timothy and Titus, he chose his literary forms based on his unique audiences.

The point is this: throughout Scripture, we see a great variety in communication style, demonstrating that we have freedom to communicate creatively, using forms and methodologies that help us teach and preach the Word of God to people in many different cultures—and at any moment in history.

Teaching the New Testament Letters

These biblical documents in themselves illustrate an effective way to communicate biblical truth to believers as well as unbelievers. They were written to various churches and individual believers to help them mature and grow in all aspects of the Christian life. They were not meant to be read in segments but as a whole. If we're going to communicate this Holy Spirit–inspired information effectively, we must teach the content in a way that is coherent and in harmony with the grammatical structure and purpose inherent in these letters and intended for their recipients.

This means that believers need to be exposed to the unfolding message in these letters sentence by sentence, paragraph by paragraph. In other words, when we preach and teach from these letters, we need to maintain proper continuity. We must be careful not to take texts out of context. If we do, people will naturally miss the comprehensive meaning the Holy Spirit designed for the original listeners. In some instances, this can also result in superficial or even false interpretation and misapplication of biblical truth.

There are indeed a variety of ways we can make the content in these letters understandable and applicable in any culture of the world and at any moment in history. The guiding principle is to make sure that listeners understand God's specific messages as they are revealed and unfolded in these letters, and to then see how each section of these letters applies to their lives.

For example, to help my audience understand the total message, I've at times presented these letters dramatically. On one occasion I simulated Paul in prison as he wrote the letter to the Ephesians. Dressed in Roman garb, I sat at a small table, with one of my associates dressed as a Roman soldier standing behind me. As I simulated Paul writing this letter—reciting his words as I wrote—I presented the whole letter. This method was particularly impactful when I came to Ephesians chapter 6 and gestured to the "Roman guard" as I read each piece of armor (Eph. 6:16–17). It set the stage for more messages as I taught this letter paragraph by paragraph, ending each message with "Principles to Live By."

Teaching Old Testament Personalities

To teach the Old Testament, I've discovered that focusing on character studies is very effective. Large segments in the Scriptures describe the lives of Abraham, Jacob, Joseph, Moses, Joshua, Samuel, David, Elijah, Nehemiah, Daniel, and others. Through biblical exposition, it's possible to make these biblical personalities come alive and then to end each message with "Principles to Live By" that come from the biblical text. They were all human beings just as we are human beings, and their successes and failures apply to all of us today in all cultures of the world. Frankly, as I reflect on this series of sermons I did over a period of years, I received the most positive feedback compared with any other series of messages.[1]

Applying Biblical Truth

Without question, it's important that we teach the Scriptures so people clearly understand God's truth. However, we must not assume that simply comprehending the message of Scripture automatically results in internalization and application. In fact, understanding alone can lead to "head knowledge" without "heart knowledge." We must help people understand the way this biblical truth applies to their lives.

Unfortunately, some of us have concluded that our task is to help listeners understand the scriptural message, but it's the Holy Spirit's responsibility to apply that message in listeners' lives. This is only partially true. People can understand and interact with scriptural knowledge and fail to see how it applies in their day-to-day lives. As teachers, we must also share principles to live by that come from the biblical story and share ways these principles can be applied in various life experiences. Furthermore, to help listeners personalize and apply these principles, we need to provide them with opportunities to ask the Holy Spirit to help them practice what they have learned.

This whole process raises an important question: What about unbelievers? I personally believe that when the Bible is clearly taught, both saved and unsaved can understand most aspects of Scripture. This is particularly true when people are seeking the truth. In this sense, they are like the Bereans who "examined the Scriptures daily" in order to discover if the redemptive message was true (Acts 17:11). At the same time, believers will continue "growing into maturity with a stature measured by Christ's fullness" (Eph. 4:13).

Vital Relational Experiences with One Another and with God

Principle 2: To equip communities of faith to become the church God intended, we must help all believers to have meaningful relational experiences with one another that are intricately related to meaningful relationships with God.

As a result of Peter's message in Jerusalem, the three thousand who came to faith as a result of Peter's message not only "devoted themselves to the **apostles' teaching**"—but also "to the **fellowship**." As we've noted in the previous chapter, this *koinonia* or fellowship included four relational experiences, which are both horizontal and vertical.

The *Agape* Meal

In having this relational experience, Luke has recorded that these new believers first of all "devoted themselves . . . to the **breaking of bread**."

"They **ate their food** with joyful and sincere hearts" (Acts 2:42, 46).

As we've also noted in chapter 12, believers in Jerusalem remembered the Lord's broken body and shed blood with a full meal. The rather complex Passover meal Jesus ate with the apostles in the upper room became a simple communal meal as believers met in their homes.

A Change in Form

At some point in early church history, this full meal or supper was reduced to a "token meal" involving a small substance and a sip of juice. This change illustrates "freedom in form" and it's certainly appropriate since the meaning is what is most important, not the quantity or substance. Engaging in a "token meal" is more workable in a variety of social situations when believers gather for fellowship.

However, there is a major lesson we can learn from this change. When church leaders eliminated the full meal associated with remembering the Lord's Supper, it changed the natural environment that lends itself to having deep and meaningful fellowship with one another and with God.

In reflecting on what happened in first-century churches, I was challenged to re-create some of the more meaningful experiences associated with the Lord's Supper. I suggested to our leaders that we attempt to reproduce to a certain extent what happened at both the human and divine level. We didn't eliminate the "token meal," but we felt it was also possible at times and in some ways to duplicate the New Testament *agape* meal.

A Leadership Experience

I have vivid and pleasant memories when I recall pioneering this experience with our elders and their wives. Each couple brought food for the meal that we placed on a table in our home. As we met together, we first spent time sharing God's special blessings in our lives and praying for one another. We then passed a large loaf of bread as each of us broke off a sizable piece. And before taking our first bite, we prayed and thanked the Lord for His broken body. We then joyfully filled our plates and moved to small tables throughout our home. In fact, we continued to eat the same bread—from what was left following our first bite and additional loaves we had placed on the table.

Following this "supper" together, we then—at each table—remembered the shed blood of Christ, using the very "juice" we had been drinking during the meal. This whole sequence and experience somewhat simulated what Jesus did—as Paul recorded in his letter to the Corinthians:

> For I received from the Lord what I also passed on to you: On the night when he was betrayed, the Lord Jesus **took bread**, and when he had given thanks, **broke it**, and said, "This is my body, which is for you. Do this in remembrance of me." In the same way also he **took the cup**, **after supper**, and said, "This cup is the new covenant in my blood. Do this, as often as you drink it, in remembrance of me." (1 Cor. 11:23–25)

In a very real way, we felt we were also practicing what John taught in his first epistle when he wrote:

> What we have seen and heard we also declare to you, so that you may also have **fellowship with us**; and indeed **our fellowship is with the Father and with his Son, Jesus Christ**. (1 John 1:3)

Small Group Experiences

After engaging in this *agape* meal as leaders, we encouraged members of the body generally to have the same experience. Since we had divided our congregation into small groups that met in homes, we had already set the stage for this to happen. We encouraged these mini-churches to also remember the Lord in association with a full meal. In that sense, it had similarities to what happened in Jerusalem when believers "broke bread from house to house" and "ate their food with joyful and sincere hearts" (2:46).

Family Experiences

Not only did we encourage our small groups to experience the *agape* meal, but I also suggested individual families periodically remember the

Lord in this way—particularly when children were old enough to participate with understanding and had personally received the Lord Jesus Christ as Savior. This is a powerful way to engage in family worship—which no doubt happened in many homes in the first century, since extended families particularly functioned as the "church in miniature."

As we engaged in these small group experiences, we were obviously not duplicating all aspects of the *agape* meal first practiced in the New Testament churches. However, we were engaging in similar *koinonia* experiences—having fellowship with one another and at the same time having fellowship with God. This indeed helped us to relate to our heavenly Father whom we could not see as we related to our brothers and sisters in Christ whom we could see. This is why these integral relational experiences, both with one another and with God, are so significant. It's the basis of true and meaningful worship.

Corporate Prayer

When the church was born in Jerusalem, these believers not only ate together—as they remembered the Lord's death—but they "devoted themselves . . . to prayer" (Acts 2:42b). They had discovered that every believer can enter God's presence through their eternal high priest, the Lord Jesus Christ (Heb. 4:14–16).

Small Group Prayer

As we started our new church, I also asked myself and my fellow elders how we could make corporate prayer more meaningful—for ourselves and for the total body of believers. We determined to answer this question in our own lives. We began to pray for one another at a deeper level as we shared our needs and concerns.

We then began to pray for the needs of others in the church. To discover these needs, each elder was assigned a number of couples and singles. We made telephone calls, asking for personal prayer requests. Then, as we met together, we prayed specifically for these congregational needs. What was particularly encouraging was to discover how God was answering our prayers. Of course, this was a practical way to serve as shepherds to our own people, and a function prescribed in Scripture (see chapter 20).

As the church grew, we multiplied these small groups and appointed other spiritual leaders to lead these groups. The prayer process we began as elders became a significant modeling process for these leaders. We were able to maintain contact with most of the congregation, which also modeled the importance of prayer in the lives of all our fellow believers.

Congregational Prayer

The second major approach to prayer involved the total congregation. Following our teaching and worship hour, we continued to meet for a time of sharing—what the late Ray Stedman called a "body life" experience. During this hour we shared what God was doing in our lives, which involved requests for prayer and answers to prayer. We also worshiped the Lord with music. Fortunately, we had musicians who could respond to particular requests spontaneously.

This time of mutual sharing and worship became one of our most meaningful times together. Witnessing answers to prayer became a powerful spiritual dynamic and a memorable part of our experience. In fact, I still have specific memories that go back nearly fifty years—and, upon reflection, I could fill pages with what happened in these services.

As the church grew, however, we had to change our forms, particularly in our corporate meetings. The congregation became too large for open sharing. We also shortened the meetings to be able to have multiple services in the same facility, so we shifted this emphasis to our small groups. Our challenge was to keep these prayer and sharing experiences ongoing and meaningful.

In essence, our goal was to have similar experiences as those in the Jerusalem church when they "devoted themselves . . . to prayer." Just as these believers "ate together" and "remembered the Lord," so we wanted to experience "talking to one another" in the context of "talking to God." Prayer became very meaningful and exceptionally personal.

Mutual Sharing of Material Possessions

The third relational experience in Jerusalem was indeed very horizontal. Those who lived in the vicinity of the city and the surrounding area actually sold houses and lands and "brought the proceeds of what was sold, and laid them at the apostles' feet," who in turn "distributed to each person as any had need" (Acts 4:34–35).

This semi-communal arrangement was temporary. We're not told how long these God-fearing Grecian Jews—now believers—stayed in the Jerusalem area. They eventually returned to their homes in various parts of the Roman world, particularly when persecution became intense. They in turn started churches in their local communities.

Materialism in the First-Century World

Some who returned certainly continued to be generous believers. However, like many Christians today, they succumbed to the pressure of the world, thinking only of themselves. And those who later became believers in various areas of the Roman world had not seen generosity modeled in Jerusalem.

This materialism is obvious when James, the lead elder in Jerusalem, wrote "to the twelve tribes dispersed abroad" (James 1:1b). Many who had means were neglecting the poor who were literally "without clothes" and "daily food" (James 2:14–17). This was a direct contrast to what happened in Jerusalem when the church was born. Consequently, James addressed these materialistic attitudes and behavior.

Materialism in Today's World

As a pastor, I on one occasion faced a significant challenge related to materialism. It happened during an economic crisis in our own American culture when we faced a serious recession. In Texas we were particularly hard-hit because of the oil crisis, which in turn devastated the real estate market. And once the real estate market began to crater, an unusual domino effect took place that also impacted the banking industry.

All of this brought me face to face with the results of this economic recession and the way it impacted Christians in their patterns of giving.

Because economic times had been good over the years, many Christians had been giving out of what was "leftover," rather than out of what was set aside regularly as "first fruits."

I distinctly remember having a revealing conversation with one of our elders who at the time served as CEO of a large banking industry. "Gene," he said, "I've approved loans for many Christians. When I do, I always ask for their budgets. To be honest, I can count on one hand the number who have regular giving in their financial planning. They have everything else in their budgets—but not God, who should be at the top of the list."

This was a revealing conversation. To be more specific, the majority of Christians attending our church (and many other churches) were not regular, systematic, and proportional givers—which is a clear biblical principle in Scripture (1 Cor. 16:2). When they felt the economic crunch, they had very little left over—virtually no excess to give. It took everything they were earning to handle their indebtedness. Furthermore, they were concerned about their own future and even stopped giving from any excess. Had they been giving God their first fruits all along, the ministry would not have been the first place to feel the financial crunch.

As a result of this crisis, the elders asked me to do a series of messages on giving. To do so, I invited them to join me in a detailed study of the Word of God on what it teaches about generosity. Our challenge was to look at the totality of Scripture—which we did—and as a result I developed a series of messages. Since this was a corporate effort, these messages were well received and indeed brought a positive response in terms of generosity.

I was amazed at what we discovered in this study. We outlined over a hundred supracultural principles that should determine the way we, as believers, should handle our material possessions. The elders then encouraged me to write a book on our findings, which I did. Initially it was entitled *A Biblical Theology of Material Possessions*, later published by Howard Publishing Company under the title *Rich in Every Way*.[2]

Generosity should be part of our relational experience as believers. The primary emphasis in Scripture is helping those who have serious material needs as well as meeting the financial needs of the church—including the needs of those who are in full- and part-time ministries.

However, as with the other relational experiences, when we meet one another's needs, we are engaging in meaningful worship and a relationship with God our Father. Jesus said, "Whoever gives even a cup of cold water to one of these little ones because he is a disciple, truly I tell you, he will never lose his reward" (Matt. 10:42). This indeed is an act of worship.

Corporate Praise

This fourth relational experience with one another and with God certainly involved the use of music. Luke never used the terms *psalms*, *hymns* and *spiritual songs*, as later mentioned by Paul in his letters to the Ephesians and Colossians (Eph. 5:18b–19; Col. 3:16). But we can assume that the reference to the Jerusalem believers "praising God" included some form of music—such as when the disciples sang "a hymn" as they left the upper room (Matt. 26:30).

As we noted in chapter 12, "psalms" probably refers to the Old Testament psalter, and "hymns" refers to "praise songs"—poetic expressions that reflect the very words and thoughts of Scripture. "Spiritual songs" or "spiritual odes" are words set to music that simply express a love for God and for one another.

Cultural Relevance

It's significant that we have no reference in the New Testament to musical instruments and to specific "forms" that were used to express this biblical and spiritual content—either instrumentally or vocally. It's my opinion that the Holy Spirit purposely avoided referring to scales, pitches, rhythms, chords, and instrumentalities in order to allow musical experiences to be supracultural.

By contrast, there are many references in the Old Testament to various instruments that were used to worship God. These instruments clearly related to the Old Testament culture, which was basically limited to the Middle East. However, when Jesus gave the Great Commission, He made it clear that the message of the gospel should be carried to "all nations" and all cultures of the world where musical forms vary greatly. In other words, as with many absolute biblical functions, music was to be expressed in a way that people could worship in their own social settings.

Again, I believe this is why instruments are not mentioned in the New Testament—only content and purpose—which are supracultural. Thus, believers are free to use musical forms that are culturally relevant at any moment in history and any place in the world in order to communicate biblical truth with one another and, at the same time, to worship God.

Creating Mutual Understanding

When we began the first Fellowship Bible Church, we recognized that there were various cultures represented among those we were ministering to—including both believers and unbelievers. We determined to use a variety of musical instruments and forms to worship God as one body of believers. This called for mutual understanding and appreciation of these various cultural expressions. Since I had already taught on the subject of absolutes and non-absolutes in Scripture, most of our people understood how this concept related to music.

A Very Encouraging Experience

On one occasion I had invited Dr. John Walvoord, then president of Dallas Seminary, to speak in what had already become multiple services. He had just written a book on events in the Middle East, and I asked him to address his perspectives on the second coming of Christ.

All services were packed—with people actually sitting on pillows on the floor since we ran out of seats. But on that particular Sunday we had invited a Bluegrass band to lead us in worship. This was a new experience for me as well. They came highly recommended. However, I wondered how the president of Dallas Seminary—who was indeed quite traditional in his thinking—would respond. Frankly, I was a bit nervous.

However, this group was amazingly professional and led us in some great songs of praise and worship. Following the service, I was greatly encouraged when Dr. Walvoord said, "Gene, God is indeed blessing this ministry." I breathed a sigh of relief!

To resolve the musical tensions that exist, many congregations have gone to both traditional and contemporary services. This is certainly not inappropriate. But there's something very special and unifying about learning to worship God as one body using a variety of musical forms.

I remember one significant observation by one of our elders. "Gene," he said, "I don't particularly identify with certain kinds of contemporary music. However, when I see young people sincerely lifting their hands and voices in praise and worship, I then worship too, regardless of the forms."

Unfortunately, this is not the perception and attitude among many believers today. Those in the younger generation should be taught to appreciate the great historic hymns of the faith. On the other hand, many of the older generation should be taught to appreciate and participate in the variety of contemporary expressions. We must not absolutize something God has created to be a non-absolute. In other words, we must remember that the absolutes in music involve the content—and the purpose. We are to use biblical truth to teach and admonish one another but also to sing to God with gratitude in our hearts (Col. 3:16). The non-absolutes—pitches, rhythms, chords, and various instruments—are the way we express this truth to worship God. It's a freedom that He has created so believers all over the world in various cultures and subcultures can freely and naturally worship and praise Him.

In teaching people to appreciate various musical forms, we must help them understand that music—particularly in certain forms—involves very significant emotional memories. We must help them understand and accept this reality. If we don't, it's easy to confuse what is absolute (content and function) and what is non-absolute (structure and forms). Learning to appreciate new forms is a process and often involves a certain number of emotional memories that are difficult to understand. This is another reason why all believers representing all generations need to learn to appreciate different forms, even though we all have certain preferences.

A Unique Cultural Experience

I'll never forget ministering to a group of six hundred pastors and wives way out in the bush in Nigeria. Before I spoke, these men and women worshiped and praised God with music. Their initial songs—both content and form—were familiar to me since they learned them from American missionaries. They were singing in English, but midway through this time of worship, they segued into their own cultural experience, using instruments that were common in their culture. In fact, their rhyme, rhythm, and harmony were totally different than what I was used to. Even though they were singing and worshiping in their own unique way and in their Hausa language, my heart was lifted in praise to God. In fact, just watching them was a personal worship experience.

In conclusion, let's remember that the way music is presented and used is a non-absolute, a cultural expression. This is clearly why the Holy Spirit focuses on content and purpose, not musical forms. Obviously, the content should be biblically and theologically accurate. This is the most important criteria for evaluating these experiences. But whatever the form, it should be an appropriate means of "teaching and admonishing one another through psalms, hymns, and spiritual songs, singing to God with gratitude in [our] hearts" (Col. 3:16).

Having said this, I sometimes wonder what music will be like in heaven when "every tribe and language and people and nation" sing "a new song." One thing is certain! Whatever the form, we'll all be united in eternal love (Rev. 5:8–14; 14:3; 15:2–3).

Vital Witnessing Experiences with the Unsaved World

Principle 3: To equip communities of faith to become the church God intended, we must help all believers love one another and become unified in Spirit and truth, demonstrating Christ's oneness with the Father to those who are unsaved; and, at the same time, we should equip these believers to share the gospel message personally with unbelievers.

This principle is based on the way the Jerusalem church engaged in the ministry of evangelism. While continuing to learn the Word of God and having dynamic relationships with one another and with God, they were "enjoying the favor of **all the people**"—namely, the thousands of unbelievers in Jerusalem. And so "every day the Lord added to their number **those who were being saved**" (Acts 2:47).

As we've noted in chapter 6, this vital experience was to continue—which is obvious in the directives and objectives in the New Testament letters. This then introduces us to this specific supracultural principle associated with these three vital experiences.

This principle is a succinct but comprehensive description and application of what Jesus taught the apostles in the upper room as well as what He prayed for on the way to the garden of Gethsemane. They were to "love one another" as He had loved them, demonstrating they were His disciples (John 13:34–35). They were to be one as He was one with the Father so that the world would believe that He had come from the Father (John 17:20–23).

Unfolding God's Plan

As we've noted in previous chapters, there are an abundance of biblical events and directives that relate to corporate witness. When we started the first Fellowship Bible Church, I began to teach this biblical material, beginning with Jesus' directives to the apostles to "love one another as He had loved them" in order to make it clear to the unbelieving world that they were His disciples.

From this point, I followed the unfolding events, including Jesus' prayer for these men—and all future believers—that we'll all be one as He is one with the Father, demonstrating this great truth to the unsaved world.

To help all of us develop this "oneness," I did a number of messages on the "one another concepts" in Scripture. I emphasized how important it is to follow the Jerusalem model so that we, too, might "enjoy the favor of all the people"—namely, unsaved people with whom we come in contact (see chapters 12 and 13).

These messages in turn related to our small group ministry. We encouraged all our people to be involved in small groups meeting in homes. Initially we called these groups "mini-churches." These were believers who met together in various neighborhoods, enabling them to demonstrate love and unity to their unsaved neighbors and inviting them to attend these home meetings.

In conjunction with this series on the "one anothers," I also did a series on God's plan for the family, demonstrating from Scripture that as households we are in essence the "church in miniature." By demonstrating love and unity, we can also build bridges to our unsaved neighbors.[3]

Personal Witness

This emphasis on love and unity, of course, is not a substitute for personal witness. As pastors, we need to equip all believers to communicate how we're saved. To achieve this goal, I attempted to model a simple gospel presentation—in my messages, during communion services, and when baptizing believers. We also conducted seminars with a focus on helping people to learn to present the gospel as well as how to invite the unsaved to respond.

In terms of remembering the broken body of Christ and His shed blood, I will never forget one experience. It's so memorable I can still see the couple sitting in the audience. Prior to inviting people to participate, I explained what Jesus meant when He startled people with the statement, "Truly I tell you, unless you eat the flesh of the Son of Man and drink his blood, you do not have life in yourselves" (John 6:53).

At this point, I explained the true meaning of what Jesus meant. When we receive Christ by faith, we partake of Him in the sense that He becomes a part of our inner being through the person of the Holy Spirit. Just as the bread becomes a part of our material and physical beings, so Jesus becomes a part of our immaterial being—our soul and spirit.

I then invited anyone who had not received Christ in this way to do so at that very moment—and then upon receiving Christ, to participate in the communion service to illustrate and commemorate what they had just done spiritually.

To this very day I can see the tears that flowed from their eyes as they listened, responded spiritually, and received the bread and cup. Later they shared that this was their moment of salvation—not participating in communion but receiving Christ by faith prior to remembering what Christ had done for them.

Family Edification

Principle 4: To equip communities of faith to become the church God intended, we must help parents to rear their children "in the training and instruction of the Lord" (Eph. 6:4).

When we study the three vital experiences that are illustrated and explained in Scripture, it may appear that there is a serious element missing—namely, a focus on family nurture and edification. In fact, at one point in my own ministry, I decided to do a series of messages on the family. Initially I was puzzled. Where do we find a significant number of passages in the New Testament that focus on family nurture? In actuality, we don't—with the exception of Paul's succinct instructions in Ephesians and Colossians (Eph. 6:1–4; Col. 3:20–21).

The Old Testament, of course, sets the stage for parental responsibility in a very powerful passage in Deuteronomy. Prior to entering the land of Israel, Moses proclaimed these instructions to parents:

> These words that I am giving you today are to be in your heart. Repeat them to your children. Talk about them when you sit in your house and when you walk along the road, when you lie down and when you get up. Bind them as a sign on your hand and let them be a symbol on your forehead. Write them on the doorposts of your house and on your city gates. (Deut. 6:6–9)

Though succinct and only alluded to in the rest of the Old Testament story, Moses' challenge is certainly applicable to Christian parents. In fact, Paul emphasized and elaborated on his commitment to Moses' directive by applying this Old Testament parental model of nurture to the personal ministry of his missionary team. He wrote these words to the Thessalonians:

> We were gentle among you, as a **nurse** [literally a nursing mother] **nurtures her own children**. . . . Like a **father with his own children**, we encouraged, comforted, and implored each one of you to walk worthy of God, who calls you into his own kingdom and glory. (1 Thess. 2:7, 11–12)

Beyond these brief references, we have few instructions regarding family nurture. However, as I reflected on this reality, I realized the family in the New Testament story is virtually synonymous with the church. In other words, what is written to the church was, for the most part, written to the family. This is especially true since the family was considered to be the church in miniature.

Three vital experiences can be seen at two levels: the family setting and the church setting.

The Family Setting

First, parents should help their children learn the Word of God, primarily through modeling biblical truth as well as appropriate instruction at various age levels.

Franz Delitzsch's translation of Proverbs 22:6 captures this pedagogical approach: "Give to the child **instruction conformably to His way**; so he will not, when he becomes old, depart from it."

He then comments on this verse: "The instruction of youth, the education of youth, ought to be conformed to the nature of youth; the matter of instruction, the manner of instruction, ought to regulate itself according to the stage of life, and its peculiarities; the method ought to be arranged according to the degree of development which the mental and bodily life of the youth has arrived at."[4]

Second, parents should help their children have meaningful relationships with one another and with their heavenly Father.

Again, this should happen primarily through modeling. Ideally, children should see love and unity demonstrated by their parents. And when conflicts arise—which they will—children should see these tensions resolved through mutual confession and forgiveness. As stated earlier, sharing an *agape* meal together is a powerful way to help children—at an appropriate age—understand and be thankful for Christ's sacrifice and provision for our salvation.

Third, parents should help the entire family be an example of love and unity to their unsaved neighbors, looking for opportunities to share the gospel message.

Sharing the gospel should be primarily modeled by parents so that as children mature and enter their teen years and become mature enough, they'll be able to engage appropriately in personal evangelism.

The Church Setting

The second level for family edification involves the church. Without question, parents need support and help in nurturing their children, but the biblical story gives no specific illustrations or instructions regarding how this should be done. Again, this is by divine design, giving us scriptural functions and principles that can be applied in all cultures of the world. Again, the three vital experiences apply.

First, leaders in the church should provide children and youth vital learning experiences with the Word of God—communicating biblical truth for their age levels.

Fortunately, many countries in the world enable local churches to provide educational experiences that are designed specifically for children and youth. These experiences should be the best they possibly can be, conducted by spiritually qualified teachers.

Second, leaders in the church should provide children and youth with relational experiences with one another and with God—again, adapted for their age level.

Those who provide these relational experiences should model them among themselves, both horizontally and vertically.

Third, leaders in the church should provide children and youth with witnessing experiences with the unsaved world.

As with adults, this should happen by helping the younger generation model Christlike love and unity with one another and to those who have not made decisions for Christ. However, explaining the gospel is generally an exercise for older youth and adults.

To sum up, these then are biblical guidelines for family nurture. And again, this allows for freedom in form, developing curricula and programs that apply to all age levels and in all cultural situations.

Following biblical instruction and illustrations, these educational leaders should certainly be qualified spiritually in order to teach and model these principles. They should also be as creative as possible, utilizing the most effective methods, means, and technology. In other words, we must do all we can to bring our children and youth to Christ and to help them mature in their Christian faith. Though, ideally, this should be the primary responsibility of Christian parents, they need qualitative help and support from the church. This is a must in our cultures today.

Principle 5: To equip communities of faith to become the church God intended, we must develop forms and structures that reflect a divine sequence and consistently provide all believers with these three vital experiences.

As we study the biblical story, it's obvious that these three vital experiences are functionally interrelated. However, there is also a divine sequence that is clearly illustrated in the Jerusalem model. In this sense, function and form blend together.

Considering Divine Sequence

First, learning the Word of God is foundational for spiritual growth. Jesus established this priority when He commissioned the apostles to teach authentic disciples all that He had taught them (Matt. 28:19–20). This priority is also illustrated in the church in Jerusalem when the three thousand believers "devoted themselves to the **apostles' teaching**" (Acts 2:42).

Second, relationships with God and one another follow naturally and are also vital for spiritual growth. However, it's the Word of God that keeps these second experiences in harmony with divine written revelation. As we relate to one another and with God, we are "built on the foundation of the apostles and prophets"—namely, what they taught and recorded as God's truth (Eph. 2:20).

Third, learning the Word of God and having authentic relationships with one another and God also provides the foundation for being effective witnesses in the world, both corporately and personally. In essence, this is what Jesus prayed for in John 17—that as believers we'll be one in "the faith" and with one another "so that the world may believe" that Jesus came from the Father.

Maintaining Proper Balance

Unfortunately, various churches throughout history have used "freedom in form" to focus on one or two of these experiences rather than all three. This creates an imbalance that interferes with God's plan for corporate and personal spiritual growth. For example:

- Some churches structure for **learning the Word of God** and neglect relational experiences and evangelism.
- Some churches structure for **relational experiences**, both with God and one another, while neglecting a learning experience with the Word of God and evangelism.
- Some churches structure for **evangelism** and neglect biblical teaching and relational experiences.
- Some churches structure for **Bible teaching** and **relational experiences** while neglecting evangelism.
- Some churches structure for **relational experiences** and **evangelism** while neglecting Bible teaching.
- Some churches structure for **Bible teaching** and **evangelism** and neglect fellowship.

Though these categories may be overly simplified and overly categorized, I've discovered they help all of us, particularly as spiritual leaders, to evaluate church structures to see if we are providing believers with all three experiences in proper sequence and in proper balance. When we fail to maintain this balance, it interferes with God's plan for believers to continue "growing in maturity with a stature measured by Christ's fullness" (Eph. 4:13). (To see what can happen when a church fixates on one or two of these experiences, see chapter 27.)

A Question for Thought and Discussion

What happens in churches when there's a failure to develop forms and structures to provide believers with all three vital experiences?

14

The Functioning Body

Video Intro from Gene

3lenses.org/c14

We cannot discuss the church as God intended it to be without looking carefully at how all believers are to function. Utilizing a very practical and universal metaphor, Paul used this analogy exclusively in Scripture to describe the church (see chapter 4). Here in Romans, he succinctly referred to the physical body and then applied it to the church:

The Human Body:

Now as we have **many parts** in **one body**, and **all the parts** do not have the same function,

The Church:

in the same way we who are many are one body in Christ and individually members of one another. (Rom. 12:4–5)

Spiritual Gifts

Immediately following the application of this metaphor, Paul made reference to spiritual gifts:

According to the grace given to us, we have different gifts: If prophecy, use it according to the proportion of one's faith; if service, use it in service; if teaching, in teaching; if exhorting, in exhortation; giving, with generosity; leading, with diligence; showing mercy, with cheerfulness. (Rom. 12:6–8)

Paul's description of these spiritual gifts raises a relevant question: How does the biblical concept of spiritual gifts relate to the functioning body of Christ today? This indeed is an important question since there are so many opinions concerning the answer. Regarding these opinions, this is verified in a scholarly treatise compiled and edited by Dr. Wayne Grudem, *Are Miraculous Gifts for Today? Four Views*. These four views are comprehensive presentations by four well-respected professors and teachers who are all committed to the full authority and inspiration of Scripture. Yet, Grudem states a significant conclusion in the preface of this book. After having spent significant time together discussing their perspectives, Grudem concludes there is little consensus regarding spiritual gifts among evangelical Christians today.[1]

It should also be noted that within these general viewpoints are additional and varied opinions, which raises another important question: In view of these varied viewpoints regarding spiritual gifts, is it possible to discover what the Bible actually teaches on the subject and how they relate to body function today?

A Personal Challenge

During the process of discussing this subject with my students at Dallas Theological Seminary, and with fellow professors, pastors, and missionaries, I decided to try to discover the answer to this question. I was still in the process of writing the original *Sharpening the Focus of the Church*. Consequently, I attempted to put aside my own opinions and conclusions to study the New Testament once again, noting every reference to spiritual gifts and the context in which they appear.

Significant Variation

1. The number and kinds of gifts varied significantly from church to church in the New Testament world.

This observation is based on the list of gifts mentioned in the letters written to various churches. Note the following:

Paul's Letter to the Corinthians

• Wisdom	• Apostles
• Knowledge	• Prophets
• Faith	• Teachers
• Healing	• Miracles
• Performing of miracles	• Healing
• Prophecy	• Helping
• Distinguishing between spirits	• Leading
• Different kinds of tongues	• Tongues
• Interpretation of tongues	(1 Cor. 12:28)
(1 Cor. 12:8–10)	

Letter to the Romans	**Letter to the Ephesians**
• Prophesy	• Apostles
• Service	• Prophets
• Teaching	• Evangelists
• Exhorting	• Pastors
• Giving	• Teachers
• Leading	(Eph. 4:11)
• Mercy	
(Rom. 12:6–8)	

Peter's Letter to Various Churches

• Speaking
• Serving
(1 Peter 4:10–11)

As we compare these lists, it's clear that the Corinthian church had more gifts manifested than any other New Testament church. Paul affirmed this in his introductory remarks in his first letter when he wrote that they were gifted "in all speech and all knowledge . . . so that" they did "not lack any spiritual gift" (1 Cor. 1:5, 7).

The Roman church was also a gifted church. However, only two of the gifts mentioned in the Roman list (prophecy and teaching) are mentioned in the Corinthian list. Likewise, the "Ephesian list," though shorter, included two additional gifts—evangelists and pastors—which are not included in the Corinthian or the Roman list. And Peter simply summarized all gifts under two categories—"speaking" and "serving."[2]

This variation indicates that there was a significant difference in the kinds of gifts manifested from church to church in the New Testament. Some seemed to have many gifts; others had fewer.

Correcting Improper Use

2. The passages where gifts are referred to most extensively were written to correct the improper use of spiritual gifts.

The Corinthian Church

The believers in the Corinthian church were misusing their gifts. It was not a matter of knowing what their gifts were, but rather using them inappropriately. In fact, when Paul wrote to them, he classified them as immature and carnal believers:

> For my part, brothers and sisters, I was not able to speak to you as spiritual people but as **people of the flesh**, as **babies in Christ**. I gave you milk to drink, not solid food, since you were not yet ready for it. In fact, you are still not ready, because you are still **worldly**. (1 Cor. 3:1–3a)

As we study this letter carefully, we can make the following observations. *First,* some were using their spiritual gifts to "build themselves up" while "putting others down." They were guilty of spiritual pride. This is why Paul spent most of chapter 12 using the body metaphor to illustrate that all parts of the body of Christ are necessary. Note the following key statements that emphasize this point:

If the foot should say, "Because I'm not a hand, I don't belong to the body," it is not for that reason any less a part of the body." (1 Cor. 12:15)

And if the ear should say, "Because I'm not an eye, I don't belong to the body," it is not for that reason any less a part of the body. (12:16)

If the whole body were an eye, where would the hearing be? If the whole body were an ear, where would the sense of smell be? (12:17)

And if they were all the same part, where would the body be? (12:19)

The eye cannot say to the hand, "I don't need you!" Or again, the head can't say to the feet, "I don't need you!" (12:21)

Second, the Corinthians were giving attention to the "lesser gifts" while neglecting the "greater gifts."

Paul clearly stated what the "greater gifts" were: "first apostles, second prophets, third teachers." He then listed the "lesser gifts": "miracles, then gifts of healing, helping, leading, various kinds of tongues" (1 Cor. 12:28).

Paul then made his point. The Corinthians should "desire the greater gifts" (12:31). The context in Paul's letter clearly indicates that they were giving attention primarily to those with the lesser gifts (see 1 Cor. 14). Some were rejecting Paul, Peter, and Apollos who had the "greater gifts" (1 Cor. 1:12–13).[3]

Third, the Corinthians were not only giving priority to the "lesser gifts," but they were misusing them in the church (again, carefully read 1 Cor. 14). There was disorder and confusion. Thus, Paul ended chapter 14 with this exhortation: "Everything is to be done decently and in order" (14:40).

Fourth, the gifts that were being used in the Corinthian church were certainly not a sign of their spiritual maturity. The Holy Spirit had sovereignly bestowed these gifts when these Corinthians became believers, affirming their salvation experience (1 Cor. 1:4–8). And as we've seen, they were able to continue using these gifts regardless of their carnality and sinful behavior, which led to the inappropriate use their gifts.

The Roman Church

The believers in Rome evidently did not have as many problems as the Corinthians relative to the way in which they were using their spiritual gifts. However, one problem seems to be the same—the presence of spiritual pride. Thus, before listing the gifts, Paul wrote:

> For by the **grace** given to me, I tell everyone among you **not to think of himself more highly than he should think**. Instead, think sensibly, as God has distributed a **measure of faith** to each one. (Rom. 12:3)

Here Paul evidently used the term *grace* and the phrase "the measure of faith" to refer to his and their giftedness. Again, it's obvious these believers knew what their gifts were. Paul was simply admonishing them to use them in non-prideful ways.

The Ephesian Church

We see the same emphasis in the Ephesian letter. Before listing the gifts, Paul exhorted them to be humble and patient, "making every effort to keep the unity of the Spirit through the bond of peace" (Eph. 4:2–3). Then before listing the gifts, he said, "Now **grace** was given to each one of us according to the **measure of Christ's gift**" (4:7). Again, Paul was evidently using "grace" and "measure" to refer to the "grace gifts."

In conclusion, Paul was exhorting all of these first-century believers not to use their gifts to elevate themselves in the local assembly. They were to strive for oneness and unity through humility. This is the primary theme in all of the spiritual gift passages, and this was Peter's emphasis as well. Using "grace" to refer to their gifts, he admonished them to use their gifts to serve one another, not themselves:

> Above all, maintain constant **love for one another**, since love covers a multitude of sins. Be hospitable to one another without complaining. **Just as each one has received a gift, use it to serve others**, as good stewards of the **varied grace of God**.
> (1 Peter 4:8–10)

Sovereign Bestowal

3. Nowhere in these gift passages are believers told to seek to receive these gifts or to try to discover them in order to function in the body of Christ; rather, they were distributed by the Holy Spirit apart from human effort and according to God's sovereign will.

This is one of the most important observations when discerning what the Bible teaches about spiritual gifts. I initially found this observation difficult to acknowledge and accept since I believed and taught that all believers have at least one gift. I had been encouraging believers to attempt to discover what their gifts were in order to function in the body of Christ. However, as mentioned in the previous observation, that is not the thrust of what the biblical writers were saying. Again, it seems clear these New Testament believers knew what their gifts were. They weren't searching for them. Rather, they were often misusing these gifts.

This observation, however, frequently leads to another question: What about Paul's exhortations to the Corinthians at the end of chapter 12 and at the beginning of chapter 14?

The Greater Gifts

Paul wrote:

- But desire the greater gifts (1 Cor. 12:31)
- Desire spiritual gifts (14:1)

A careful evaluation of these specific texts, as well as their contexts, demonstrates that Paul was not encouraging individual believers to seek to be apostles, prophets, and teachers—which were the "greater gifts" (1 Cor. 12:28; Eph. 4:11). Rather, he was exhorting them to give priority to those who were seeking them and had these greater gifts. Thus, he used the second person plural in the Greek text. We can legitimately paraphrase this statement in 12:31 as follows: "But, as a local community of believers, desire that those who possess the greater gifts be given priority rather than those with the lesser gifts."

In 1 Corinthians 14:1, Paul broadened his statement. Again, we can paraphrase: "As a body of believers pursue love, yet as a body desire earnestly that the **greater gifts** be manifested but give particular attention to those who have the gift of prophecy."

Imparting Gifts

We also need to address Paul's statement to the Roman believers when he wrote to them and said, "For I want very much to see you, so that I may **impart to you some spiritual gift** to strengthen you, that is, to be mutually encouraged by each other's faith, both yours and mine" (Rom. 1:11–12).

On the surface, this may appear to be a reference to encouraging believers to seek the gifts of the Spirit. However, we must remember that Paul had apostolic authority. With this supernatural giftedness he was able in turn to impart gifts, such as to Timothy. Thus, he wrote to his missionary companion: "Therefore, I remind you to rekindle the **gift of God** that is in you **through the laying on of my hands**" (2 Tim. 1:6). Paul was hoping to use his apostolic authority in harmony with God's sovereign will to impart some gifts to the Romans so they could grow spiritually. This supernatural power was affirmed in that he had "the signs of an apostle . . . including signs and wonders and miracles" (2 Cor. 12:12).[4]

Thus, we must conclude from the whole of Scripture that individual Christians are not instructed to search for or to try to discover their spiritual gifts. To do so would be to emphasize something the Bible doesn't emphasize. Paul particularly implied that if a person is gifted in some way, that individual will know it and other Christians will know it too. It has nothing to do with human effort, for God has chosen to sovereignly and miraculously bestow these gifts apart from any searching or asking (Acts 2:1–4; 10:44–48; 1 Cor. 1:4–7; 2 Cor. 1:6). Thus, we read in the Hebrew letter that **God Himself verified** the message of the gospel, both "by **signs** and **wonders**, **various miracles**, and **distributions of gifts from the Holy Spirit according to his will**" (Heb. 2:4).

As we've seen, these gifts were also bestowed on believers by the Holy Spirit **regardless of their spiritual maturity**. Again, this is obvious among the Corinthians. They were the most gifted church in the New

Testament and yet they were the most worldly and carnal. They were even "behaving like mere humans"—namely, unbelievers (1 Cor. 3:3).[5]

A Better Way

4. The New Testament emphasizes that there is a "better way" than an emphasis on the gifts of the Spirit.

As we've noted, Paul told the Corinthians to desire that the greater gifts be active and manifested among them rather than the lesser gifts (1 Cor. 12:28–31a). He then went on to say, "I will show you an **even better way**" (1 Cor. 12:31). Paul then made it clear that these believers may have the gift of **tongues** (13:1), the gifts of **prophecy**, **knowledge**, and **faith** (13:2) as well as the gift of **giving** (13:3), and yet lack love, which is the most important quality in measuring up to the fullness of Christ's stature. If they lacked love, their gifts were like a "noisy gong or a clanging cymbal" (13:1). Without love, their gifts were as "nothing" (13:2). Without love their gifts would "gain nothing" (13:3). And then at the end of this chapter, Paul shared the better way than focusing on their gifts: "Now these three remain: faith, hope, and love—but the greatest of these is love" (1 Cor. 13:13; see chapter 16).

Character Qualities

5. When local church leaders were to be appointed, Paul did not instruct Timothy and Titus to look for spiritual gifts; rather, he instructed them to look for character qualities.

This is another very significant observation. When I first noticed the absence of any reference to gifts in the qualifications for eldership, several questions went through my mind. Why didn't Paul tell Timothy and Titus to look for the gifts of administration and leading? After all, these men were to manage the church (1 Tim. 5:17). Why didn't Paul instruct them to look for the gifts of pastor? And teacher? Again, this was to be their responsibility (1 Peter 5:2; Acts 28; Titus 1:9). And since they were to pray that the sick might be made well, wouldn't they need the gift of healing (James 5:14)? Though these elder functions are outlined in Scripture, Paul said nothing about selecting these men on the basis of spiritual gifts.

We see the same emphasis in the appointment of deacons and deaconesses. Since these people were to be involved in "serving" roles, why didn't Paul specify that they were to be selected based on having the gifts of serving, helps, mercy, and hospitality? And certainly, their cultural responsibilities required that they be good administrators and organizers. And yet there is nothing stated about the gifts of leading or administration. Again, we must ask why?

Some have pointed out that Paul in his letter to Timothy does mention that elders must "**be able to teach**" (1 Tim. 3:2). Is this not the gift of teaching?

Paul beautifully illustrates what *didaktikos* (being "able to teach") means in his second letter to Timothy. He mentioned this concept in the context of a number of other spiritual characteristics. Writing to Timothy, he said:

> The Lord's servant must **not quarrel**, but must **be gentle** to everyone, **able to teach**, and **patient**, instructing his opponents **with gentleness**. (2 Tim. 2:24–25a)

To understand the meaning of *didaktikos* in both letters to Timothy, we need to note the cluster of words highlighted in these verses. It's clear that Paul was dealing with a quality of life that demonstrates an **even temper, kindness, patience,** and **gentleness**—namely, the **fruit of the Holy Spirit** (Gal. 5:22–23). In essence, Paul was saying that when a spiritual leader faced those who opposed what he is teaching, if he was "able to teach" he would respond in a nondefensive and nonthreatened way. In other words, being able to teach (*didatakos*) is a quality of spiritual maturity along with all the other qualities outlined for spiritual leaders (1 Tim. 3:1–7). It's a reference to the foundational and spiritual characteristic that enables a leader to communicate in a mature Christlike way.

In conclusion, nowhere in the list of qualifications for serving as elders or deacons does Paul list spiritual gifts. And this leads to a final observation, which is perhaps most helpful of all.

The "One Another" Injunctions

6. There are many "one another" directives described in Scripture that state how all believers are to be functioning members in the body of Christ.

The Greek word *allelon*, frequently translated "one another," is used approximately sixty times in the New Testament letters to describe what believers are to do to build up one another. Paul leads the list for frequency, having used the word in a positive sense at least forty times.[6] And just as basic doctrines are repeated from letter to letter in the New Testament, so are many of these "one another" injunctions. It's understandable since these letters were originally designed to be self-contained for particular churches.

Paul's letter to the Romans includes the most extensive "one another" profile. There are nine positive directives in chapters 12–16:

1. We are to function as "members of one another" (Rom. 12:5).
2. We are to "love one another deeply as brothers and sisters" (12:10a).
3. All of us are to "take the lead in honoring one another" (12:10b).
4. We are to "live in harmony with one another" (12:16; 15:5).
5. We are "to love one another, for the one who loves another has fulfilled the law" (13:8).
6. We are to "pursue what promotes peace and what builds up one another" (14:19).
7. We are to "accept one another, then, just as Christ accepted you" (15:7 NIV).
8. We are to "instruct [admonish] one another" (15:14 NKJV).
9. We are to "greet one another" (16:16).

Several other New Testament letters include additional "one another" directives. They are as follows:

1. We are to "welcome one another" (1 Cor. 11:33).
2. We are to have "concern for one another" (1 Cor. 12:25).

3. We are to "serve one another through love" (Gal. 5:13).

4. We are to "carry one another's burdens" (Gal. 6:2).

5. We are to "bear with one another in love" (Eph. 4:2; Col. 3:13).

6. We are to "submit to one another" (Eph. 5:21).

7. We are to "encourage one another" (1 Thess. 4:18; 5:11).

8. We are to "confess our sins to one another" (James 5:16a).

9. We are to "pray for one another" (James 5:16b).

10. We are to "offer hospitality to one another" (1 Peter 4:9).

11. We are to "fellowship with one another" (1 John 1:7).

And here is one of the most comprehensive exhortations that is directed to all believers:

> Let the word of Christ dwell in you richly, **teaching and admonishing one another** in all wisdom, singing psalms and hymns and spiritual songs, with thankfulness in your hearts to God. (Col. 3:16 ESV; see also Eph. 5:19)

As we study these "one another" directives as well as others mentioned in the New Testament, it's clear that all members of the body of Christ are to participate in carrying out these exhortations. In fact, they are clearly associated with doing the will of God.

Freedom in Form

7. As with all aspects of carrying out the Great Commission, the New Testament does not prescribe absolute forms for carrying out the supracultural "one another" functions and directives in order to build up the body of Christ.

As we've seen, the body of Christ is to function in all of its parts—which is a supracultural directive and principle. However, as with all biblical functions, forms are not described for practicing the "one another" directives. Once again, this is a tribute to the supracultural nature of Scripture.

Concluding Thoughts

The functioning body is essential for growth and maturity to take place in any given church. The very nature of the body of Christ makes it important for every member to function and contribute to the process of edification. Christians cannot grow effectively in isolation. They need to experience each other.

It's certainly true that the New Testament describes spiritual gifts in conjunction with body function and mutual edification. However, the emphasis is not on searching for or trying to discover and identify spiritual gifts. Rather, believers are told again and again the importance of becoming mature in Christ, both as individual believers and as a corporate body. As we've seen from the study of the "one another" directives, all believers are told to help one another mature in Christ by carrying out a number of "one another" functions and directives.

In addition, any person who desired to be a spiritual leader in the church should be primarily concerned about developing and manifesting the qualifications of maturity specified in the New Testament rather than attempting to identify their spiritual gifts. It follows that those responsible to select and appoint leaders should not look for gifts but rather manifestations of Christlike character.

Having made these observations, I in no way wish to restrict the Holy Spirit's ministry. God is God and what He revealed and enacted in the first century He can do at any moment in history. Regardless of our viewpoints on spiritual gifts, there is certainly general agreement that we need to manifest the "fruit of the Spirit," which means to "live by the Spirit" and to "keep in step with the Spirit" (Gal. 5:22, 25). However, to be consistent with what we observe in the New Testament era, it seems clear that spiritual gifts will always be "distributed . . . according to His will," not ours (Heb. 5:4).

I've shared the observations in this chapter with a number of spiritual leaders over the years who represent various viewpoints. In all instances, most have agreed that what I've shared is in harmony with what we read in Scripture. This has been reassuring, since I believe in doing theological studies in community, not in isolation—and in the process, to create unity in the body of Christ, not division.

I've also taught the "one another" concepts for many years as a pastor, which I explain in the following chapter, "Biblical Principles of Edification—Part 2" in the section titled "Building Up the Body of Christ." The results have been very encouraging in terms of body function and mutual edification.

In conclusion, I'd ask that you carefully evaluate these seven observations by studying the Scriptures on your own, preferably with a group of serious Bible students. If you conclude that I'm in error on any particular observation, please give me your feedback. As a result of my involvement in ministry for nearly seventy years, I've discovered that there is always more to learn when it comes to understanding and applying the eternal Word of God.

A Question for Thought and Discussion

Whether or not you agree or disagree with my observations and conclusions in this chapter, how can we keep differences of opinion from becoming a divisive issue in the church?

15

Biblical Principles of Edification—Part 2

Video Intro from Gene

3lenses.org/c15

Building Up the Body of Christ

In chapter 14, "The Functioning Body," we looked at the pervasive emphasis in the New Testament letters on the numerous "one another" functions and directives. Paul laid the foundation for this means of edification in his circular letter, no doubt sent first to the church in Ephesus:

> From him [Christ] the whole body, fitted and knit together by every **supporting ligament**, promotes the growth of the body for **building itself up in love** by the **proper working of each individual part**. (Eph. 4:16)

This succinct but comprehensive statement is profound in meaning. It complements Paul's previous statement in this passage that Jesus Himself gave significant gifted individuals to the church—apostles, prophets, evangelists, pastors, and teachers—"**to equip the saints** [all believers] **for the work of ministry, to build up the body of Christ**" (Eph. 4:11–12).

Paul then concluded that when "each individual part" functions properly, the body will continue "building itself up in love," and will also continue "**growing into maturity with a stature measured by Christ's fullness**" (Eph. 4:13b). I've continued to state this foundational goal when stating principles that enable every community of faith to become the church God intended.

A New Perspective

As I stated in the previous chapter, when I began to take a fresh look at how believers are to continue to mature in Christ, I developed a new perspective. Previously, I had put a strong emphasis on "looking for" and "trying to discover" spiritual gifts in order to function properly in the body of Christ. However, as a result of a more in-depth look at Scripture, I changed my emphasis based on the observations outlined and described in the previous chapter. And when I did, this new approach virtually eliminated the confusion my previous emphasis had created. Rather, it led to very positive results in terms of body function and mutual edification.

For example, I vividly remember one student who sincerely wanted to know what his gifts were. I told him that as he engaged in ministry, he would have an answer to his question—particularly as he evaluated his activities and feelings by using the list of gifts mentioned in the New Testament as criteria.

Responding positively, this student spent a whole summer in ministry. However, when he returned to campus, he sought me out and said with an element of frustration, "Prof, I spent all summer in ministry and I'm still not sure what my gifts are."

I immediately responded to his report with my own. I shared my own personal journey that very summer. I had looked carefully at every reference to spiritual gifts in the unfolding biblical story, taking a fresh, in-depth look at what the Scriptures teach on this subject.

Two observations that influenced my thinking the most are as follows:

1. Nowhere in the gift passages in Scripture are believers told to seek to receive these gifts or to try to discover them in order to function in the body of Christ; rather, they were distributed

by the Holy Spirit apart from human effort and according to God's sovereign will.

2. There are many "one another" directives described in Scripture that all believers are to practice in order to be effective functioning members of the body of Christ.

In view of these observations in Scripture, I changed my emphasis. And when I helped launch the first Fellowship Bible Church, I began teaching the "one another" directives, encouraging all believers to practice these very clear instructions.

We saw positive and rewarding results immediately. People began functioning within the body of Christ, ministering to one another and "building up one another." They were not searching for their gifts through introspection. They were not puzzled and confused, wondering what their gifts were. Nor were they comparing themselves with one another in terms of what they believed were their gifts or others' gifts. We witnessed no competition or intimidation, and I have no recall of anyone feeling they were more spiritual than others. They simply ministered to one another, humbly serving each other in a variety of ways.

I realize that this perspective and experience runs counter to a lot of viewpoints on spiritual gifts. As we've noted in the previous chapter, interpretations and applications vary greatly among qualified teachers. There is virtually no consensus among biblical scholars. In view of these various viewpoints, doesn't this indicate that the subject of spiritual gifts and how they apply today is not clear in Scripture? If it were, would we not have basic agreement among serious students of the Scriptures—just as we have agreement on a number of major doctrinal issues?

In view of this ambiguity, I decided to emphasize and teach what is *not* ambiguous in terms of body function. I'm referring to the way New Testament authors used the term *allelon*—translated "one another."

Teaching the "One Another" Directives

As stated in the previous chapter, what believers are to do for "one another" appears approximately sixty times in the New Testament. However, in my first series on the "one another" directives, I began with those referenced by Paul in his letter to the Romans. In the previous chapter, I simply outlined these positive exhortations (see chapter 14). In this chapter I'd like to develop them more fully to demonstrate how they relate to how all believers are to participate in building up the body of Christ.

There are nine directives in Romans 12–16, which in turn became the basis for my series of messages. There is substantial biblical information to go into depth on all of these exhortations. However, I simply want to mention each one and show how effective these exhortations can be in helping people do "the work of ministry," and to "build up one another." In fact, these directives translate into the following specific supracultural principles with questions for application.

Principle 1: All of us as believers in local communities of faith should believe and accept the fact that we need one another.

> In the same way we who are many are one body in Christ and individually members of **one another.** (Rom. 12:5)

This is a very enduring truth. We cannot mature in isolation. No member of the body—including yours truly—can say to any other member of the body, "I don't need you!"

Unfortunately, many believers in our culture have become influenced by a philosophy of individualism. It's easy to conclude that since each one of us has access to the Word of God, this is basically all we need to grow spiritually. We have multiple opportunities to hear Bible teaching—in our churches, on the radio, and on TV—as well as to be able to read a number of excellent books and watch thousands of videos. All of these resources and opportunities can be a great blessing. In fact, I've been greatly privileged to include 1,500 videos in my *Life Essentials Study Bible*. However, I in no way want these videos to support the erroneous conclusion that each of us has all we need on a personal level to grow spiritually.

The fact is, learning biblical truth in isolation apart from experiencing "body life" can lead to "head knowledge" rather than total life change—mentally, emotionally, and spiritually. We would then have no corporate criteria for measuring our spiritual maturity.

All of the "one another" directives in the New Testament support this supracultural principle—that we are indeed "members of one another" and we need each other. To help each other grow spiritually, we simply need to begin to practice the following "one another" directives.

A Question for Thought and Discussion

*What specific things can I do to meet
the needs of my fellow Christians?*

Principle 2: As believers, we are to love one another with deep affection.

Love **one another** deeply as brothers and sisters. (Rom. 12:10a)

Here Paul used the Greek term *philadelphia.* Perhaps the following translation makes the point clearer—"Be kindly **affectionate** to **one another** with **brotherly love** [*philadelphia*]" (12:10a NKJV).

This is a compound Greek word that is significant in understanding body function. *Phila* relates to the Greek term *phileo*, which refers to love that often focuses on the "emotional" dimension in relationships. This word also relates to *agapao*, a much more comprehensive term that is used more frequently. *Agape* love involves doing what is right and appropriate regardless of our feelings. However, when Paul used the term *philadelphia*, he was saying that we should also relate to one another with positive emotions—not just with a sense of responsibility, obligation, and obedience to Scripture.

The second part of this compound word—*delphia*—comes from the Greek term *adelphoi*, which can be translated "brothers and sisters." Paul was saying that we are a "family in Christ." This term is used more than two hundred times in Acts and the Epistles. Because of this brother-sister relationship, we are to do all we can to care for "one another" (see Appendix B for a listing of these references).

To understand the significance of what Paul was saying, we need to consider the social situation in the Roman world. We would have to look far and wide to discover households where family members understood and experienced either *agapao* or *phileo* love. Dysfunction was the norm. Consequently, God designed a wonderful plan to bring emotional and spiritual healing into the lives of husbands and wives, fathers and mothers, and their children. It involved the functioning family of God where believers express Christlike love and care for one another, both at the action and feeling levels.

Personally, I like the descriptive term "reparenting." Even today there are many individuals in our present culture who need to learn to love both at the feeling and action level. When all members of God's family function as God intended, this healing process will happen in a miraculous way.

A Question for Thought and Discussion

What can I do specifically to demonstrate Christlike affection to my brothers and sisters in Christ?

Principle 3: As believers, all of us should honor one another.

This "one another" injunction is translated in various ways:

- "Take the lead in honoring **one another**" (CSB)
- "Honor **one another** above yourselves" (NIV)
- "Showing eagerness in honoring **one another**" (NET)
- "Give preference to **one another** in honor" (NASB)

While teaching this concept, one of my fellow pastors—a very competent pianist—shared a personal experience. He went on to suggest that what happened to him might help communicate what Paul had in mind with this "one another" directive.

On one occasion he was asked to accompany a well-known soloist. He immediately thought this would be a wonderful opportunity to demonstrate his own skills. During the rehearsal he ran his fingers up and down the keyboard with an array of arpeggios. However, after a brief time accompanying this very competent musician, she quietly walked over to the piano, and with a smile on her face said, "I'm a wonderful accompanist to you!"

Her point was crystal clear. Brent was to accompany her—to make her "look" and "sound" good! However, he was overshadowing her and in essence making himself "sound good" and she was "accompanying" him.

When I heard this story, I immediately understood why Brent shared this experience. The application was obvious. As believers, we are to be "accompanists" to our fellow believers. We're to make others "look" and "sound" good. And, of course, when all believers honor others above themselves, all will be honored.

This is a concept that is uniquely based on relationships in Christ. We're not to honor others with a motive to be honored in return. It's the total opposite of what happens to those who are motivated by self-interest—that is, "I'll scratch your back if you'll scratch mine!"

This principle is based on God's love, which is unconditional. Our love for others should be unconditional as well. The wonderful reality is that when all members of the body of Christ honor one another above themselves, we will indeed experience reciprocation from other members of God's family—and especially from God Himself.

A Question for Thought and Discussion

In what ways can I minister to my fellow members in the body of Christ without expecting anything in return?

Principle 4: As believers we are to experience oneness in our relationships with one another.

Live in harmony with **one another**. (Rom. 12:16a)

This is Paul's first directive in this letter to be a unified body in Christ. Later, he prayed that this might be true among the believers in Rome (Rom. 15:5–6). However, at this point he wanted them to know and understand the basic truth that creates this unity. In essence, it's humility. Thus, he followed this directive with these very descriptive words: "Do not be proud; instead, associate with the humble. Do not be wise in your own estimation" (12:16b).

Paul elaborated on this emphasis in his letter to the Philippians. Using Jesus Christ as our greatest example, he wrote:

> Do nothing out of selfish ambition or conceit, but **in humility** consider others as more important than yourselves. Everyone should look not to his own interests, but rather to the interests of others. (Phil. 2:3–4)

A Question for Thought and Discussion

What interests do others have that I can begin focusing on rather than thinking about my own?

Principle 5: As believers, we are to love one another as Christ loved us.

> Do not owe anyone anything, except to love **one another**, for the one who loves another has fulfilled the law. (Rom. 13:8)

This principle was modeled in an incomparable way in the upper room. Jesus had just finished washing the disciples' feet. While they were still reeling from this very humbling experience, Jesus made His point:

> I give you a **new command: Love one another.** Just as I have loved you, you are also to **love one another.** By this everyone will know that you are my disciples, if you **love one another.** (John 13:34–35)

This new command to love one another was in part a fulfillment of the law—just as Paul stated in this "one another" concept in Romans. The ultimate fulfillment involves both our love for God and one another. Jesus made this clear on one occasion in His conversation with the Pharisees (Matt. 22:37–39). But here in Romans, Paul focused on our relationship with one another as fulfilling the law. Thus, he wrote:

> The commandments, Do not commit adultery; do not murder; do not steal; do not covet; and any other commandment, are summed up by this commandment: Love your neighbor as yourself. Love does no wrong to a neighbor. **Love, therefore, is the fulfillment of the law**. (Rom. 13:9–10)

Decades later, the apostle John captured the real meaning of Jesus' statement that evening in the upper room:

> This is how we have come to know love: He laid down his life for us. We should also lay down our lives for our brothers and sisters. (1 John 3:16)

A Question for Thought and Discussion

What can I do to demonstrate sacrificial love toward another brother or sister in Christ?

Principle 6: As believers we are to be peacemakers and build up one another.

> So then, let us pursue what promotes peace and what builds up **one another**. (Rom. 14:19)

This positive "one another" directive is related to what we are *not* to do in our relationships—which Paul stated earlier: we are *not* to "judge one another" (Rom. 14:13). In fact, these two "one another" directives are inseparable as Paul applied the law of love to a very practical situation. Consequently, he spent most of this chapter emphasizing that we are to avoid using our freedom in Christ in a way that causes another Christian to fall into sin.

In this case the sin involved idolatry and immorality, particularly as it related to worship in pagan temples. Some of these New Testament believers were so weak in their faith that seeing another Christian participate in any action that even appeared to be associated with this sinful behavior would cause them to engage in idolatry and immorality once again.

The true meaning of this "thou shalt not" directive is very meaningful in my own personal experience. I grew up in a religious community that was very legalistic and works-oriented. Again and again, I heard the statement that we're not to "offend" another brother or sister in Christ. This word appears in the King James Version but does not appear in the original text of Scripture (Rom. 14:21). Unfortunately, the leaders in this religious community defined "offense" as when another Christian disagrees with another Christian and has his feelings hurt. I later discovered that many of these "hurt feelings" were reflections of immaturity, selfishness, and judgmental attitudes.

Unfortunately, these believers misinterpreted what Paul was teaching in Romans chapter 14. He was referring to causing another brother or sister to "stumble" and fall into serious sin (vv. 19–21). In fact, neither the "weaker" nor "stronger" believers were to judge each other based on personal opinions and emotions. Paul went on to make it clear that the stronger believer should be particularly concerned with the weaker believer. Thus, he wrote:

> Now we who are strong have an obligation to bear the weaknesses of those without strength, and not to please ourselves. (Rom. 15:1)

It's in this context that Paul exhorted all believers to "pursue what promotes peace and what builds up one another" (14:19).

Two Questions to Think About and Answer

What are some things I can do immediately that will promote peace and help build up others within my community of faith?

What are some things I need to stop doing within the family of God, and even within my biological family, that might cause others to sin?

Principle 7: As believers, we are to live in unity with one another in order to honor God and be a witness in this world.

> Now may the God who gives endurance and encouragement grant you to live in harmony with **one another**, according to Christ Jesus, so that you may glorify the God and Father of our Lord Jesus Christ with one mind and one voice. (Rom. 15:5–6)

At this point, Paul prayed specifically for these believers to "live in harmony with one another"—the very directive he had shared earlier (12:16). It's not an accident that his prayer for oneness and unity is essentially the same as Jesus' prayer on His way to the garden of Gethsemane. Notice the nearly identical nature of these prayers.

Jesus' Prayer

> I pray not only for these [the apostles], but also for those who believe in me through their word [all believers of all time]. May they all **be one**, as you, Father, **are in me and I am in you**. May they also be in us, so that the world may believe you sent me. I have given them the glory you have given me, so that they may **be one** as **we are one**. I am in them and you are in me, so that they may be made completely **one**, that the world may know you have sent me and have loved them as you have loved me. (John 17:20–23)

These two prayers relate directly to what the late Dr. Francis Schaeffer called the "final apologetic"—a miraculous means of convincing unbelievers that Jesus Christ is indeed the incarnate Son of God (see chapter 6).

Paul clearly understood what Jesus prayed for on His way to the garden of Gethsemane. Both of these prayers are based on the foundational directives Jesus gave to "love one another" as He has loved us (John 13:34–35; Rom. 13:8). This is divine continuity.

A Question for Thought and Discussion

What are some positive and specific things I can do
that will help develop unity among my fellow believers?

Principle 8: As believers, we are to recognize and overcome any areas of prejudice toward one another.

> Therefore welcome **one another**, just as Christ also welcomed you, to the glory of God. (Rom. 15:7)

This "one another" directive becomes even clearer when it's translated, "**Accept** one another, then, just as Christ **accepted** you" (NIV).

To understand more deeply what Paul was saying, we need to remind ourselves of the way in which Christ accepted each one of us when we accepted His invitation to become a believer. He required only one thing—our faith in who He is as the Son of God who died for our sins and was resurrected so that we could have eternal life. Thus, we are to **accept our fellow believers just as Christ accepted us**.

I can relate to this directive. I was reared in a religious community where I was taught that only those in this community had a correct understanding of biblical truth. We lived isolated lives from others who claimed to be followers of Christ. However, something happened in my life a short time after my own conversion experience. As I listened to Christian radio, I discovered there were many others who claimed to be believers and who were living more in the will of God than the many in my own religious community. I was particularly impacted by their concern for those who had not heard the message of Christ.

Since the radio station I was listening to originated at Moody Bible Institute in Chicago, I decided to enroll as a student. However, due to the context I grew up in, I was not aware that deep down I continued to have feelings of superiority because of my religious upbringing.

In essence, these were feelings of prejudice. Thankfully, God used a crisis in my life to help me understand and recognize these feelings for what they were. I didn't realize it at the time that this was what in essence happened to the apostle Peter when the Lord orchestrated his meeting with Cornelius, a Gentile. His confession reveals his prejudice: "Now I truly understand that God doesn't show favoritism" (Acts 10:34).

Prejudice has deep roots—at times so deep within our souls that we don't recognize its presence.

As believers who have been accepted by Christ—regardless of our cultural backgrounds—we must experience the reality of Paul's penetrating statement in his letter to the Galatians: "There is no Jew or Greek, slave or free, male and female; since you are all one in Christ Jesus" (Gal. 3:28).

A Question for Thought and Discussion

*What are areas in my life where I may be prejudiced
in my relationship with others, and what should I be doing
to correct these sinful attitudes and actions?* (James 2:1)

Principle 9: As believers, we are to teach and admonish one another.

My brothers and sisters, I myself am convinced about you that you also are full of goodness, filled with all knowledge, and able to **instruct one another.** (Rom. 15:14)

In actuality, Principles 8 and 9 are twin exhortations. Yes, we are to accept one another as Christ accepted us. But this doesn't mean that we accept and approve of sin in the life of fellow believers. If we accept others regardless of their failures, this gives us the right—and the responsibility—to admonish fellow believers who are walking out of the will of God.

Paul lists two requirements for attempting to correct fellow believers. *First,* we are to be "**full of goodness**" (Rom. 15:14a). This simply means we are committed to living in the will of God. Though we certainly will never do this perfectly, we are continuing "to grow into maturity with a stature measured by Christ's fullness."

Paul elaborated on this requirement in his letter to the Galatians. In fact, it involves another "one another" injunction. He wrote:

> Brothers and sisters, if someone is overtaken in any wrongdoing, **you who are spiritual**, restore such a person with a gentle spirit, watching out for yourselves so that you also won't be tempted. **Carry one another's burdens**; in this way you will fulfill the law of Christ. (Gal. 6:1–2)

When Paul referred to being among those who are "spiritual," he is summarizing what he had just written in the previous chapter about walking "by the Spirit" and "living by the Spirit" (Gal. 5:16, 25), rather than engaging in the "works of the flesh" (Gal. 5:19–21). This is the first requirement that qualifies us to correct another believer who is walking out of the will of God.

Note also that restoring a brother or sister in Christ is a task for more than one individual believer. This is why Paul used the plural pronoun—"**you** who are spiritual." This is **biblical intervention** in the life of a fellow believer who is trapped in sin.

Second, another requirement for admonishing another believer is to be "**filled with all knowledge**" (Rom. 15:14b). This simply means we know what God's will is and what it isn't. Our motivation is based on biblical directives and principles, not legalistic rules and regulations.

The important message related to this "one another" injunction is that when we love others as Christ has loved us, we will do all we can to lead a believer out of sin and back into the will of God.

A Question for Thought and Discussion

*Am I aware of a fellow believer who is deliberately living in sin,
and what steps can I take with others to help this person live
in God's will once again?*

Principle 10: As believers, we are to express appropriate godly physical affection to one another.

Greet **one another** with a holy kiss. (Rom. 16:16)

This principle is based on the final "one another" directive in Romans. It's significant that Paul recorded this same basic exhortation in three other letters (1 Cor. 16:20; 2 Cor. 13:12; 1 Thess. 5:26). Peter also included it at the conclusion of his first letter (1 Peter 5:14).

This form of greeting varies from culture to culture and is a non-absolute. In the New Testament society, it probably involved a kiss on the cheek or neck. For example, when the Ephesian elders said goodbye to Paul, we read that they "fell on" his "neck and kissed him" (Acts 20:37 ASV).

This reference to Paul's farewell physical expression correlates with what happened in Ephesus when he said farewell to the disciples. The New King James makes the point clearly—"Paul called the disciples to himself, **embraced them**, and departed to go to Macedonia" (Acts 20:1).

Though we're not given a specific description of this form, there is a definite reference to physical touch. As we know, there is something special and even healing about this kind of sensitive and loving communication. However, it always must be "holy" and void of any sexual connotations.

This caution makes **verbal greetings** even more important. To a certain extent, we can compensate for lack of physical touch with **verbal words** that are always heartfelt and sincere. To do so, we need to be on guard against greetings that are purely ritualistic.

On one occasion, I learned a significant lesson as a pastor. I was in a rush on a Wednesday evening as I entered our church building. A young teenager was standing there, and as I hurried by, I managed to say, "Hi Bruce, how are you doing?"

A few moments later one of our elders tapped me on the shoulder and said—"Gene, I have to admonish you about something you just did."

I thought he was kidding! But it only took a moment to sense he was serious—and I quickly asked what I had done.

"Well," he said, "you asked Bruce how he was doing a moment ago, but in your rush, you didn't hear his response."

I immediately understood Mike's concern and asked what Bruce had said when I had asked him how he was doing. Mike's response startled me. My young friend had responded, "Not well. My brother was in a motorcycle accident today."

I immediately sought Bruce out and apologized and asked forgiveness for my insensitivity. He forgave me and thanked me for my concern and prayers. This experience taught me a great lesson. When I ask people how they're doing, I should listen carefully to what they have to say.

Though this interpretation and illustration regarding "greeting one another with a holy kiss" may not answer all the questions regarding these five exhortations in Scripture, hopefully it captures in some respects what Paul and Peter had in mind.

A Question for Thought and Discussion

What should I be doing to show sincere interest and appropriate affection in the lives of my fellow believers?

Multiple Messages

As I stated at the beginning of this chapter, all these "one another" directives can be substantiated with a number of scriptural references and passages and become the basis for multiple messages. This I did, followed by a number of other messages on the remaining "one another" directives. In fact, following this series from Romans, which I titled "Building Up One Another," I did four more complete series—

1. Encouraging one another
2. Loving one another
3. Serving one another
4. Praying for one another[1]

As one who has experienced again and again the positive results from teaching these "one another" directives, I would certainly suggest that you, as a pastor or other spiritual leader, consider doing the same.

A Question for Thought and Discussion

Regardless of our views on spiritual gifts, why is it important to teach the "one another" functions and directives in the New Testament story and to illustrate how to practice them in the church today?

16

Measuring Local Church Maturity

Video Intro from Gene

3lenses.org/c16

In the previous chapter, we've reviewed Paul's statement that as believers we are to continue "growing into maturity with a stature measured by Christ's fullness" (Eph. 4:13). Generally speaking, Paul was referring to all believers—from the time the local church was born in Jerusalem until the second coming of Christ when all "saints" will be perfectly transformed into His image and presented to Him as His "bride" at the "marriage of the Lamb" (1 Thess. 4:13–18; 1 Cor. 15:51–57; John 14:1–3; 1 John 3:2; Rev. 19:7–8).

Only God can measure this corporate and universal maturity over the centuries and in all parts of the world. However, it's His will that all local communities of faith who are waiting for this great event are to be more and more "transformed" into Christ's image.

This raises a very practical question: What does it look like for a local church to reflect the very life of Jesus Christ? Paul leads the way in answering this question. He frequently used three descriptive words that are mentioned in his succinct statement to the Corinthians: "Now these three remain:

faith, hope, and **love**—but the greatest of these is **love**" (1 Cor. 13:13).

This is one of the most quoted statements from the Bible—even among people who don't claim to be serious followers of Christ. Many believers have done so without really understanding that Paul used these three qualities to measure the degree to which a local church was becoming more and more like Christ. I confess that this was true in my own life until I began to look carefully at how Paul used the terms *faith, hope,* and *love* in the introductions to his letters.

1 Thessalonians

In this letter, note Paul's **prayer of thanksgiving** for these three qualities that were very visible in this church:

> We always thank God for all of you, making mention of you constantly in our prayers. We recall, in the presence of our God and Father, your work produced by **faith**, your labor motivated by **love**, and your endurance inspired by **hope** in our Lord Jesus Christ. (1 Thess. 1:2–3)

To underscore the importance of this threefold measurement, Paul circled back at the end of this letter with this metaphorical charge:

> But since we belong to the day, let us be self-controlled and put on the **armor of faith and love**, and a **helmet of the hope** of salvation. (1 Thess. 5:8)

A Divine Trilogy

It's obvious in this letter that **faith, hope**, and **love** demonstrated that these believers were "growing into maturity with a stature measured by Christ's fullness" (Eph. 4:13). This was indeed a corporate manifestation, which is why Paul used the terms *you* and *your*, second person plural pronouns in the Greek text. This indicates that together as a body of believers they were reflecting these three qualities of maturity.

Unfortunately, in our English language, these single and plural pronouns are the same, which can lead to a false interpretation that focuses on "individualism" rather than a corporate manifestation of these qualities. They can only be measured accurately when they are reflected by believers in relationship with one another.

A Divine Measurement

Note that Paul also used three words that measured the degree of faith, hope, and love that existed in this church—their "work," their "labor," and their "endurance." As we'll explain in the next chapter, these are very comprehensive concepts that are explained in the New Testament letters. These explanations, in turn, form a very comprehensive criteria for measuring maturity in local churches.

Colossians

The next time Paul used **faith**, **hope**, and **love** to introduce his correspondence, they appeared in his letter to the Colossians. And again, they appear in an opening prayer of thanksgiving:

> We always thank God, the Father of our Lord Jesus Christ, when we pray for you [for "all who have not seen me in person"], for we have heard of your **faith** in Christ Jesus and of the **love** you have for all the saints because of the **hope** reserved for you in heaven. (Col. 1:3–5; 2:1)

Paul had never met these believers in Colossae or Laodicea, a neighboring village. However, he had received a very positive report from Epaphras, whom Paul called a "dearly loved fellow servant" (Col. 1:7–8). It appears that Epaphras was gifted as an evangelist, pastor, and teacher, enabling him to carry out the Great Commission in this geographical area, both in "making disciples" and then "teaching them" to become mature in Christ—reflecting these three qualities.

However, Paul was particularly pleased with Epaphras' report regarding their "love in the Spirit." Though subtle, this reference correlates with his statement to the Corinthians—"Now these three remain: **faith, hope,** and **love**—but **the greatest of these is love**" (1 Cor. 13:13).

2 Thessalonians

When a church was wavering in one of these qualities, Paul also made this clear in his introductory prayers. This is obvious in his second letter to the Thessalonians:

> We ought to thank God always for you, brothers and sisters, and rightly so, since **your faith is flourishing** and the **love each one of you has for one another is increasing**. (2 Thess. 1:3)

Paul was pleased with the progress these believers were making in their "**work** produced by **faith**" and their "**labor** motivated by **love**." However, it's significant that he made no reference to their growth in **hope**. As you read further in this letter, Paul explained why this was true. Something had happened in the church in Thessalonica following Paul's first letter. They were growing in their **faith** and **love**, but Paul was deeply concerned regarding what had interfered with their "**endurance** inspired by **hope**" (1 Thess. 1:3).

A False Report

As we read on, it becomes apparent what had transpired:

> Now concerning the coming of our Lord Jesus Christ and our being gathered to him [**the blessed hope**]: We ask you, brothers and sisters, not to be **easily upset** or **troubled**, either by a **prophecy** or by a **message** or **by a letter** supposedly from us, **alleging that the day of the Lord has come**. (2 Thess. 2:1–2)

Paul was not certain regarding the exact origin of this false information. But whatever the source, he assured these believers it was a deceptive message that contradicted the truth regarding Christ's second coming. This also explains why Paul did not thank God for their continued growth in their "endurance inspired by **hope**." In fact, their "endurance" or steadfastness had turned to being "upset" and "troubled"—words Paul used to describe their lack of security, stability, and doctrinal firmness.

Eschatological Clarification

Paul proceeded to explain why the "day of the Lord" had not come; namely, that the antichrist—"the man of lawlessness"—had not appeared on the scene. Though Paul did not explain all that would happen leading up to Christ's return to bring judgment on the earth, he made it very clear that it hadn't happened (2 Thess. 2:5–12). Therefore, he encouraged them to once again "stand firm" in their "hope." They had been "chosen . . . for salvation." They would indeed "obtain the glory of our Lord Jesus Christ" when all believers are "gathered to him" (2 Thess. 2:1, 14–15; see also 1 Thess. 4:13–18). Paul then concluded these words of theological clarification and encouragement with a specific prayer and reference to the "good hope":

> May our Lord Jesus Christ himself and God our Father, who has loved us and given us eternal encouragement and **good hope** by grace, encourage your hearts and strengthen you in every good work and word. (2 Thess. 2:16–17)

Ephesians

When Paul wrote his circular letter to the churches in Asia—no doubt delivered first to the Ephesians—we discover another very interesting perspective on the meaning of our hope in Christ. Rather than thanking God for these qualities immediately, his prayer appears several paragraphs into the letter—which is in contrast to his letters to the Thessalonians and Colossians. Note what he wrote:

> This is why, since I heard about **your faith** in the Lord Jesus and **your love** for all the saints, I never stop giving thanks for you as I remember you in my prayers. (Eph. 1:15–16)

As in his second letter to the Thessalonians, Paul does not mention "hope" in this prayer of thanksgiving. But in this letter, he immediately continued his prayer—with a specific request regarding hope in Christ:

> I pray that the eyes of your heart may be enlightened so that you may **know** what is the **hope of his calling**, what is the wealth of his **glorious inheritance** in the saints, and what is the immeasurable greatness of **his power** toward us who believe, according to the mighty working of **his strength**. (Eph. 1:18–19)

In this prayer, Paul described very specifically the **hope** these believers had in Christ. They had a "glorious inheritance" because of God's "power toward" them, which is "immeasurable." Paul prayed that these believers might "know" with certainty the "hope" they had because of the Father's "calling" in their lives.

A Description of Hope in Christ

At this point, we can determine why Paul initially omitted "hope" in his prayer of thanksgiving. We can also understand the reason for his rather lengthy introduction to this letter in which he praised God for "every spiritual blessing" these believers had "in Christ" (Eph. 1:3). He then described these "blessings," clearly and rather definitively explaining the hope every believer has in Christ:

> "For he [God] **chose us** in him [Christ], before the foundation of the world." (1:4)

> "He **predestined us to be adopted as sons** through Jesus Christ for himself." (1:5a)

> "In him we have **redemption** through his blood, the **forgiveness** of our trespasses." (1:7)

> "In him we have also received an **inheritance**." (1:11a)

> "In him you [we] also were **sealed** with the promised Holy Spirit" who is "the **down payment** of our **inheritance**." (1:13–14)

It's not an accident that Paul introduced this letter with this very specific but elaborate description of the **hope** all believers have in Christ, and then segued to his prayer that these believers might "know what is **the**

hope of his calling, what is the **wealth of his glorious inheritance** in the saints" (1:18). Clearly, Paul was pleased with the **faith** and **love** in the lives of these believers, but he was concerned that they truly understand and experienced their **hope** and security in Christ.

An Elaboration on Hope in Christ

As we continue to read this letter, it's apparent that Paul continued to address the subject of hope. He explained that both Jewish and Gentile believers *have the same hope*. Evidently, some who had come to faith as Jews believed their hope was more significant than the hope of believing Gentiles. Paul addressed this issue, focusing his thoughts on Gentile believers:

> At that time, you [as Gentiles] were without Christ, excluded from the **citizenship of Israel**, and **foreigners to the covenants of promise**, **without hope** and **without God** in the world. But now in Christ Jesus, you who were **far away** [as Gentiles] have been **brought near** by the blood of Christ. . . . For through him **we both** [as Jews and Gentiles] have access in one Spirit to the Father. (Eph. 2:12–13, 18)

Paul again returned to this theme in chapter 4, making sure these Gentile believers—and Jewish believers—understood their oneness in Christ:

> There is **one body** and **one Spirit**—just as you were called to **one hope** at your calling—**one** Lord, **one** faith, **one** baptism, **one God and Father of all**, who is above all and through all and in all. (Eph. 4:4–6)

In Summary

Paul made it clear in these letters, that the way he determined the extent a community of faith was "growing into maturity with a stature measured by Christ's fullness" was to observe the degree to which these believers were manifesting faith, hope, and love. As we'll see, this observation relates directly to Paul's succinct statement in his letter to the Corinthians: "Now these three remain: **faith, hope**, and **love**—but the greatest of these is **love**" (1 Cor. 13:13).

1 Corinthians

Since Paul used these three terms to measure maturity in his introductions to his letters to the Thessalonians, Colossians, and Ephesians, this raises three very significant questions:

- How did Paul introduce his first letter to the Corinthians?
- What did he thank God for in the lives of these believers?
- Why did Paul wait until nearly two-thirds of the way into this letter to mention faith, hope, and love?

It's evident Paul's gratefulness moved in a different direction in the introduction to this letter. Rather than thanking God for their faith, hope, and love, he thanked God for the "**grace of God**" that had been "given to" them "in Christ Jesus" (1 Cor. 1:4). This difference is significant, since this is the only time Paul used this particular greeting in all thirteen of his letters.

Salvation by Grace

What did Paul mean? He was not referring to God's grace that saves us, which he referred to in his letter to the Ephesians—that is, "for you are **saved by grace through faith**, and this is not from yourselves; it is **God's gift**" (Eph. 2:8). This is the unmerited favor that saves all who believe in the Lord Jesus Christ. However, in his letter to the Corinthians, he was referring to their "**grace gifts**." Thus, Paul introduced the letter with these words:

> I always thank my God for you because of **the grace of God** given to you in Christ Jesus, that you were **enriched in him** in every way, in **all speech** and **all knowledge**. In this way, the testimony about Christ [the salvation message] was **confirmed** among you, so that you do not lack any **spiritual gift**. (1 Cor. 1:4–7)

The Grace Gifts

Unquestionably, Paul was referring to the "grace gifts" that the Holy Spirit had sovereignly bestowed on these believers when they, by faith, responded to the gospel of Jesus Christ. Paul delineated these gifts of the Spirit in chapters 12–14. And, in this introductory paragraph, Paul made it very apparent that it was these grace gifts that had confirmed the gospel message and the regenerating work of the Holy Spirit in their lives.

The author of Hebrews very specifically addressed this confirmation when he wrote:

> How will we escape if we neglect such a great **salvation**? This **salvation** had its beginning when it was spoken of by the Lord, and it was **confirmed** to us by those who heard him. At the same time, God also **testified by signs and wonders**, **various miracles, and distributions of gifts from the Holy Spirit according to his will**. (Heb. 2:3–4)[1]

This is why Paul was convinced these Corinthians were authentic disciples, in spite of their immaturity and worldly lifestyle. Most of them were living such carnal lives, they could hardly be distinguished from their pagan neighbors. In fact, their sinful lifestyle gave birth to the term "Corinthianize," which actually means "to be sensuous or sexually immoral." Consequently, Paul wrote:

> For my part, brothers and sisters, I was not able to speak to you as **spiritual people** but as **people of the flesh,** as **babies in Christ**. I gave you milk to drink, not solid food, since you were not yet ready for it. In fact, you are **still not ready**, because **you are still worldly**. For since there is envy and strife among you, are you not worldly and behaving like **mere humans**? (1 Cor. 3:1–3)

The more literal translation states they were "behaving like mere men" (1 Cor. 3:3b–4). W. Harold Mare reminds us that "to walk *kata anthrōpon* [mere men] . . . means to live only the way the ordinary sinful man lives—in selfishness, pride, and envy."[2]

A More Specific Look

To understand more fully why Paul did not thank God for faith, hope, and love in the lives of the Corinthian believers and why he waited until a much later point in the letter to even use these terms, we need to look at the immediate context—namely, 1 Corinthians 13.

The Corinthians' Gifts Were Not a Measure of Their Maturity (1 Cor. 13:1–3)

Paul's Text	An Explanation
If I speak human or angelic **tongues** . . . (1 Cor. 13:1)	Some of the Corinthians practiced this spiritual gift since they had been enriched in every way in all of their speaking (see 1 Cor. 1:5; 14:1–25).
but do not have **love** . . .	As we'll see, the Corinthians were not reflecting love in their lifestyle.
I am a noisy gong or a clanging cymbal.	The sound of their speaking gifts was as noise without true meaning because of their lack of love.
If I have the gift of **prophecy** and understand all **mysteries** and all **knowledge** . . . (1 Cor. 13:2)	Some of the Corinthians practiced these additional gifts as well (see 1 Cor. 12:1–30).
and if I have all **faith** so that I can move mountains but do not have **love** . . .	Even if they had this kind of faith—they still lacked the most important quality of maturity: the love of Christ.
I am nothing.	The way they were using these gifts (prophesying, knowledge, faith) was a meaningless exercise in God's sight.
And if I give away all my possessions, and if I give over my body in order to boast but do not have **love**, I gain nothing (1 Cor. 13:3).	The Corinthians had promised to give materially to help believers in need in Judea. However, they could have given away all their material possessions and even died as martyrs, but since they still lacked love, this kind of sacrifice would be meaningless in God's sight (see 2 Cor. 9:5).

In view of their worldly behavior, imagine how the Corinthians responded as they heard these words read from this letter. They thought their giftedness was the true measure of spirituality. However, Paul was telling them that what they valued the most meant very little in God's sight. The spiritual gifts they were so proud of were simply a reflection of God's grace—not a mature response **to His grace**.

The Corinthians' Love Was Virtually Nonexistent in This Church (1 Cor. 13:4–7c)

Paul's Text	An Explanation
Love is patient, love is kind. Love does not envy . . . (1 Cor. 13:4a).	In chapter 3, Paul told them they were impatient, unkind, and envious (see especially verse 3).
[Love] is not boastful, is not arrogant . . . (13:4b).	In chapters 3 and 4, Paul told them they were demonstrating the opposite of love with their boasting and arrogant attitudes (see 3:21; 4:18).
[Love] is not rude, is not self-seeking . . . (13:5a).	In chapter 11, Paul told them that they were engaging in terrible rudeness and selfishness during the Lord's Supper (11:20–21).
[Love] is not irritable, does not keep a record of wrongs (13:5b).	In chapter 6, Paul described their anger against one another, resulting in public disputes in a court of law (see 6:1, 6).
Love finds no joy in unrighteousness but rejoices in the truth (13:6).	In chapters 5 and 6, Paul referred to their unrighteous, immoral behavior (5:1–2; 6:15, 20).
[Love] bears all things (13:7a).	In chapter 8, Paul chided them for not caring about their weaker brothers when they purchased meat offered to idols (see 8:9).
[Love] believes all things . . . (13:7b).	In chapter 9, Paul had to defend his apostleship. They no longer trusted him, even though he led them to Christ (see especially 9:1–2).
[Love] hopes all things (13:7c).	In chapter 15, Paul addressed the fact that some no longer believed in the resurrection of Christ—the basis of a Christian's hope (see 15:17–19).

In this brief paragraph, Paul summarized what he had written, particularly in the first twelve chapters, demonstrating that the Corinthians had little (if any) love. They were woefully falling short of "growing into maturity with a stature measured by Christ's fullness" (Eph. 4:13). If they were listening at all, they could not deny this indictment.

The Corinthians' Focus Was Misdirected (1 Cor. 13:7d–13)

Paul's Text	An Explanation
[Love] endures all things. Love never ends. But as for **prophecies**, they will come to an end (1 Cor. 13:7d–8a).	Their prophecy gifts were temporal, whereas **love is eternal**.
As for **tongues**, they will cease . . . (13:8b).	Their tongue gifts were temporal, whereas **love is eternal**.
As for **knowledge**, it will come to an end (13:8c).	Their knowledge gifts were temporal, whereas **love is eternal**.
For we know in part, and we prophesy in part, but when the perfect comes, the partial will come to an end (13:9–10).	Paul seemed to be using the word "perfection" in this context to refer to their total transformation into the image of Christ at the second coming. At that moment, the temporal or the "partial" will cease to exist. Then "we will be changed" (1 Cor. 15:52). We will see Christ "face to face" (1 Cor. 13:12).
When I was a **child**, I spoke like a **child**, I thought like a **child**, I reasoned like a **child**. When I became a **man**, I put aside childish things (13:11).	Paul used his personal life as an illustration to tell them that he was once like them—acting like a child. But when he began to measure up to the fullness of Christ, he no longer focused on the gifts of the Spirit but on developing **faith**, **hope**, and **love**, and especially **love**.
For now we see only a reflection as in a mirror, but then face to face (13:12a).	Their corporate lifestyle was a very poor reflection of Christ as they looked into the mirror of God's truth. What came back from the mirror was impatience, unkindness, jealousy, bragging, arrogance, etc. However, someday they would be transformed into Christ's likeness. There would be no mirror, for they will see Jesus Christ face to face and they will be like Him. This is the "perfect" they would see and someday experience (see 1 Cor. 13:10).

Now I know in part, but then I will **know fully**, as I am **fully known** (13:12b).	At this point, their knowledge of God was limited, but when they were ultimately transformed into Christ's image, they would have full knowledge.
Now these three remain, **faith, hope,** and **love**—but the greatest of these is **love** (13:13).	From this point forward, they should focus on what's most important: **faith, hope,** and **love**—but especially **love**.

It's clear from this letter that the Corinthians were the most gifted church in the New Testament era—and yet they were the most immature and worldly. They were not manifesting faith, hope, and love. Even in Paul's second letter to this church, he often encouraged them to "become mature" (2 Cor. 13:11). In fact, leading up to this specific challenge to grow spiritually, he said, "Test yourselves to see if you are in the faith" (13:5a). This indicates that Paul was beginning to wonder about the validity of their salvation experience. But, at the same time, he concluded with a gracious benediction: "The **grace** of the Lord Jesus Christ, and the love of God, and the fellowship of the Holy Spirit be with you all" (13:13).[3]

Hebrews

The trilogy of faith, hope, and love is not only a Pauline measurement. We see the same emphasis in the letter to the Hebrews.[4] Though not as immature and carnal as the Corinthians, these believers were still infants in Christ. They needed someone to teach them "the basic principles of God's revelation." They needed "milk, not solid food" (Heb. 5:12). Their challenge was to "leave the elementary teaching about Christ and go on to maturity" (Heb. 6:1). In other words, they were to grow up spiritually.

After carefully explaining that Christ is every believer's great high priest and the one final and perfect sacrifice for sin, the author went on to spell out the true criteria for measuring maturity in a body of believers. As in the Corinthian letter, these qualities of maturity appear much later in Hebrews, and for the same reason. These believers lacked maturity. Thus, we read:

Let us draw near with a true heart in full **assurance of faith** . . . (10:22a)

Let us hold on to the confession of our **hope without wavering** . . . (10:23a)

And let us consider one another in order to promote **love** and **good works** . . . (10:24)

Once again, we see the unity of Scripture. The author of Hebrews is in perfect agreement with Paul regarding the basic criteria for measuring a church.

Concluding Thoughts

Without question, the qualities of faith, hope, and love, but especially love, are the true measure of a healthy church. They describe specifically what it means to be "growing into maturity with a stature measured by Christ's fullness" (Eph. 4:13).

In our next chapter, we'll consider the supracultural principles that come from these observations. We'll also look more specifically at what Paul meant by "**work** produced by faith," "**labor** motivated by love" and "**endurance** inspired by hope."[5]

A Question for Thought and Discussion

When a church is growing rapidly in numbers, why is it easy to measure success quantitatively rather than qualitatively?

17

Biblical Principles of Edification—Part 3

Video Intro from Gene

3lenses.org/c17

The Measure of a Healthy Church

In chapter 16, we looked at several letters Paul wrote to prominent churches in the New Testament world. At the beginning of the letters to the Thessalonians, Colossians, and Ephesians, he included the concepts of **faith**, **hope**, and **love**. He also included a **prayer of thanksgiving**, for these qualities of maturity that were being demonstrated within these local communities of faith.

By contrast, these qualities do *not* appear in 1 Corinthians and Hebrews until *much later* in each letter. And rather than thanking God that these qualities exist, Paul and the author of Hebrews exhorted these believers to develop these qualities in their lives (1 Cor. 13:13; Heb. 10:22–24).

There's another similarity in these two letters. Paul identified the Corinthians as "babies in Christ." They still needed "milk to drink, not solid food" (1 Cor. 3:1–2). The author of Hebrews also classified the recipients of his letter as "infants" who were also living on milk. He then encouraged them to "leave the elementary teaching about Christ and **go on to maturity**" (Heb. 5:13; 6:1).

Quality Not Quantity

These three concepts indicate that spiritual maturity in a local church should be measured **qualitatively** rather than **quantitatively**. However, this does not mean numbers are unimportant. Attendance can certainly indicate that a local church is effectively carrying out the Great Commission, both in making and teaching disciples. Initially, the church in Jerusalem modeled both quantitative and qualitative growth. Thousands were responding to the gospel and growing spiritually (Acts 2:41–47; 4:32–37; 5:14–16; 6:7).

The churches in Antioch of Syria and in Ephesus also multiplied greatly as both Jews and Gentiles became believers. Since these cities were among the largest in the Roman Empire, there was great potential for numerical growth. However, as we'll see, Luke also indicated these churches were growing **qualitatively**—which is the most significant measurement.

The Church in Antioch

When Barnabas arrived in Antioch and saw that many had become believers, "he was glad and **encouraged** all of them to remain true to the Lord with **devoted hearts**"—which is the basis for growing in **faith**, **hope**, and **love** (Acts 11:23). And when Saul (Paul) arrived and joined Barnabas, "for a whole year they met with the church and **taught large numbers**." We certainly can assume that what they taught these believers enabled them to continue to grow in these three qualities.

The Church in Ephesus

When Paul arrived in Ephesus on his third journey, we can only imagine the spiritual growth that took place because of Paul's intense two-year daily ministry in "the lecture hall of Tyrannus" (Acts 19:9–10). Though Paul was engaged in a strong evangelistic ministry, he was also involved in an in-depth ministry to the thousands who came to faith in Christ. In terms of the number of conversions, consider those who became "believers" and "came confessing and disclosing their practices," and burned their magic books valued at "50,000 pieces of silver." Today these manuscripts would have been valued in multimillions of dollars.

The Majority of Churches

Though these three large churches were prominent in the New Testament world, the vast majority throughout the Empire were no doubt relatively small. For example, when Paul, Silas, and Timothy planted a church in Philippi, some estimate the city population at 46,000 and a church that numbered fifty to a hundred people.[1]

The same was likely true of the church in Corinth, although this city was probably much larger. Thessalonica may have numbered 85,000, and when Paul wrote his two epistles, the number of believers was probably about the same as the churches in Philippi and Colossae. Whether large or small, New Testament leaders used the same criteria for measuring success. It was qualitative rather than quantitative.

A Contemporary Experience

When we started the first Fellowship Bible Church in Dallas, we also experienced rapid growth. Within a short period of time we exceeded a thousand and planted several branch churches. In retrospect, there are definite reasons for this unusual numerical growth. Just as was true in Jerusalem, Antioch, and Ephesus, Dallas is a huge metropolis with great potential for church growth. And like those Jews in Jerusalem particularly, the Dallas population included large numbers of people who had religious backgrounds. Many were churchgoers but did not have either a salvation experience or an in-depth relationship with Jesus Christ. Others were believers looking for a more satisfactory worship and teaching experience. And, because we were offering a unique church experience built on expositional Bible teaching, fellowship with God and one another, and presentation of the gospel, our numerical growth was instant. Word spread rapidly.

Since we were experiencing such rapid growth numerically, we were very committed to following the biblical model regarding measuring success. With our quantitative growth, we wanted to produce qualitative growth, measured by **faith**, **hope**, and **love**—but especially **love**. I immediately began to share the importance of these qualities with our leadership.

I was particularly encouraged after we built our worship center at Fellowship Bible Church North—the third church where I served as founding and lead pastor. Again, I preached messages on this divine trilogy. A husband and wife in our church who were both skilled in creating stained glass designs prepared a beautiful window depicting **faith**, **hope**, and **love**. It was located front and center in our sanctuary, very visible above the platform from which I preached those very sermons. Over the years, I often sat in the front row of the worship center and looked up at this inspiring window and reflected on the amazing concepts embodied in these three words. It continued to remind me of what should be the ultimate goal for our church—and every church—to continue "growing into maturity with a stature measured by Christ's fullness" (Eph. 4:13, which is a reflection of these corporate qualities.

A Series of Messages

To help our total congregation understand and be committed to this biblical concept, I delivered a series of messages on these qualities which soon became a part of our DNA. Paul, of course, stands out in using faith, hope, and love to measure maturity in the local church. And in his first letter to the Thessalonians, he succinctly defined the meaning of these words.

"Work Produced by Faith" (1 Thess. 1:3a)

Principle 1: To equip believers to grow into maturity with a stature measured by Christ's fullness, we must help them reflect that we are God's "workmanship, created in Christ Jesus for good works" (Eph. 2:10).

In his letter to the Ephesians, Paul stated that we "are saved by **grace through faith**," and this is not from ourselves; "it is **God's gift—not from works**, so that no one can boast" (Eph. 2:8–9). However, once we receive the gift of eternal life, we're to grow in our relationship with Jesus Christ, more and more reflecting His perfect life. Paul went on to state that we are now "his **workmanship**, created in Christ Jesus **for good**

works, which God prepared ahead of time for us **to do**" (Eph. 2:10).

When Paul wrote to the Thessalonian believers and commended them for their "**work produced by faith**," he was referring to what should happen in our lives as a community of faith once we're saved. "Works" have no part in our salvation, but once we are "saved by grace through faith," we are to produce "good works."

In this same letter, Paul mentioned three very visible and measurable aspects of this quality of maturity.

Transformed Lives

Even though these believers had worshiped idols and engaged in the worst kinds of immorality, they had not returned to their paganistic lifestyles (1 Thess. 1:8–10). In fact, by the time Paul wrote his first letter, their "work produced by faith" had become known all over Macedonia and was even being talked about in the neighboring region of Achaia (1 Thess. 1:5–7).

Faithfulness

These believers had continued to serve Jesus Christ in spite of persecution. They hadn't turned their backs on God and denied that they knew and loved Him. This is certainly inherent in the encouraging report Timothy later shared with Paul and Silas. Paul responded with these encouraging words: "For now we live, if you stand firm in the Lord" (1 Thess. 3:8).

Generosity

The Thessalonians, along with other Macedonian churches, demonstrated a remarkable and sacrificial spirit in sharing their material possessions. Though Paul didn't mention this particular "work produced by faith" in his initial letters to the Thessalonians, he noted their generosity in his second letter to the Corinthians:

> We want you to know, brothers and sisters, about the grace of God that was given to the churches of Macedonia [which included the Thessalonians]: During a severe trial brought about by affliction, their abundant joy and their extreme poverty overflowed in a wealth of generosity on their part. I can testify that, according to their ability

and even beyond their ability, of their own accord, they begged us earnestly for the privilege of sharing in the ministry to the saints, and not just as we had hoped. Instead, they gave themselves first to the Lord and then to us by God's will. (2 Cor. 8:1–5)

Walking Worthy

To understand an even more comprehensive definition of "work produced by faith," consider once again Paul's letter to the Ephesians. When referring to the fact that we are "God's workmanship created in Christ Jesus for good works," he used a very descriptive metaphorical concept. The Greek word is *peripateo*, which literally means "to walk." Paul used this word when he stated that "we are his **workmanship**, created in Christ Jesus for good works, which God prepared ahead of time for us **to do** [*peripateo*]" (Eph. 2:10).

Paul continued to use this basic word in the very practical section of this letter to exhort these believers **to do** [*peripateo*] these good works, which are measurable. In fact, what Paul wrote provides every community of believers throughout history with a criteria for evaluating the way our salvation experience is producing "good works." In other words, we can measure our corporate lifestyle as a church reflects "work produces by faith."

A General Exhortation

"Therefore I, the prisoner in the Lord, urge you to **walk** worthy [*peripateo*] of the calling you have received." (Eph. 4:1)

Specific Exhortations

Following this general exhortation, Paul stated four specific directives, using the term *peripateo*. And under each of these four directives, he stated more specific ways to make this happen.

Directive #1: "Therefore, I say this and testify in the Lord: You should no longer **walk** as the Gentiles do, in the futility of their thoughts" (Eph. 4:17).

- They were to stop lying and "speak the truth" (4:25).

- They were not to sin by allowing anger to linger resulting in bitterness (4:26, 31).
- They were never to steal; rather they were to have a strong work ethic where they could even be generous and help others (4:28).
- They were never to use foul language but to use words to build up one another (4:29).
- They were to be "kind and compassionate to one another, forgiving one another (4:32).

Directive #2: "Therefore, be imitators of God, as dearly loved children, and **walk** in love, as Christ also loved us and gave himself for us, a sacrificial and fragrant offering to God" (Eph. 5:1–2). Note: here Paul zeroed in on the false view of love:

- They were to avoid any form of "sexual immorality and any impurity and greed" (5:3).
- They were never to use "obscene" language and "crude joking" (5:4).

Directive #3: "For you were once darkness, but now you are light in the Lord. **Walk** as children of light" (Eph. 5:8).

- They were to reflect "goodness, righteousness, and truth" (5:9).
- They were never to "participate in the fruitless works of darkness" (5:11).

Directive #4: "Pay careful attention, then, to how you **walk**—not as unwise people but as wise" (Eph. 5:15).

- They were to make good use of their time (5:16).
- They were to understand what the Lord's will is (5:17).
- They were never to be excessive drinkers (5:18).
- They were to teach one another with "psalms, hymns, and spiritual songs" (5:19).
- They were to give "thanks always for everything" (5:20).
- They were to submit to one another (5:21).

When as Christians we "walk worthy" as Paul described it, we are demonstrating "**work** produced by **faith**" (1 Thess. 1:3). This is, in essence, why Paul was commending the Thessalonians. He had heard about the way they had left "the road" that is "broad that leads to destruction," and were traveling down the "narrow . . . road that leads to life" (Matt. 7:13–14). They were walking the path Jesus described as "the way, the truth, and the life" and as a body of believers, they were reflecting what He taught and how He lived (John 14:6).

The Thessalonians then are positive examples of believers who were reflecting "**work** produced by **faith**" through their walk with Christ. In fact, it was a growing work of faith. This is why Paul commended them once again in his second letter. Their "faith" was "flourishing" (2 Thess. 1:3). In other words, this dimension of their Christian lives was becoming even more obvious. Unlike the Corinthians, they were moving beyond infancy into adulthood, no longer talking like children, thinking like children, and reasoning like children. They were putting their childish ways behind them (see 1 Cor. 13:11).

"Endurance Inspired by Hope" (1 Thess. 1:3c)

Principle 2: To equip believers to grow into maturity with a stature measured by Christ's fullness, we must help them understand the "blessed hope" regarding Christ's return, knowing with certainty that their eternal destiny is secure.

Early in my Christian life, if you had asked me if I was sure I'd go to heaven when Christ returned or when I died, I would have said—"I hope so." I was not certain. Unfortunately, I was echoing the corporate membership of the church I attended at that time. In their theology, no one could know for sure if they were going to "make it" all the way to heaven. In their thinking, it depended on their "good works."

Fortunately, my perspective changed. As I began to study the Scriptures, I discovered that God wants all of His children to be able to respond to the question about their eternal destiny with assurance. This is a biblical definition of **hope**, and it is a measurement of maturity among believers in a local church.

When I became a pastor, I wanted all of us to grow together in our hope—the assurance of our salvation. As the author of Hebrews wrote, we can "seize the **hope** set before us" and "we have this **hope** as an **anchor** for the soul, **firm** and **secure**" (Heb. 6:18b–19a). With deep meaning we can sing together that old gospel song:

> *Blessed assurance, Jesus is mine!*
> *Oh, what a foretaste of glory divine!*
> *Heir of salvation, purchase of God*
> *Born of his Spirit, washed in His blood* [2]

This doesn't mean that we'll never be tempted to doubt the reality of our hope. But when we do, it doesn't affect the certainty of our hope. This is why the writer of Hebrews also exhorted us to "hold on to the confession of **our hope without wavering**, since he who promised is faithful" (Heb. 10:23). Once we become believers, our hope is based on God's faithfulness, not on our human effort.

Our Hope in Christ

In his letter to the Ephesians, Paul also addressed the need for all believers to understand they all had one hope in Christ. Clearly, this was a misunderstanding among the Asian Christians. Many Jews and Gentiles had become believers, but since the children of Israel were given the "covenants of promise" (Eph. 2:12), the Jewish believers concluded that they had a unique hope—a special position in God's kingdom. Like some of the early Jewish believers in Jerusalem, which included Peter—they believed that God "shows favoritism." This, of course, changed in Peter's thinking when he met Cornelius (Acts 10:34–36).

To reassure these Gentile believers in Ephesus and the other Asian churches regarding their "hope" in Christ, Paul wrote:

> At that time you were without Christ, excluded from the citizenship of Israel, and foreigners to the covenants of promise, **without hope** and **without God** in the world. But now in Christ Jesus, you who **were far away** have been brought near by the blood of Christ. (Eph. 2:12–13)

To make sure these believers really understood that both believing Jews and Gentiles had access to the Father by one Spirit and had "one hope," Paul culminated his thoughts with this reassuring paragraph (note the metaphors Paul used to describe the church):

> So, then, you [as believing Gentiles] are **no longer foreigners** and **strangers**, but fellow citizens with the saints, and **members of God's household**, built on the foundation of the apostles and prophets, with Christ Jesus himself as the cornerstone. In him the **whole building**, being put together, grows into a holy temple in the Lord. In him you are also being **built together** for God's dwelling in the Spirit. (Eph. 2:19–22)

The Foundation of Hope

The hope of true believers is described throughout the New Testament letters. Jesus Christ came to provide this hope, but those who became authentic disciples didn't fully understand and appreciate this reality in all its fullness until after Jesus suffered, died, and **rose again**. This is true because our **hope in Christ** is inseparable from **His resurrection**. That He lives is the foundation of our hope, which Thomas came to believe and deeply appreciate when he saw the wounds on Jesus' hands and side (John 20:24–29).

The apostle Peter also referred to this hope in his sermon on the day of Pentecost. Quoting from one of David's messianic psalms, Peter described Christ's own hope and how it related to His own resurrection:

> Therefore my heart is glad and my tongue rejoices. Moreover, my flesh will rest **in hope**, because you will not abandon me in Hades or allow your holy one to see decay. (Acts 2:26–27)

We have hope because Christ lives. It's because of the Lord's resurrection that we, too, can claim the promise that someday we will also be raised (Eph. 1:18–20; 1 Cor. 15:16–20). Jesus had a new and glorified body following the resurrection—and when He comes, so shall we.

When he addressed their question, Paul wanted the Thessalonians to understand what has happened to the believers they have known who have died. As Paul wrote:

> We do not want you to be uninformed, brothers and sisters, concerning those who are asleep, so that you will not grieve like the rest, **who have no hope**. For if we believe that Jesus **died and rose again**, in the same way, through Jesus, God will bring with him those who have fallen asleep. (1 Thess. 4:13–14)

The apostle Peter also addressed this great truth as a "living hope":

> Blessed be the God and Father of our Lord Jesus Christ. Because of his great mercy he has given us new birth into a **living hope** through the **resurrection of Jesus Christ from the dead** and into an **inheritance** that is **imperishable**, **undefiled**, and **unfading**, kept in heaven for you. (1 Peter 1:3–4)

Hope Reflects Joy

Paul captured this reality beautifully in his prayer for the believers in Rome:

> Now may the God of **hope** fill you with all **joy** and **peace** as you believe so that you may overflow with **hope** by the power of the Holy Spirit. (Rom. 15:13)

One of the most inspiring stories that touched my own life and that relates to Paul's prayer involved Kefa Sempangi. Kefa pastored the 14,000-member Redeemed Church in Uganda when Idi Amin held control of this country as a ruthless dictator. On Easter morning, 1973, more than seven thousand people were gathered from miles around to celebrate. Kefa ministered most of the day.

When the service and events were complete, he pushed his way through the crowd and arrived at the place where he was staying. He quickly noticed that several men had entered his room and had closed the door behind him. They were Amin's assassins. The tallest of the men pointed his rifle at Kefa's face and told him that they were going to kill him, but first he would allow Kefa to share some final words.

Kefa could only stare at this man in shock and unbelief. Fear gripped his soul. But suddenly he regained his composure and uttered words that could only have come from God's supernatural guidance:

> I do not need to plead my own cause. I'm a dead man already. My life is dead and hidden in Christ. It is your lives that are in danger. You are dead in your sins. I will pray to God that after you have killed me, He will spare you from eternal destruction.[3]

Hearing these words, the hatred in these men's faces changed to curiosity. The leader directed them to drop their rifles and they asked Pastor Kefa if he'd pray for them—right then. Amazed and bewildered, Kefa began to pray for their eternal salvation.

When Kefa completed what was a very simple and direct prayer, Amin's men turned to leave, assuring him of their protection. These men later became believers and eventually assisted Pastor Kefa and his family in their escape from Uganda.

That evening as Kefa drove home, he was deeply puzzled but had joy in his heart. He felt that he had passed from death to life and that he now understood Paul's words to the Galatians: "I have been crucified with Christ, and I no longer live, but Christ lives in me. The life I now live in the body, I live by faith in the Son of God, who loved me and gave himself for me" (Gal. 2:20).

What motivates followers of Jesus Christ to face this kind of oppression so triumphantly? The answer is their focus on the eternal hope in Jesus Christ. This is what motivated Paul to write to the Philippians from a Roman prison, "For me, to live is Christ and to die is gain" (Phil. 1:21). He knew that if a soldier ended his mortal life, he still had eternal life—a supernatural life—in heaven. "For we know," he wrote to the Corinthians, "that if our earthly tent we live in is destroyed, we have a building from God, an eternal dwelling in the heavens, not made with hands" (2 Cor. 5:1).

"Labor Motivated by Love" (1 Thess. 1:3b)

Principle 3: To equip believers to grow in maturity with a stature measured by Christ's fullness, we must help them grow in their love for one another.

In his first letter to the Corinthians, Paul stated that love is greater than "faith" and "hope" (1 Cor. 13:13). This is true since "love" is more comprehensive in meaning and certainly includes "work produced by faith." For example, in Ephesians Paul stated that the way we demonstrate that we are God's "workmanship, created in Christ Jesus for good works" is to "**walk in love**, as Christ also loved us and gave himself for us, a sacrificial and fragrant offering to God" (Eph. 5:1–2).

As we continue in our study of the New Testament letters, it's clear that **faith**, **hope**, and **love** are interrelated virtues. But where there is faith and hope—foundational qualities—love is all encompassing. In his first epistle, the apostle John tells us why: "God is love" (1 John 4:8, 16). And, as we've emphasized throughout this study on the church, when local communities of faith love one another as Christ loved them, they bear witness to the incarnation—the most essential doctrine of Christianity—"that is, in Christ, God was reconciling the world to himself" (2 Cor. 5:19a).

Jesus' incarnation is indeed the essence of our message to the world. When we love others as Christ loved us, we miraculously visualize and verify the reality of this message. Our love for one another is the ultimate measure of a healthy church.

As we read the New Testament letters, we repeatedly encounter Christ's new commandment. In fact, the directives and exhortations to love others appear approximately fifty times in the Epistles. To evaluate the degree our churches are measuring up to Jesus' commandment, we can use scriptural directives as basic criteria. Following are selected references:

"The Greatest of These" (1 Cor. 13:13)

Indeed, if you fulfill the royal law prescribed in the Scripture, **Love your neighbor as yourself**, you are doing well. (James 2:8; see also Gal. 5:14)

For you were called to be free, brothers and sisters; only don't use this freedom as an opportunity for the flesh, but **serve one another through love**. (Gal. 5:13)

Do everything in love. (1 Cor. 16:14)

With all humility and gentleness, with patience, **bearing with one another in love**. (Eph. 4:2)

But **speaking the truth in love**, let us grow in every way into him who is the head. (Eph. 4:15)

And **walk in love**, as Christ also loved us and gave himself for us, a sacrificial and fragrant offering to God. (Eph. 5:2)

Husbands, **love your wives**, just as Christ loved the church and gave himself for her. (Eph. 5:25; see also Eph. 5:28, 33; Col. 3:19)

Make my joy complete by thinking the same way, **having the same love**, united in spirit, intent on one purpose. (Phil. 2:2)

Above all, **put on love**, which is the perfect bond of unity. (Col. 3:14)

Now **the goal of our instruction is love** that comes from a pure heart, a good conscience, and a sincere faith. (1 Tim. 1:5)

so that they may encourage the young women to **love their husbands** and to **love their children**. (Titus 2:4)

And let us consider one another in order to **provoke love and good works**. (Heb. 10:24)

Since you have purified yourselves by your obedience to the truth, so that they show sincere **brotherly love** for each other, from a pure heart **love one another constantly**. (1 Peter 1:22)

Honor everyone. **Love the brothers and sisters**. (1 Peter 2:17)

Finally, all of you be like-minded and sympathetic, **love one another**, and be compassionate and humble. (1 Peter 3:8)

Above all, maintain constant love for one another, since **love** covers a multitude of sins. (1 Peter 4:8)

For this is the message you have heard from the beginning: We should **love one another**. (1 John 3:11)

We know that we have passed from death to life because we **love our brothers and sisters**. (1 John 3:14)

Little children, **let us not love in word or speech, but in action and in truth**. (1 John 3:18)

Now this is his command: that we believe in the name of his Son, Jesus Christ, and **love one another** as he commanded us. (1 John 3:23)

Dear friends, let us **love one another**, because **love** is from God, and everyone who **loves** has been born of God and knows God. (1 John 4:7)

Dear friends, if God loved us in this way, we also must **love one another**. (1 John 4:11)

And we have this command from him: The one who loves God must also **love his brother and sister**. (1 John 4:21)

This is how we know that we **love God's children**: when we love God and obey his commands. (1 John 5:2)

So now I ask you, dear lady—not as if I were writing you a new command, but one we have had from the beginning—that we **love one another**. (2 John 1:5)

This is **love**: that we walk according to his commands. This is the command as you have heard it from the beginning: that you **walk in love**. (2 John 1:6)

Freedom in Form

As with all of the biblical functions, we have freedom to develop forms to help believers grow in **faith**, **hope**, and **love**. However, when considering forms, we need to carefully review the three vital experiences and functions described in chapters 12 and 13. When we provide believers with these three experiences in proper sequence and balance, the result is the development of **faith**, **hope**, and **love**, and especially **love**!

Concluding Thoughts

As a pastor, I've had multiple opportunities to participate in a number of conferences for pastors where I've spoken on the measure of a healthy church.[4] These servants of the Lord have represented churches of all sizes—from very small to very large. In these conferences, I've shared the essence of what I've written in these two chapters. Regardless of our church growth numerically, we need to measure our success by the degree of faith, hope, and love that is being manifested among believers.

I've been particularly rewarded by the response from pastors from relatively small churches. Many have been discouraged because they've been given the impression they were unsuccessful because their churches were not growing substantially in numbers—even though they were located in population centers that were also relatively small.

Some of these small churches may have been more successful quantitatively than larger churches when measured percentagewise by the potential for growth. They may have already been more successful qualitatively than some larger churches when measured by faith, hope, and love. Perhaps this was true of the Thessalonians and other small churches in the Roman world, since Paul thanked God for these three qualities.

A Question for Thought and Discussion

How does Paul's statement in 1 Corinthians 13:13 that "love is the greatest of these" relate to Jesus' new command in the upper room (John 13:34–35)?

18

New Testament Church Leadership—Phase 1

Video Intro from Gene

3lenses.org/c18

To understand leadership in the New Testament church, we need to look at two phases. Though they overlap, each is distinctive.

- **Phase 1** describes God's plan for launching and establishing local churches.
- **Phase 2** grows naturally out of Phase 1 and relates to permanent leadership in local churches.

The New Testament Setting

As the apostles began to carry out the Great Commission and to make disciples, their only inspired, enscripturated guidance was embodied in the Old Testament, a source these men used primarily to convince people that Jesus Christ was the promised Messiah. However, they had no New Testament literature. With the exception of the small letter composed by the Jerusalem Council, the New Testament as we know it today did not even begin to come into existence for approximately another fifteen or twenty years after Pentecost (Acts 15:23–29). Consequently, God implemented a supernatural plan to not only make disciples but to equip them to become like Christ.

The Greater Gifts

To initially plant churches and to help them mature in Christ, God's plan included "the greater gifts." These supernatural gifts refer both to **individuals** themselves as well as to their **supernatural abilities** to communicate divine truth. Following is the way Paul listed them in his letters to the Ephesians and the Corinthians. Note how these two lists compare:

Ephesians	1 Corinthians

And he [Jesus] himself gave
  some to be **apostles,**
  some **prophets,**
  some **evangelists,**
  some **pastors** and **teachers** (4:11)
 	
to equip the saints
for the work of ministry,
to build up the body of
Christ (4:12)
	And God has appointed these in the church:
	
	  first **apostles,**
	  second **prophets,**
	  third **teachers,**
	  next miracles,
	  then gifts of healing,
	  helping,
	  leading,
	  various kinds of tongues
	  (12:28).

until we all reach unity
  in the faith and
  in the knowledge of God's Son,
growing into maturity
with a **stature measured by Christ's fullness** (4:13).
	But desire the greater gifts.
	  And I will show you an even
	  better way (12:31) . . .
	Now these three remain:
	  faith, hope, and **love**—
	  but the greatest of these is **love**
	  (13:13).

Comparisons

When we look carefully at these two passages, there are at least three significant comparisons.

First, in the Ephesian letter Paul listed only "the greater gifts," whereas in the Corinthian letter he also listed "the secondary gifts." This appears to be true since the Corinthians were focusing on the "secondary gifts" and even rejected some of those who were and had the "greater gifts." Consequently, Paul instructed these believers to desire that the "greater gifts" (apostles, prophets, and teachers) and their supernatural abilities be active in their church (1 Cor. 12:31).

Paul verified this emphasis in his opening comments in the Corinthian letter. He had received a report from a respected family that some were saying, "I belong to Paul," or "I belong to Apollos," or "I belong to Cephas," or "I belong to Christ" (1 Cor. 1:11–12). In other words, some were actually refusing to listen to some who had and were the greater gifts—which included Paul, Silas, and Timothy, who started this church. Paul "was not able to speak to [them] as spiritual people but as people of the flesh, as babies in Christ" (1 Cor. 3:1).

Second, in the Ephesians passage Paul referred to the ultimate way to measure a healthy church—the extent to which believers are "**growing into maturity with a stature measured by Christ's fullness**" (Eph. 4:13). However, in the Corinthian letter, he actually specified how to determine the degree to which a community of believers are actually measuring up to Christ's stature—the way they were growing in faith, hope, and love—but especially love (1 Cor. 13:13). As we've noted in chapter 16, the Corinthians were lacking in all three qualities.

Third, there is specific **similarity** but yet a lack of **conformity** when Paul listed the "greater gifts" in the two letters. The sequence is basically the same, but Paul added "evangelists" in the Ephesian letter and combined the "pastor" gift with the "teaching" gift (Eph. 4:11). To understand this variance, we need to look more specifically at "the greater gifts" which are mentioned in both letters.

Apostles

In terms of this gift to the church, there are two groups of leaders that are identified as "apostles." The late Dr. George Peters has written about these two classifications: "The unique position of **the apostles** in the beginning ministries of the church is recognized throughout the New Testament—only they're known as **the apostles of Jesus Christ**, while others are known simply as **apostles** or as **apostles of the church.**"[1] Personally, I like the terms *primary apostles* and *secondary apostles*.

The Primary Apostles. The term "apostle" (*apostolos*) almost without exception is used in a very distinct and primary way to describe the men Jesus selected out of the larger group of disciples and identified them as "apostles." Luke made this point very clear in his gospel when he recorded that Jesus "summoned his **disciples**, and he chose **twelve of them**, whom he also named **apostles**." These men were to become "the greater gifts," particularly to the church at large (Luke 6:13; see also Matt. 10:1–4; Mark 3:13–19). They were unique representatives of Jesus and were His messengers, to whom He initially gave the Great Commission.

Judas, of course, turned his back on the Lord and was replaced by Matthias, who was "added to the **eleven apostles**" (Acts 1:26). Later, Paul was also directly called by Jesus to be a primary apostle. It happened on the Damascus Road when Jesus audibly spoke to Saul (Paul) from heaven (Acts 9:4–16).

Luke's record in the book of Acts verifies Paul's apostolic calling. He was recognized and affirmed by the Jerusalem Council as "an **apostle** to the Gentiles" (Acts 15:25; Rom. 11:13; Gal. 1:15; 2:6–9). Through the power of the Holy Spirit, Paul was able to perform "the **signs of an apostle** . . . including **signs** and **wonders** and **miracles**" (2 Cor. 12:12, see also Rom. 15:18–19). However, in spite of his enormous influence in carrying out the Great Commission, Paul always humbly considered himself "the least of the **apostles**" because he had "persecuted the church of God" (1 Cor. 15:9).

The Secondary Apostles. The term *apostle* is also used in a secondary sense. Luke identified Barnabas as an apostle when referring to his "missionary ministry" with Paul (Acts 14:4, 14). And Paul himself called Silas and Timothy "Christ's apostles" (1 Thess. 2:6–7).

These men were "apostolic messengers" in proclaiming the gospel, but the primary apostles were selected directly by Jesus Christ and were eyewitnesses of His ministry from John's baptism. In fact, it's clear this was a requirement in selecting someone to replace Judas (Acts 1:21–22).

Paul was an exception in terms of witnessing Christ's earthly ministry. However, as we've noted, he encountered the resurrected and ascended Christ on the road to Damascus and he is classified as a primary apostle who especially reached Gentiles with the gospel.

Luke's Focus on the Twelve Apostles. In the first twelve chapters of Acts, Luke almost exclusively recorded the acts of the twelve apostles, focusing particularly on the ministry of Peter and John. It appears these men spent much of their time in Jerusalem in the early years of the church, although they probably traveled back and forth to their homes in Galilee just as they had done with Jesus. But when persecution drove many disciples out of the city, the apostles stayed (Acts 8:1).

It was in this context that these men, with the elders in Jerusalem, hammered out the theological issues facing the expanding church. Luke devoted a lengthy section in his narrative describing when and how these men resolved the conflict regarding law and grace (Acts 15:6–29).

Tradition tells us that eventually most of the apostles left Jerusalem and even their homes in Galilee and carried out Christ's command in Acts 1:8—to be his "witnesses"—not only "in Jerusalem, in all Judea and Samaria" but "to the ends of the earth."[2]

Luke's Focus on the Apostle Paul. Following Peter's enlightening experience with Cornelius, Paul's ministry along with his missionary companions received primary attention in Luke's narrative (see Acts 13:1–2ff). Clearly, Paul had a unique apostolic ministry in planting churches throughout the Roman world. He was multi-gifted since he was "appointed a **herald, apostle,** and **teacher**" (2 Tim. 1:11; see also 1 Tim. 2:7). In terms of the "greater gifts" listed in the Ephesian letter and Paul's ministry, it appears he was an **apostle, prophet, evangelist, pastor,** and **teacher.** He functioned in all of these roles in founding and establishing churches.

In Summary. The ministry of the primary apostles was foundational, which is also described by Paul: "So, then, you are no longer foreigners and strangers, but fellow citizens with the saints, and members of God's household, built on the **foundation of the apostles and prophets,** with Christ Jesus Himself as the cornerstone" (Eph. 2:19–20).

In view of this larger picture, we can also conclude that Paul placed apostles at the top of the list in both his letters to the Ephesians and Corinthians because he was using the word in a **primary sense.** He was not just describing an "apostolic ministry or work," but he was describing a specific calling, an appointment made by God to specific individuals who were **called directly by Jesus Christ** to have a unique foundational ministry of evangelism and edification in launching local churches. Paul made this clear when he wrote, "**He** [Jesus Christ] **gave some to be apostles**" (Eph. 4:11).

Prophets

In the Old Testament. Though the term *apostles* is basically a New Testament concept, the term *prophets* is used again and again in the Old Testament to refer to those who declared and announced God's will to the people of Israel. As Merrill F. Unger states, "The true prophet was God's spokesman to man, communicating what he had received from God."[3]

When we look carefully at the Old Testament documents, it's clear that the prophets declared and announced doctrinal truth about God and His will as well as predictive truth regarding God's will in the future. When true prophets spoke, they were divinely inspired by God Himself (2 Peter 1:20–21). False prophets were severely judged (Deut. 18:20). In fact, the true test of a prophet in the Old Testament was that every prediction without exception must come true. Otherwise, they were considered false prophets (Deut. 18:22).

In the Book of Acts. In the book of Acts, twenty-five out of thirty-four statements about "prophecy" or "prophets" (74 percent) refer to **Old Testament prophets** who predicted the coming of the Messiah.[4] However, seven of these thirty-four statements refer to New Testament prophets.

In addition to the "prophets from Jerusalem" who went down to Antioch (Acts 11:27), eight men are specifically named:

1. Agabus: "One of them, named Agabus, stood up and **predicted** by the Spirit that there would be a severe famine throughout the Roman world" (Acts 11:28; see also 21:10–11).
2. Barnabas, Simeon, Lucius, Manaen, and Saul: "Now in the church at Antioch there were **prophets** and **teachers**" (Acts 13:1a).
3. Judas and Silas from Jerusalem: "Both Judas and Silas, who were also **prophets themselves**, encouraged the brothers and sisters and strengthened them with a long message" (Acts 15:32).

In the Epistles. In the New Testament letters there are approximately thirty references to "prophets" or "prophesying."

1 Thessalonians: When Paul penned his first letter to the church in Thessalonica, he gave some specific instructions regarding how to evaluate those who supposedly had the gift of prophecy. He wrote: "Don't stifle the Spirit. **Don't despise prophecies but test all things**. Hold on to what is good" (1 Thess. 5:19–21).

Clearly, Paul was cautioning these believers to discern between "false prophets" and "true prophets." On the one hand, they were not to restrict the Spirit's voice through gifted believers; on the other hand, they were to evaluate everything that was being said and to only listen to prophetic messages that were from God.

To help these believers determine what was a true prophetic message, God gave some the "gift of discernment" (1 Cor. 12:10). They were also able to evaluate these messages with the "apostles' teaching," as illustrated in 2 Thessalonians 2:1–12.

1 Corinthians: Fifteen references to the prophetic gift appear in Paul's first letter to the Corinthian church (1 Cor. 3:1–4). Since these believers were misusing and abusing their gifts of the Spirit, Paul gave very specific instructions regarding how to use this prophetic gift—namely, to give priority attention to this gift since it was designed by God to edify and build up believers (1 Cor. 14:1–4).

Ephesians: In this letter, no doubt a circular epistle, we see how clearly the prophetic gift is aligned with the apostolic gift in God's overall plan for the body of Christ. Paul wrote: "And he himself [Jesus] gave some to be **apostles**, some **prophets**" (Eph. 4:11a). Later, he told believers that they were "built on the foundation of the **apostles** and **prophets**" (Eph. 2:19–20). Paul then elaborated on this apostolic and prophet association when he referenced the mystery of the church. "This was not made known to people in other generations as it is now revealed to his holy **apostles** and **prophets** by the Spirit" (Eph. 3:5). "So, then, you are . . . built on the foundation of the **apostles** and **prophets**" (Eph. 3:3, 5).[5]

Revelation: Finally, there are ten references to prophets or prophesying in the book of Revelation. It's my opinion that most of these refer to those who will receive and exercise this gift after Jesus Christ has removed the church from this world.[6]

Evangelists

Though Paul included "evangelists" in the list of "greater gifts" in his letter to the Ephesians (4:11), there are only two other references to the title (*euangelistes*) in the New Testament. We've already mentioned "Philip the **evangelist**" (Acts 21:8). On the other hand, Paul told Timothy to "do the **work** of an **evangelist**" (2 Tim. 4:5b), which raises a very interesting question. Did Timothy have the gift of "evangelism," or was he simply to do the same work as a man like Philip who had the gift of evangelism? It's my opinion that Paul was instructing Timothy to share the gospel just as all spiritual leaders are to "do the work of an evangelist" even though they don't have this special gift.

Like the apostles, Philip stands out as being exceptionally gifted. As an evangelist, he cast out unclean spirits and healed the lame and the paralyzed (Acts 8:7). He received a direct revelation from the Lord regarding the Ethiopian eunuch (8:29) and after he led this man to Christ "the Spirit of the Lord carried Philip away" (8:39). It appears the Lord supernaturally transported him to Azotus—a different location—and he then continued with his evangelistic work, that of "preaching the gospel" (8:40).

Though Luke's reference to Philip as an evangelist is his only direct reference to this kind of gifted person in the New Testament, there are other ways to recognize those with this gift. For example, there were "men from Cyprus and Cyrene, who came to Antioch and began speaking to the Greeks also, **proclaiming the good news** about the Lord Jesus" (Acts 11:20). The phrase "proclaiming the good news" describes their evangelistic ministry. The phrase means "to evangelize." We see the results of their ministry since "a large number who believed turned to the Lord" (Acts 11:21).

The apostles, and particularly Paul, certainly had the gift of evangelism. Jesus directed these men to make disciples—which is an evangelistic ministry. It appears that all of these New Testament pioneers were multigifted. This gives us a significant clue as to why the list of the "greater gifts" is not exactly parallel as listed in the Ephesian and Corinthian letters but in essence represents the same individuals. This will become even more obvious when we look at the gifts of pastor and teacher mentioned next in this list.[7]

Pastors and Teachers

It's obvious throughout the book of Acts that the **primary apostles** also had the gift of teaching. This gift enabled them to not only "make disciples" but also to "teach them" how to become mature in their faith. This two-fold charge was an inseparable part of the Great Commission (see chapter 5).

Some of the New Testament prophets who were not apostles in a primary sense also had the gift of teaching. Barnabas, Simeon, Lucius, and Manaen are called **prophets** and **teachers**. These men received a direct, verbal message from the Holy Spirit who said, "Set apart for me Barnabas and Saul for the work to which I have called them" (Acts 13:2b). Even prior to this event we see Barnabas and Saul using their teaching gifts in Antioch. Luke has recorded that "for a whole year they met with the church and **taught** large numbers" (11:26).

This leads to another interesting observation. When Paul categorized the "greater gifts" in his letter to the Corinthians, he specified only **teachers**. However, in his letter to the Ephesians, he listed **pastors** and **teachers**. In this sense, he was referring to combination gifts just as Luke referred to **prophets** and **teachers**.

Some may also have been gifted as **evangelists** and **teachers**. Apollos illustrates this possibility. He was "an eloquent man who was competent in the **use of the Scriptures**" (18:24). While in Achaia, "he was a great help to those who by grace had believed"—using his **teaching** gift. But it seems he also used his "**evangelism and teaching** gifts" when "he vigorously **refuted the Jews** in public, **demonstrating through the Scriptures** that Jesus is the Messiah" (18:27–28).

Timothy: A Pastor and Teacher. This young man is perhaps the most outstanding example of having what may have been the gifts of **pastoring** and **teaching**.[8] Paul frequently used him in this capacity, leaving him to help a new and struggling church. He sent him back to Thessalonica "to **strengthen** and **encourage**" these Christians in their faith (1 Thess. 3:2).[9] Likewise, he asked him to go to Corinth to **teach them** the doctrines that he himself was **teaching** "everywhere in every church" (1 Cor. 4:17). He also asked Timothy to "remain in Ephesus" that he might "**instruct**

certain people not to **teach** false doctrine" (1 Tim. 1:3). And later Paul wrote to him, "What you have heard from me in the presence of many witnesses, **commit to faithful men** who will be able to **teach others also**" (2 Tim. 2:2).

When we look at the exhortations Paul gave Timothy in his two letters, we see more possible verification of his **pastoral** and **teaching** gifts:

- Command and **teach** these things (1 Tim. 4:11).
- Until I come, give your attention to **public reading, exhortation**, and **teaching** (4:13).
- Don't neglect **the gift** that is in you; it was given to you through prophecy, with the laying on of hands by the council of elders (4:14).[10]
- Pay close attention to your life and **your teaching** (1 Tim. 4:16).

Titus: Another Pastor and Teacher. Titus, too, may have had the gifts of **pastoring** and **teaching**. He, like Timothy, was closely associated with Paul in establishing churches (2 Cor. 2:13; 7:6–7, 13–14). He left him in Crete to carry out a teaching-pastoral ministry: "To set right what was left undone" and "to appoint elders in every town" (Titus 1:5). While there he was "to proclaim things consistent with **sound teaching**" (2:1) and to "**encourage** and **rebuke** with all authority" (2:15).

Other Possible Pastors and Teachers. Paul particularly referred to a number of other individuals who may have had the same **pastoring** and **teaching** gifts as Timothy and Titus.

- Paul planned to send "Artemis or Tychicus" to the island of Crete to continue the ministry that Titus had begun (Titus 3:2).
- Luke stayed in Philippi for at least eight years to establish the church (Acts 16:11; 17:1; 20:6). Later he wrote his gospel and the book of Acts. This revelatory ability may have been related to the gift of **pastoring** and particularly **teaching**.
- Mark joined Barnabas in ministry and eventually was inspired by the Holy Spirit to record his gospel. Again, this required a

revelatory gift—perhaps "teaching."

- In his letter to the Colossians, Paul made reference to Aristarchus (4:10); Justus (4:11), Epaphras (4:12), Demas (4:14), Archippus (4:17)—all of whom may had the gifts as pastor and teacher. If not, they were "to do the work" of pastoring and teaching just as Timothy was to "do the work of an evangelist" (2 Tim. 4:5b). Perhaps this was also true of Epaphroditus (Phil. 2:25), Erastus and Trophimus (2 Tim. 4:15–16), and Gaius (Acts 19:29).

Most of these observations are based on conjecture, but even if half of these men had the supernatural gifts of pastoring and teaching, it helps clarify Paul's reference to these gifts in his circular letter to the Ephesians.[11]

An Old Testament Precedent

A Physical Tabernacle

At Mount Sinai, God also also revealed a plan so that His people could develop an intimate relationship with Him. It involved the Tabernacle—a place for worship. Moses received this plan directly from the Lord and communicated it to all Israel:

> Moses then said to the Israelites, "Look, the Lord has appointed by name **Bezalel** son of Uri, son of Hur, of the tribe of Judah. He has **filled him with God's Spirit**, with **wisdom, understanding**, and **ability** in every kind of craft to design artistic works in gold, silver, and bronze, to cut gemstones for mounting, and to carve wood for work in every kind of artistic craft. He has also given both him and **Oholiab** son of Ahisamach, of the tribe of Dan, **the ability to teach others**. He has **filled them with skill** to do all the work." (Ex. 35:30–35a)

In this Old Testament setting, God by His Spirit gifted Bezalel with supernatural "wisdom, understanding, and ability" to construct the **earthly tabernacle**. The Spirit also gifted both Bezalel and his associate Oholiab with "the ability **to teach others**" how to construct this place of worship.

But there was one more important step. The Holy Spirit also gifted a select number of others to join in this effort—"**every skilled person in whose heart the Lord had placed wisdom**, all whose hearts moved them, to come to the work and do it" (Ex. 36:2).

A Spiritual Tabernacle

In the New Testament, the Lord had a plan to build a **living spiritual tabernacle**, metaphorically described by the apostle Peter as "living stones, a spiritual house" (1 Peter 2:5a). This was a description of local communities of faith located throughout the Roman world.

Initially—as with God's people at Mount Sinai—believers had no written documents to instruct them on how to build up this spiritual body. Consequently, the Holy Spirit gifted the apostles and other key individuals with wisdom and knowledge and skill—just as He had by His Spirit gifted Bezalel and Oholiab so that they could build the earthly tabernacle. He gave some the supernatural gift of teaching—the ability to **teach all members of the body of Christ** how to build up one another—just as the Holy Spirit gifted Bezalel and Oholiab with the ability to teach others how to build the earthly tabernacle.

There's another beautiful parallel. In the Old Testament, God's plan was to build a place where He would be present in the Holy of Holies and accessible through the High Priest. In the New Testament, God's plan was to create the living body of Christ where He could dwell in the hearts of all believers who are "a **holy priesthood** to offer **spiritual sacrifices** acceptable to God through Jesus Christ" (1 Peter 2:5b). Paul joined Peter in describing God's will for this new covenant reality. As believers, we are to present out "bodies as **living sacrifice**, holy and pleasing to God" which is our "true worship" (Rom. 12:1). Both apostles were describing God's glorious plan for the church.

Concluding Thoughts

The study of the book of Acts and the New Testament letters gives us significant insights as to *who* and *what* were the "greater gifts" and why they were given. Some were individuals who were supernaturally gifted by Jesus Christ Himself to launch and establish churches, and some were particularly gifted to give us the corpus of trustworthy, divine truth that is recorded in our New Testament.

Whenever and wherever local churches were founded, God instituted His **second phase**—a plan that clearly relates to permanent leadership in local churches. As will be shown in the next chapter, this called for church leaders who were able to have a ministry primarily because of their godly character rather than supernatural gifts and abilities.

A Question for Thought and Discussion

What is the practical significance in understanding the correlation between 1) the supernaturally gifted individuals who helped build the earthly tabernacle in the Old Testament setting and 2) the supernaturally gifted individuals who helped build the church in the first century (God's spiritual tabernacle)?

19

New Testament Church Leadership—Phase 2

Video Intro from Gene

3lenses.org/c19

During the period of time I was preparing to pass my lead pastor baton to my successor, I received an invitation to join three men for dinner. One was my good friend Bob Buford (now with Jesus), who served as founder and CEO of Leadership Network. Brad Smith was Bob's associate and Jeff Jones eventually became my successor.

Shortly into the meal it became clear that all three had agreed on an agenda. In essence, they said, "Gene, in view of your years of pastoral experience, we're convinced you need to write a book on church leadership."

I was surprised—but certainly honored. I had been thinking a lot about the importance of doing theology in community and I couldn't help but see this as a Spirit-directed opportunity. Consequently, I invited my own fellow elders—eleven men—to join me in this endeavor. Several of us had served together in this pastoral leadership role for many years.

They agreed and we met weekly for several months. Together we studied every reference to local church leadership in the New Testament. We began in the book of Acts and followed the unfolding story in Scripture. As a result, I wrote the book I was encouraged to write—*Elders and Leaders: God's Plan for Leading the Church*. This chapter includes a comprehensive summary of what we discovered in Scripture.[1]

The Elders in Jerusalem (AD 45)

Luke never mentioned local church leaders (elders) until approximately twelve years after Pentecost. The setting was the church in Antioch of Syria. Some prophets from Jerusalem traveled to this city and "one of them, named Agabus, stood up and predicted by the Spirit that there would be a severe famine throughout the Roman world" (Acts 11:28). As prophesied, it happened—and Luke reported what happened in Antioch:

> Each of the disciples, according to his ability, determined to send relief to the brothers and sisters who lived in Judea. They did this, sending it to the **elders** by means of Barnabas and Saul. (Acts 11:29–30)

As stated, this was Luke's first reference to **permanent** local church leaders in the book of Acts. They're called **elders**—and since Agabus and his fellow prophets had come from Jerusalem, we can assume he was referring to the "elders" in the Jerusalem church.

Important Questions

Luke's rather brief but descriptive reference to these spiritual leaders raises some important questions. Since approximately twelve years had passed since Pentecost, when did these men become elders in Jerusalem? We can only speculate that it probably happened after the seven were chosen and appointed to care for the Grecian widows (Acts 6:1–6). If there had been elders already functioning at this point in time, the apostles would certainly have involved them in solving this problem.

This raises a second question: Who selected and appointed those who were serving as elders in Jerusalem? Based on the apostles' involvement in appointing the seven who cared for the widows, we can speculate it was probably the apostles themselves who were also involved in appointing elders. As the New Testament story unfolds, we'll see this possibility affirmed.

These speculations raise a third and very important question: What qualifications would the apostles have looked for in selecting and appointing elders? This question is even more significant since it would be at least another thirty years before Paul outlined in writing the qualifications for these permanent church leaders (1 Tim. 3:1–7; Titus 1:5–9). Consequently, we cannot be certain regarding any specific maturity profile prior to that time.

The Foot Washing Experience

To explore a possible answer to this question, we must not forget what the apostles had personally learned about spiritual maturity and qualifications for leadership just a short time before Christ's death and resurrection. Ironically, these men were arguing among themselves who was to be the greatest in Christ's kingdom when Jesus humbled Himself and washed their feet. However, after the ascension and when the "Spirit of truth" came, they would certainly have remembered what Jesus had said in the upper room:

> "The kings of the Gentiles lord it over them, and those who have authority over them have themselves called 'Benefactors.' It is not to be like that among you. On the contrary, whoever is greatest among you should become like the youngest, and whoever leads, like the one serving." (Luke 22:25–26)

What happened following this experience, plus the coming of the Holy Spirit, would have impacted the apostles and helped them formulate criteria for selecting those who would oversee local churches. First and foremost, they should be **humble servants following the example of Jesus Christ**.

Economic Responsibility and Accountability

Based on Luke's account, these spiritual leaders were to oversee the distribution of the financial gifts from the disciples in Antioch to the believers throughout Judea. Luke recorded that this "relief"—obviously currency—was sent "**to the elders**" (Acts 11:30).

This would have been an enormous task, particularly in making sure that those in need were cared for equitably. Since they had **received the gift**, it would be their managing responsibilities to **distribute the gift**. They no doubt appointed qualified individuals to help with the distribution of these funds, just as they had done in caring for the Grecian widows (Acts 6:1–7).[2]

A Prayer and Healing Ministry (AD 45–47)

The next chronological reference to "elders" in the New Testament story appears in the letter James—Jesus' half-brother—wrote "to the twelve tribes dispersed abroad" (James 1:1b). At this point, James was probably already serving as the lead elder in the Jerusalem church. This position becomes clear as the leadership story in the book of Acts unfolds (Acts 12:17; 15:13–21; 21:18; Gal. 2:9, 12).

As James closed out this letter, he penned these words:

> Is anyone among you sick? He should call for the **elders of the church**, and they are to pray over him, anointing him with oil in the name of the Lord. (James 5:14)

James did not limit prayer requests to certain kinds of illnesses. Whether the sickness was rooted in the physical, the psychological, or the spiritual, believers were to be free to ask for prayer from the elders of the church (5:15–16). And since this reference to praying for those who were sick happened early in the biblical story, we can conclude this was to be another priority for elders in terms of their spiritual responsibilities.

The First Church Planting Mission (AD 47)

Luke's next reference to "elders" enables us to witness for the first time the actual appointment of these local church leaders. It happened on the first missionary journey into the Gentile world. After starting churches in four significant cities in southern Galatia, Paul, and Barnabas "returned to Lystra, to Iconium, and to Antioch" and "**appointed elders** for them in **every church**" (Acts 14:21b, 23).

This was a somber event. As they appointed these individuals "they committed them to the Lord" in the context of prayer and fasting (14:23b). Just as Paul and Barnabas had faced persecution in starting these churches, these elders would also face "many hardships" in leading these churches (14:22a).

As we reflect on the "appointment of elders" in these communities of faith, we are once again faced with a very intriguing question: How were Paul and Barnabas able to discover leaders who were qualified after such a brief time—probably a year or so after the churches were founded?

The answer to this question relates to what happened in the church in Jerusalem. As we've noted, there were many devout Jews who had come from all over the New Testament world (Acts 2:5). When they became believers, their spiritual growth happened quickly, building on their knowledge of the Old Testament, followed by the "apostles' teaching" (Acts 2:42).

The same was true in these Galatian cities. There were a number of committed Jews and even devout Gentiles. For example, in Pisidia Antioch, Luke reported that "many of the **Jews** and **devout converts** to Judaism followed Paul and Barnabas" (Acts 13:43). Once these eager listeners responded to the gospel, many would have matured quickly in their Christian faith. Among them would have been men like those who were appointed to care for the widows such Stephen and Philip—and even men like Barnabas and Silas who obviously became believers when the church was born in Jerusalem. Since these men were devout, God-fearing, Grecian Jews with a significant knowledge of the Old Testament, once they believed in the Lord Jesus as Messiah, they very quickly began to grow "into maturity with a stature measured by Christ's fullness" (Eph. 4:13).[3]

Here's another significant question: To what extent were the believers in each church involved in selecting these men to be elders? Again, we can only speculate. But we have a precedent when the apostles laid hands on the seven men chosen to care for the widows in Jerusalem. Though they were not elders, they occupied a very significant leadership role. The apostles told the representatives from the Hellenistic community to select from among them "seven men of good reputation, full of the Spirit and wisdom" (Acts 6:1, 3). However, it's logical Paul and Barnabas consulted a significant segment of the believers in these Galatian churches to recommend men who were already emerging as spiritual leaders.

The Law–Grace Controversy (AD 49)

When Paul and Barnabas returned to Antioch of Syria from their first missionary journey, they faced a serious theological problem. A group of men came down from Judea and tried to convince these Gentile converts that they could not be saved unless they were circumcised according to the Jewish law. Paul and Barnabas took on this challenge in heated public debates—but to no avail. Consequently, they "and some others were appointed to go up to the **apostles** and **elders in Jerusalem** about this issue" (Acts 15:1–2).

Here for the first time, we see both the apostles and the elders "working together." We also see something happening in terms of God's plan for human responsibility. Even Paul and Barnabas were not able to resolve this theological issue in Antioch. This certainly could have happened through miraculous intervention, but it didn't. It was obviously not God's will.

After Paul and Barnabas arrived in Jerusalem, the apostles and elders continued to engage in a very human process. After having a lengthy "discussion," Peter (representing the apostles) shared a **previous revelatory experience** he had on a rooftop in Joppa—and later how Cornelius (a Gentile) was saved by grace through faith in the Lord Jesus Christ—and nothing more (Acts 10:1–11; 18:15; 15:7–11). Paul and Barnabas then confirmed Peter's experience by reporting what they had experienced on their first missionary journey—how God had done "signs and wonders" to confirm the message of salvation to the Gentile world (Acts 15:12b).

James, serving as a lead elder in Jerusalem, followed next and verified Peter's testimony regarding Gentile conversion by quoting from **God's revelation to the prophet Amos and then sharing his opinion or judgment** (Acts 15:13–21).

Once these men had engaged in this lengthy process involving debate, reports, dialogue, and discussion, and had arrived at a solution, God then **directly** affirmed their conclusions. The Holy Spirit spoke through Judas and Silas who were both "prophets" (15:32). Consequently, these men were also chosen by the apostles and elders "with the whole church" to help Paul and Barnabas deliver the letter (15:22).

Luke's reference to the involvement of the "whole church" in selecting Judas and Silas raises another question: How many other believers other than the apostles and elders were involved in this decision? To answer this, we need to review the meaning of the term "church" (*ekklesia*) once again. In most instances in the biblical record, this term simply referred to a local community of believers—such as all the believers in Jerusalem. More literally it refers to "an assembly"—in this case those believers who were gathered with the apostles and elders. This would have been a relatively small group compared with the total number of believers who were part of the church in Jerusalem. In other words, Luke's use of "whole church" simply referred to the "whole assembly" who had gathered—perhaps in a large, spacious home such as Mary's, Mark's mother (Acts 12:12–13). We must remember that the church at this point in time could not meet in public places—certainly not in Jerusalem.

As we look at this specific event in the context of the unfolding story in the book of Acts, it's clear that a gradual transition was taking place as God gave more and more responsibility to spiritual leaders to make decisions based on previous revelation by the Holy Spirit. They also learned lessons from their ongoing church planting experiences. God did not always reveal to believers what to do and say—even during the early years of the church. However, something else is very apparent. **The Holy Spirit decided when to speak directly** and when to be a "**silent encourager**" so believers could make decisions based on what He had already revealed.

Character-Based Judgments (AD 49–50)

As the biblical story continued to unfold, we once again see God entrusting believers with more human responsibility in making judgments regarding the appointment of leaders. This becomes apparent when Paul returned to Lystra on his second journey. He reconnected with these believers and particularly with the elders. It was then he heard about Timothy, which Luke has recorded: "He was **well spoken of** by the **brothers** at Lystra and Iconium" (Acts 16:2 ESV).[4]

It's my opinion that when Luke used the term "brothers" (*adelphoi*) to describe Timothy's reputation, he was referring to the "elders" that were appointed on the first missionary journey (Acts 14:21–23). This conclusion is also based on a statement Paul made when he later wrote his first letter to Timothy. He reminded him of "the council of elders" who had laid their hands on him—probably to commission him once Paul chose him to be his missionary companion (1 Tim. 4:12). It's logical to conclude that these were the same men Paul and Barnabas had appointed as elders on their first missionary journey (Acts 14:21b, 23). They were now giving Paul very positive comments regarding Timothy's spiritual growth.

Paul was obviously very encouraged—not only with this positive report from the elders in Lystra, but also in Iconium. Timothy's reputation had spread to this sister church. Consequently, **Paul chose him based on his character**.

This was especially important in Paul's thinking since he did not want to make the same mistake that he felt he and Barnabas had made when they chose John Mark to accompany them on their first missionary journey. Paul had become very agitated that Mark "had deserted them in Pamphylia and had not gone with them to the work" (Acts 15:38–39). This also reflects the human element on what was also a divine process.

These two stories involving John Mark and Timothy certainly demonstrate that God was putting more and more responsibility on even the apostles in discerning whether or not spiritual leaders were qualified. When we read Paul's letters to Timothy and Titus outlining the qualifications for elders/overseers, we'll see how important it is to select leaders based on character.[5]

Respect and Esteem (AD 51)

During Paul's second missionary journey he also wrote his first letter to the Thessalonians. In the closing section of this epistle, he wrote, "Now we ask you, brothers and sisters [*adelphoi*], to give recognition to those **who labor** among you and **lead you** in the Lord and **admonish you**, and to regard them very highly in love because of their work" (1 Thess. 5:12–13). Here Paul did not identify these leaders with a specific title.

Rather, he simply described their leadership role in managing the church and admonishing these believers.[6]

Again, we face two interesting questions. What were the spiritual leaders called in the church in Thessalonica? And who appointed them? We're not given specific answers to these questions, but it's very likely they were called **overseers** rather than elders. This conclusion is based on the fact that Paul used the term *episkopoi* (overseers) to address church leaders in Philippi, which was a neighboring church in Macedonia (Phil. 1:1b).

We must remember that on the second journey, Luke stayed on in Philippi for at least six to eight years after Paul, Silas, and Timothy left for Thessalonica. He certainly became involved in appointing spiritual leaders in the Philippian church. We can also be sure that during this lengthy period of time, Luke made a number of trips to both Berea and Thessalonica—a distance of just seventy-five to a hundred miles—and helped establish these churches, which probably involved helping appoint spiritual leaders. It's logical that the leaders in Thessalonica were also called **overseers** rather than **elders**.

This leads to another question: While in Philippi, why would Luke choose the term "overseer" (*episkopos*) rather than "elder" (*presbuteros*)? The answer to this question also comes from the unfolding story in the New Testament. Since the Macedonian churches in Philippi, Thessalonica, and Berea were composed of many Gentile converts (1 Thess. 1:9), and since Luke himself was a Gentile Christian, he would have been very culturally sensitive to the needs of these churches. These cities were Roman colonies (see Acts 16:12), and the term "overseer" (*episkopos*) was used to identify a leader or superintendent of each colony. The term for *overseer* would be far more familiar to these believers than "elder."

The Ephesian Elders (AD 58)

The next episode in the biblical story is the most descriptive and comprehensive regarding elder/overseer functions. It's also a very touching exposure of Paul's heart. The once tough-minded, task-oriented Pharisee who had approved Stephen's death had become a sensitive and compassionate shepherd of shepherds.

Paul was headed for Jerusalem. Knowing that he would be delayed if he entered the province of Asia, he decided "to sail past Ephesus" (Acts 20:16). However, he could not ignore his deep concern for the Ephesian elders/overseers. So he disembarked at Miletus, a coastal village, and sent someone to ask "the **elders** of the church" to make the day's journey to join him.

When these men arrived, Paul reflected on his own three-year ministry in Ephesus and then charged them and warned them very specifically:

> Be on guard for yourselves and for all the flock of which the Holy Spirit has appointed you as **overseers**, to **shepherd** the church of God, which he purchased with his own blood. I know that after my departure **savage wolves** will come in among you, **not sparing the flock.** Men will rise up even from your own number and distort the truth to lure the disciples into following them. Therefore be on the alert, remembering that night and day for three years I never stopped warning each one of you with tears. (Acts 20:28–31)[7]

As Paul reunited and fellowshipped with these men, he reminded them of the way he lived when he ministered among them for three years. He had shown:

- Humility and compassion (Acts 20:19)
- Faithful teaching and preaching (20:20)
- An evangelistic ministry (20:21)
- A nurturing ministry (20:27)
- Pure motives (20:33–35)

Before Paul finally said goodbye and boarded ship, he exhorted these men to remain diligent in their various tasks:

- To be accountable (20:28)
- To give oversight (20:28a)
- To shepherd (20:28b–30)
- To be faithful (20:31)

Note also that both terms are used in this account to describe these church leaders. Luke used "elders" and Paul used "overseers." Again, this demonstrates that these terms were used interchangeably, particularly in churches that had a significant number of both Jewish and Gentile converts.

Leadership Qualifications (AD 63)

Paul's Letter to Timothy

Following Paul's first imprisonment, he left Timothy in Ephesus to handle a leadership crisis. Apparently, what Paul warned against at Miletus had happened (Acts 20:28–31). Some of the elders began teaching "false doctrine" (1 Tim. 1:3–5). However, the current elders/overseers were not the only cause of the problem. There were others who wanted to become leaders and were not qualified. Consequently, Paul outlined a standard for selecting and appointing these men. Interestingly, this happened more than fifteen years after Paul and Barnabas first appointed elders on the first missionary journey in Lystra, Iconium, and Antioch of Pisidia.

Before listing these qualities of maturity, Paul implied that any believing man **could seek the role of eldership**.[8] However, anyone selected and approved should be "growing into maturity with a stature measured by Christ's fullness" (Eph. 4:13).

In this sense, an elder's calling and position was different from those who were the **greater gifts** to the church. Paul made it clear that Jesus Christ "himself gave **some** to be apostles, **some** prophets, **some** evangelists, **some** pastors and teachers" (Eph. 4:11). However, here in his letter to Timothy, Paul also made it clear that "if **anyone** aspires to be an overseer [elder], he desires a noble work" (1 Tim. 3:1). But he must measure up to certain qualifications.

Quality 1—"Above Reproach" (1 Tim. 3:2a)

Paul began this list with an overarching quality: "an **overseer** . . . must be **above reproach**." In essence, this means a spiritual leader should have a "good reputation" among believers as well as unbelievers (3:7a).

Quality 2—"The Husband of One Wife" (1 Tim. 3:2b)

There are various interpretations as to what Paul meant with this phrase. It's my opinion that Paul was dealing primarily with a man's present marital faithfulness to one woman. He was referring to moral purity, and this is why he lists this quality immediately. There is nothing that builds a man's reputation more significantly than being faithful to one woman—his wife. Paul repeats this same requirement in the same sequence in his letter to Titus (Titus 1:6).[9] Essentially, this word means a "good reputation."

Quality 3—"Self-Controlled" (1 Tim. 3:2c)

Paul was describing a man who is stable and steadfast, and his thinking is clear, reflecting faith, hope, and love (1 Thess. 5:8).

Quality 4—"Sensible" (1 Tim. 3:2d)

The Greek term literally means to be "sound in mind." In fact, the word can be translated in various ways—to be "discreet," "sober," "sensible."

Quality 5—"Respectable" (1 Tim. 3:2e)

The most descriptive use of the word for "respectable" [*kosmios*] appears in Paul's letter to Titus when he refers to slaves who are to "**adorn**" [*kosmeo*] the "teaching of God our Savior in everything" (Titus 2:10). Note that the English word "cosmetics" comes from the Greek word *kosmios*. Paul was saying that a man who serves as a spiritual leader should have a life that is like "**cosmetics** to the gospel"—to make the gospel attractive by the way he lives.

Quality 6—"Hospitable" (1 Tim. 3:2f)

Generally speaking, being "hospitable" refers to the way we use our material possessions to serve others—particularly with the homes we live in and the food we eat.

Quality 7—"Able to Teach" (1 Tim. 3:2g)

Paul used the basic Greek word *didaktikos*, translated "able to teach," twice in his letters. The second time he used it was in the second letter to Timothy to describe how this young man should relate to those who disagree with him (2 Tim. 2:23–25). He was to communicate in nonargumentative, nondefensive, and nonthreatening ways. In other words, *didaktikos* refers to a man's character—not his teaching skills per se.

Quality 8—"Not an Excessive Drinker" (1 Tim. 3:3a)

From a larger biblical perspective, most scholars agree that this is primarily a reference to wine. Paul was saying that spiritual leaders should (1) never overindulge and overdrink (Prov. 23:29–30); (2) never cause others to sin by using their freedom in Christ (Rom. 14:21); and (3) never become addicted to anything, including food (Prov. 23:20–21).

Quality 9—"Not a Bully" (1 Tim. 3:3b)

Paul warned leaders to avoid having anger out of control—physically and verbally. Such a violent person is one who is ready to strike out physically.

Quality 10—"Gentle" (1 Tim. 3:3c)

Being "gentle" is in direct contrast to being "violent." There are several Greek words that are translated "gentle," and here Paul chose *epieikes*, which describes a person who is "forbearing," "equitable," "fair," and "reasonable."

Quality 11—"Not Quarrelsome" (1 Tim. 3:3d)

Stated positively, this quality refers to being "peaceable"—a person who avoids arguments. This is a very basic character quality that also describes a leader who is "able to teach."

Quality 12—"Not Greedy for Money" (1 Tim. 3:3e)

A more literal translation is "not a lover of money." This does not mean money in itself is evil. Rather it's "the **love** of money" that is "a **root** of all kinds of evil" (1 Tim. 6:10). Paul was stating that a spiritual leader must model generosity and nonmaterialistic attitudes and actions to those they shepherd.

Quality 13—"Manage His Own Household Competently" (1 Tim. 3:4–5)

If a man is married and has children, a basic criterion for determining whether he is ready for a key leadership role in the church is how well he is functioning as a spiritual leader in his home. Paul viewed a well-ordered family as a true test of a man's maturity and ability to lead other believers. Clearly, he was thinking of grown children who were already married and living in the same compound. However, as Paul wrote to Titus, these grown children should not be "accused of wildness or rebellion"—in other words, extreme forms of sinful behavior (Titus 1:6).

Quality 14—"Not Be a Recent Convert" (1 Tim. 3:6)

Paul warned against appointing men to leadership who were new believers. If we do, we're setting that person up for a direct attack from Satan—and that point of attack will be pridefulness.

Paul's Letter to Titus

At some point following his first prison experience, Paul joined up with Titus and the two of them ministered on the island of Crete. They had a fruitful ministry. Paul then traveled on alone, leaving Titus to "set right what was left undone and . . . to **appoint elders in every town**" (Titus 1:5).

On the way to Necropolis, he penned a follow-up letter, including the qualifications that Titus should look for in selecting and appointing men as elders/overseers (Titus 1:5–9). When we combine the list of qualities Paul outlined in Titus, with the list of qualities in his letter to Timothy, we see a number of them are essentially the same, with minor variation in wording. However, a careful look demonstrates that there are some qualities that were unique in his letter to Timothy and there were also some qualities that were unique in his letter to Titus. This is clear from the following charts:

Characteristics in 1 Timothy and Titus

Qualification	Greek Term
Above reproach (1 Tim. 3:2); blameless (Titus 1:6)	*anegkletos**
Husband of one wife (1 Tim. 3:2; Titus 1:6)	**
Manage his own household competently (1 Tim. 3:4–5)	**
Faithful children (Titus 1:6)	**
Self-controlled (1 Tim. 3:2; Titus 1:8)	*sophron*
Hospitable (1 Tim. 3:2; Titus 1:8)	*philoxenos*
Not an excessive drinker (1 Tim. 3:3; Titus 1:7)	*paroinos*
Not a bully (1 Tim. 3:3; Titus 1:7).	*plektes*
Not greedy (1 Tim. 3:3; Titus 1:7)	*aischrokerdes***

* These two Greek words are basically synonyms.
** Paul used a Greek phrase to describe this concept, not a single term.
*** This Greek word is translated "not greedy for money" in Titus.

Characteristics Unique in 1 Timothy

Qualification	Greek term
Sensible (3:2)	*nephaleos*
Respectable (3:2)	*kosmios*
Able to teach (3:2)	*didaktikos*
Gentle (3:3)	*epieikes*
Not quarrelsome (3:3)	*amachos*
Not be a new convert (3:6)	*neophutos*
Good reputation among outsiders (3:7)	*marturia*

Characteristics Unique in Titus

Qualification	Greek Term
Not arrogant (1:7)	*authades*
Not hot-tempered (1:7)	*orgilos*
Loving what is good (1:8)	*philagathos**
Righteous, just (1:8)	*dikaios*
Holy (1:8)	*hosios*

Self-controlled (1:8)	*egkrate*
Holding to the faithful message (1:9)	**

* Literally, "a lover of good men"
** Paul used a Greek phrase to describe this concept, not a single term.

As we look at the variation in these two lists, it shouldn't surprise us that Paul addressed unique circumstances when he wrote to Timothy in Ephesus and then to Titus in Crete. Though many of the challenges were the same, there were also special problems these men would have to face, and he prescribed certain requirements accordingly. However, each list would certainly stand alone in appointing qualified elders/overseers.[10]

Assistants to Elders/Overseers: Deacons (AD 63)

When under house arrest in Rome, Paul wrote to the Philippians and greeted not only the "overseers" [elders] but also those he identified as "deacons" (Phil. 1:1). This is the first time the term "deacons" (*diakonoi*) is used in the biblical story to designate a group of people who were to serve in this kind of official capacity. During the six to eight years Luke ministered as an apostolic representative in the church in Philippi, he apparently appointed not only those who were to "shepherd the flock" but also those who would assist the overseers/elders in their ministry.

A couple of years later—after Paul was released from prison—he once again used this terminology when he wrote his first letter to Timothy, listing not only the qualifications for elders/overseers, but also for deacons (1 Tim. 3:18–23).

The Elders/Overseers and Deacons: A Supracultural and Cultural Sequence

When Paul and Barnabas returned to Lystra, Iconium, and Antioch of Pisidia on the first missionary journey, they first "appointed **elders** for them in every church" (Acts 14:23). There's no reference to "deacons." And when Paul left Titus in Crete, he was "to appoint **elders** in every town" (Titus 1:5). Again "deacons" are not mentioned.

Does this mean that "deacons" were never appointed in these churches? Not at all. They were no doubt appointed at a later time and for very pragmatic reasons. Initially, these churches were relatively small, and the elders/overseers did not need deacons to assist them in overseeing the church. As the churches increased in numbers, so did special cultural needs, and the elders/overseers faced a similar challenge as the apostles faced in Jerusalem—relative to the neglected widows. They needed to maintain their managing and shepherding priorities.[11]

This overall perspective also helps clarify why Paul and Peter listed and described specific "functions" for elders/overseers but not for deacons. Elder/overseer roles are supracultural and the specific tasks for deacons are cultural.

A Comparison of Elders/Overseers and Deacons

Terms	Qualifications	Functions
Elders/Overseers: First to be appointed; also permanent positions.	Described in detail (1 Tim. 3:1–7; Titus 1:5–9)	Manage/shepherd in ways that are supraculturally defined, e.g., overseeing the total ministry, teaching, admonishing, praying.
Deacons: Appointed only when necessary; position may have been temporary since needs change.	Described in detail (1 Tim. 3:8–13)	Serve in various ways that are culturally defined.

God's people "from every tribe and language and people and nation" (Rev. 5:9) and at any period in history need oversight, teaching, admonishing and prayer. However, by God's design the specific "functions" for deacons are never spelled out in detail—except what is inherent in the title—simply "to serve" [*diakoneo*]. This generic "function" was to be fleshed out in various ways from place to place and at different points in time and history.

Men and Women Deacons

When outlining the qualifications for selecting men to serve as "deacons," Paul inserted four qualifications for women. He used the Greek word *gunaikas*, which can be used to describe any adult woman who is married, who has never been married, or is widowed or divorced (1 Tim. 3:11). Personally, I favor the interpretation that Paul was addressing special qualifications for "women" who would also serve as deacons. If this is correct, we have the following character profile for both men and women who serve as deacons.

Qualifications for Men Who Serve as Deacons

Qualification 1—"Worthy of respect" (1 Tim. 3:8a)

Qualification 2—"Not hypocritical" (3:8b)[12]

Qualification 3—"Not drinking a lot of wine" (3:8c)

Qualification 4—"Not greedy for money" (3:8d) [13]

Qualification 5—"Holding the mystery of the faith with a clear conscience" (3:9)

Qualification 6—"Blameless" (3:10)[14]

Qualifications for Women Who Serve as Deacons

Qualification 1—"Worthy of respect" (3:11a)[15]

Qualification 2—"Not slanderers" (3:11b)

Qualification 3—"Self-controlled" (3:11c)[16]

Qualification 4—"Faithful in everything" (3:11d)[17]

Qualifications for Men (Continued)

Qualification 7—"Husbands of one wife" (3:12a)

Qualification 8—"Managing their children in their own households competently" (3:12)

Men and Women Assistants

In essence, men and women who serve as assistants to elders/overseers in the church were to be very qualified. This is understandable since these individuals were to represent the elders in helping them carry out managing and shepherding responsibilities.[18]

Material Support (AD 63)

Paul's letter to Timothy gives us more information about local church leaders than any other New Testament document. Thus, he addresses the need to support some elders/overseers financially. Consequently, he wrote: "The **elders** who are **good leaders** [who manage well] are to be considered worthy of **double honor**, especially those who work hard at **preaching** and **teaching**" (1 Tim. 5:17).

When interpreting this directive by Paul, some believe that he was dividing the elders/overseers into two categories with separate responsibilities: namely, those who are "managers" or "administrators" and those who **teach**. However, the leadership story that unfolds in the New Testament does not support this interpretation. First of all, *manage* is an overarching responsibility and function and is synonymous with the term *pastor* or *shepherd*. It means to give overall direction to the local church, just as fathers are to manage their families. In other words, elders/overseers were to function like multiple fathers to the church family.

What Paul was actually saying to Timothy is that there will be some elders/overseers who will spend more time than others managing and shepherding the church, particularly in carrying out major "teaching and preaching" functions. Because they were devoting this time to their local church ministries, they needed financial support. They were "worthy of **double honor**," which is related to the word *honorarium*. **All** elders/overseers were to be worthy of honor, but some would be worthy of "double honor" (1 Thess. 5:12–13).

Protection and Discipline (AD 63)

After instructing Timothy regarding the need to make sure the material needs of certain elders/overseers in Ephesus were met, Paul went on to outline guidelines for both **protecting** and **disciplining** spiritual leaders who may be accused of wrongdoing:

> Don't accept an accusation against an **elder** unless it is supported by **two or three witnesses**. **Publicly rebuke those who sin**, so that the rest will be afraid. (1 Tim. 5:19–20)

Protecting Elders

Paul was attempting to protect any leader from false accusations. This was the basic intent of the Old Testament law, which Paul was alluding to (Deut. 19:15). This guideline was designed to protect **any person** from being falsely accused—not just leaders in Israel. However, when Paul wrote to Timothy, he applied it to elders/overseers.

It's a tragedy when a spiritual leader's character is maligned by evil people—which happened to Paul himself (2 Cor. 6:3–13). However, he wanted Timothy to make sure that any elder in Ephesus who was falsely accused was protected.

Disciplining Spiritual Leaders

If an elder/overseer was guilty of a serious accusation, being in violation of the qualifications outlined earlier in his letter to Timothy, Paul stated that he was to be "publicly rebuked." Interpreted properly, this does *not* mean that it should always be before the whole community of believers. Rather, Paul was referring first of all to the other elders. The goal should be to bring about repentance and restoration within the leadership of the church.

This does not mean that this kind of discipline should never be made public to the larger church community. For example, if the accusation involves unfaithfulness and adultery and it proves to be true, an elder should be removed from his role as a shepherd. When this happens, it is virtually impossible to keep this kind of information within the leadership circle. However, when it does become necessary to go before the total congregation (especially to avoid rumors), hopefully the elder/overseer guilty of this kind of sin has already experienced true repentance, even if he must step aside because he is no longer "above reproach" in this area of his life.

Shepherding God's Flock (AD 63)

When the apostle Peter wrote to the churches scattered throughout Asia Minor (1 Peter 1:1), he addressed the elders/overseers as "shepherds" rather than "managers." Though the two words describe the same function in the biblical story, this pastoral title captures in a beautiful way the role of an elder/overseer. Thus, Peter wrote:

I exhort the **elders** among you as a **fellow elder** and witness to the sufferings of Christ, as well as one who shares in the glory about to be revealed: **Shepherd God's flock** among you, not **overseeing** out of compulsion but **willingly**, as God would have you; not out of greed for money but **eagerly**; not lording it over those entrusted to you, but being **examples to the flock**. (1 Peter 5:1–3)

Peter demonstrated sincere humility in identifying himself as a "fellow elder" and a "fellow shepherd." Though he had been called and appointed by Jesus Christ to the highest leadership position in the church—the leader of the apostles—he addressed local church elders as equals.

One of the most encouraging points Peter made in this paragraph relates to the fact that all shepherds have a "chief Shepherd" who will be with them, even "to the end of the age" (Matt. 28:20). And someday He will reward all faithful elders/overseers with "the unfading crown of glory" (1 Peter 5:4). Though we do not understand what this metaphor refers to specifically, one thing is certain. This recognition will endure forever, and these faithful servants will use their rewards, not to glorify themselves, but to honor and worship the Lord Jesus Christ throughout eternity (see Rev. 4:9–11).

Serving with Joy (AD 66–70)

"Remember Your Leaders"

By the time the author of Hebrews wrote about spiritual leaders, both Paul and Peter had probably experienced martyrdom. This may help us understand what the author of Hebrews meant when he wrote: "**Remember your leaders** who **have spoken** God's word to you. As you carefully observe the outcome of **their lives**, imitate **their faith**" (Heb. 13:7).

This exhortation is in the past tense. The reference to "the outcome of their lives" may refer to the way they died since the Greek term *ekpasis*, translated "outcome," may refer to their martyrdom. Could this be a reference to Paul and Peter and others who gave their lives so that the recipients of this letter could become true believers in Jesus Christ?

"Obey Your Leaders"

In his next reference to leaders, it appears that the author moved his thoughts from those who had an "apostolic" and "church planting" ministry among them (past tense) to those who were elders/overseers in local churches (present tense): "Obey your leaders and **submit to them**, since they keep watch over your souls as those who will give an account, so that they can do this with joy and not with grief, for that would be unprofitable for you" (Heb. 13:17).[19]

Concluding Thoughts

The study of local church leadership in the New Testament is an unfolding story. This is in harmony with many biblical subjects. And as we follow this story, which began in Jerusalem and continued throughout the Roman world, a definite profile emerges that yields principles that are enduring truths. When accurately stated, they are supracultural and just as applicable today as they were in the churches in the first century. These principles are outlined, explained, and illustrated in the following chapter.

A Question for Thought and Discussion

Though leadership in the church in Phase 1 and Phase 2 are uniquely different in calling, appointments, and function, what are some of the areas of overlap and correlation?

20

Principles of Leadership

Video Intro from Gene

3lenses.org/c20

As previously noted, there are two phases of leadership described in the New Testament story. Phase 1 involved those who are described as the "greater gifts"—namely, the apostles, prophets, evangelists, pastors, and teachers. They were appointed, gifted, and supernaturally enabled to carry out the Great Commission. They were chosen by Jesus Christ Himself to launch and help establish local communities of faith throughout the then known world (Eph. 4:11–12).

For the most part, these Christ-appointed leaders in Phase 1 also **selected** and **appointed** the leaders in Phase 2—those who were to **manage** and **shepherd** these local communities of faith. Servants, called deacons, were subsequently **appointed** to assist these leaders.

Though those who were and had the greater gifts had a foundational ministry in launching the church, their activities and functions blend with the ministry of local church leaders in yielding supracultural principles.[1]

Titles

Principle 1: Every local church should choose titles for their spiritual leaders that are culturally relevant.

This principle is obvious in the unfolding biblical story. When local communities of faith were predominantly Jewish, the leaders were called elders (*presbuteroi*). This term is directly related to the Jewish culture from the time of Moses. However, when used to refer to leaders of the church, the term took on a different meaning, namely, to manage and shepherd believers in the Lord Jesus Christ.

Paul also used *episkopoi* to describe local church leaders. This term translated "bishop" or "overseer," related directly to the Gentile culture. They were superintendents of Roman colonies. Converts from the Gentile community would understand this terminology but would also be taught that the spiritual leaders had a unique function related to God's divine plan for the church.

A Contemporary Illustration

To illustrate the freedom we have in what we call local church leaders, I'm reminded of the late Jim Peterson's outstanding missionary ministry among university students and professionals in Brazil. These students who were becoming doctors, dentists, architects, and executives were greatly influenced by Marxist ideology. Many didn't believe in God, and most had negative attitudes toward the "institutional church." In fact, to use the Portuguese term for church (*igrejas*) created barriers in communication. They also had negative reactions to the term for "pastor" or "priest" (*padre*). Both terms reminded them of institutionalized religion, which they had rejected.

To overcome this communication barrier, Jim used the Portuguese term *turmas* rather than "churches" to describe the "groups" of believers—in reality "house churches." And to overcome negative reactions to "pastor" or "padre," he used the Portuguese term *mestres*, which means "teachers" to identify these leaders in each of these *turmas* or "groups" of believers. This is certainly in harmony with Jesus' commission when He told the apostles to make disciples and then to **teach** groups of these disciples (Matt. 28:19–20). The term *turmas* is almost synonymous in meaning with the Greek word *ekklesia* (church).

In essence, this is what the apostles did, particularly in using "elders" or "overseers" to describe those who managed and shepherded local churches. Even the author of Hebrews simply used "leaders."

Jim wanted these "teachers" to understand principles of church life and leadership. Consequently, he invited me to conduct seminars in strategic locations in Brazil, focusing on both their pastoral and teaching roles within these *turmas* or house churches.

Pastoral Reflections

When we launched the Fellowship Bible Church movement in the Dallas area, we chose to use the biblical term "elders" because it was a familiar title to most of us. However, as just pointed out, the supracultural principle that focuses on titles allows terminology that communicates best in particular cultural situations. Since we have used the term *elders* to describe our spiritual leaders, I've chosen to use this title in conjunction with the following principles—with the understanding that we did not consider this title biblically necessary. Leadership functions are the absolutes—not how they are identified.

Qualifications

Principle 2: All elders should be appointed based on the maturity profile outlined by Paul in the pastoral epistles.

A Dynamic Bible Study

When I helped launch the first Fellowship Bible Church in 1972, I began to meet with a group of men for Bible study. As a basis of our discussion, I suggested that we use the character qualities outlined by Paul for elders in his letters to Timothy and to Titus (1 Tim. 3:1–7; Titus 1:6–9). We quickly discovered that these character qualities were not just for church leaders but for all men who desired to grow "into maturity with a stature measured by Christ's fullness." This becomes clear when you look at the way these characteristics are used throughout the New Testament letters to describe character development for all believers.

It became a dynamic and life-changing twenty-week experience for all of us. We spent one session on each character quality, defining each one biblically and then spending time sharing with each other how we could develop this quality in our lives to help us be better husbands, better fathers, and better servants of the Lord—wherever that might be.

Shortly after this study, I was encouraged to write a book based on these twenty qualities, *The Measure of a Man* (Baker). Little did I realize this book would continue to be used as a training tool to this day. It's been translated into a number of languages and has never gone out of print since it was first published in 1974. I often say this has happened not because I wrote it but because I used the character qualities recorded by the apostle Paul who received this information directly from the Holy Spirit. Consequently, these are supracultural qualities of maturity.

Elder Appointments

As a result of this study, we eventually selected and appointed our first elders. Initially, we simply directed prospective elders to use this list of qualities for self-evaluation. However, since the man selected to be a prospective elder "must manage his own household competently," we soon discovered it was necessary to involve wives in the evaluation process. We then developed an evaluation scale for both based on these qualities.

We asked these couples to personalize this scale, asking both husbands and wives to evaluate themselves. But over a process of time, we discovered it was important to have others evaluate these couples, using the following form:

"A Stature Measured by Christ's Fullness"
(Eph. 4:13; 1 Tim. 3:1–7; Titus 1:6–9)[2]

Above Reproach

How do you evaluate his/her reputation as a Christian both among fellow believers as well as among non-Christians?

Dissatisfied   1   2   3   4   5   6   7   Satisfied

The Husband of One Wife

How do you evaluate his/her relationship with his/her spouse?

Dissatisfied   1   2   3   4   5   6   7   Satisfied

Temperate

How do you evaluate the degree to which he/she is maintaining balance in his/her Christian experience?

Dissatisfied   1   2   3   4   5   6   7   Satisfied

Prudent

How do you evaluate his/her ability to be wise and discerning?

Dissatisfied   1   2   3   4   5   6   7   Satisfied

Respectable

How satisfied are you with the way his/her life reflects the life of Jesus Christ?

Dissatisfied   1   2   3   4   5   6   7   Satisfied

Hospitable

How do you evaluate his/her level of generosity?

Dissatisfied   1   2   3   4   5   6   7   Satisfied

Able to Teach

How do you evaluate his/her ability to communicate with others who may disagree with him/her?

Dissatisfied   1   2   3   4   5   6   7   Satisfied

Not Addicted to Wine

To what degree are you satisfied with his/her ability to control various kinds of obsessions and compulsions?

Dissatisfied   1   2   3   4   5   6   7   Satisfied

Not Self-Willed

How satisfied are you with his/her ability to relate to other people without being self-centered and controlling?

Dissatisfied   1   2   3   4   5   6   7   Satisfied

Not Quick-Tempered

How satisfied are you with the way he/she handles anger?

Dissatisfied   1   2   3   4   5   6   7   Satisfied

Not Pugnacious

How satisfied are you with his/her ability to control any form of verbal or physical abuse?

Dissatisfied   1   2   3   4   5   6   7   Satisfied

Gentle

How objective and fair-minded is he/she in his/her relationships with others?

Dissatisfied   1   2   3   4   5   6   7   Satisfied

Uncontentious

How satisfied are you with his/her ability to avoid arguments?

Dissatisfied   1   2   3   4   5   6   7   Satisfied

Free from the Love of Money

How satisfied are you with his/her ability to be nonmaterialistic?

Dissatisfied   1   2   3   4   5   6   7   Satisfied

One Who Manages His/Her Own Household Well

If they are a father or mother, how satisfied are you with his/her ability to function in this role according to God's plan?

Dissatisfied   1   2   3   4   5   6   7   Satisfied

Loving What Is Good

To what degree are you satisfied with his/her efforts at "overcoming evil with good"?

Dissatisfied   1   2   3   4   5   6   7   Satisfied

Just ["Upright"]

How satisfied are you with his/her ability to be just and fair in his/her relationships with others?

Dissatisfied   1   2   3   4   5   6   7   Satisfied

Devout ["Holy"]

To what degree are you satisfied with the way his/her life reflects God's holiness?

Dissatisfied   1   2   3   4   5   6   7   Satisfied

Disciplined

How satisfied are you with his/her ability to live a disciplined Christian life?

Dissatisfied   1   2   3   4   5   6   7   Satisfied

Overall Spiritual Maturity

How do you evaluate his/her overall maturity as a Christian?

Dissatisfied   1   2   3   4   5   6   7   Satisfied

Pastoral Reflections

After fifty years involved in church planting, I'm convinced that selecting and appointing elders and wives (if married) based on this maturity profile is absolutely essential to become the church God intended us to be. By the time I was in process of passing my leadership baton to my successor as lead pastor, we had arrived at the following methodology:

Step 1: Selecting Potential Candidates

As elders, in consultation with our wives, we discussed potential candidates—couples we felt measured up to the biblical qualifications and who had faithfully served as small group leaders for a significant period of time.[3]

Step 2: An Invitation to Evaluation

When we narrowed the list, we approached these couples and explained why they had been chosen as potential candidates. We then asked if they would be open to going through an evaluation process, which is described in the following steps. We also made it clear that they were under no obligation to accept this role, even if they were willing to take the following steps.

Step 3: Studying the Biblical Qualifications

If open to taking this step, we asked these prospective couples to meet with the lead pastor and his wife and to spend a number of weeks studying the twenty-character qualities outlined by Paul. In this case, we used my book *The Measure of a Man* as a basis for discussion, interaction, and application. During this process these couple were able to use the evaluation scales to measure the extent that they felt they were ready to become spiritual leaders.[4]

Step 4: A Deeper Relational Experience

At the end of this evaluation process, the lead pastor spent several days with these prospective elders along with several current elders in a wilderness setting—in our case on a secluded ranch in the Big Bend country of Texas. Here we had the opportunity to get to know each other at a deeper level—studying the Word together, praying together, sharing together, and spending time recreationally.

Step 5: Evaluating the Candidates

Our next step was to use the character qualities to evaluate both "husband and wife" candidates. The following church leaders filled out the evaluation form:

1. The current elders and their wives,
2. The senior staff people who knew these couples well, and
3. The people who were part of the small groups these couples were leading.[5]

Step 6: A Final Invitation

Once the elders had assessed all of these evaluations and there were no serious reservations, we then approached the couples and formally invited them to accept the role as an elder couple.

Step 7: Presentation to the Congregation

We then presented these couples to the entire congregation, explaining why they had been chosen and the extensive process they had gone through. We reviewed the qualifications from Paul's letters and asked anyone who may have any serious concerns to contact the lead pastor—in this case yours truly! We also made it clear that the elders would not consider any unsigned responses since these couples would like to meet personally with anyone who had concerns so that they, as a prospective elder couple, could address these issues in their lives.[6]

Step 8: Publicly Commissioned

If there were no reservations stated, we then presented these couples to the total church body. All of our elders and their wives laid hands on these couples and prayed for them and publicly welcomed them into this official position.

Note: Once we instituted this very thorough process, we had virtually no concerns expressed. In fact, people were deeply impressed with the spiritual commitment, openness, and vulnerability of these prospective elders and their wives. It engendered great respect and admiration. These couples served as great models for all believers in terms of "growing into maturity with a stature measured by Christ's fullness" (Eph. 4:13).

Multiple Fathers and Mothers

Principle 3: Elders, along with their wives, should manage and shepherd the church just as fathers and mothers are to care for their families and shepherds are to tend their sheep.[7]

It's clear from the New Testament story that the way local church leaders are to function is based on the family model. To review, Paul made this point clear in his first letter to Timothy. Any man selected to be an elder "must manage his own household competently and have his children under control with all dignity." He then added these words of clarification as to how this qualification relates to the church: "If anyone does not know how to manage his **own household**, how will he take care of **God's church**?" (1 Tim. 3:4–5; see also Titus 1:6).[8]

In essence, Paul was saying that elders who qualify as effective fathers in their own biological families now become "multiple fathers" in managing the spiritual family of God. It follows naturally that their wives and the mothers of their children are to serve with these elders as "multiple mothers" within the church family. Each couple becomes a father-mother team.

"God's Household"

To comprehend how the household model should function, it's important to understand that each local church in Scripture is also defined as a family. Both Paul and Peter have reminded us that we are "members of God's household" (Eph. 2:19; see also 1 Peter 2:5; 4:17). This concept is reinforced manyfold with nearly two hundred references that describe believers as "brothers and sisters in Christ" (see Appendix B).

God's Household

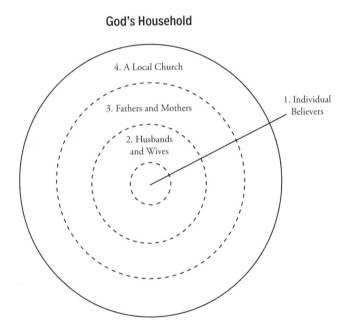

More specifically, note the chart to discover why each community of faith is a spiritual family. This visual describes the local church and the social units within this "spiritual family."

1. The Scriptures teach that as individuals, we become members of God's family by putting our faith in the Lord Jesus Christ

and experiencing the new birth (John 3:3; Eph. 2:8–9).

2. According to God's design, most individual believers will marry, creating marital relationships and couples within God's family (Gen. 2:24; Matt. 19:5; Eph. 5:31).

3. Again, according to God's design, most married couples will have children, creating physical families. Husbands and wives become fathers and mothers. Note: Many New Testament churches were started as individual households (see chapter 7).

4. Every local church is God's family or household composed of believers—individuals, married couples, and physical families.[9]

A Biblical Leadership Model

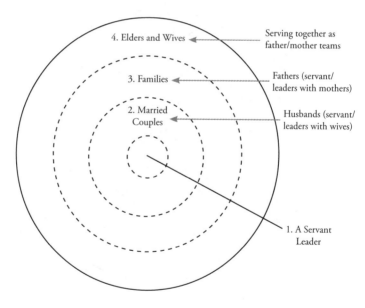

The chart illustrates how the family model should function in terms of leadership within the family of God.

1. Any Christlike believer who is selected and approved can become a servant-leader in the church (1 Tim. 3:1ff).[10]

2. Husbands are to function as Christlike servant-leaders with their wives who together become mutual servant-leaders (Eph. 5:22–23, 25).[11]

3. Within God's ideal plan, Christlike fathers are to function as the primary servant-leaders, managing their own families well (1 Tim. 3:4–5; Titus 1:6). Christlike mothers are to be servant-leaders with fathers in nurturing their children (1 Thess. 2:7, 11). Mature fathers also lead with a teachable spirit.[12]

4. Christlike elders and their wives are to serve together as servant-leaders within the family of God, just as they serve together as fathers and mothers in leading their physical families. Though elders occupy this official position, their wives assist them in their leadership role—just as they help nurture their children in their own households.

Managing and Shepherding Functions

Principle 4: All elders should make sure they manage and shepherd the church well by maintaining six important functions:

Praying for the Sick (James 5:13–16)

As my fellow elders and I studied local church leadership in the biblical story, we noticed that this responsibility is mentioned early in the biblical story. Consequently, we needed to communicate more deliberately that we were available to pray for anyone who requested prayer for healing—regardless of the nature of the illness.[13]

Teaching the Word of God (Titus 1:9a)

Most formal teaching naturally involves those elders/pastors who devote significant time to the ministry. Paul describes them as those elders who "are to be considered worthy of **double honor**, especially those who work hard at **preaching** and **teaching**" (1 Tim. 5:17).[14]

In my own role as an elder "considered worthy of double honor," I served as the lead pastor/teacher, regularly explaining the Scriptures in a formal sense to the total congregation. At times I shared this role with other staff pastors. In some unique situations, I also invited non-staff elders/pastors to present messages to the total congregation. In fact, I still remember a message titled "Love, Love, Love" that was presented by a non-staff elder nearly fifty years ago. Though his full-time profession was dentistry, he was an excellent Bible teacher.[15]

Though our non-staff elders/pastors had full-time jobs in the business world, they were also uniquely involved in shepherding and teaching small groups. In addition, they had many one-on-one opportunities to "teach" as people sought guidance as how to live day by day in the will of God. This is what "spiritual fathering" is all about.

On one occasion a businessman and his wife asked me for wisdom regarding a potential business venture. To answer their questions, I suggested they consult with two of our elders—a retired banking executive and another elder who was operating his own employee benefit consulting company.

After listening carefully and considering biblical principles and various pragmatic factors, both elders shared they had reservations because of potential financial risks. However, they recommended that this couple consult further with another elder who was involved in more entrepreneurial business ventures. Again, they did—and received the same advice regarding serious risks—affirming the wisdom from the two previous elders.

Though these three men were not "teaching the Word of God" in a formal setting, they were functioning in a very important "teaching role." They had far more wisdom than I did in terms of evaluating this potential business venture. This is why those of us who have been equipped theologically in educational institutions should look to elders who have this kind of business experience to help with this kind of advice, counseling, and "teaching."

Disciplining Unruly Believers (Gal. 6:1–2)

On one occasion, a well-known Christian businessman in our church decided to leave his wife and family to have a relationship with a married woman. I knew this man well and was shocked. One of my fellow elders and I, following Paul's instructions in Galatians 6:1–2, went to his place of business, walked into his office, and told him we had come to plead with him to return to his wife and family.

He was angry and asked us to leave. However, we firmly insisted that we talk—and seeing that we were not to be deterred, he consented to meet in a private place. At one point, my fellow elder—himself a businessman—placed his hand on this man's arm and, with tears streaming down his cheeks, pleaded with him to reconsider his decision. After a two-hour session, he finally consented to see a Christian counselor.

Weeks went by, but I'll never forget the day I saw this man enter the back of the church. After the service, he walked up to me with tears in his eyes. Putting his burly arms around me—and with a trembling voice—he said, "Thank God, you didn't let me go!" His relationship had been restored with his wife and God gave them another ten wonderful years together before she died of cancer. After a period of time, he was also restored to serving on several significant Christian ministry boards.

On another occasion during this whole process of restoration, he said, "Gene, I'll be indebted to you the rest of my life." That makes being a "shepherd" worth all the time and effort.

This, of course, is a wonderful story. I love to tell it. But I also remember another elder and I going through the same process with another man who had left his wife and family. Though we pleaded with him to reverse his decision, he rejected our words of concern and refused to seek counseling and help. He had also stopped attending our church services.

The Lord has never promised that we'll always be successful in attempting to restore "sheep" who have wandered into the "thicket" of sin. But hopefully, in the final analysis, this man never forgot our love and concern for him and ultimately repented and sought forgiveness.

Overseeing the Material Needs of the Church (Acts 11:29–30)

Some believe that the oversight of the financial and other material needs in the church is the responsibility of a different group of leaders—not the elders. They often tend to classify a shepherding ministry as "spiritual" and "financial concerns" as "nonspiritual." However, in helping with the economic crisis in Judea, it's important to remember that the disciples in Antioch sent their financial gifts to "the elders." These leaders had ultimate responsibility to make sure these funds were distributed properly (Acts 11:29–30).

The household model does not separate "spiritual" and "financial concerns." Biblically, a "father" is ultimately responsible for the material welfare of his family. He may, of course, "delegate" many aspects of this task to his wife. This I've done over the years because of my wife's budgetary and financial skills—which has given me more time for other responsibilities. We must recognize, however, that some wives do not feel comfortable with this task.

But here's the important point. Elders have the same ultimate responsibility for the family of God. They can certainly delegate this task to qualified assistants—such as deacons. They should not get bogged down with details that sidetrack them from other important priorities, which the apostles certainly modeled when the Grecian widows were being neglected in the daily distribution of food. However, elders are ultimately accountable for the financial and material welfare of the church family—definitely a spiritual task and duty.

Maintaining Doctrinal Purity (Acts 20:28–31)

On one occasion, we faced this challenge when a prominent leader of one of the women's Bible study groups began to disseminate a very inaccurate view regarding the second coming of Christ. Unfortunately, she was influenced by a man who claimed to know who the antichrist was and when Jesus would return. She was so forceful in communicating this information that a number of women became very confused.

As elders, we had to deal with this matter sensitively but directly. We delegated the matter to one of our competent staff pastors who met with this group of women and exposed this erroneous view of eschatology. He then privately and sensitively asked this teacher to resign. She did so, but predictably, left our church believing she was still right.

Fortunately, the damage was minimal, but had we not stepped in when we did, we would have faced a much more serious problem of confusion and disunity because of false teaching. In fact, it was beginning to affect husband-wife relationships. Our responsibility as elders was and is to maintain doctrinal purity. Incidentally, this staff pastor who helped resolve this problem demonstrated unusual pastoral skills and eventually became my successor.

Modeling Christlike Behavior (1 Cor. 11:1; 1 Tim. 3:1–7; Titus 1:6–9)

Though it's certainly important to communicate God's Word didactically, it's what people see in our lives that gives weight to our words. This is why the qualifications for elders are so important. If we are to "teach the Word of God" effectively, we must simultaneously "live the Word of God."

Over the years, I've found this to be one of the most significant factors in helping our people to grow and mature in Jesus Christ. Again and again, I have gotten feedback as to how much our people admire our elders and their commitment to godliness. This becomes particularly effective in terms of the family model. When mature spiritual leaders and their wives serve effectively as "fathers and mothers" to the church family, people can see positive marital and family role models.

This does not mean spiritual leaders have perfect relationships. When they and their wives are also vulnerable role models who share their own relational challenges, it motivates others to grow in their relationships in a powerful way. It demonstrates we are all in process of "growing into maturity with a stature measured by Christ's fullness" (Eph. 4:3).

A Primary Leader

Principle 5: The elders in a local church need a primary pastoral leader who both leads and serves, and who is also accountable to his fellow spiritual leaders.

New Testament authors record very little regarding having a primary leader among the elders. However, it's important to remember that this biblical record is an unfolding story that is open-ended. Taken out of biblical and historical context, this lack of specificity in ecclesiology can lead to some very erroneous and impractical conclusions.

We need to understand that this principle that focuses on a primary leader is obvious in the Old Testament with leaders like Moses, Joshua, Ezra, and Nehemiah—and others. It's also illustrated in the larger setting in the New Testament. Jesus prepared Peter to become the leader of the apostles, which is very obvious in the Gospels. Peter assumed this role as recorded in the book of Acts. Paul was also clearly the leader of his various missionary teams and in terms of the local church, James, the half-brother of Christ, emerged as the primary leader among the elders in Jerusalem (Acts 12:17; 15:13–21; 21:18).[16]

Both Timothy and Titus also illustrate how important it is to have a primary leader in any given situation. In these New Testament settings, they were apostolic representatives. Though their positions were not permanent in local churches, they were to take a strong, primary leadership role in Ephesus and Crete to make sure that qualified leaders were appointed.

In the early days of my church planting ministry, I was so committed to plurality in leadership—which I believe is a biblical concept—that I often denied that I was indeed the primary leader. If you asked me who led the church, I would say "the elders." In essence, that was a true statement. If you then asked me who led "the elders," I would answer, "We lead the church together." Again, this was a true statement. However, I did not answer the questions adequately. The facts are that "I led the elders" and together "we led the church." In those early years, I communicated a model of leadership I was not actually practicing.

Since then, I have made it clear that as the primary leader of the elders, I have functioned at three levels.

Leadership Accountability Model

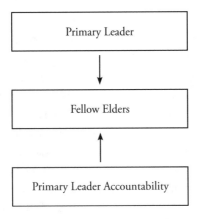

First, I looked to my fellow spiritual leaders as my counselors and advisors. Ultimately, I was accountable to them. I asked them to take final responsibility to make sure I was fulfilling my role properly. They had final authority to guide me, correct me, and, if need be, remove me from my position should I fail to function as a competent spiritual leader. I put this in writing so I would be fully accountable.

Second, I viewed my role as an elder/pastor as "one among equals" in the decision-making process. Though I brought recommendations and proposals to the elders, final decisions were made by the total body of elders. Though I also led the elders, I considered myself as one of the decision-makers.

Third, I viewed my role as serving as pastor and leader of the elders—as did they. In fact, I eventually chaired the elder board. In this role, I served as a "pastor to the pastors" and "leader of the leaders."[17] I was also responsible to take the lead in consultation with the other elders to make sure all staff and non-staff leaders measured up to biblical qualifications and fulfilled their functions. I felt this overall arrangement was in harmony with what Jesus modeled and then taught Peter and the other apostles—that He who is greatest is to be a servant (Matt. 20:26; Luke 22:26).[18]

Carrying Out the Great Commission

Principle 6: Though the apostles and some other New Testament leaders had an unusual calling and supernatural enablement to carry out the Great Commission, those who serve as elders in local churches should lead in carrying out the Great Commission.

To apply this principle, local church elders should first of all help all believers to communicate and verify the gospel in their own sphere of influence by manifesting love and unity. As I've stated throughout this book, this is what Jesus commanded in the upper room and prayed for on the way to the garden of Gethsemane. He made it crystal clear why this is so vital in "making disciples." Twice in His prayer, He made this purpose clear:

"That the world may **believe** you sent me" (John 17:21).

"That the world may **know** you have sent me" (17:23).

As a pastor, I made it a point to teach these passages of Scripture creatively at least once a year, sometimes more. In terms of being and doing what Jesus commanded and prayed for, we need constant reminders. More importantly, the way believers relate to one another is also a constant reminder of whether or not this is happening. Love and unity in itself are the greatest means to practice what I like to call "body evangelism." Though we cannot change water to wine or raise the dead, we can participate in another miraculous manifestation—loving one another as He loved us, demonstrating the oneness Jesus Christ had with the Father, enabling Him to be the incarnate Son of God.[19]

Second, elders should model this love and unity to all believers. However, the "message incarnate" is not sufficient in itself. People need to not only "see" the gospel message—they need to "hear" it as well.

This kind of training involves two significant learning experiences. All believers need to hear the gospel message presented publicly. I've attempted to use the natural opportunities that are particularly associated with both communion and baptism. Not only can we explain the reason for Christ's death and resurrection, but we can invite people to receive the Lord Jesus Christ as personal Savior.

Pastors should also present the gospel in conjunction with messages to the total congregation. I'm not implying that we turn teaching situations into simple gospel messages that leave people "unfed" with the Word of God. I've discovered there are many opportunities within in-depth portions of Scripture that enable us to explain the gospel. In fact, the Holy Spirit has woven these opportunities into the very fabric of Scripture. I've discovered that unsaved people appreciate understanding the unique depth inherent in Scripture. We simply need to teach the totality of the Word of God clearly, imaginatively, and always "speaking the truth in love" (Eph. 4:15).

Third, we should teach all believers that our mission field today is not only our local communities, but the world. Metaphorically, we are to be witnesses in our own "**Jerusalem**, in all **Judea** and **Samaria**, and to the **ends of the earth**" (Acts 1:8). There are those who desire to participate in "apostolic, prophetic, evangelistic and pastoral and teaching ministries" in areas where there is no gospel witness or where churches are few and far between.

Today, there are many unique ways to help make this happen. For example, it includes short term mission trips as well as settling into countries virtually for a lifetime. These dedicated believers serve as our representatives in carrying the gospel to the world. Biblically, they need our prayers and financial support.

At one point, I challenged my fellow non-staff elders to think in terms of how they might have a unique ministry in other parts of the world. I suggested they consider how they might utilize their financial resources to enable them to make this happen. More specifically, I suggested they plan their retirement income to enable them to have a self-supported mission ministry.

Without interfering with their financial giving to our church, some began immediately to have a ministry in various countries. In fact, one elder who was very well off took early retirement and he and his wife made a dozen trips to a foreign country to have a Bible teaching ministry. Since they served as an Aquila-Priscilla team, they supported themselves financially in making these trips.

Obviously not all of these men could afford this kind of mission activity. However, most of them participated in a unique way. They acknowledged that without my suggestion, they would have not considered these opportunities.

As I was preparing this chapter for publication, I became aware of an incredible ministry in Kenya, Africa. Dr. Bob Mendonsa and his wife, Julie, started taking yearly trips to Kijabe, Kenya, where he worked as a volunteer orthopedic surgeon in a mission hospital. During that time, Bob and Julie developed a vision and a plan to move to Kenya and build a children's home. They retired from their full-time jobs as surgeon and teacher in Texas, and they now work together full-time in a ministry called Naomi's Village. This village provides complete care for almost a hundred Kenyan children who were left orphaned by terrorism, AIDS, disasters, and domestic violence in the Great Rift Valley. Not only do they serve these children who have no parents, but they serve community families struggling with the burden of generational poverty. As I pen these words, they have a staff of 211 Kenyans who help operate this ministry.

I was deeply impressed with Bob and Julie's life story—a successful surgeon and teacher in North Dallas who gave up their professions to dedicate their life to this ministry. It is a privilege for local churches to be involved in supporting this kind of ministry.

Adequate Forms

Principle 7: Elders are responsible to make sure that adequate forms and structures are developed to carry out the biblical functions inherent in the previous principles.

Under the leadership and inspiration of the Holy Spirit, the authors of Scripture purposely left unanswered a number of "form" questions in order for us to be both biblically accurate and culturally efficient. For example, here are ten form questions that need to be answered in today's churches:

1. How old should these elders be?
2. What specific methodologies should be used to select and appoint qualified spiritual leaders?
3. How many elders should be appointed to lead a single church?
4. How long should these leaders serve?
5. How should elders make decisions?
6. How do elders and staff pastors work together?
7. Shouldn't all staff pastors be elders?
8. Which is more biblical—a congregational form of church government or an elder-led church?
9. What "form changes" need to be made as the church grows numerically?
10. How should the "family model" work to be in harmony with other biblical principles?

A Question for Thought and Discussion

If elders/overseers were to shepherd, teach, and manage local churches, why is there no reference to the gifts of pastoring, teaching, and administration in the list of qualifications?

21

Biblical Examples of Administration and Organization

Video Intro from Gene

3lenses.org/c21

The subject of administration and organization in Scripture is simply an extension of how to develop cultural forms and utilize creative methods to carry out the Great Commission. There is, though, one specific difference from what we've observed thus far. Up to this point our focus has been on the New Testament story and the way the apostles and subsequently the body of Christ carried out the Great Commission. But in terms of administration and organization, the *whole* biblical story gives us the same basic process and principles.

Following are two Old Testament and two New Testament situations that demonstrate how Moses, Nehemiah, and the apostles administered and organized God's work.

A Comparative Study

The Old Testament example in Exodus involved multiplied thousands of Israelites camped in the wilderness. The New Testament example involved a rapidly growing group of Christians in Jerusalem, also numbering in the thousands.[1]

The following chart outlines the **problems**, the **solutions**, and the **results** recorded in these passages.

The Israelites in the Wilderness (Ex. 18:13–27; Deut. 1:9–18)	The Church in Jerusalem (Acts 6:1–7)
The Problem: Exodus 18	**The Problem: Acts 6**
v. 13—The people stood in line from morning until evening. v. 14—Moses sat alone trying to solve their problems, serving as a **judge** in matters of interpersonal relationships, and **teaching them the laws of God**. v. 18—This never-ending process created undue stress for Moses and discontentment among the people as well.	v. 1—The disciples were multiplying rapidly, and the Hellenistic widows were being neglected in the daily serving of food. Consequently, the Grecian Jews began to complain. v. 2—The twelve apostles were concerned but couldn't neglect their primary responsibilities . . . to **teach the Word of God** and **devote themselves to prayer**.
The Solution: Exodus 18	**The Solution: Acts 6**
v. 19—Moses' father-in-law, Jethro, advised Moses to establish priorities —to serve as a **mediator between the people and God**. —to **teach the people the laws of God**. vv. 20–21—In turn, he should **delegate** handling the interpersonal problems of everyday life to a **select group of qualified men**—"able men, who fear God, men of truth, those who hate dishonest gain" (NASB). v. 22—These qualified men were to handle the **minor matters**, and only the **major problems** should be filtered through to Moses. **Deuteronomy 1** vv. 9–12—Moses **communicated** his problem to the people.	v. 2—The Twelve called a meeting of the Grecian disciples. vv. 3–5—They informed them regarding their major priorities: **prayer** and the **ministry of the Word**. v. 3—The apostles instructed the **Grecian believers** to **select seven qualified individuals** from among them to care for the widows' needs—"men of good reputation, full of the Spirit and wisdom" (NASB). The apostles would then be able to focus on their priorities. v. 6—The **apostles then confirmed** these men through prayer and by laying their hands on them.

The Solution: Exodus 18	The Solution: Acts 6
v. 13—He further instructed **each tribe to choose** those who were "wise and discerning and informed"; **Moses then appointed** them as heads. vv. 16–18—Moses **carefully instructed** the leaders in everything they were to do.	

The Results: Exodus 18	The Results: Acts 6
vv. 22–23—Moses was assisted in his responsibilities and **able to endure** the demands of his leadership role. Furthermore, the **people's needs were met**.	v. 7—The widows' **needs were met, unity was restored**, and the apostles were able to fulfill their primary responsibilities. Consequently, the Word of God kept on spreading and the number of believers kept on increasing greatly.

The Nature of the Problems

Both Moses and the apostles had more than they could do personally, and both were becoming involved in details that kept them from fulfilling their primary responsibilities. Since the children of Israel lined up to state their grievances and to have Moses solve their problems, he was unable to endure the physical and psychological stress. Evidently, some stood in line all day long and perhaps even by nightfall did not have a hearing with Moses (Ex. 18:13).

It doesn't take much imagination to reconstruct the tense mood and emotional outbursts that must have taken place among these people. Remember, too, that the children of Israel had already demonstrated their desire to return to Egypt. They were not happy people.

In the New Testament setting, the God-fearing Grecian Jews who had come to Jerusalem to worship and had become believers faced a similar problem. This cultural segment of the Jewish people became very unhappy when their widows were being neglected in this semi-communal system.

We must understand that the local Jewish widows—called Hebrews—who lived in Judea and particularly in the vicinity of Jerusalem were being cared for. The Grecian widows who had come from other countries to worship—such as Mesopotamia, Cappadocia, Pontus, Asia, Egypt, and Rome—were being neglected in the daily distribution of food. They, too, had stayed in Jerusalem following the birth of the church. It's understandable how they could have been neglected—especially because of favoritism.

The Way the Problems Were Solved

Note the four important similarities in these two settings. *First,* both Moses and the apostles *established priorities.* Furthermore, these priorities were similar. Both Moses and the apostles were to teach the Word of God and were to continue a ministry of prayer.

The *second* similarity is that both Moses and the apostles were to delegate *responsibilities to qualified leaders.* This correlates with what we've observed more in-depth in the chapters on leadership in the church (see chapters 19 and 20).

Without question, the requirements in both circumstances were essential in solving the problems. Both Moses and the apostles needed honest and wise men they could trust. If these qualities were lacking, these men would have compounded the problems.

The *third* similarity involved *representation.* The people themselves were involved in selecting those who were responsible for resolving the problems. In the Old Testament setting, each tribe was involved in selecting those who would represent them. In the New Testament setting, the Grecians themselves selected the seven men.[2]

A *fourth* similarity is that in both circumstances, the *organizational structures set up were temporary.* When the children of Israel settled in the land, the system changed. And in a relatively short period of time, persecution drove the believers from other parts of the Roman world out of Jerusalem and Judea. The semi-communal system ceased to exist and some of the men who were serving tables became traveling evangelists (Acts 7–8). In both examples, the cultural dynamics changed, creating new needs, which called for new forms and structures.

The Significance of the Results

The results are clearly delineated in the biblical record. Both Moses and the apostles were able to carry out their primary tasks and the people's needs were met. Had they not addressed the problems administratively and organizationally, the spiritual and social dynamics would have deteriorated, resulting in growing dissatisfaction, resentment, and disunity.

Nehemiah's Leadership Model (Neh. 1–6)

Nehemiah stands out on the pages of the Old Testament as a man who understood and practiced outstanding leadership skills. From the moment he faced the morale problem in Jerusalem until it was resolved, he practiced outstanding administrative and organizational principles.

Rebuilding the Walls in Jerusalem

The Problem

1:2–3   Nehemiah, cupbearer to the king of Persia, received a report that the remnant in Judah who had returned were in great distress because the walls of Jerusalem were broken down and burned with fire.

1:4   Nehemiah's response was one of depression and sadness.

The Solution

1:4–11   Nehemiah fasted and prayed, waiting for an opportunity to share this problem with the king.

2:6   Eventually, the king responded to Nehemiah's request for help.

2:12–16   When Nehemiah arrived in Jerusalem, he spent three nights secretly surveying the situation and developing a comprehensive strategy.

2:17–3:32 Nehemiah then revealed his plan and asked the people to help him rebuild the walls. Because of this detailed proposal and Nehemiah's testimony regarding God's answer to his prayers, the people overcame their morale problems and responded positively.

4:1–13   When the enemies of Israel tried to stop their work, the people prayed and set up a guard day and night.

4:14   When the people grew fearful, Nehemiah told them (1) not to be afraid, (2) to remember the greatness of God, and (3) to fight for the sake of their families.

6:15   They completed the walls in an amazing fifty-two days.

The Results

6:16   When the enemies of Israel witnessed this incredible feat and heard the rejoicing of Israel, "they lost their confidence." They recognized that this could have been achieved only "with the help of God."

12:27–43 The people sang and praised God, purifying themselves and the city, and offered sacrifices to God.

The Nature of the Problem

The broken walls of Jerusalem resulted in ridicule, reproach, and humiliation for the people of Judah. They were mistreated and abused. Many of the Jews were afraid to even live within the city. They remained a scattered, fearful people, even though they were living in the land of Judah. They had little security from their enemies and lived in constant fear and anxiety. To make matters worse, many were living out of fellowship with God.

The Way the Problem Was Solved

Nehemiah's approach to solving this problem is a marvelous example of God-oriented administrative and organizational skills that included both divine and human dimensions.

First, Nehemiah sought wisdom and help from God (1:4–11). Struck with the terrible plight of his people, Nehemiah's initial step was to pray and fast.

- He acknowledged God's greatness.
- He confessed Israel's sins (including his own).
- He reminded God of His promises to regather the children of Israel if they repented.

- He then prayed specifically, asking the Lord to grant him favor with the king whom he served.

Second, Nehemiah did all he could from a human perspective to build bridges to the king (2:1–10). Nehemiah had already laid the groundwork for this bridge. He had been a good servant, and his sadness was obvious to the king in view of his previous happy countenance.

As Nehemiah's specific prayer was beginning to be answered, he was both spiritually and pragmatically ready with the appropriate responses. Then, when the king asked why he was so downcast, at that moment Nehemiah again asked God for wisdom as he requested that the king might send him to rebuild the walls.

When given a favorable reply, Nehemiah took another bold step! He asked for official letters from the king to be able to pass unhindered through various regions. He even asked for the privilege of cutting down trees from the king's forest that was in the vicinity of Jerusalem. These requests reveal that while Nehemiah was initially praying and fasting, he was also doing significant research and developing a potential solution to the problem.

Third, when Nehemiah arrived in Jerusalem, he secretly evaluated the damage and then developed his administrative and organizational strategy (2:11–16; 3:1–32).

On three successive nights, Nehemiah carefully inspected and evaluated the damage to the walls. He knew that he needed to have his facts in hand, even before he reported on why he had come. He understood the low morale and knew he had to have his plan developed before he challenged the people to rebuild the wall. To release this information prematurely may have allowed details of the plan to leak out to the enemies of Israel, who would have scoffed even more and planned retaliation even before the people began the rebuilding process.

Nehemiah mapped out this plan carefully and with wisdom. Over twenty-five times the phrase "next to him/them" or "after him/them" is used to designate the organizational structure. Every person or group who could work were assigned to a task. Furthermore, they were assigned by residence.

Nehemiah knew why this was necessary:

- Those who were assigned to sections of the wall near their homes would be more personally involved and more highly motivated.
- They would not have to travel to another part of the city to do the job, wasting valuable time.
- In case of attack, they would not be tempted to leave their posts, but would stay and protect their families.
- The task would be a family effort, using all available talent.

Obviously, this was a brilliant administrative and organizational strategy.

Fourth, Nehemiah at the right moment revealed the plan to the people, motivating them with both human and divine factors (2:17–20).

He appealed first to their wretched condition—the reproach they were bearing because of the broken walls, and the desolate condition of Jerusalem. Next, he told them how God had miraculously helped him win the favor of the king and his support in this venture. Consequently, the people responded positively and corporately—and no doubt shouted, "Let's start rebuilding" (2:18b). With God's help and this well-ordered strategy, people believed they could accomplish this goal!

Fifth, Nehemiah supervised the work closely, facing and solving unforeseen problems as they arose during the process (4:1–12; 6:15).

Even though the people were willing to tackle this enormous task, they faced constant ridicule and hostility. When it became obvious their enemies were planning to attack to stop the work, Nehemiah prepared for the battle by placing people all around the wall. As just stated, he stationed them by families (4:13). If the worker's family members had been in another place in the city or outside the walls, the temptation would be to run to them. Now they would have to fight to protect them—on location!

From that moment on some worked and some guarded; some worked with one hand and carried a weapon in the other; those who had to work with both hands kept their swords at their sides. And in case of attack, a trumpet call would quickly gather them together.

No one was to go out of Jerusalem at night; rather they were to stand guard. And in the final days of building, Nehemiah and many of his workers and guards never removed their clothes nor laid down their weapons, even when they stopped for a drink of water (4:23). Against almost impossible odds, they completed the wall in fifty-two days.

The Significance of the Results

The results of Nehemiah's administrative and organizational skills are obvious all the way through this enormous task. At every step along the way, he achieved certain significant goals. And while supervising the work, Nehemiah also helped straighten out some difficult social and financial problems (5:1–19) and warded off a subtle attack on his own life (6:1–14).

The final results of this project were phenomenal and intensely rewarding. Imagine how Nehemiah felt when he heard the people singing and praising God at the dedication of the wall (12:27–29, 31–42).

The Apostles and Elders in Jerusalem (Acts 15:1–35)

The following New Testament illustration has similarities to the way Nehemiah led the Jews to rebuild the walls in Jerusalem. However, this problem was basically theological.

The Problem

15:1   Certain religious Jews from Jerusalem were teaching false doctrines in Antioch—that the Gentiles must be circumcised to be saved.

15:2   Paul and Barnabas debated the issue publicly but could not solve the problem.

The Solution

15:2–3 The church leadership in Antioch decided to seek guidance and help from the apostles and elders at Jerusalem.

15:4   They sent a delegation with Paul and Barnabas who reported to the apostles and elders and some additional believers how Gentiles were being converted through faith alone.

15:6   The apostles and elders then met in a closed session to discuss the matter.

15:7–11   Peter reminded those gathered of the conversion of the Gentile Cornelius and his household—definitely a part from being circumcised and keeping other aspects of the law.

15:12   Paul and Barnabas affirmed Peter's report and gave specific testimony regarding the "signs and wonders God had done through them among the Gentiles."

15:13–21   James then made reference to Old Testament prophets and how they had predicted Gentile conversion; he then proposed a solution to the problem—a letter clarifying the theological issue.

15:22   The apostles, elders, and others who were assembled agreed to this proposal.

15:22–32   Judas and Silas were chosen by everyone gathered to accompany Paul and Barnabas as they delivered the letter.[3]

The Results

15:31   The church in Antioch rejoiced when they heard the contents of the letter.

15:33   Judas and Silas were sent back to Jerusalem in peace.

15:35   The work of God continued unhindered.

16:4–5   The letter was also delivered by Paul, Silas, and Timothy to many of the new churches.

The Nature of the Problem

This was a serious theological issue involving God's plan of salvation. If this problem had not been solved, it would have affected all the newly formed churches. Antioch was a prominent center of Christian activity, and it would not be long until the news of the disagreement and debate would have spread to the new believers scattered throughout the New Testament world who were already facing this theological issue because of false teachers. The results would be continued confusion, disillusionment, disunity, and rejection by many of the redemptive message.

The Way the Problem Was Solved

It did not take long for the leaders in the Antiochian church to recognize the explosive nature of this problem. They acted quickly and with wisdom. They met together and decided this problem was beyond their ability to handle. They needed assistance, so they chose a delegation to accompany Paul and Barnabas who set off for Jerusalem—the birthplace of the church.

When these representatives arrived, there were no attacks on personalities. There were no accusations against the Jerusalem church. They simply reported what God was doing in the Gentile world. And it was this noncritical and objective tactic that set the tone for this whole conference. And, step by step under the leadership of men who were seeking God's will, the confusion regarding how we're saved was clarified. Salvation is by grace through faith!

The Significance of the Results

When this theological problem was solved, the results were immediate. Most importantly, there was peace and unity among believers—the very thing Jesus had prayed for on His way to the garden of Gethsemane (John 17:20–23). The work of God continued without interruption and without being sidetracked onto peripheral issues.

Summary

Here, then, are four biblical examples of developing administrative and organizational structures and procedures. Though all vary, they have several things in common: a problem arose, a solution was sought, and results were achieved. More than that, all four examples yield some very significant supracultural principles. These principles are outlined and explained in the chapter to follow.

A Question for Thought and Discussion

As you continue to reflect on these four examples, what would have happened in each situation if those in leadership failed to face reality?

22

Principles of Administration and Organization

Video Intro from Gene

3lenses.org/c22

As we've noted in the previous chapter, there are relatively few references to detailed administrative actions and organizational structures in the New Testament. Those that are recorded are only partially described. Consequently, this lack of conformity and incompleteness in the biblical record cannot be prescriptive, absolute, or normative. Without doubt this lack of specificity is by divine design so we would not absolutize forms and structures.

However, as we've observed in the previous chapter, there are four very illuminating examples in the Old and New Testaments. In this chapter, we'll look at the enduring, supracultural principles that come from these examples that can guide us in facing challenges and solving problems in our churches today, regardless of our cultural situations.

Principles of Administration
Facing Reality

Principle 1: We must never ignore people problems; rather we must face reality.

The Biblical Examples

As stated in the previous chapter, it doesn't take much imagination to conclude what would have happened among the children of Israel if Moses had ignored Jethro's advice at Mount Sinai (Ex. 18:19–23), or if the apostles had not listened to the report regarding the murmuring of the Hellenists in the church in Jerusalem (Acts 6:1). Moses would have faced an unresolvable problem, and the first church may have splintered. Humanly speaking, Moses may have "died of a heart attack," and the apostles would have been seriously side-tracked in carrying out their God-ordained priorities.

In view of the law and grace theological issue, what if the disciples in Antioch had not faced the reality regarding the heresy that was being taught in Jerusalem? It would have had negative repercussions throughout the New Testament world. In fact, this was already beginning to happen in the churches throughout Galatia, which certainly prompted Paul's letter to these churches.

Nehemiah's circumstances were certainly different. Humanly speaking, he had a good reason to ignore the plight of his people. After all, he was in captivity serving as cupbearer to a pagan king hundreds of miles away. However, he could not escape the pain he felt in his heart, especially since his own immediate family was involved (Neh. 1:1–4). Though Nehemiah knew the task would be tough and filled with unpredictable events—some that might even threaten his life—yet he acted on what he firmly believed was the will of God.

Contemporary Situations

Throughout the New Testament record, church leaders faced people problems and it should not surprise us that the same is true today. Some of these problems relate to numerical growth and changing needs. Some are serious theological and cultural challenges. Some are as old as humankind, and some are new and contemporary. However, as illustrated in both the Old and New Testaments, these problems must be solved in order to faithfully carry out the Great Commission.

As pastoral leaders, we must never ignore these problems. If we do, they may overwhelm us, defeat us, and even cause us to give up. We may even feel hostile and bitter or depressed and discouraged. Unfortunately, we may also rationalize our failures, putting the blame on others for our own unwillingness to face problems.

Unsolvable Problems

There are some church difficulties that seem impossible to resolve. For example, on one occasion I had opportunity to consult with a pastor who had again and again faced serious challenges with the lay leadership in the church. The obstacles he faced in leading the church effectively were clearly related to carnal and outright sinful attitudes and actions.

After listening carefully to what he had consistently tried to do, I concluded that he had made "every effort to keep the unity of the Spirit through the bond of peace" (Eph. 4:3). I also noted the negative impact on his family, and advised him to resign with dignity and to trust the Holy Spirit to deal with certain members of the church board.

Fortunately, when we encounter even the most difficult circumstances realistically and faithfully practice this supracultural principle, we can successfully solve most problems. However, we must always seek God's wisdom to enable us to develop concrete solutions that are in harmony with His will (James 1:5).

Gaining Perspective

Principle 2: We must develop a proper perspective on problems before proposing concrete solutions.

The Biblical Examples

In terms of the Grecian widows who were being neglected, it did not take long for the apostles to see the nature of the problem (Acts 6:1–7). These men acted quickly, developed a plan, arrived at a solution and the positive results were immediate. Luke has recorded that "the word of God spread" and "the disciples increased greatly in number" (Acts 6:7).

313

For Nehemiah, it was a totally different story. It took time to develop a proper perspective. When he arrived on the scene, he devoted three nights to carefully inspecting and evaluating the walls of Jerusalem. Because of the low morale of his fellow Jews and the explosive nature of the situation, he knew he had to gain proper perspective so he could develop a workable plan to rebuild the wall and then publicly announce his strategy—probably to key leaders in Jerusalem.

The problem in the Antiochian and Jerusalem churches was yet different. It was basically a theological problem that needed input from a number of key leaders. It called for a process of reports, debate, and discussion, both in public and in private. And it was the result of this process that led to perspective and an "administrative and organizational" answer—namely, a letter and its deliverance to the churches.

In Moses' situation, he was so close to the problem that he couldn't see the forest for the trees. He knew he faced tremendous demands on his time and energy. He also knew he was leading a group of "unspiritual" and "unpredictable" people. However, he needed perspective and a plan that would help him facilitate his responsibility. Fortunately, his father-in-law Jethro served as a consultant and helped Moses gain perspective, which in turn enabled him to solve the problem.

Contemporary Situations

A great danger that faces every Christian leader today is to ignore the fact that we need help and advice in solving problems. Like Moses, we may act out of ignorance. Or we may feel it will reveal our incompetency. It's easy to allow feelings of insecurity to become a problem of pride.

Either way we tend to ignore the problem, or we proceed to try to solve it alone. This can be disastrous since it will inevitably make the problem worse and actually reflect on our ability to lead. These biblical examples demonstrate that to seek advice is a sign of strength and not of weakness.

This principle also illustrates why a commitment to multiple leadership is so important. Frankly, this is one of the greatest lessons I've learned in pastoral ministry. Early on, I felt it was my personal responsibility to solve problems—not to bother my fellow leaders. Or on second thought, was it because I felt seeking their help might reveal my incompetency or inability to solve problems? Probably at times it involved both reasons.

Thankfully, I quickly learned that people respect us more when we seek advice. They also take ownership in helping solve the problems. And when plans fail, everyone shares in the failure. Most importantly, corporate insight leads to success in resolving problems. There is indeed wisdom that can come from a "multitude of counselors" (Prov. 11:14 KJV).

Prioritizing

Principle 3: We must establish priorities.

The Biblical Examples

In solving the problem with the widows in Acts 6, the apostles specifically practiced this principle. They quickly established their priorities and made them known to those who brought the complaint. They were not suggesting that "serving tables" was unimportant—far from it—but their actions demonstrated that they had certain spiritual responsibilities that they had to fulfill. To maintain their priorities to teach the Word of God and devote themselves to prayer, they needed assistance from other competent men.

One of the main reasons we may have difficulty solving administrative and organizational problems effectively is that we try to solve them all by ourselves. This was Moses' dilemma until he took his father-in-law's advice. He was actually in danger of physical and psychological deterioration caused by undue stress. Fortunately, he recognized this fact and did something about it. Jethro helped him establish his priorities.

Contemporary Situations

Today as pastors and other spiritual leaders, we are often bombarded with many demands on our time. Contemporary culture and its pressures have complicated the lives of people, creating greater needs. Consequently, it is absolutely essential to establish priorities. As pastors particularly, if we don't, we will neglect our primary calling to "teach" and "shepherd" our people.

Personally, I have struggled practicing this principle most of my ministry life—particularly as a lead pastor in a dynamic, growing churches. At times I've allowed my concern for people generally to cause me to neglect my expanding pastoral staff.

For example, on one occasion, two couples that I was very close to faced a moral issue. After confronting the situation successfully and establishing accountability groups, I continued to be involved in their restoration—timewise and emotionally.

Then to my surprise, one of my fellow pastors asked me to meet with him and several other pastors on staff. They lovingly but very directly confronted me relative to my priorities. In essence, they said—"Gene, we appreciate your concern for these couples. However, there are other issues—and people—that need your attention." In fact, one pastor said, "*We* need your attention too."

I must add that they were not being selfish. They were right! I needed to be available to my fellow pastors. And furthermore, I immediately realized that I had allowed my loving concern for these couples to interfere with other important priorities.

I must confess one other issue related to establishing priorities. It has involved my family. Though the New Testament says very little about this priority, it is certainly implied in the qualification for an elder—that we must manage our families competently (1 Tim. 3:4–5).

Over the years, particularly as a pastor, I feel I had at times failed to be available to my children when they needed me the most. I periodically needed to ask their forgiveness—which they have graciously given. Thankfully, I also have a wonderful wife who often covered for me—explaining that I wish I could be with them, but I had other important matters to care for. I'm indeed grateful, but if I had my ministry life to live over, with God's grace I would do a better job of establishing priorities!

Delegation

Principle 4: When we delegate responsibility, it must be to qualified people.

The late Peter Drucker, who made a careful study of executives, concluded that a significant mark of all successful leaders is that they know how to "use all the available strengths—the strength of associates, the strength of supervisors, and one's own strength."[1] Drucker's conclusions are certainly in harmony with God's revelation in Scripture. This principle was demonstrated by Moses, by Nehemiah, by the apostles, and by the church. More specifically, they enlisted *qualified people* to help resolve each problem.

This is one of the most important administrative and organizational principles illustrated and emphasized in the New Testament. For example, most all of the qualifications for elders and deacons relate to a person's reputation, morality, ethics, temperament, habits, and spiritual and psychological maturity (see chapter 20).

Many churches today are guilty of delegating responsibility to unqualified people. They often make judgments based on "skills" and popularity, which can lead to serious problems. Unfortunately, "ability" and "carnality" can mix well and cause problems. It is much better to have a person with undeveloped skills but who is strong spiritually and psychologically, and teachable. These people can learn quickly, particularly through modeling.

In chapter 28, I'll share some significant lessons I've learned. Though some have been painful, they helped me apply this principle of delegation in a much more effective and productive way.

Divine and Human Factors

Principle 5: We must maintain a proper balance between divine and human factors.

Incredible Balance

Nehemiah demonstrated the balance between divine and human factors in a remarkable way. He "prayed" and then "acted." And sometimes he "acted" and then "prayed." Often, he "prayed" while he "acted." In other words, Nehemiah consistently sought guidance from God and at the same time used his mind, energy, and skills to do what needed to be done.

Perhaps the clearest example of this balance was when he arrived in Jerusalem and "got up in the night" and went out and *inspected the walls*. This involved hard work and human responsibility. At the same time, he stated: "I did not tell anyone **what my God was putting into my mind** to do for Jerusalem" (Neh. 2:12 NASB). In other words, Nehemiah was formulating his plans as he inspected the walls; however, he was relying on God's wisdom and power to achieve his goals. In fact, he had demonstrated this balance even before he arrived in Jerusalem.

As church leaders today, we should strive to maintain the same balance as Nehemiah. In our humanistic world it's easy to attempt to solve problems using our own strengths and abilities and to neglect the power of prayer, faith, and God's help. On the other hand, since it often takes a lot of time and energy to solve problems in a ministry, it's easy to rationalize our lack of human responsibility and to withdraw and spend time in prayer or in Bible study. To be leaders who are acting in God's will, we must maintain a proper balance.

A Great Learning Experience

I must confess that practicing this principle is not easy for me. As a leader, I'm a Type A personality. But my greatest lessons came when I faced problems I couldn't solve. This, of course, was Nehemiah's predicament.

In the second church plant where I served as founding pastor, we had looked hard and long for property to build a permanent facility. But to no avail. In fact, my leadership team was ready to give up.

I was very discouraged. But then I remembered Nehemiah's challenge. I prepared a message on his prayer experience and then led the congregation to go through the same process.

- Like Nehemiah we acknowledged God's greatness using Scripture and hymns (Neh 1:4–5a).
- Like Nehemiah we reminded God of His promises to us—particularly in the Great Commission (1:5b).
- Like Nehemiah we confessed our sins and claimed God's forgiveness (1:6b).
- Like Nehemiah we became specific in our request for help (1:11b).

In terms of our specific requests, we asked God to lead us to someone—anyone who could help us. Since He used Artaxerxes, a pagan king, certainly He could move on someone's heart to assist us in locating a permanent place to worship.

To my amazement, God began to answer our prayers the very next day. I was stunned—and I had to confess elements of unbelief that I had following the prayer process with the congregation.

To make a long story short, God opened one door after another—as we continued to pray and at the same time do all we could to act responsibly. And step by step we were able to use our own **human capabilities** to walk through those **divine doors**. We were able to secure a piece of property that humanly speaking would never have become available. As a result, we were able to build a facility in which our growing congregation could worship and be taught the Word of God. To this very day, it stands as a testimony and witness to what God can do—through us— even though we faced what seemingly was an impossibility. Yes, this was a great learning experience for me. In fact, I have used Nehemiah's prayer process in other challenging situations and in every instance, we have seen remarkable answers to our prayers.

Appropriate Constituency

Principle 6: We must take an approach to problem solving and decision-making that takes into consideration the attitudes and feelings of all those who are directly involved.

The Biblical Examples

We see this principle illustrated in all four biblical examples described in the previous chapter. Before Moses took specific steps to solve his problem, he explained to all the people he was not able to fulfill this heavy responsibility without help (Deut. 1:1, 9). Nehemiah also called the people together and explained his strategy (Neh. 2:17).

We see this same action when the apostles in Jerusalem "summoned the congregation" of Hellenistic believers and explained the situation (Acts 6:2). And in Acts 15, the apostles and elders communicated to all those who gathered who then agreed upon a solution to the theological problem (Acts 15:22–29).

In all four of these examples, the circumstances varied in what was said, how much was said, when it was said, and to whom. But there was always communication with as many people as *necessary*.

In these biblical case studies, there was also a certain amount of group involvement in the decision-making process. Again, we see variance in the particulars. Moses instructed *each tribe* to select leaders to represent them and to meet their needs (Deut. 1:13). The apostles charged the group of Grecian representatives to choose seven men to serve tables (Acts 6:1–3). And though the apostles and elders initially met in closed session to hammer out some of the aspects of the problem of law and grace, the larger community of believers that had gathered helped make the final decision (Acts 15:22).

Nehemiah's problem was a different one indeed. The primary responsibility of rebuilding the walls lay on his shoulders. He had to serve as a strong, dynamic primary leader who initially had to act alone. But Nehemiah also knew he could never achieve his goals without the cooperation of the people. He carefully developed a plan, communicated his ideas to the people, and then issued a call to "come" and as a team rebuild the walls of Jerusalem. The results of his success as a leader are reflected in their response.

Contemporary Situations

Many problems are created in our churches today when we ignore this important biblical principle. Naturally, there are some challenges and even problems that need to be brought to the whole church for discussion and support. But overcommunicating and involving people who need not be involved can also cause serious problems—especially when inexperienced believers who also may be spiritually and emotionally immature are involved in making serious decisions. But again, our biblical examples give us significant guidelines in applying the principles regarding who should be involved directly in solving the problems.

I've learned that having a group of godly elders has helped greatly in practicing this principle. When people discovered how seriously we took our commitment to being "above reproach" in our own personal lives as well as our commitment to making decisions that benefit the church body, they responded with great respect and trust—and cooperation!

There's one additional factor that is absolutely essential is taking into consideration the attitudes and feelings of all those within the body. It can be summarized with three words: **communication, communication, communication!** Seriously, to be successful leaders, this is foundational in winning trust and securing cooperation and support from the total body.

Obviously, there are issues that must be kept confidential within the group that has ultimate responsibility for leading the church—in our case, those we called elders. This is particularly true during decision-making that involves a significant process. But in the most part, much of what happens at the highest level of leadership can be wisely communicated—first of all to the staff and then to the broader leadership team—and then to the body at large. This is why we have put a strong emphasis on written "elder reports," sharing much of our conversations and decisions with the total congregation.

Creative Resolutions

Principle 7: We must solve every problem creatively under the leadership of the Holy Spirit.

We must remember that in the Bible there was no one particular way of either addressing or solving these kinds of problems. Situations were different. Circumstances varied, the nature of the problem varied, and solutions varied. Consequently, we must never allow ourselves to get locked into administrative methods and routines.

Principles of Organization
Means to Divine Ends

In addition to the seven previous principles of administration, four additional principles of organization come from chapter 21 and demonstrate how to apply the never-changing truths in the Word of God.

Principle 1: We should organize to apply biblical principles that are supracultural, enduring truths, never allowing forms and structures to become ends in themselves.

Structures are not ends in themselves. If we violate this principle in our ministries, we have allowed non-absolutes to become absolute. We have allowed patterns and procedures to hinder our ability to engage in supracultural functions. To use a rather simple metaphor, we must not allow the "cart to get in front of the horse." Using another analogy, we must never allow organizational structure to "get in the driver's seat." If we do, we've allowed the church to become institutionalized (see chapter 27).

Human Essentials

Principle 2: We should organize to meet needs.

The first and most all-inclusive and continuous need faced by the New Testament church was to carry out the Great Commission. They were under obligation to make disciples and to teach those disciples, and they were to organize to do so. But as pointed out already, very few illustrations are given as to "how" this was done.

This was a distinctive mark of a New Testament church that was functioning according to the will of God. In the examples we have looked at, the church organized when the need arose, whether it was to feed the people in need or to solve a theological problem.

Unfortunately, some today interpret the lack of organizational detail in the New Testament as an indication that the church is to function without form and structure. This, of course, is impossible. Yes, the church in essence is an organism. But as an organism, it cannot function without some form of organization. As we've stated already, wherever there are people, there is function, particularly as it relates to human needs. And wherever there is function, there is form. This is a God-ordained reality.

Simplicity

Principle 3: As much as possible, we should keep organization simple.

This principle is closely aligned with "organizing to meet needs." If organizations are to be functional, they must be as simple as possible. Unfortunately, organizational patterns can become complex and rigid, which actually hinders efficient ministry with people. This can happen naturally with numerical growth.

This does not mean that organizational patterns are never complex. For example, the structure in Exodus 18 was very intricate, but it was also designed for a multitude of people who were traveling through the wilderness. Even though it was complex, it *was* functional, and carefully designed to meet the needs of the children of God at that particular time in their lives.

Today, what we would call a megachurch certainly calls for a great deal of organizational structure. This is inevitable. However, this can very quickly lead to institutionalism. People begin to serve the structures of the church rather than effectively carrying out biblical directives and applying biblical principles. The structures become "silos" where people are functioning, sometimes in isolation, not communicating with one another.

The Need for Alignment

When I began the process of passing my leadership baton to my successor, I asked him to lead our growing church staff in an alignment process. Thankfully, he had a significant passion to take on this challenge.

Both of us agreed that this was a special need—and our elders agreed. Ministries were multiplying, and as often happens, groups of people within the church at large began to develop their own objectives that can quickly become unrelated to the overall corporate objectives of the church.

This was actually a two-year process as the total leadership team met together to review *why* we existed as a local community of faith and then to evaluate and establish objectives in harmony with the overall God-designed purposes that relate to the Great Commission. This in turn helped determine, develop, and restructure appropriate forms and structures for each ministry within the church.

There was also a unique benefit that resulted in having my successor lead this process. He developed significant trust on the part of the total staff. This facilitated in a remarkable way the process when he ultimately replaced me as lead pastor.

A Serious Caution

At this point, we also need a word of warning. A "smooth running church" does not necessarily mean it is as successful as it should be. It's possible for groups of people, whether believers or nonbelievers, to develop dynamic organizations to achieve certain goals. The fact is, effective structures can be used to reach any purpose—biblical or nonbiblical. This is why we must use a God-ordained way to measure a church—namely, the degree of faith, hope, and love that is being developed and manifested (see chapters 16 and 17).

Flexibility

Principle 4: We must keep organizational structures flexible.

The patterns and methods set up in the wilderness for a people "on the move," were changed when they "settled in the land." And, when the walls were complete under Nehemiah's leadership, a new approach was devised to govern Jerusalem. And centuries later after the church was born, the structure of Acts 6 was terminated when persecution drove people out of Jerusalem and back to their homes in other parts of the New Testament world.

Later, when the specific "law and grace" problems recorded in Acts 15 were solved, the churches went on to develop *new* ways of solving *new* problems. Biblical leaders who were committed to these principles were never locked into organizational structures.

Organizational patterns that become rigid are in danger of being treated as authoritative and absolute. This violates Scripture. We are not free to make unchangeable what God intended to be changeable. "In a rapidly changing age like ours," said Dr. Schaeffer, "an age of total upheaval like ours, to make non-absolutes absolute guarantees both isolation and the death of the institutional, organized church."[2] Though Schaeffer was addressing issues in the second half of the twentieth century, what he wrote is still true today.

A Question for Thought and Discussion

As you reflect on these principles of administration and organization, can you describe a church situation where these principles were violated, or on the other hand, where they were practiced effectively?

23

Models of Communication

Video Intro from Gene

3lenses.org/c23

We've already noted how New Testament believers communicated with the world and with one another in carrying out the Great Commission. As the apostles, along with other gifted leaders, "made disciples," they taught, declared, spoke, proclaimed, preached, testified, witnessed, exhorted, praised, reasoned, refuted, explained, demonstrated, persuaded, and gave evidence for what they believed. And, as people responded to the gospel, they were taught, encouraged, strengthened, implored, exhorted, established, and admonished.

However, to gain a foundational and broader perspective, it's very helpful—and challenging—to look at the way Jesus Christ communicated with a variety of people. He stands out on the pages of Scripture as the greatest teacher who ever lived.

Darrell L. Bock and Benjamin I. Simpson set the stage for this observation in their classic volume, entitled *Jesus According to Scripture*: "Just as a three-dimensional portrait gives depth to an image in a way that two dimensions cannot, so these four Gospels reveal a many-sided Jesus whose fundamental claims still challenge us today. Such a look at Jesus according to Scripture gives us a glimpse of how unique a figure Jesus was."[1] This uniqueness is definitely seen in Jesus' teaching.

Jesus Christ's Communication Model

Jesus' Communication with People Generally

When we look carefully at the way Jesus communicated to a variety of groups and individuals, there are approximately 184 specific situations described in the Gospels.[2] These are listed in the following table, which demonstrate the unique balance in Jesus' ministry. Also note the balance in numbers as they relate to a variety of different individuals and groups in Table 2.

Number of Times Christ Spent Ministering to Various Individuals and Groups (as listed in the four Gospels)

Communications Situations	Number
The disciples (larger group of followers)	29
The scribes and Pharisees (as a group)	28
Sick people (individual and group healings)	27
Two or more apostles (the Twelve)	24
A general group of people*	20
Individuals generally**	19
Individual apostles (the Twelve)	19
The multitudes	18
TOTALS	**184**

*Indicates such groups as the "Jews," the "servants," etc.
**Such as Nicodemus, the woman at the well, a scribe, etc. This does not include individuals who are classified as disciples. They are included under the first item in the table. Out of twenty-nine references to the disciples, only eight are "individual" disciples.

The Number of Times Christ Spent with Individuals Compared with the Number of Times He Spent with Groups

Individuals		Groups	
Sick people	22	Disciples	29
Individuals generally	19	Scribes and Pharisees	28
Individual apostles (the Twelve)	19	Two or more apostles	24
		General group (other than disciples)	20
		Multitudes	18
		Sick people (a group)	5
TOTAL	**60**		**124**

As we look at both the situations and the statistics in Table 1 and Table 2, it's obvious Christ balanced His ministry by communicating with a variety of people with various backgrounds, needs, attitudes, and cultural perspectives. In essence, Jesus neglected no one. He came to be the Savior of the world, not only in His death and resurrection but in His ministry. He maintained a unique balance to individuals and groups.[3]

Jesus' Communication with the Apostles

As Jesus communicated with people generally, He at the same time focused on twelve men. This involves an outstanding communication model. The apostles were His special group. Though Jesus balanced His time with a variety of individuals and other groups, He actually spent most of His time with the Twelve:

- Most every time He spoke to the multitudes, the apostles had opportunity to hear what He said.
- Most every time He healed people, they observed these miraculous events.
- Most every time He dialogued and debated with the Pharisees, they looked on with amazement—and questions.

- Most every time He talked with individuals, they also listened in—or at least got firsthand feedback—such as with Nicodemus or the woman at the well.

Note, too, the unique process in Christ's communication model. At times He would be teaching the multitudes. He would then use this opportunity to speak more in-depth to a smaller group of disciples who were following Him. Then, on some occasions, He would turn to the Twelve and speak even more specifically about the truth He was teaching to both the multitudes and the smaller group of disciples. Going a step further, He would at times turn to one individual or perhaps to two or three of the Twelve to share with them some truth even more forcefully.

A Communication Pattern in Christ's Ministry

It's clear that while Jesus ministered to a multitude involving a variety of people, His primary focus was to equip the apostles to continue His ministry once He had returned to the Father. And while He was equipping these twelve men, He also focused on Peter and John in order to prepare them for a more foundational ministry that would go beyond that of the other apostles. This is obvious from the ministry of these two men as recorded in the book of Acts, as well as by the New Testament literature they wrote. Jesus was also preparing Peter to become the leader of the other apostles, which is verified by the way He singled him out for special instruction. Luke also described this leadership role beginning with Peter's message on the day of Pentecost (Acts 2:14–41).

Paul's Communication Model

Jesus commissioned the eleven apostles, not only to make disciples but to teach these disciples everything He had commanded them. In terms of leadership, Peter became an apostle primarily to the Jews and Paul became an apostle primarily to the Gentiles (Gal. 2:7–8). However, we know more about Paul's communication style than any of the other apostles, so in this section we'll look at Paul's communication model.

To illustrate, I've chosen Paul's first letter to the Thessalonians since it includes very specific references to the way he and Silas and Timothy communicated with these people, both while ministering among them and after they had to leave. It is one of the most comprehensive communication models found among those who founded and established churches in the first-century world. Furthermore, it demonstrates Paul's commitment to a "team approach."

The Founding of the Church in Thessalonica

Luke recorded the basic events leading to the founding of the church in Thessalonica (Acts 17:1–9). To "make disciples," Paul "reasoned" in the synagogue for three Sabbaths, probably covering a three-week period (17:2–3). Some Jews plus a large number of Greeks and leading women became believers (17:4). Other than these basic facts, Luke tells us very little about the actual ministry of these three men in this Macedonian city, but the first letter Paul wrote to this church demonstrates a powerful communication model with these people—before and after they became believers.

The Letter to the Thessalonians

The First Thessalonian Letter	Communication Characteristics
1:1 Paul, **Silvanus**, and **Timothy** to the church of the Thessalonians in God the Father and the Lord Jesus Christ. Grace to you and peace.	Paul wrote this letter representing his two coworkers who served with him when the church was founded in Thessalonica.
1:2 We always thank God for all of you, making mention of you **constantly in our prayers**;	Part of their follow-up was to let these believers know they were praying for them.
1:3 We recall, in the presence of our God and Father, your work produced by **faith**, your labor motivated by **love**, and your endurance inspired by **hope** in our Lord Jesus Christ.	They gave these believers positive feedback when they heard of their spiritual growth, manifesting faith, hope, and love.

The First Thessalonian Letter	Communication Characteristics
1:4–5a For we know, brothers and sisters loved by God, that he has chosen you, because our gospel did not come to you **in word only**, but also **in power, in the Holy Spirit**, and **with full assurance**.	They reminded these believers of God's sovereign work in their lives and that they had not depended upon their communication skills alone, but on the power of the Holy Spirit.[4]
1:5b–6 You know **how we lived among you** for your benefit, and you yourselves became **imitators of us and of the Lord** when, in spite of severe persecution, you welcomed the message with joy from the Holy Spirit.	These missionaries lived in such a way as to be living models of the Christ-life that these people could imitate.
1:7–8 As a result, you became **an example to all the believers in Macedonia and Achaia**. For the word of the Lord rang out from you, not only in Macedonia and Achaia, but in every place that your faith in God has gone out. Therefore, we don't need to say anything,	They commended the Thessalonians for being a corporate witness and example to other believers.
1:9–10 for **they themselves report what kind of reception we had from you**: how you turned to God from idols to serve the living and true God and to wait for his Son from heaven, whom he raised from the dead—Jesus, who rescues us from the coming wrath.	They also gave them positive feedback regarding the way other believers were responding to their example.
2:1–2 For you yourselves know, brothers and sisters, that our visit with you was not without result. On the contrary, after we had previously suffered and were treated outrageously in Philippi, as you know, we were **emboldened by our God** to speak the gospel of God to you in spite of great opposition.	They reminded these believers of their first encounter, that their commitment to communication was because of God's empowerment.
2:3 For our exhortation didn't come from **error** or **impurity** or an intent to **deceive**.	These men were **honest, open**, and **sincere** in their communication.

The First Thessalonian Letter	Communication Characteristics
2:4 Instead, just as we have been approved by God to be entrusted with the gospel, so we speak, **not to please people**, **but rather God**, who examines our hearts.	They wanted to **please God first of all**, not men.
2:5 For we never used **flattering speech**, as you know, or had **greedy motives**—God is our witness—	Their speech and motives were **sincere** and **pure**.
2:6–7a and we didn't seek glory **from people**, either from you or **from others**. Although we could have been a burden **as Christ's apostles**,	They did not demand honor because they were Christ's representatives; rather they won **respect** through their behavior.
2:7b instead we were **gentle** among you, as a nurse nurtures her own children.	They communicated with these people in a spirit of **gentleness**—like a mother nursing her child.
2:8 We cared so much for you that we were pleased to share with you not only the gospel of God but also **our own lives**, because you had become dear to us.	They were **unselfish**, being willing to literally give their lives if necessary to win these people to Christ.
2:9 For you remember our **labor and hardship**, brothers and sisters. Working night and day so that we would **not burden any of you**, we preached God's gospel to you.	They worked night and day to care for their material needs so as not to have their **motives** misinterpreted.
2:10 You are witnesses, and so is God, of how **devoutly**, **righteously**, and **blamelessly** we conducted ourselves with you believers.	They lived **exemplary lives** among those who came to Christ (see 1:5–6).
2:11–12 As you know, like a father with his own children, we **encouraged**, **comforted**, and **implored each one of you** to walk worthy of God, who calls you into his own kingdom and glory.	They maintained an **individualized ministry** among these new Christians; they literally taught and encouraged "each one," just like a father would communicate with each one of his children.

The First Thessalonian Letter	Communication Characteristics
2:13 This is why we constantly thank God, because when you received the **word of God** that you heard from us, you welcomed it **not as a human message**, but as it truly is, the **word of God**, which also works effectively in you who believe.	They **exalted the Word of God**; not their own ideas or philosophy.
2:17–18 But as for us, brothers and sisters, after we were **forced to leave you** for a short time (in person, not in heart), we greatly desired and made every effort **to return and see you face to face.** So we wanted to come to you —even I, Paul, time and again—but Satan hindered us.	They **continued their sincere interest** in these people after they had to leave them, letting them know they wanted to minister to them personally once again.
3:1–3a Therefore, when we could no longer stand it, we thought it was better to be left alone in Athens. And we **sent Timothy**, our brother and God's coworker in the gospel of Christ, to **strengthen** and **encourage** you concerning your faith, so that no one will be shaken by these afflictions.	They **followed up** their ministry by having Timothy return to Thessalonica to strengthen and encourage these believers.
3:3b–5 For you yourselves know that we are appointed to this. In fact, when we were with you, we told you in advance that we were going **to experience affliction**, and as you know, it happened. For this reason, when I could no longer stand it, I also sent him to find out about your faith, fearing that the **tempter had tempted you** and that our labor might be for nothing.	They were **straightforward** and **honest** with these people about the realities of Satan, and the trials they would have to endure because of their decision to follow Christ.

The First Thessalonian Letter	Communication Characteristics
3:6–9 But now Timothy has come to us from you and brought us good news about your faith and love. He reported that you always have **good memories of us** and that you long to see us, as we also **long to see you.** Therefore, brothers and sisters, in all our distress and affliction, **we were encouraged** about you through your faith. For now we live, if you stand firm in the Lord. How can we thank God for you in return for all the joy we experience before our God because of you,	They **did not hesitate to share their human feelings** with these people—that they were very concerned about them. And when they received a positive report of their progress in the faith, they were encouraged in the midst of their own trials and tribulations. They did not hesitate to share these inner feelings.
3:10–13 as we **pray very earnestly night and day** to see you **face to face** and to **complete what is lacking in your faith**? Now may our God and Father himself, and our Lord Jesus, direct our way to you. And may the Lord cause you to **increase and overflow with love for one another and for everyone,** just as we do for you. May he make your **hearts blameless in holiness** before our God and Father at the coming of our Lord Jesus with all his saints. Amen.	They continued their **prayer ministry** for these believers and reassured them that they **wanted to return as a team** and assist them further in their Christian development.
4:1ff. Additionally then, brothers and sisters, we ask and encourage you in the Lord Jesus, that as you have received instruction from us on how you should live and please God—as you are doing—**do this even more.**	Paul **used this letter as an additional means of follow-up**. Certain areas needed additional instructions—about morality (4:2–8); business life (4:10–12); the second coming of Christ (4:13–17); attitudes toward their spiritual leaders, those in special need, and all believers (5:12–15; as well as in their church life (5:16–21).

A Powerful Example

In this profound communication model representing Paul, Silas, and Timothy, we see how they carried out the Great Commission by both "making disciples" and "building disciples":

Their Functions as a Team

1. They were living examples of Christ's life.
2. They were sincere and honest, and kept their motives pure.
3. They were bold and unintimidated.
4. They were gentle and loving.
5. They were unselfish and sincerely interested in people.

Their Functions at the Divine Level

1. They engaged in a ministry of prayer.
2. They acknowledged God's sovereignty.
3. They relied upon the Holy Spirit.
4. They exalted the Word of God.

Their Functions at the Human Level

1. They won respect through their attitudes and actions.
2. They maintained an individualized ministry as well as a ministry to groups.
3. They followed up by sending Timothy back to teach them.
4. They were honest and open about their own humanness.
5. They hoped to return as a team.
6. They gave positive feedback to these new believers regarding their progress in the Christian life.
7. They maintained a written ministry by sending letters to encourage and instruct them.

Functional Evaluation

1. They evaluated their communication by the way these believing communities manifested faith, hope, and love.
2. They evaluated their communication by the way these believers were multiplying themselves in their sphere of influence.

Concluding Thoughts

Jesus' communication model has been an inspiration to multitudes over the centuries. However, it's impossible for any one human being to emulate how He taught—and, of course, to verify His message with the various "signs and wonders" and "various miracles" He performed (Heb. 2:3–4). Even the apostles, as gifted as they were, could not totally emulate Jesus' model.

Paul and his missionary team take us a step closer to practicing Jesus' model of communication. They were uniquely called and gifted to carry out the Great Commission. On the other hand, they were human beings just like all of us, demonstrating a model we can emulate.

As we'll see in the chapter to follow, both Jesus' model and Paul's provide us with enduring principles that can be applied by every community of believers at any moment in history and throughout the world. We'll look at these principles in the next chapter.

A Question for Thought and Discussion

What are some additional reasons we need to understand both the divine and human dimensions that are illustrated in the communication ministry of Jesus, the apostles, and other supernaturally gifted leaders in the New Testament story?

24

Principles of Communication

Video Intro from Gene

3lenses.org/c24

As we've noted in the previous chapter, Jesus Christ stands out on the pages of Scripture and in all history as an incomparable teacher and communicator. The reason is obvious. He was, and is, the Son of God. With His omniscience, He could address the deepest needs of His listeners. For example, when He communicated with the woman at the well, He knew the details of her life and adjusted the way He communicated (John 4:16–19). And when He addressed the large crowd in a home in Capernaum, He read the thoughts of some scribes and said, "Why are you thinking these things in your hearts?" (Mark 2:8). We see this again and again as He ministered to both individuals and groups of people.

In addition to His omniscience, Jesus was also omnipotent, able to verify His verbal communication with signs and wonders. His most miraculous verification was His teaching regarding His resurrection when He said: "Destroy this temple, and I will raise it up in three days." He, of course, "was speaking about the temple of his body" (John 2:19–21).

However, even though it's humanly impossible for any one of us to ever communicate like Jesus, every local community of believers can use His model as a divine standard. Even as human beings we can emulate some of His insights and skills. Here are several principles to guide us in carrying out the Great Commission.

A Welcoming Community

Principle 1: As a community of believers, we are to do all we can to communicate with as many different people as possible.

As we've seen in the previous chapter, Jesus communicated with a variety of people in a variety of different situations. As already stated, He ministered as the divine Son of God, utilizing His divine insight and supernatural power.

We, of course, will never be able to come close to emulating Jesus' communication model just as we'll never be able to measure up to "the stature of the fullness of Christ" while on this earth. However, as every member of the body does its part, we can communicate with many different individuals and groups—just as Jesus did. And together we can more and more reflect Christ's image.

This does not mean we should never have target audiences, people we want to reach in a special way. But when we evaluate our overall ministry as local churches, we should focus on all kinds and classes of people within our cultural environment—and beyond. Let's remember that Jesus neglected no one.

Following Jesus' Example

I have vivid memories of the early years at the first Fellowship Bible Church. The Jesus revolution, coming out of the hippie movement, was in full force. Our goal as leaders was to follow Jesus' example and to create an environment where all people were welcome.

As I looked out at the congregation in the early 70s, I saw people from all walks of life representing various economic levels. There were older men who were dressed in suits with ties and some younger men who were incredibly casual. Some had beards and long hair, but some were closely shaven. Some adults and youths sat on pillows together on the floor because we had run out of chairs. I saw this multicultural representation among both men and women—young and old.

A Very Special Memory

I remember one young man who was new in the faith. With guitar in hand, he stood on the platform. He had long hair, a full red beard and was dressed in overalls. With a friend who was clean cut—who also played the guitar—they sang a song the bearded one had just written based on his recent conversion experience.

To make a long story short, Jim eventually adjusted his external decorum, entered seminary, graduated, and served as a successful pastor in one of our Fellowship Bible Churches for thirty-two years. He never lost his passion to reach people from a variety of backgrounds.

Our culture has changed since then—but the same supracultural principle applies. As communities of faith, we should follow Jesus' example and attempt to communicate with as many different people as possible. I like the theme in the last church I founded and served as lead pastor— "Come as you are, be transformed, and make a difference."

My successor Jeff Jones and his leadership team have continued with this emphasis—even to a greater degree. As I pen these words, my wife and I just attended a worship service last Sunday. I was deeply moved as I witnessed a variety of cultural backgrounds among those who served on the worship team—African American, Asian, Latino, and Caucasian people. I then looked around at those who were worshiping—and saw the same cultural mix. I was deeply thankful for what I observed and the continued emphasis on reaching as many different people as possible. Jesus, of course, set the example.

Love and Unity

Principle 2: To verify that Jesus Christ was and is the incarnate Son of God, as a community of believers we should communicate love for one another that results in oneness and unity.

As Jesus communicated with people, He performed miracles to verify who He is and why He came. And the apostles, including Paul, were able to verify the salvation message by doing the same. As believers today, we are able to verify this divine message in a remarkable and miraculous way by allowing unbelievers to see our love for one another and our oneness in Christ. It's possible at any moment and in every culture of the world.

First, it's possible because Jesus Christ prayed for all of us—that it might be true (John 17:22–23). *Second,* through the power of the Holy Spirit, we're able to achieve this goal by "making every effort to keep the unity of the Spirit through the bond of peace" (Eph. 4:3). And as believers, together we can "take up the full armor of God" and defeat Satan's tactics to destroy unity in our local churches (Eph. 6:13–18, see chapter 8.)

At the time I was rewriting this book, my successor Jeff Jones has just written *Rebranding Christianity.*[1] His emphasis is on what he has called "the Jesus brand," and of course that brand is what Jesus taught the apostles in the upper room and what the authors of the New Testament letters emphasized again and again. We are to "love one another as Christ has loved us." Unfortunately, Satan has been working hard to create a "branding problem" in many of our churches today. Needless to say, I'm thankful for this continued emphasis.

Equipping Leaders

Principle 3: As pastoral leaders particularly, we should follow Jesus' example in training the apostles in order to equip individuals for special leadership roles.

Part of our biblical responsibility as shepherds and teachers is to communicate the Word of God to all members of the church. As we do, we will be setting the stage to build into the lives of those we are preparing in a special way for leadership. As we teach the Scriptures to all believers, we can follow up these messages by going more deeply into biblical truth with a more select group in order to multiply our own teaching and shepherding ministry. And as we communicate with those in these smaller groups, we can spend even more time with individuals within that group. As we've seen in the previous chapter, this was often Jesus' communication strategy.

Following this model calls for intentional communication. For example, it's one thing to share the gospel as the church gathers, but it's another thing to train individuals to communicate the gospel one-on-one and to make disciples. It's one thing to teach all members of the body of Christ passages of Scripture that will help them mature in their faith, but it's another thing to help **individuals** in the church to have a deepener understanding of Scripture and then to be able to teach the Word of God to others. Again, this will not happen unless we are intentional in our communication strategy. Paul beautifully modeled this principle, particularly with Timothy (2 Tim. 2:2).

A Dynamic Bible Study

As I look back over my years of pastoral ministry, one of my most memorable experiences happened shortly after I helped plant the first Fellowship Bible Church. I mentioned this experience briefly in chapter 20, but I would like to expand on what actually happened and how it relates to this principle.

I issued an open invitation to the men of the church to join me for an early morning Bible study. I was excited when about twenty showed up. We met in a motel conference room and then ate breakfast together before beginning our regular daily activities.

As I thought about an appropriate study, the maturity profiles outlined by Paul in 1 Timothy 3 and Titus 1 came to mind. Though Paul was addressing the need to appoint qualified men to be elders, he also made it clear to Timothy and Titus that this was a measurable spiritual criterion to help all men to become mature men of God.

The first quality in both passages is to be "above reproach" or "blameless" (1 Tim. 3:2; Titus 1:6). Interpreted properly, these characteristics simply mean to have "a good reputation."

I taught this concept for about twenty-five to thirty minutes, looking at other scriptural passages that explained this quality. I then led the group in open discussion for about the same amount of time. We shared with one another how we could continue to develop a reputation as men who wanted to "[grow] into maturity with a stature measured by Christ's fullness" (Eph. 4:13).

Following this opening session, I asked these men to volunteer to teach and lead future discussions just as I had done. In fact, as I reflect on those who taught and led the next discussions, several became dynamic elders in the church. Several focused on becoming outstanding, Christ-centered businessmen. Several men had effective full-time ministries, such as John Breneman, who is still serving in Sweden with his wife, conducting a strong Christ-centered counseling ministry. I think of John Maisel, who launched East-West Ministries International. Even today, East-West focuses on church planting in closed countries.

To be honest, this was one of the most dynamic Bible studies I have ever been involved in. As the men led these studies I simply folded into the group and became one of them. Again, this was indeed an experience that related to what Paul wrote to Timothy: "What you have heard from me in the presence of many witnesses entrust to faithful men, who will be able to teach others also" (2 Tim. 2:2).

An Unexpected Opportunity

Something else happened that I didn't anticipate. A publishing friend of mine asked me to write the book *The Measure of a Man* based on these qualities that Paul outlined in these passages. Little did I realize that this book would still be in print fifty years later and available in numerous languages.[2]

I must add that the reason this has happened is because I borrowed the outline from the apostle Paul, and we know where he got it—directly from the Holy Spirit. These qualities are indeed supracultural manifestations of maturity for all Christ-followers, in every culture of the world, at any time. I'm indeed thankful to the many pastors and church leaders who are still using this book to equip men to become spiritual leaders in their families and the local church—and beyond. I'm greatly humbled and encouraged as I receive regular emails and letters from men sharing how this book has changed their lives.

Again, as pastoral leaders particularly, we should follow Jesus' communication model. Without neglecting our local community of faith, we should focus on key individuals who can multiply our ministry.[3]

Human Effort

Principle 4: As pastoral leaders, we need to follow the example of the apostles and other New Testament leaders who used communication skills that involved significant human effort.

A Personalized Ministry

Even though the apostles and other New Testament leaders had miraculous gifts to help them teach and verify the Word of God, they also used their human ingenuity and skills. We've seen this modeled by Paul and his missionary team. This is why they spent time with these believers individually, utilizing the God-ordained parental model. As stated in the previous chapter, Paul wrote: "Although we could have been a burden as Christ's apostles, instead we were gentle among you, as a nurse [literally as a nursing mother] nurtures her own children" (1 Thess. 2:7). Paul continued: "As you know, **like a father** with his own children, we **encouraged**, **comforted**, and **implored each one of you** to walk worthy of God, who calls you into his own kingdom and glory" (1 Thess. 2:11–12).

In the Greek text, Paul used redundancy to emphasize the personal nature of his missionary team's communication. In essence, they "implored each one of" these believers **one by one** "to walk worthy of God." And, of course, the reference to a "nursing mother" is very intimate and personal. To follow this model of communication, we cannot ignore engaging in a **personalized ministry**.

A Time Commitment

This kind of effort is also illustrated in the **time commitment** of this missionary team. While in Thessalonica, they worked "night and day so as not to be burdensome to these people." In fact, Paul was so intent on not communicating false motives that he at times did not take what was rightly his (1 Cor. 9:1–15).

In terms of time and effort, it's not possible for most of us to be involved to the same extent as Jesus and Paul and other New Testament leaders. God has established priorities for all of us—such as to provide for and to nurture our families. As spiritual leaders devoted to full-time

342

ministry, we cannot effectively carry out the Great Commission without hard work and engagement in people's lives. To reach all classes of people—both groups and individuals—and to build our lives into certain people in-depth, calls for diligence and hard work.

A Caution

At this point, I feel I must issue a word of caution. As those who are "worthy of double honor" (financial support) and who "work hard at **preaching** and **teaching**" (1 Tim. 5:17), we must not neglect our **shepherding role**. Part of that role is to "feed the sheep" through teaching, but it also involves personal care and concern.

In fulfilling this God-ordained and prescribed role, it's easy to follow our natural comfort zones in teaching and preaching the Word of God in a public setting. At the same time, it's easy to neglect a personal, "one-on-one," or small group ministry that follows the example of Jesus and Paul and his missionary team.

On the other hand, it's also easy to follow our natural comfort zones in being with people and to neglect to spend time adequately preparing to teach and preach the Word of God. It takes a lot of effort to adequately study the biblical text in order to communicate God's truth to people and then help them apply God's Word in their personal lives.

It becomes increasingly difficult not to go to extremes when we are ministering to a large and growing congregation. We must not lock ourselves away in our studies. But, at the same time, we have to be sensitively selective in terms of a small group and personal "one-on-one" ministry. Part of that selectivity certainly focuses on spending quality time with our own families and other staff leaders.

Creative Thinking

In practicing this principle, as a lead pastor I was able to blend my athletic interests with mentoring my fellow pastors. Following our time on the racquetball court, we spent many hours in the spa simply talking about ministry and personal issues. Even to this day, many years later, some of these pastors have related how significant that time was in their spiritual and ministerial growth.

In terms of adding a personal touch with members of the body who have special needs, my executive assistant suggested a plan that helped me greatly. Paul would call her a "deacon" par excellence. She kept a careful record of people who had special needs. As I left to travel to and from the office, she gave me information regarding these situations along with telephone numbers. As I drove, I was able to make phone calls—legitimately so—letting these people know that I was concerned. Invariably, I was also able to pray with these individuals. To this day, people remember those personal conversations.

We developed one other form that paid great dividends in meeting people's needs within a large congregation. It involves small groups led by qualified lay leaders who we also called pastors. Their responsibility, along with their wives, was to teach and shepherd the people in these groups. However, there were special needs where I felt I needed to be personally involved.

And, as lead pastor, I remember people who had serious health issues. For example, when I received information regarding serious crises, I made it a priority to visit these individuals—particularly in hospital situations. I remember often arriving on the scene only to find the leaders of small groups, along with other members, already ministering to these individuals. In a relatively small amount of time, I was able to add my personal touch. This became doable even within a large congregation.

Here again we see the uniqueness of the body of Christ. God did not call each one of us to carry out the Great Commission alone. He did not call each one of us to be "an apostle Paul" or even "a Timothy." But He does expect each member of the body to function and contribute to communicating the Word of God and meeting people's personal needs. And as pastors and leaders, we need to do our best to make this happen.

Seeking God's Enablement

Principle 5: Though Christian communication takes time and effort, it is also a very unique and distinctive process involving supernatural elements.

This principle is foundational in being able to communicate effectively with both unbelievers and believers. Though we may not experience the miraculous manifestations and experiences as often happened in the New Testament setting, we are always to rely on the Holy Spirit to help us communicate the Word of God. We must remember that the message of Scripture is supernatural in itself, having been revealed by the Spirit of truth (John 15:26; 16:13). It is He whom Jesus sent to "convict the world about sin, righteousness, and judgement" (16:8).

Furthermore, we must not forget the power of prayer. Since Paul wrote more letters than any other New Testament author, we see how important this divine element was in his communication.

Note particularly his prayers in the Ephesian letter, which serves as a model for all of us:

> I pray that the God of our Lord Jesus Christ, the glorious Father, would give you the Spirit of wisdom and revelation in the knowledge of him. I pray that the eyes of your heart may be enlightened so that you may know what is the hope of his calling, what is the wealth of his glorious inheritance in the saints, and what is the immeasurable greatness of his power toward us who believe, according to the mighty working of his strength. . . . For this reason, I kneel before the Father from whom every family in heaven and on earth is named. I pray that he may grant you, according to the riches of his glory, to be strengthened with power in your inner being through his Spirit, and that Christ may dwell in your hearts through faith. I pray that you, being rooted and firmly established in love, may be able to comprehend with all the saints what is the length and width, height and depth of God's love, and to know Christ's love that surpasses knowledge, so that you may be filled with all the fullness of God. Now to him who is able to do above and beyond all that we ask or think according to the power that works in us—to him be glory in the church and in Christ Jesus to all generations, forever and ever. Amen. (Eph. 1:17–19, 3:14–21; see also Paul's prayers in Phil. 1:9–11 and Col. 1:9–12)[4]

Modeling God's Truth

Principle 6: In all of our communication we must remember that a Christlike example is basic to effective communication.

Words alone can never achieve what the power of positive examples can achieve. This was a distinctive characteristic of Paul, Silas, and Timothy. Paul wrote: "You are witnesses, and so is God, of how **devoutly, righteously,** and **blamelessly** we conducted ourselves with you believers" (1 Thess. 2:10). These men demonstrated with their lives what they were communicating with their lips.

This principle is to be applied by all of us, regardless of our particular positions and roles in the body of Christ. This is why Paul wrote to the Corinthians: "Imitate me, as I also imitate Christ" (1 Cor. 11:1).

Leadership Qualifications

This is also why Paul put such a great emphasis on proper moral and ethical behavior as a criterion in selecting church leaders (1 Tim. 3:1–13; Titus 1:6–9). This is a distinctive reason why Paul also chose Timothy to be his missionary companion. Luke has reported: "The brothers and sisters at Lystra and Iconium **spoke highly of him**" (Acts 16:2). Timothy had a very good reputation.

We see the power of example throughout the New Testament—individually and in corporate examples of the church. As Christ becomes incarnate within the body of Christ, our words become more and more meaningful.

Unforgettable Moments

As I reflect on this principle, two memorable experiences come to mind. Though they both relate to my experiences at Moody Bible Institute, they particularly apply to our role as pastors and leaders.

The first experience happened when I was a student. One of my professors took a personal interest in me, actually believing in me when I didn't believe in myself. But the most impactful experience happened when he took me with him on a ministry trip. As we were headed to Texas via train (which dates me), he turned to me and said, "Gene, there are two things I aways pray for. First, that I'll never just serve as a professional."

346

Even in my youthfulness and immaturity, I knew what he meant. He didn't want his ministry to be just a job. And then he said, "I also pray that I'll always be thankful that someone comes to hear me speak."

I'll never forget these two powerful statements. But what makes them so memorable is what happened when we arrived at our destination—a small church way out in the boonies of Texas. My professor friend spoke to a small group of Sunday school teachers. You would think he was speaking to thousands. Again, I'll never forget that experience.

The second memory also relates to Moody Bible Institute. After graduating and going on for more education, I was invited to join the faculty. One day I was seated in chapel with my fellow professors. Then-president Dr. William Culbertson was speaking. Looking at all of us, he directly, but with a serious and sensitive tone, addressed us, "Men and women, these students [and he then paused and gestured to the student body], will forget much of *what you say*, but [and he once again looked directly at us] they will never forget *who you are*."

I'll never forget those words. Dr. Culbertson's message took on even greater meaning because they came from a man that I knew practiced what he preached. I know this by experience—whether leading the multifaceted ministry at Moody Bible Institute, addressing the faculty and students, interacting with many of us personally, or on the volleyball court where we played together for a number of years.

Freedom in Form

Principle 7: We should always be free and flexible in our communication methodology; however, we should use methodology that best facilitates communicating the biblical message.

As with all functions that are described in Scripture, communication forms are not prescribed in the New Testament. Whether it involved Peter's words recorded by Mark or Paul's communication with various individuals and groups on his missionary journeys, there is no consistent pattern in the way their content was presented. And, as is true throughout the book of Acts and the New Testament letters, there is very little description of methods. And those that are described vary greatly. This again illustrates divine design. The authors of the New Testament focused on the message and functions, not forms.

The New Testament letters also reveal variety in literary style. For example, when we look at Paul's thirteen letters, there is no consistent approach in form and structure. Paul had "freedom" in his written communication methodology. This was part of his strategy when he wrote— "I have become **all things** to **all people**, so that I may by every possible **means** [or methods] save some" (1 Cor. 9:22).

We must then choose methods that help us communicate the Word of God to various individuals and groups of people in the best possible way and within their cultural settings. This again calls for creativity, and today we're very fortunate to have access to some amazing technology. For example, while working on the revision of this book, I sat in my living room in Dallas, Texas, teaching a group of spiritual leaders in São Paulo, Brazil. They could see and hear me as if I was in the same room—and I could see and hear them as we utilized our computers and the internet to communicate with one another via Zoom.

This illustration only touches the tip of the iceberg in terms of creative communication in today's world, which includes the advent of artificial intelligence. Though the world's system has always used technological developments to achieve evil goals, this does not mean that these tools and methods in themselves are evil. Let's use them to effectively communicate the Word of God.[5]

A Question for Thought and Discussion

As you reflect on the principles in this chapter, which ones do you believe are violated the most in the average church?

Section 3

THE LENS OF HISTORY

Video Intro from Gene

3lenses.org/sc3

To carry out the Great Commission effectively, we must learn from function and form as we follow the New Testament story. When we do, we can eliminate what violates biblical principles and accentuate what is in harmony with these enduring truths.

Paul made this clear in his first letter to the Corinthians. Referencing the sins of the children of Israel and God's subsequent discipline, he wrote:

> These things happened to them as examples, and they **were written for our instruction**, on whom the ends of the ages have come. So, whoever thinks he stands must be careful not to fall.
> (1 Cor. 10:11–12)

We can apply the same process to God's revelation in the New Testament. However, to develop an effective philosophy of ministry, we must also learn lessons from church history generally, from social history, and from our own personal ministerial histories.

Needless to say, I've had to be selective since volumes have been written following the first century. Therefore, I've chosen to focus on what we can learn about leadership.

25

Lessons from the Seven Churches of Asia

Video Intro from Gene

3lenses.org/c25

Without question, the church today is under fire. Though I've purposely avoided naming authors and titles, there are many books and articles that have focused on the way local communities of faith are failing in various ways to be the church God intended for them to be.

As I've reflected on these concerns, my thoughts have gravitated to the letters to the seven churches in Asia that were dictated by Jesus Himself. Though what John heard Jesus say definitely fits more accurately under the "Lens of Scripture," I've included this material as an introductory chapter in this section, entitled the "Lens of History." The reason is simply that the spiritual condition of these seven churches helps us develop an historical perspective, not only on the condition of churches at the end of the first century, but also throughout the next two thousand years.

In these letters, Jesus addressed serious dysfunctional issues that make concerns regarding churches today seem almost mild—at least in the Western culture. However, in making this comparison, I in no way wish to downplay the fact that many churches in today's world are failing to continue "growing into maturity with a stature measured by Christ's fullness" (Eph. 4:13).

These letters serve as a constant reminder that even though Jesus was disappointed in several of these churches, He did not give up on them. Neither should we give up on the church today! His promise to Peter is still true—"I will build my church, and the gates of Hades will not overpower it" (Matt. 16:18).

The Historical Setting

It appears these communities of faith came into existence because of Paul's two-year daily ministry in Ephesus in the school of Tyrannus. Men and women came to this city from all over Asia to shop, to recreate, and to visit the Roman baths. They also visited the pagan temple of Diana, where they engaged in worship characterized by various forms of immorality and idolatry.

During their stay, many heard about this unusual Jewish teacher who had become a follower of a man called Jesus Christ. No doubt out of curiosity, they went to hear Paul teach and many responded to the gospel. Luke has recorded that "**all the residents of Asia, both Jews and Greeks, heard the word of the Lord**" (Acts 19:10). Many evidently returned to their own cities throughout Asia and established local churches.

When Jesus appeared to John on the isle of Patmos, He dictated letters to seven of these churches. In fact, because John eventually took up residence in Ephesus, he had probably visited many of these Asian churches prior to the time he was exiled on the isle of Patmos. He was no doubt already aware of the serious problems in some of these communities of faith and would have been deeply concerned. He would've been encouraged to hear Jesus address these issues directly.

The Seven Letters

Some respected Bible teachers believe that Jesus was not only addressing current issues in these seven churches, but what He dictated was prophetic. They have concluded that each letter and each church represent an unfolding story regarding the state of local churches generally in various periods of history, with the church of Laodicea representing the final period of church history before Jesus returns.

I certainly respect this interpretation. My opinion is that the spiritual conditions of these churches simply serve as first-century examples that yield powerful lessons, both positive and negative. These lessons, in turn, are divinely designed to challenge church leaders throughout the centuries to help all believers to continue "growing into maturity with a stature measured by Christ's fullness." Since several of these churches were terribly dysfunctional, it should help us gain perspective in evaluating more objectively the maturity level of local churches today.

An Historical Profile

Following are some of Jesus' exact words which were written about twenty-five to thirty years after Paul became a martyr in Rome. Assuming these churches at that moment represented local churches throughout the Roman world, these letters give us an historical perspective on the state of the New Testament churches toward the end of the first century. In many respects, it's a dismal picture. If we think churches today are in a mess, compare our present situation with these seven churches in Asia. Consider the following profile:

Churches That Were Immature (40%)

Thyatira:

"You tolerate the woman Jezebel, who . . . deceives my servants to commit sexual immorality."

Note: This is the only letter where Jesus used a singular pronoun to address the spiritual leader. In all the other letters he used plural pronouns to address each community of faith.

Sardis:

"You have a reputation for being alive, but you are dead."

Laodicea:

"You are wretched, pitiful, poor, blind, and naked."

Churches That Had Elements of Both Maturity and Immaturity (30%)

Ephesus:

"You have persevered and endured hardships for the sake of my name."

"You have abandoned the love you had at first."

Pergamum:

"Yet you are holding on to my name and did not deny your faith in me."

"You have some there who hold to the teaching of Balaam . . . and the teachings of the Nicolaitans."

Note: To interpret Jesus' reference to "some," it's helpful to understand the structure of these churches. In most cases these believers were not able to meet together as a total congregation. Consequently, they met in house churches. It's possible that when Jesus referred to "some" of these believers, He was referring to a single house church out of several that had begun to engage in immorality and idolatry. For example, the "woman Jezebel" may have emerged as a leader in one of these house churches in Thyatira.

Churches That Were Mature (30%)

Smyrna:

"I know your affliction and poverty, but you are rich."

Philadelphia:

"You have kept my word and have not denied my name."

Lessons from Jesus Christ

What are some lessons that emerge from these letters that can help all of us become the churches that God intended us to be?

Lesson 1: We must understand that when we fail to provide believers with the three vital experiences illustrated in the early days of the

church, it can take only one generation for relatively mature churches to become worldly and immature.

This seems to have happened to the majority of the seven churches. If they came into existence at the time Paul was in Ephesus teaching in the school of Tyrannus, it would have been approximately a generation later—about twenty-five to thirty years—when Jesus sent these letters via the apostle John. Assuming these churches were relatively mature in the early years of their existence, three out of seven were woefully immature and worldly thirty or more years later and only two were highly commended by Jesus.

Why did this happen? Here we can learn a valuable lesson from the Old Testament. After the children of Israel settled into the promised land, Joshua issued commands:

> "Therefore, fear the LORD and worship him in sincerity and truth. Get rid of the gods your ancestors worshiped beyond the Euphrates River. . . . or the gods of the Amorites in whose land you are living. As for me and my family, we will worship the LORD." (Josh. 24:14–15)

Unfortunately, God's people did not obey these directives, nor did they follow Joshua's example. Little by little they failed to teach their children God's commandments and how He had provided for them when they obeyed these commands. We read that after Joshua and his generation had died, "another generation rose up who did not know the LORD or the works he had done for Israel" (Judg. 2:8–10). They "did what was evil in the LORD's sight" and "worshiped the Baals and abandoned the LORD" (Judg. 2:8–12). Tragically, it only took *one generation* for degeneration to happen.

This evidently happened to the majority of the seven churches in Asia, no doubt for the same reasons it took place within the nation of Israel. And like today, churches can cease being dynamic communities of faith when pastoral leaders fail to:

- Provide believers with vital learning experiences with the Word of God

- Provide believers with vital relationships with one another and with God
- Provide believers with vital witnessing experiences with the unsaved world

Note: See chapters 12 and 13 to explore an in-depth look at these three vital experiences.

Lesson 2: We must understand that even though Jesus has a deep love and compassion for all communities of faith, He will also discipline those churches that knowingly and willingly depart from living in the will of God.

Jesus' love and compassion for all churches is obvious when he wrote to the church in Sardis—a worldly church. Addressing the majority, he said, "You have a reputation for being alive, but **you are dead**" (Rev. 3:1). Jesus also stated, "But you have a few people in Sardis who have not defiled their clothes, and they will walk with me in white, because they are worthy" (Rev. 3:4).

We also see Jesus' compassion and love when He addressed the church in Laodicea. Writing to the immature majority, He said, "For you say, 'I'm rich; I have become wealthy and need nothing,' and you don't realize that you are wretched, pitiful, poor, blind, and naked" (Rev. 3:17). However, at the end of the letter He once again revealed his love: "See! I stand at the door and knock. If **anyone** hears my voice and opens the door, I will come in and eat with him and he with me" (3:20).

Though Jesus loved all of these believers, we also see Jesus' intense disciplinary warnings. Note the graphic metaphors, which indicates Jesus' displeasure with various groups within these churches:

The Church in Ephesus

Remember then how far you have fallen; repent, and do the works you did at first. Otherwise, I will come to you and **remove your lampstand** from its place, unless you repent. (Rev. 2:5)

The Church in Pergamum

So repent! Otherwise, I will come to you quickly and fight against them with the **sword of my mouth**. (Rev. 2:16)

The Church in Thyatira

But I have this against you: You tolerate the woman Jezebel, who calls herself a prophetess and teaches and deceives my servants to commit sexual immorality and to eat meat sacrificed to idols. . . . Unless they repent of her works, **I will strike her children dead**. (Rev. 2:20, 22b, 33a)[1]

The Church in Sardis

Remember, then, what you have received and heard; keep it, and repent. If you are not alert, **I will come like a thief**, and you have no idea at what hour I will come upon you. (Rev. 3:3)

The Church in Laodicea

So, because you are lukewarm, and neither hot nor cold, **I am going to vomit you out of my mouth**. . . . As many as I love, I rebuke and discipline. So be zealous and repent. (Rev. 3:16, 19)

The Church in Corinth

These disciplinary warnings are also a stark reminder of Paul's admonitions in his first letter to the Corinthians. He addressed those in the church who were intentionally divisive and destructive:

Don't you yourselves know that you are God's temple [church] and that the Spirit of God lives in you? If **anyone** destroys God's temple [church], God will destroy **him**; for God's temple [church] is holy, and that is what you are. (1 Cor. 3:16–17)

Because Paul used "temple" rather than "church," it's easy to miss his message. He was certainly referring to this local community of faith in Corinth. To paraphrase, he was saying that if any individual Christian

356

purposely set out to destroy the love and unity in a local church, God will bring severe discipline into that person's life.

Paul does not define how God will "destroy" this erring believer. I've seen some tragic events happen in people's lives where this may have been God's discipline. We must not judge one another as to how God is carrying out this discipline. On the other hand, I take these statements by Paul very seriously, including his positive exhortations to the Ephesians:

> Therefore I, the prisoner in the Lord, urge you to walk worthy of the calling you have received, with all humility and gentleness, with patience, bearing with one another in love, **making every effort to keep the unity of the Spirit through the bond of peace**. (Eph. 4:1–3)

Lesson 3: We must understand that God holds spiritual leaders responsible for not dealing with sinful behavior in the church.

As pointed out in Jesus' letter to the church at Thyatira, He addressed the spiritual leader directly regarding his toleration of the woman Jezebel (Rev. 2:20). No doubt by design, we're not told who this pastoral leader was, but we can assume that he was probably the primary overseer.

James, the half-brother of Jesus, who became the lead elder in Jerusalem, would have identified with this lesson. In fact, he addressed this issue in his letter when he wrote: "Not many should become teachers, my brothers, because you know that we will receive a stricter judgment" (James 3:1).

This exhortation is not meant to discourage any one of us from Jesus' commission to teach other's the Word of God. However, it demonstrates that serving in a pastoral or teaching role is a serious effort. But the good news is, we can count on God's blessing and help—which leads to the next lesson.

Lesson 4: We must remember that Jesus Christ is still the great shepherd and founder of the church, and He will ultimately reward spiritual leaders for being faithful.

Toward the end of the apostle Peter's ministry on earth, he wrote these encouraging words:

> I exhort the **elders** among you as a **fellow elder** and witness to the sufferings of Christ, as well as one who shares in the glory about to be revealed: Shepherd God's flock among you, not overseeing out of compulsion but willingly, as God would have you; not out of greed for money but eagerly; not lording it over those entrusted to you, but being examples to the flock. **And when the chief Shepherd appears, you will receive the unfading crown of glory.** (1 Peter 5:1–4)

Regardless of our circumstances and challenges as spiritual leaders in the church, let's remember Jesus will reward us for being faithful. Let's also remember that when He gave the Great Commission to the apostles, He promised, "I am with you always, to the end of the age" (Matt. 28:20b). As pastoral leaders of local churches, we can claim this same promise. The author of Hebrews reminds us that Jesus "will never leave" us "or abandon" us (Heb. 13:5).

When Paul wrote to the Philippians, he specifically addressed the "overseers [elders] and deacons," along with all believers in this church, and then prayed for them all—a prayer request that we can certainly rely on for ministry today:

> And I pray this: that your love will keep on growing in knowledge and every kind of discernment, so that you may approve the things that are superior and may be pure and blameless in the day of Christ, filled with the fruit of righteousness that comes through Jesus Christ to the glory and praise of God. (Phil. 1:9–11)

Concluding Thoughts

In evaluating the state of the church today, we need to remind ourselves of what the apostle Paul wrote to the churches he and his missionary companions planted in the region of Galatia. He made the following metaphorical and passionate declaration: "**My children, I am again**

suffering labor pains for you until Christ is formed in you" (Gal. 4:19). Clearly, Paul agonized over the spiritual condition in the lives of those he led to Christ and he never ceased to do all he could to help these believers become more and more like Christ.

Jesus Christ, who "loved the church and gave himself for her to make her holy" (Eph. 5:25–26), continues to love believers of all times. His goal then and now is to "present the church to himself in splendor, without spot or wrinkle or anything like that, but holy and blameless" (5:27). This is both an eternal and present perspective. And toward the end of the first century, Jesus demonstrated this love at that moment in history—even though in some of the churches in Asia this involved "tough love."

I'm deeply committed to the church, regardless of some difficult and "messy situations." I can testify to the fact that when we are devoted to applying the enduring truths and supracultural principles that emerge from a careful study of Scripture, we can experience what Jesus prayed for—love and unity that is miraculous and deeply fulfilling (John 17:20–23). And let's remember: the darker the world becomes, the brighter our light can—and should—shine.

A Question for Thought and Discussion

When facing difficult situations in a local church, why is it so important to have godly men and women in leadership?

26

Leadership Lessons from Church History

Video Intro from Gene

3lenses.org/c26

There are a number of reasons why we should study history—the multi-faceted story that has continued beyond the biblical record. John Payne stated that "serious reflection on the past protects us from error, reminds us of God's faithfulness, and motivates us to persevere."[1]

Andrew Davis gives us another significant reason: "Studying church history has the power to humble us." We realize that "we are a part of something immeasurably immense, the dimensions of which it will take eternity to comprehend."[2]

Church history is an enormous study with a multitude of subjects and lessons that have already filled voluminous documents. In this single chapter I've chosen to focus on foundational lessons that relate to leadership. We'll look particularly at what transpired beyond the New Testament story at the end of the first century and at the beginning of the second century, and what impacted the church thereafter.[3]

The Earliest Church Fathers

It's difficult to imagine the challenges church leaders faced when direct messages from the "Spirit of truth" ceased in terms of the inspired Scriptures (John 14:15–17, 25; 15:26; 16:13; 2 Tim. 3:16). In fact, false apostles and prophets already existed during the New Testament period. Paul warned the Corinthians about "false apostles, deceitful workers, disguising themselves as apostles of Christ" (2 Cor. 11:13). Peter wrote that there would be "false prophets" and "false teachers" who would "bring in destructive heresies" (2 Peter 2:1). Jude called some of them "shepherds who only look after themselves" (Jude 1:12b). And after the Holy Spirit–inspired and supernaturally gifted apostles and prophets passed off the scene, this problem multiplied.

The Didache

Perhaps the first significant document following New Testament literature is the *Didache*, meaning "teaching" in Greek. The more elaborate title is "The Lord's Teaching Through the Twelve Apostles." The author or authors are anonymous and were not the original apostles appointed by Christ Himself. They appear to be Jewish believers who had significant knowledge of the Gospel of Matthew, and the writing is usually dated from late in the first century.

The *Didache* addresses leadership in the church, both Phase 1 and Phase 2 (see chapters 18 and 19). Regarding Phase l, the following words were written regarding apostles, prophets, and teachers (see Eph. 4:11–12; 1 Cor. 12:28a):

> Whosoever, therefore, comes and teaches you all these things that have been said before, receive him. But if the **teacher** himself turns and **teaches another doctrine** to the destruction of this, hear him not. But if he teaches so as to **increase righteousness** and **knowledge of the Lord**, receive him as the Lord. But concerning the **apostles** and **prophets,** act according to the decree of the Gospel. Let every **apostle** who comes to you be received as the Lord. But he shall not remain more than one day; or two days, if there's a need. But if he remains

three days, he is a **false prophet.** And when the apostle goes away, let him take nothing but bread until he lodges. If he asks for money, he is a **false prophet**. And every **prophet** who speaks in the Spirit you shall neither try nor judge. . . . But not everyone who speaks in the Spirit is a **prophet**; but only if he holds the ways of the Lord. Therefore, from their ways shall the false prophet and the **prophet** be known. . . . And every **prophet** who teaches the truth, but does not do what he teaches, is a **false prophet**. . . . But whoever says in the spirit, **Give me money**, or something else, you shall not listen to him.[4]

The rather austere guidelines in the *Didache* indicate the pervasive presence of false teaching. It also demonstrates that very soon following the events in the New Testament, direct revelation basically ceased or was rare. It would take a significant period of time before the New Testament documents both in part and as a whole were available.

Consequently, local churches had to develop specific criteria for determining false motives among those who claimed to be authentic apostles, prophets, and teachers. The *Didache* indicates that these supernaturally gifted individuals still lived, which may substantiate the conclusion that this document was written late in the first century. In fact, these references may have referred to some of the other Christ-appointed and gifted apostles who ministered with and perhaps outlived Peter, John, and Paul.

The authors of the *Didache* next addressed Phase 2, which is leadership in the local church. Many of these individuals were initially appointed by the apostles, following the example of Paul and Barnabas on the first missionary journey (Acts 14:21–23). The authors of the *Didache* indicate that these leaders were selected and appointed by the churches themselves, rather than by the apostles:

Appoint, therefore, for yourselves, **bishops** and **deacons** worthy of the Lord, men meek, and not lovers of money, and truthful and proved; for they also render to you the service of the **prophets** and **teachers**. Therefore do not despise them, for they are your honored ones, together with the **prophets** and **teachers**. And reprove one another, not in anger, but in peace, as you have it in the Gospel.[5]

At this point, it's important to review the nomenclature that emerged in the New Testament story to describe permanent local church leaders. The first term was *presbuteroi*, which is translated "elders." It was used to describe spiritual managers and shepherds of communities of believers who were predominantly Jewish, such as was true in the church in Jerusalem (Acts 11:30). This term was familiar to these converts since it was used for centuries to refer to the elders in Israel.

The second term was *episkepoi*, translated "overseers" or "bishops." This terminology was used interchangeably with "elders" and was familiar to Gentile believers since it was used to refer to leaders of Roman colonies. For example, the spiritual leaders in Ephesus—a Roman city—were identified by Luke with both terms since there were both Gentiles and Jews living in this city (Acts 20:17, 28). In both cultures, the titles were well-known, but the functions for these leaders changed to describe their managing and shepherding roles in local churches.

It's significant that the authors of the *Didache* used the term *episkepoi* (bishops). This no doubt indicated they were referring to leaders who ministered in local churches throughout the Gentile world. This also helps explain the warnings regarding false apostles, prophets, and teachers who were active in the predominantly Grecian and Roman culture.

Lessons from the *Didache*

Lesson 1: We must be cautious in giving credence to spiritual leaders who claim to be "apostles, prophets, and teachers" on par with those in the New Testament era who had gifts that were bestowed by Jesus Christ Himself.

These so-called spiritual leaders abound in many parts of the world today and are often guilty of communicating false doctrine. Sadly, many Christians—and even non-Christians—have fallen prey to what is often false teaching and even manipulative behavior.

The Scriptures are clear about how believers were to identify these individuals who were chosen and gifted by Jesus Christ Himself. Paul testified to his own calling when he made reference to miraculous gifts: "The **signs** of an apostle were performed with unfailing endurance among you, including **signs** and **wonders** and **miracles**" (2 Cor. 12:12). The author of Hebrews also references these apostolic signs (Heb. 2:2–4).

In view of Paul's reference as to how to identify a true apostle, this seems to be a significant omission in the *Didache*. This perhaps indicates that the authors lacked specific exposure to certain New Testament documents.

Lesson 2: We must take seriously the complete list of leadership qualities listed by Paul in the pastoral epistles.

The *Didache* demonstrates that leadership in the church was beginning to focus on Phase 2 involving the appointment of elders or bishops and deacons who were to serve as permanent leaders in local communities of faith. As we've noted earlier, we see an emphasis on character, but it is limited. These leaders were to be "worthy of the Lord, men meek, not **lovers of money**, and truthful and proved." Though these are valid qualities of maturity, Paul mentioned at least eighteen more in his letters to Timothy and Titus (1 Tim. 3:3; Titus 1:7).

The reference to not being "lovers of money" is significant since this was a serious problem among those who were false apostles, prophets, and teachers—long before the *Didache* was written. Paul specifically warned against this problem in his letter to Titus. Following the list of character qualities for selecting and appointing elders/overseers, he stated why taking these qualities seriously was so important:

> For there are many rebellious people, full of empty talk and deception, especially those from the circumcision party. It is necessary to silence them; they are ruining entire households by **teaching what they shouldn't in order to get money dishonestly**. (Titus 1:10–11)

It's no surprise that this serious problem continued to exist and multiply at the close of the first century and on into the second. This has continued to be a troublesome issue throughout church history, and is a serious problem even today. Religious leaders particularly who occupy high levels of leadership in Christianity have persistently used the false teaching embodied in "prosperity theology" to manipulate Christians materially to benefit themselves.

Clement of Rome

Clement served as bishop of Rome and penned an epistle to the Corinthians. It may have been written in the late 90s and was eventually eliminated from being in the canon of inspired Scripture. Nevertheless, what Clement wrote to this church nearly a half century after Paul's letters presents us with a serious issue faced by those who were appointed bishops in the Corinthian church.

Interestingly, the following quotation from Clement's epistle indicates these spiritual leaders were evidently appointed by some of the apostles who were chosen by Jesus Christ Himself:

> Christ therefore was sent forth by God, and the **apostles** by Christ. . . . Having therefore received their orders, being fully assured by the resurrection of our Lord Jesus Christ, and established in the word of God, with full assurance of the Holy Ghost, **they went** forth proclaiming that the kingdom of God was at hand. And thus preaching through **countries** and **cities**, **they appointed** the first-fruits [of their labors], having first proved them by the Spirit, to be **bishops** and **deacons** of those who should afterwards **believe**.[6]

In the book of Acts, Luke was selective in his references to the ministry of the apostles who were chosen, gifted, and "sent forth" by Jesus Christ. He focused primarily on Peter and John and then later on Paul. Clement may have given us a clue as to the ministry of at least one of the eleven apostles who were given the Great Commission on the mountain in Galilee (Matt. 28:16–20). Tradition indicates that Peter's brother, Andrew, ministered in Greece toward the end of his life, where he became a martyr. Though speculative, he may have been one of the apostles who helped appoint the "bishops and deacons" in Corinth.

Clement went on to describe other serious problems in the Corinthian church—which is reminiscent of the blatant carnality Paul addressed in his first letter decades before (see chapter 16). Evidently, there were once again some unspiritual individuals in the church who had orchestrated the dismissal of qualified spiritual leaders. Thus, Clement wrote:

> Our apostles also knew, through our Lord Jesus Christ, [that] there would be strife on account of the office of the **episcopate** [that is, bishops]. . . . We are of the opinion, therefore, that those appointed by them, or afterwards by other eminent men, with the consent of the whole Church, and who have blamelessly served the flock of Christ in a **humble, peaceable,** and **disinterested spirit,** and have for a long time possessed **the good opinion** of all, cannot be justly dismissed from the ministry. For our sin will not be small, if we eject from the **episcopate** those who have **blamelessly** and **holily** fulfilled its duties.[7]

Clement went on to address this same issue in a later chapter of this letter:

> It is disgraceful, beloved, yea, highly disgraceful, and unworthy of your Christian profession, that such a thing should be heard of as that the most steadfast and ancient church of the Corinthians should, on account of one or two persons, engage in sedition against its **presbyters.**[8]

A Powerful Lesson from Clement

Lesson: It only takes one or two strong, immature, and carnal individuals in the church to destroy unity and orchestrate rejection of qualified spiritual leaders.

When this happens it is a tragedy. As Paul wrote by inspiration of the Holy Spirit, it's dangerous to deliberately destroy unity in the church. He warned the believers in Corinth: "If anyone destroys God's temple [the church], God will destroy him" (1 Cor. 3:17a). No doubt aware of Paul's warnings, Clement underscored the same concern when he warned of "danger brought upon yourselves."

We can take this lesson one step further. If one or two carnal Christians can force qualified leaders to step away from ministry, it's certainly true when one or two of these individuals serve on a leadership team. They can destroy unity among the spiritual leaders that will filter down into the total church family. This is why it's so important to take the biblical qualifications for leadership seriously—something we'll address in more detail later in this chapter.

The good news is that when we have spiritually qualified leaders who function as a unified team, it's possible to deal with divisive people in the church body generally. But when there is also immaturity and carnality in the leadership, the door is wide open for a lethal attack from Satan. It can be devastating to a local community of faith. This is why it is so important that local churches have a system to make sure elders (including the lead pastor and other associates) be selected based on the qualities outlined by Paul in 1 and 2 Timothy. (See chapter 20 and 28, where I share a personal and painful lesson that illustrates what can happen when one carnal individual is appointed to be an elder.)

Ignatius, Bishop of Antioch

The following quotation regarding Ignatius is included as an introduction to his letters:

> Little is known of the early life of Ignatius, but his seven surviving letters describe his journey to Rome where he was condemned to die in the Coliseum. Ignatius was taken by a group of Roman soldiers from his home in Antioch, brought overland to Smyrna, then taken by ship to Greece, and eventually to Rome. Along the way he seems to have been allowed to meet with Christian congregations in various cities, to whom he composed his letters. Through them, we can see that Ignatius was familiar with Paul's epistles, as well as the Gospels of Matthew and John. In the 19th and 20th centuries, there was a great deal of scholarly debate as to whether the letters of Ignatius were authentic, or if they were forgeries written in his name after his death, but the current scholarly consensus is that the seven presented here [in this document] were in fact written by Ignatius.[9]

Ignatius' Letters. As we look at the letters Ignatius wrote to several churches, it appears that a significant amount of time had passed following the New Testament story. He definitely focused on Phase 2, namely, leadership in local churches and he made very little reference to those involved in Phase 1—apostles, prophets, and teachers. It seems apparent that most, if not all, of these supernaturally gifted individuals had entered heaven's gates.

Ignatius focused on what had developed into a three-tier system within local churches. He used "bishop" (*episkopos*) to refer to the primary leader of a local community of believers. He used "elders" (*presbuteroi*) to describe those men who reported to the bishop, and he used "deacons" (*diakonoi*) to describe those who served both the elders and the bishop.

Ignatius' Leadership Role. Since there is significant scholarly consensus that Ignatius served as the bishop of Antioch in Syria, it's helpful to reconstruct how he may have come to occupy this position. We can only speculate since we're not given details in the book of Acts as to how any of these elders were appointed in this church. Based on other events recorded in the biblical story, we can conjecture that it happened at some point after Luke referred to "Barnabas, Simeon . . . Lucius of Cyrene, Manaen . . . and Saul [Paul]" whom he identified as "**prophets** and **teachers**" (Acts 13:1).

Clearly, several of these men were leaders involved in Phase 1, since they received a direct revelatory message from the Holy Spirit. They were to commission Barnabas and Saul to begin the first missionary journey to the Gentile world (Acts 13:1–2). Luke has recorded that "**the Holy Spirit said**, 'set apart for me Barnabas and Saul for the work to which I have called them'" (13:2). Again, this specific message came directly from the Lord which indicates these men had at least two of the greater gifts, namely **prophet** and **teacher** (Eph. 4:12; 1 Cor. 12:28, 31).

This hypothesis that Ignatius and others were later appointed to be "elders" (*presbuteroi*) after this revelatory experience is based on what happened in Jerusalem. Again, we're not certain when elders were appointed in the Jerusalem church, but we can speculate it happened at some point following the apostles' involvement in the selection and appointment of the seven men to care for the widows (Acts 6:1–6). If elders had been appointed, it seems that they would have solved this problem. So, just as the apostles were involved in solving the widows' problems, we can also assume they were even more directly involved in the appointment of the Jerusalem elders (see chapter 19, "The Elders in Jerusalem (AD 45)").

At some point following this event, we know that the apostle Peter spent time in Antioch. Perhaps he and some of the other apostles were involved in the appointment of elders in the rapidly growing church in Antioch. Paul and Barnabas may have also participated when they returned from the first missionary journey, just as they were involved in appointing elders in the churches in Lystra, Iconium, and Antioch (Acts 14:21–22).

Regardless, Luke chose to omit this information from the book of Acts. We can certainly conclude that Ignatius was one of the elders in Antioch who eventually emerged as the leader of the other elders and was called a bishop (*episkopos*). In other words, just as James, the Lord's brother, had emerged as the primary leader among the elders in Jerusalem, Ignatius became the primary leader of the leaders in Antioch. To clarify his role, they called him the "bishop" (Acts 12:17; 15:13–21; 21:18). This was a new designation and definition, but it was still in harmony with the cultural freedom associated with the terms *elders* and *bishops* that were used interchangeably.

Bishop of Bishops. With this new title and leadership role, and because of the influence of false prophets and teachers throughout the Roman world, Ignatius emerged in the New Testament world as the "bishop of bishops" and took on himself unusual authority. This is predictable, since so many churches were being impacted by false doctrine. Furthermore, the bulk of the New Testament letters were not readily available.

Ignatius was a dedicated disciple of Jesus Christ. He was concerned that believers were being led astray by false views regarding the deity of Jesus Christ and the means of salvation—that we are saved by grace through faith. In many respects, the statements in his letters sound similar to what we read in Paul's epistles.

Because of Ignatius' example and emphasis on the bishop's leadership role, other bishops eventually emerged and took on themselves virtually apostolic authority. The local church elders in turn supported and reported to each bishop. Though Ignatius taught that the bishop and elders should humbly serve together in giving direction to the church, each bishop eventually came to have the final word in many aspects of the life of the church.

As stated, deacons in turn supported both the elders and the bishop, but recognized the bishop as the primary leader with significant spiritual authority. They, too, were to be highly respected, but they were servants to the other leaders.

Following are some selected quotes from various letters indicating what Ignatius taught in this three-tier system.[10]

The Epistles of Ignatius to the Ephesians

Chapter 1

And that being, **subject to your bishop**, and the **presbytery** [elders], ye may be holy and thoroughly sanctified . . . (v. 9).

For even Jesus Christ, our inseparable life, is sent by the will of the Father; as the bishops, appointed unto the utmost bounds of the earth, are by the will of Jesus Christ (v. 12).

Wherefore it will become you to run together according to the **will of your bishop**, as also ye do (v. 13).

Chapter 2

Let us take heed therefore, that **we do not set ourselves against the bishop,** that we may be subject to God . . . (v. 3).

It is there evident that we ought to **look upon the bishop,** even as we do **upon the Lord Himself** (v. 4).[11]

We see this same emphasis in what Ignatius wrote to the Magnesians, the Trallians, the Philadelphians, and the Smyrnaeans. In one letter he wrote that the bishop presides "in the place of God." In another letter he wrote that "it is not lawful without the bishop, neither to baptize, nor to celebrate the Holy Communion."[12] This demonstrates authority that is never specified in the New Testament.

In many respects, however, it's inspiring to read the letters of Ignatius. He was a godly, humble leader—willing to give his life as a martyr, which happened. He had a deep concern for unity and godliness among the leaders of the church as well as for the whole church family. Perhaps most importantly, he was concerned about doctrinal purity.

It's also understandable why Ignatius promoted the three-tier system of leadership in the local church with the bishop serving as the primary leaders of the elders. This in itself is in harmony with what we see developing in the biblical story, beginning in Jerusalem with James serving as the lead elder. We also see this development in the letters Jesus dictated to the "angels," or "messengers" in the seven churches of Asia. Most Bible interpreters agree they were the primary leaders.

Lesson 1: All church leaders need a leader, but one who is a servant-leader and also accountable to those he leads.

Unfortunately, Ignatius' emphasis on every local church bishop being answerable only to God helped lead to a lack of accountability. And though it was a biblical and practical role, serving as "bishop of bishops" evolved into an abuse of power, which began to take place in churches throughout the Roman world. It led to the non-biblical leadership hierarchy in the Roman church and continued in some of the Reformation churches—which in more ways than one violated the servant-leadership model in the New Testament.[13]

Sadly, much of what we see throughout church history violates what Jesus taught the apostles in the upper room following the foot washing experience. Asking these men if they understood what He had done for them, Jesus answered His own question:

> You call me Teacher and Lord—and you are speaking rightly, since that is what I am. So if I, your Lord and Teacher, have washed your feet, you also ought to wash one another's feet. For I have given you an example, that you also should do just as I have done for you. (John 13:13–15)

As we follow the unfolding biblical story, it's clear that the real issue is not the "foot washing" experience per se; rather, Jesus was teaching them that "the greatest among you will be your servant" (Matt. 23:11; see chapters 6 and 19).

Even though Jesus told Peter in a clear statement that he would be a primary leader in laying the foundation and building the church, he learned this lesson well (Matt. 16:18; Eph. 2:19–20). Toward the end of his life on earth, he wrote these descriptive and humble words to all local church leaders. Speaking as the primary leader of the apostles—one of the most significant and important leadership roles in Christendom—he wrote:

> I exhort the elders among you as a **fellow elder** and witness to the sufferings of Christ, as well as one who shares in the glory about to be revealed: Shepherd God's flock among you, **not overseeing out of compulsion** but **willingly**, as God would have you; **not out of greed for money** but eagerly; **not lording it over those entrusted to you**, but being examples to the flock. (1 Peter 5:1–3)

It's true that every body of elders in a local community of faith needs a primary leader—with authority to to lead. But the New Testament teaches and illustrates that he is to be a servant-leader—to be accountable to the other elders. Paul made this clear when he addressed the Ephesian elders at Miletus (Acts 20:28–31). And since all these men were to be servant-leaders, they were to be accountable to each other and to Jesus Christ (see chapter 20, principle 5).

For this to happen, there's another important lesson that emerges, not only from the epistles of Ignatius, but from the story of the church to the present day.

Lesson 2: All spiritual leaders within the local church and within larger communities of faith should be selected and appointed to leadership based on the specific qualifications outlined by the apostle Paul in his letters to Timothy and Titus.

This lesson from the letters of Ignatius elaborates on what we also learn from both the *Didache*, and the epistle written by Clement of Rome. To review, the authors of the *Didache* stated that both "bishops and deacons" were to be "worthy of the Lord, men meek, not lovers of money, and truthful and proved." In addition, Clement implied that spiritual leaders should serve the church "blamelessly . . . in a **humble**, peaceable and disinterested spirit" and were to have "the good opinion of all." Neither document made reference to the numerous qualifications for leadership outlined by Paul.

It's possible that these authors never had access to the pastoral epistles. Clement does imply that he knew what Jesus taught the apostles about humility. However, the unfolding biblical story makes it clear that it is not sufficient for evaluating prospective church leaders. In fact, this is one of the most significant lessons that I've learned from my years of church planting. Even though we took all of the qualities seriously, initially we did not develop a procedure to measure these qualities (see chapter 20, principle 2).

Ignatius also implied that local church leaders were to imitate Jesus Christ in their character, but beyond humility there's no specific reference to what this looks like. Paul is definitive in the list of qualifications in both 1 Timothy and Titus.

Ongoing Church History. These observations lead to a thought-provoking question. Following these rather brief references to the qualifications for local church leaders by these early church fathers, as church history continued to unfold, where do we discover a strong emphasis on appointing leaders in the church who measure up to this biblical standard and criteria? It's certainly not true in Roman Catholic church history. In fact, Augustine, who is one of the most influential theologians in early church history, "argued that the grace of God is not dependent on the qualities of the minister, but upon the wonder of God's grace."[14]

Augustine further argued that "the church" is a repository of God's grace and the means of the distribution of grace to people. In other words, because the spiritual leader had an official recognized function in "the church," he was able to convey God's grace to others regardless of his character. This perspective in in total contradiction with what Paul wrote in the pastoral epistles.[15]

But let's take this a step further. Where do we have a significant emphasis on these qualifications in the writings of the major Reformers? Though their greatest emphasis was on the authority of Scripture and justification by faith and not works, a specific emphasis on utilizing these qualities in the appointment of local church leaders appears to be missing.

As I was researching and reflecting on this subject, I met with my good friend and church historian, John Hannah. After sharing my observations regarding the church fathers, I posed the question I raised earlier: "Where in church history do we have a strong emphasis on the importance of utilizing the specific qualifications outlined by Paul in selecting church leaders?"

John paused, reflected, and then said, "I really don't remember any!" He then stated that in most situations it seems it was simply assumed that these qualities are important.

Theological Education. In the twentieth century, we experienced a great movement in the United States resulting in Bible institutes, Bible colleges, and seminaries, which influenced other institutions in many other parts of the world. These academic ministries were established to replace seminaries that had become theologically liberal. In turn, curriculum was designed primarily to prepare people for ministry.

But here's another pointed question: Where do we have examples of graduation requirements that include the specific qualifications in 1 Timothy and Titus? We do indeed have consistent references to Christian character as a requirement for graduation, but where do we have the actual biblical criteria for measuring this Christian character?

This observation is not to downplay the importance of theological and academic requirements, but rather, it implies that we have continued to neglect an important foundational biblical emphasis and priority on Christlike character and maturity for Christian leaders.

Based on Scripture, church history, and my experience as a professor and a church planting pastor, I'm convinced that selecting and appointing church leaders based on these requirements is foundational for leading a church to continue "growing into maturity with a stature measured by

Christ's fullness" (Eph. 4:13). It's significant in modeling for all believers in the church what God intended regarding mature marriages, effective parenting, and godly living in general. The qualities are indeed the measure of a mature Christian. My prayer is that as we continue to sharpen the focus of the church in the twenty-first century, we recapture more and more the emphasis Paul outlined in his pastoral epistles.

In the last couple of decades, some helpful books have been written on the subject on elders and deacons and the biblical qualifications for serving in the local church. I personally recommend several![16]

A Question for Thought and Discussion

As you consider the leadership lessons we can learn from early church history, what would you consider to be the most significant?

27

Forms and Institutionalism

Video Intro from Gene

3lenses.org/c27

What follows in this chapter are significant lessons that we can learn from social history generally and church history particularly. Both involve people groups and relate to the way organizational structures have been developed to function in order to meet physical, emotional, social, and spiritual needs.

The Phenomenon of Fixation

Wherever people live on planet earth at any moment throughout the ages, they function in various ways. This is what life and living is all about. God created us to engage in a variety of activities. Regarding Adam, we read, "The LORD God took the man and placed him in the garden of Eden to **work it** and **watch over it**" (Gen. 2:15).

Since the original creation, people have developed forms in order to function. Over time, we develop a sense of security in doing things a certain way and change can feel threatening. Consequently, we tend to fixate on those forms.

Dr. Robert Nisbet, a renowned social historian, demonstrates this phenomenon among people groups. This involves both function and form. In his insightful book *Social Change and History*, he concludes that change is "not normal, much less ubiquitous and constant." He then goes on to state that "fixity is."[1]

Fixation on both function and form also happens within our local churches. As believers who meet together, we use the freedom God has given us to develop forms in order to function. And, like all people groups, we tend to fixate. We develop a sense of security in doing things in a certain way.

However, there's another reason we persist or fixate. Over the centuries we have failed to differentiate between biblical absolutes and cultural non-absolutes. In other words, Christians often believe the methodological ways they do church are prescribed in the Bible and should never change.

There are some Christians—even in our enlightened Christian society—who believe that their traditional order of worship is a biblical order. They resist change, believing they have theological reasons for this resistance.

This creates a double challenge for pastoral leaders who want to change the structures of the church in order to more effectively carry out biblical functions in our changing culture. On the one hand, Christians, too, are not exempt from resisting change because they feel insecure. On the other hand, they justify their resistance for what they believe are scriptural reasons.

Crises Bring Change

This is another lesson we can learn from Nisbet's research. To make the point regarding crises and change, he quotes Newton:

> "Every body continues in its state of rest, or of uniform motion in a straight line, unless it is compelled to change that state by forces impressed upon it."[2]

Ironically, fixation in itself will eventually create a crisis. To make this additional point, Nisbet references another prominent social historian. Paraphrasing W. E. Thomas, he states:

The very tendency of social behavior to persist, to hold fast to values and convenience, makes a degree of crisis inevitable in all but the most minor of changes. A given way of behaving tends to persist as long as circumstances permit. Then . . . the way of behaving ceases to be possible, as a result of some intrusion, some difficulty which is the consequence of event or impact, and a period of crisis ensues. The crisis, with all its social and psychological accompaniments of conflict and tension, which have been occasioned by the shattering of old ways, continues until some new form of an adaptation is reached; one in which elements of the old—usually a good many of these—are fused with new elements drawn in part from the precipitating intrusion.[3]

We can illustrate this observation in our current culture. At the beginning of the twenty-first century, there was a growing concern regarding problems created by hydrocarbon-fueled vehicles and damage to the environment created by their emissions. There was a renewed interest in developing electric vehicles by private industrialists, and their success in turn impacted the automotive industry. These dramatic changes would not have happened as they did apart from this crisis in our present culture.

This historical insight that crises bring change in society is helpful in bringing needed changes in our churches. We have divine resources that will enable us to bring about a supernatural crisis. The first resource is the divinely inspired Word of God. The second resource is the Spirit of truth who both inspired the authors of Scripture to record the Word of God and to convict those who hear the Word of God.

Practically speaking, this involves teaching what the Word of God says about absolutes and non-absolutes. As we've demonstrated in the previous section, "The Lens of Scripture," supracultural functions that yield supracultural principles are absolute. However, forms, structures, and methodology are non-absolutes. God has given us freedom to develop forms that will enable us to function biblically in all cultures of the world and at any moment in history.

"Speaking the Truth in Love"

This also means we should never compromise the teachings of the Word of God, but at the same time we should always "speak the truth in love" (Eph. 4:15). This is a specific directive from the apostle Paul. It's in this context that the Holy Spirit can create a crisis in people's lives that causes them to be open to change.

This dynamic is true in all areas of our Christian lives. Any time the truth of Scripture impacts our lives in areas that are out of God's will, it should create a spiritual and emotional crisis leading us to renew our minds so that we can walk in God's "good, pleasing, and perfect will" (Rom. 12:1–2).

A Life-Changing Personal Crisis

At this point, I want to once again relate how a crisis had a dramatic impact on my own life and ministry. As a professor in a seminary classroom, my students raised some challenging questions about the relevance of the church—challenging what I was currently teaching. It didn't take long for me to realize that I wasn't prepared to answer their questions, and it created a personal crisis.

It was then I decided midsemester to have the students "trash the syllabus"—my very words to them. I then told them we were going to back to *the* Syllabus, Jesus' Great Commission, to see how God's plan for the church unfolded throughout the biblical story.

This was an exacting and uncomfortable experience—even threatening. However, had I not faced this challenge, I would not have taken this dramatic and life-changing step. I would never have written the original copy of this book, nor would I have eventually left the seminary classroom to become a full-time church planting pastor.

I've shared this story to demonstrate that "crises" are often necessary to make significant changes in our lives. There's another significant reason I faced this particular crisis with a great deal of confidence. I firmly believed that I could find the answers to my students' questions from the inspired Word of God. My feelings of insecurity subsided as I discovered answers with the support and help from fellow professors. And, when some of my colleagues felt I was departing—at least in some respects—from a biblical ecclesiology, I was reassured by what was happening in the lives of my students. Most of the criticisms that came my way were, in essence, opinions about "forms"—not biblical functions.

Additional Anxiety

In terms of insecurity that is often associated with changes in form, let me review another personal experience. I started the first Fellowship Bible Church with a small group of keenly interested couples. I had shared the three vital experiences, along with the concept of freedom in form. This led us to launch the first Fellowship Bible Church. In the process, we developed some new forms and structures that we felt would enable us to be the church God intended us to be for our unique moment in history and in our present culture in Dallas, Texas.

It was an exciting adventure for all of us. But for a number of months, I also experienced unusual anxiety. One day it dawned on me why I was experiencing this discomfort. For a number of years, I had been involved in one kind of church structure—a system I knew well. But I was now under scrutiny by some of my colleagues as well as being involved in some dramatic form changes. In terms of my past experience, I knew the forms forward and backward within a traditional church. I had not been down this new path before. But—and this is important—once I understood the source of my anxiety, I developed a new sense of security and confidence.

This leads to a significant lesson we can learn from both social and church history:

Lesson: Since structural changes can be threatening and create insecurity, we must do all we can to help people understand from Scripture the difference between function and form; between biblical principles and cultural patterns; between organism and organization. In essence, we must help them understand the difference between absolutes and non-absolutes.

Institutionalism

A common term that has been used to describe a significant aspect of "fixation on form" is **institutionalism**. When this happens, an institution or organization tends to become more important than the people these structures were designed to serve.

John W. Gardner, speaking essentially as a secularist, defined this as "organizational dry rot."[4] Though he addressed this issue decades ago, what he wrote still applies, not only to institutions generally, but also to local churches and denominations.

Following are some specific symptoms of institutionalism which I've paraphrased from literature and my own personal experiences:

- The structural arrangements in the organization become rigid and inflexible.
- Individuality and creativity are often lost in the structural mass.
- Communication breaks down within the organizational structure as described by this descriptive metaphor: "The right hand doesn't know what the left hand is doing."
- As the organization increases in size, "silos" come into existence, which can cause serious misunderstandings and even competition within the organization.
- People often begin to focus on their own interests and develop their own forms within the organization. When this happens, the corporate objective of the organization is diluted because of the number of self-serving objectives.

When all of this happens, it affects the morale and motivation within the organization. People begin to function more out of duty and obligation than privilege and opportunity. And, as the organization continues to increase in size, the process of institutionalism speeds up. A hierarchy of leadership often develops which intensifies the problems of communication from the top to the bottom of the organization.

Institutionalism in Judaism

Religious organizations are certainly not exempt from this kind of "dry rot." We see this graphically illustrated in Judaism in the first century. In fact, Jesus put His finger on the devastating results of institutionalism. He reminded the religious leaders that they had successfully preserved their religious system and that their traditions had led the majority of people into an external conformity with an outward expression of their religion, but they had lost the individual who had no deep understanding of God's truth. Their followers had no vital and real experience with the living God. This is the ultimate manifestation of legalism.

We have a specific example when Jesus' disciples were criticized by the Pharisees for plucking the heads of grain on the Sabbath. Jesus retorted, "The Sabbath was made for man and not man for the Sabbath" (Mark 2:27). In other words, Jesus was saying, "You have taken a means and made it an end in itself. You have completely lost sight of the spirit of the law. You've lost the individual in your religious system. All you have left is an empty form."

Institutionalism in Christianity

Unfortunately, as believers and members of the body of Christ, we are not exempt from the process that leads to institutionalized Christianity. This is obvious from church history. Vibrant New Testament churches gave way to "organizational dry rot," which was further intensified by false doctrine and unrighteous living. Though there have been encouraging pockets of renewal within local churches and movements, history reveals significant institutionalism within both Roman Catholicism and Protestantism. Spiritual life and vitality and authentic relationships with God have often gotten lost in the structural mass.

All of this leads to an important lesson:

Lesson: As Christian leaders, we must be aware that our churches can become institutionalized; however, it need not happen if we continue to evaluate our forms and structures in the light of biblical functions and supracultural principles.

For organizational renewal to happen continually it must happen based on a solid theological foundation "with Christ Jesus himself as the cornerstone" (Eph. 2:20). However, even solid doctrine does not guarantee that a church or denomination is exempt from institutionalism. Unfortunately, our forms can become more important than the people we serve. Individuals can get lost in the structural mass. Our organization can become rigid and inflexible. Morale and unity among believers can deteriorate. And when our churches begin to increase in size, debilitating institutionalism can seriously interfere with our efforts to carry out the Great Commission.

On the one hand, numerical growth can be a great blessing and a result of diligent and effective ministry. On the other hand, we must be continuously on guard against becoming institutionalized.

Again, this need not happen if we continually sharpen the focus of our churches by using the lenses of Scripture, history, and culture. Practically speaking, this means we are continually evaluating our overall ministry to make sure that we are applying the supracultural principles that emerge from the biblical story. We must also learn lessons from church history and, without compromise, understand and penetrate our particular cultural situations and environments with the eternal Word of God.

Imbalance in Function and Form

Without question, most of us who believe that Scripture was inspired by the Holy Spirit are committed to providing believers with the **three vital experiences** so beautifully modeled initially by the Jerusalem church (see chapter 12).

1. We're committed to solid **Bible teaching**.
2. We believe in leading believers to **worship God** and to **relate to one another** in various ways.
3. We're committed to **reaching people with the gospel**.

Most Christian leaders today also believe we have freedom to create unique structures to provide believers with these three experiences. This is the essence of evangelical ecclesiology.

However, even current church history reveals that we tend to develop forms to emphasize one or two of these vital experiences rather than all three. To illustrate this reality, consider the following categories of churches. But, as you do, please understand that by design these descriptions are somewhat oversimplified and overgeneralized. Nevertheless the categories help demonstrate an important lesson regarding church function and church form.

Some churches have structured primarily to teach the Word of God.

It appears this has happened in our American culture particularly because of what transpired at the turn of the twentieth century. In my own research, I discovered that there were at least seventy Protestant seminaries that became theologically liberal, departing from a strong belief in the authority and inspiration of Scripture. This gave rise to the popular Bible conference movement that flourished for a number of years. People were hungry for the Word of God. It gave birth to Bible institutes and colleges and eventually to evangelical seminaries that replaced those that had become liberal. Predictably, the founders of these theological institutions developed curricula that focused primarily on learning the Scriptures. Bible courses were front and center.

Pastoral graduates of these institutions in turn focused on Bible teaching in many churches, recapturing what liberalism had removed from many American pulpits. This was particularly true where new churches were planted. Programs were structured to provide believers with a knowledge of the Word of God. In some cases, these churches functioned more like miniature Bible institutes.

Needless to say, this was an important and foundational emphasis. Believers need to be taught Scripture. This is the first vital experience described in the Jerusalem model. These new believers "devoted themselves to the **apostles' teaching**"—which was indeed the Word of God being revealed by the "Spirit of truth" just as Jesus had promised (John 14:16–17, 26).

However, with this emphasis, there has been a tendency to neglect the other two vital experiences that are essential in helping believers continue "growing into maturity with a stature measured by Christ's fullness" (Eph.

4:13). In fact, Bible knowledge alone can subtly lead to spiritual pride and isolationism from other believers.

With this emphasis came another problem. Many Christians became ardent "listeners" to what in essence were "Bible lectures" with little opportunity for personal interaction and mutual ministry. In fact, biblical functions that God designed for the body of Christ were replaced with a trained and talented Bible teacher.

Some churches have structured primarily to provide believers with vital relational experiences with one another and with God.

Interestingly, this emphasis also gained momentum at the beginning of the twenty-first century. Renewed emphasis on spiritual gifts gave rise to the charismatic movement. There was a strong focus on body function as well as meaningful worship, which led to an emphasis on both the emotional and experiential dimensions of Christianity. This became a counterbalance to the focus on "head knowledge" alone that can naturally result from learning Scripture in isolation from dynamic relationships with one another and with God.

God designed the body of Christ to function in all its parts (see chapters 14 and 15). However, this focus often led to a vacuum in understanding some important doctrines. The emphasis on experience sometimes affected the way Bible passages were interpreted rather than interpreting experiences in light of solid biblical exposition.

In some instances, this strong emphasis on experience has led to spiritual pride, just as a strong emphasis on Bible teaching has also led to the same tendency. Believers within this **affective movement** tended to judge fellow believers who did not have the same experiences as they did, just as believers within the **cognitive movement** judged fellow believers who did not have the same theological viewpoints.

This strong emphasis on body function and worship created meaningful personal and corporate experiences. Unfortunately, this emphasis sometimes led to extreme and questionable manifestations. Clearly, experiences without solid biblical teaching can lead believers astray.

Some churches have structured primarily for evangelism, with a strong emphasis on reaching the unsaved.

In our particular culture, it's difficult to pinpoint when Bible-believing Christian leaders first began to emphasize soul winning as the primary function of the church. Though the Bible is front and center, messages are often based on isolated texts rather than an exposition of biblical passages. And even though what is shared—at least for the most part—doesn't contradict Scripture, listeners are not exposed to the total unfolding story in Scripture (2 Tim. 3:6). The primary purpose of these messages is often to end with an invitation for salvation.

In terms of making disciples, this purpose is certainly in harmony with the Great Commission. However, as we've seen, when churches were planted in the biblical story, the major purpose of the church gathered was edification rather than evangelism.

A more current movement that has often focused on evangelism when the majority of believers gather has been called the "seeker movement." This emphasis has developed particularly within the megachurch movement, and has contributed significantly to creating large churches. Services are purposefully structured to create an atmosphere that is appealing to those who are not believers but who are exploring the message of Christianity and biblical content is selected and delivered in such a way so as to reach unbelievers.

Most leaders who take this approach also recognize the importance of equipping believers to become mature in Christ. Consequently, in addition to the main services, Bible-teaching programs are planned and structured for edification of believers, such as midweek classes and small groups.

Since the Scriptures are divinely designed to allow freedom in form, attempting to be "seeker friendly" certainly does not contradict this supracultural principle per se. However, since weekends and Sundays particularly have been the most culturally accepted time for believers to attend church services in order to be edified, this approach has often resulted in ambivalence and disappointment on the part of many believers. On the one hand, they're excited to see unbelievers interested in attending church and responding to the gospel. On the other hand, they desire a more in-depth exposure to Scripture to be encouraged and edified, which is one of the major purposes of the church.

There is yet another problem with this structure. Even though new believers are encouraged to attend classes for nurture, they often choose to attend only one main service, which is not designed primarily for spiritual growth. This is indeed a cultural factor affecting all attendees that we cannot ignore.

As stated earlier, these three observations are somewhat overstatements and generalizations. However, they help illustrate the way evangelical leaders have often used freedom in form to structure local church ministries. They have chosen to focus on just one of the three vital experiences illustrated and taught throughout the New Testament.

Obviously, we can also cite churches that emphasize two of these experiences rather than all three. For example:

- Some churches structure for **Bible teaching** and **relational experiences** and neglect **evangelism**. This can definitely create an ingrown mentality. Christians can become satisfied to focus on themselves without a concern for those who are lost without Christ.
- Some churches structure for **relational experiences** and **evangelism** while neglecting **Bible teaching**—which can lead to serious theological issues. In some cases, it can lead to sectarianism and even cultic beliefs and practices.
- Some churches structure for **Bible teaching** and **evangelism** and neglect **fellowship**—which can lead to superficial relationships with God and one another. The numerous "one another" injunctions that relate to "body function" are neglected.

Again, these three additional emphases are overly simplified. However, all of these categorizations can help all of us as spiritual leaders to evaluate our church structures to see if we're providing believers with **all three experiences in proper sequence** and **in proper balance**. I've discovered in my own church planting experiences that it was helpful and productive to review the Jerusalem model at least once a year for the total congregation.

The reason is obvious—which leads to an important lesson:

Lesson: No matter what our commitment to "freedom in form," it's easy to allow non-absolutes to become absolute and to become imbalanced in our emphases on these three vital experiences.

A Question for Thought and Discussion

As you reflect on your own experience in the local church, what have you observed regarding function and form?

28

Lessons from My Personal History

Video Intro from Gene

3lenses.org/c28

As pastoral leaders particularly, some of the most practical and productive lessons can come from our own experiences. This has certainly been true for me. We need to learn from our personal histories.

I'm thankful for God's blessings in my own church planting ministry. After starting the first Fellowship Bible Church, we were able to start a number of successful church plants in the Dallas area. And, to our surprise, this precipitated the Fellowship Bible Church movement, resulting in hundreds of churches. What happened beyond the Dallas area became spontaneous. For example, several families who helped launch our original church moved to Little Rock, Arkansas, and founded a Fellowship Bible Church. This church then launched a church planting ministry involving dozens of local communities of faith, and some of these churches also multiplied churches.

As I reflect on these church planting and pastoral experiences, there are things I would certainly attempt to improve and even do differently. What follows are some of those areas.

Making Disciples

In some respects, I'm reflecting on opportunities to communicate the gospel because this is where Jesus began when He charged the eleven apostles to go and "make disciples"; to share the good news with unbelievers and bring them to a saving relationship with Jesus Christ.

This is a major part of the book of Acts, particularly the apostolic teams that carried out the Great Commission. Church planting was at the heart of their ministry. From the very beginning of the church in Jerusalem, as a community of believers they were also involved in evangelism. Luke made this clear: "They devoted themselves to the apostles' teaching" as well as to "fellowship" with one another and with God. They were "**enjoying the favor of all the people**"; namely, those who were coming to faith in Jesus Christ (Acts 2:42–47). Thus, Luke recorded: "Every day the Lord added to their number **those who were being saved**" (Acts 2:47). In context, people were putting their faith in Christ, not because of the apostles' evangelistic ministry per se, but because of the functioning body of Christ in Jerusalem.

Subsequently, we see this happening in churches throughout the Roman world (1 Thess. 1:7–10; Rom. 1:8). As each church came into existence because of apostolic teams, believers were to be a living witness personally and corporately to unsaved neighbors and associates. This involved exemplifying the gospel in their business lives, social lives, church lives, and in their lives in general (see chapter 6).

The Agape Meal

As we look more specifically at the Jerusalem model and at those who responded to the gospel, a significant part of their witness happened as they "broke bread from house to house" and "ate their food with joyful and sincere hearts" (Acts 2:46). This is certainly a reference to the *agape* meal—a meal that included breaking bread to remember the Lord's pierced and broken body and partaking of a cup of wine as a reminder of the Savior's shed blood. In other words, throughout Jerusalem and the surrounding area, *the rather complex Passover meal in the upper room became a simple communal meal throughout the Jerusalem area* (see chapter 12).

A Practical Question. How did these new believers learn to engage in this *agape* experience? To answer this, we must remember that those who believed and received Jesus as the Messiah first and foremost "devoted themselves to the **apostles' teaching**" (Acts 2:42a). Here Luke obviously used a generalization to describe what would have been a significant learning process. This would have included specific teaching regarding what the apostles had just experienced and learned at the Passover meal. Furthermore, Jesus' promise to the apostles in the upper room that the Father would send the Holy Spirit to "**remind**" them of "everything" He had taught them could have included an immediate **reminder** and **explanation** of the true meaning of the bread and the cup He had shared with them during the Passover meal (John 14:26; Luke 22:19–20). Next to the humbling foot washing experience, this would have been uppermost in their minds.

Years later, Paul reviewed the true meaning of the Lord's Supper in his first letter to the Corinthians—an explanation that he also "received from the Lord" (1 Cor. 11:23–26). Unfortunately, some of these believers were abusing this sacred meal designed to remember God's gift to the world when He gave "His one and only Son" to die on the cross (11:27–33; John 3:16).

An Application for Today. There were certainly unique Jewish cultural dynamics involved in this first-century experience. However, there's a significant supracultural element that is a part of our lives as human beings in all cultures of the world and throughout history. This element involves **eating together**. For believers, this experience provides a wonderful opportunity to remember the Lord's sacrifice on the cross. And, as we do, we can demonstrate Christlike love and oneness to our unsaved neighbors—just as this happened in Jerusalem and later throughout the Roman world.

Here's the significant lesson I've learned from my own pastoral ministry. On the one hand, I've seen the positive value of encouraging believers to meet together in small groups—a function and form we introduced early in our church planting ministry. But as I reflect back on this experience, I firmly believe we could have more effectively maximized the evangelism potential within these small groups by following the Jerusalem model. More specifically, I'm convinced we could have reached more unsaved neighbors by inviting them to experience the *agape* meal. It's in this context that believers can demonstrate in a dramatic way not only the love and unity Jesus taught and prayed for, but—as we partake of these elements—we can naturally share why Jesus Christ had to give His life in death.

The challenge is to blend "edification" with "evangelism." But this can happen as unbelievers see believers demonstrating love and oneness as they engage in the *agape* meal (John 13:34–35; 17:20–23). This becomes a powerful apologetic in convincing unsaved people that Jesus Christ is really who He claimed to be—**the Son of God who is one with the Father.** It can become the experience that enables unbelievers to understand more clearly what John wrote: "But to all who did **receive him** [Christ], he gave the right to be children of God, to those who **believe** in his name" (John 1:12).

But here's something important we tend to miss in the Jerusalem story. When we look more carefully at what Luke recorded, it would be natural that unsaved Jews—and perhaps unconverted God-fearing Gentiles—actually participated in this experience. And while **receiving** the bread and **drinking** from the cup—a significant part of the *agape* meal— they later in a simple act of faith **received** the living Christ and **believed** He was indeed the promised Messiah (John 1:11–13). We read that it was during this experience that the believers were "enjoying the favor of all the people," namely, unbelievers "who were being saved" (Acts 2:47).

Understandable Objections. One of the objections to this interpretation relates to the assumption that unbelievers should never participate in the communion experience. To support this conclusion, they reference Paul's directives regarding self-examination in order to avoid God's discipline (1 Cor. 11:27–32). However, it's my opinion that we should not apply this warning to unbelievers. Paul was addressing the sinful actions among these Corinthian believers. They were abusing the *agape* meal, gorging themselves with the food that was to illustrate Christ's broken body, and even becoming inebriated with the wine that was to illustrate Christ's shed blood (1 Cor. 11:21).

They may have even been behaving just as they had done as they participated in the meals in the pagan temples. It's possible they even engaged in immoral acts following the meal, just as they had done when they were unbelievers worshiping pagan gods.

This may be why Paul warned against this kind of immorality and even alluded to temple prostitution earlier in this letter (1 Cor. 6:12–20). Regardless, this serious and almost unbelievable carnality and sinful behavior on the part of the Corinthian believers brought God's severe discipline, including sickness, and even death (11:30).

An Unparalleled Opportunity. If this interpretation is correct, the *agape* meal provides all believers with an unparalleled opportunity to illustrate and communicate the gospel. This experience can be nonthreatening to unbelievers, enabling the Holy Spirit to convict them to invite Christ to become a part of their **innermost being**—just as they had received the bread and wine, and it became a part of their **physical bodies**. And as the bread and wine is explained, the Holy Spirit can also use the love and unity that is displayed among believers as they participate in remembering the Lord's broken body and shed blood. Again, it appears that this was happening to a multitude of God-fearing Grecian Jews during the early days of the church. Consequently, new believers were added to the church every day (Acts 2:47)!

Please understand—I'm not suggesting that **receiving** the bread and wine is the **means** that brings salvation. Rather, it is an experience that demonstrates what it means to personally believe in Christ and to **receive Him** by faith, and, as a result, experience the new birth. It illustrates in a symbolic but dramatic way what Jesus truly meant when He said: "The one who eats my flesh and drinks my blood has eternal life" (John 6:54).

In summary, if I had my years of church planting and pastoral experiences to do over again, I would make more effort to cause this to happen within our small group ministries.

Lessons in Leadership

As my seminary students and I took a fresh look at God's plan for leadership in the local church, two factors greatly impacted my own thinking and convictions. First and foremost, I was deeply impressed by Jesus' model when He washed the disciples' feet and then told them to serve one another as He had served them. Even though I had researched and studied this event before, it took on new meaning. Jesus' example was the ultimate illustration of servant-leadership.

The second factor that greatly impacted my thinking related to what I perceived was a serious abuse of power on the part of lead pastors in many churches, accompanied by a lack of accountability. Clearly, this style of leadership is in direct contradiction with what Jesus modeled and taught the disciples.

Leading and Serving

These two observations influenced my approach to leadership when I became the founding pastor of the first Fellowship Bible Church. I was determined to model servant-leadership. When I was asked who led the church, I simply responded—"the elders." But this was only partially true. In actuality, the elders looked to me as their primary leader—and following my leadership, the elders and I led the church as a team.

Unfortunately, my initial response was interpreted by some fellow pastors and elder boards that we simply had a corporate leadership model—that no one was really the primary leader. This in turn led to dysfunction as other churches attempted to implement what they thought was our model.

When I saw what was happening and realized I had given a false impression, I immediately clarified what was true. From the very beginning of our church planting experience, I was indeed the primary leader of the elders and the church. However, I also clarified that as lead pastors we can both lead and serve and at the same time be accountable (see chapter 20, principle 5).

The Problem of Co-leadership

As the church grew and we added staff pastors, I gave another false impression—that we had a successful co-leadership model. Again, this was not accurate. Though I shared the primary teaching ministry with one or two of the other staff pastors, I was always the primary leader. We were not co-leaders.

This also led to misunderstanding and dysfunction. For example, here is a testimony from one of our pastoral interns who later became pastor-leader of another church.

> There are a number of things I've appreciated about the co-leadership model that I have been a part of for the last few years . . . [including the "shared load" and the team approach in the pulpit]. However, I must admit I've grown more frustrated with the co-leadership model as time has gone by. God has designed me to be a leader, but the co-leadership structure cannot allow the full expression and exercise of my giftedness. Even in a co-leadership situation that works very well, like the one I'm in where the two of us share a very similar philosophy of ministry, we still have different ideas and slightly different views on where the church needs to go strategically. That means that pastors are held back from really leading the church forward. There is no primary visionary leader, and I believe our church has suffered because of that.
>
> In my mind, the co-leadership model has been a healthy counterbalance to the idea of the domineering pastor who never fully truly operates as part of the team with other elders and staff. But after a few years of experiencing co-leadership, it feels like the pendulum has swung too far the other way, to where the idea of teamwork and co-leading is so over-emphasized that no one can give primary leadership to the church. In my next pastorate, I'm planning on having a strong emphasis on teamwork and ministry together, but I'll be the primary leader and visionary and hopefully I'll have the best of both worlds.

In essence, I was not only the primary leader of the elders, but also of other staff pastors. My goal was once again to always be a servant-leader. And if I failed to both lead and serve in this role, I wanted my fellow pastors to be free to call this to my attention. In no way did I want to give the appearance of being autocratic—which would contradict what Jesus modeled to the disciples at the Last Supper. Once again, when I understood my miscommunication, I clarified my role as lead pastor—also a reason I've included this experience in this chapter on lessons from my personal ministry.

Appointing Unqualified Leaders

From the very first day we planted the first Fellowship Bible Church, I took the qualifications for eldership seriously. However, I did not take the lead in developing a specific and thorough plan for evaluating whether or not prospective elders measured up to the Holy Spirit–inspired list in 1 Timothy and Titus. We simply asked them to read these lists and evaluate whether or not they felt qualified. As I've shared in chapter 20, this was not sufficient.

But at this point, I made other mistakes. Since elders are "to shepherd the church of God" (Acts 20:28), I concluded that *only* official elders should serve as pastoral leaders within our small group ministry. And since we were multiplying small groups rapidly, we also multiplied elders to serve as pastors. To keep up with this growing need, we appointed some men to be elders who were definitely unqualified. In some respects, I actually allowed our cultural "forms" to drive biblical "functions"—a violation of an important biblical principle.

To make a long story short, one of the young men we appointed was very educated and brilliant. However, he was also shrewd in covering up his own sinful attitudes and actions. Because of his status and ability, he influenced some other young elder leaders who were also unqualified to join his cause. Though a complicated story, he helped orchestrate a coup against me as the founding pastor. Ultimately this led to a serious division in the church.

But there's another sad aspect to this story. I had an associate pastor who became my successor as I left the home base to help start another Fellowship church. I had every confidence that in my absence he could lead the elders and with the elders lead the church.

Even though this young man was a capable Bible student and teacher as well as a seminary graduate, I and others did not really know the deep emotional and spiritual issues in his life and marriage. My successor ended up being accused of sexual assault and ended up imprisoned for many years.

I must add that before appointing this man to be my successor, one of my mature elders raised questions regarding his qualifications, particularly in his ability to relate to people and to be in touch with his own feelings. I convinced this elder that this young man was growing in this area in his life and was indeed qualified. Though I was sincere, I was sincerely wrong!

However, there is a redeeming aspect to this story. While in prison, he experienced true repentance and upon his release he asked me and others for forgiveness. He became involved in a fruitful behind-the-scenes ministry in one of our branch Fellowship churches. In the process, he asked to go public before the whole church in order to ask forgiveness—from me—and from all those that were affected by his sin. Just as in Joseph's situation, God used this evil deed and accomplished good in the lives of a lot of people who witnessed this event (Gen. 50:19–20).

This was indeed a painful leadership lesson that impacted the rest of my years as a church planting pastor. I've already shared how it contributed to developing a more comprehensive plan for selecting elders (see chapter 20, principle 2). Furthermore, I learned something about myself. One of the elders who had walked through this difficult period of time met with me one day and shared these words of wisdom: "**Your greatest strength is to trust people. However, your greatest weakness is to trust people you shouldn't trust**."

He was right. It's natural for me to trust people—and I still do. We can't lead effectively without demonstrating this quality. However, I've learned to be much more cautious and discerning, especially when selecting and appointing elders.

Note: We continued to multiply small groups and appointed leaders for the groups. We looked for couples particularly who had emerged as faithful assistant leaders in these groups. We were able to select future elders and their wives from those who pastored small groups successfully for a significant period of time and were recommended by those they led.

Expanded Accountability

As I reflect back on my church planting experiences, particularly in the early years, I learned a valuable lesson regarding the need for accountability beyond the local church structure. Elders/overseers are to maintain accountability among themselves. Paul made this crystal clear when he addressed the Ephesian elders at Miletus and said, "Be on guard for **yourselves**" (Acts 20:28a).

However, there was definitely accountability beyond themselves. The fact that Paul was addressing them as an apostle illustrates this point. And, when he later appointed Timothy to remain in Ephesus to solve leadership problems, he was demonstrating the need for expanded accountability. Timothy was operating as Paul's apostolic representative. Paul's follow-up letter to Timothy says more about this accountability than any other New Testament epistle (1 Tim. 1:3–4, 7; 3:1–13; 5:17–20, 22; 6:3–5).

Once the apostles and their direct representatives passed off the scene, we have no biblical directives as to how to maintain this kind of expanded accountability—only the supracultural principle which is as follows:

> *To follow the model that unfolds in the New Testament story, every body of local church leaders should have some kind of accountability system that extends beyond themselves.*

Some believe the Bible teaches that this final accountability should be the church congregation. Though the Scriptures allow freedom to develop this kind of form, it's my opinion there are no direct biblical illustrations and directives to support having official church membership that would give these believers this kind of authority.[1] On the other hand, the Scriptures are clear that elders/overseers have the responsibility to manage and lead local churches, just as fathers are responsible to manage and lead their families (1 Tim. 3:4–5; see chapter 20, which describes the "household model").

Regardless, following the biblical record it quickly became apparent that there was a need for supervision beyond local church structures. We've addressed this issue in chapter 26, particularly when Ignatius, who served as "bishop of Antioch," became "bishop of bishops." As a lead elder or pastor, he developed and maintained authority to give direction to other church elders and pastors throughout the Roman world. Though a system eventually evolved that violated servant-leadership, this in itself does not invalidate having a plan for expanded accountability.

As we were multiplying churches—six in the first five years—I vividly remember a comment from Dr. John Walvoord, president of Dallas Theological Seminary. With tongue in cheek, he addressed me as the "bishop of north Dallas." Knowing what he was implying, I quickly clarified that I was simply the lead pastor at the home base church. To be honest, I did not want to assume any authority and responsibility beyond this role. In retrospect, this may have been a self-serving decision. I believe I was just naïve, believing these pastors and their elders did not need expanded accountability.

However, something happened in two of these churches that I did not anticipate. Tension developed between the lead pastors and their elders. One of these situations involved pastoral incompetence and the other pastor had some serious character flaws. The body of elders in both situations were in disagreement among themselves as to how to resolve the problem.

In both cases, several elders in these churches asked for help. Unfortunately, we had no official prearranged agreements that allowed me or our elders at the home base to assume this role. There was resistance on the part of some of the elders in these churches to seek outside help.

In both of these churches, we had no choice but to allow the problem to run its course and to be solved by each body of elders. Eventually it happened, but not until serious divisions developed and people were unnecessarily hurt in the process.

Obviously, there is no perfect methodology for resolving issues like these. Biblical examples and directives plus real-life experiences demonstrate an organizational weakness in churches that are independent and where lead pastors and elders are not accountable to anyone beyond themselves. And even in churches that have some form of church membership, history demonstrates that it's not always a successful system for resolving serious problems in leadership. Churches have often split in spite of a membership structure.

One solution to this problem relates to developing denominational structures for local church pastors and fellow church leaders who are accountable to a recognized spiritual leader who is responsible for a number of churches. The Scriptures certainly allow this type of form. Furthermore, history demonstrates there are indeed various benefits within this kind of structure.

For example, I remember a crisis situation in a large and influential denominational church in the Dallas area. The lead pastor was accused of trying to murder his wife, leaving her in a vegetative state. Because of prearranged agreements within this denominational structure, a bishop was able to step in and helped solve the problem. Though the pastor denied his guilt, he immediately stepped aside, and this denominational representative temporarily took over the pastoral responsibilities.

Though this was a painful experience for this congregation, they hardly missed a beat in terms of function and operation. Had this been a typical independent church, there probably would have been a terrible split. In these situations, pastors tend to proclaim their innocence—even when it is later revealed that they were covering up their sin. The results are tragic, and the witness among unbelievers in the larger community is terribly marred.

With this illustration I'm not suggesting that the New Testament story dictates that we develop denominational structures. However, the biblical story illustrates expanded accountability for local churches and leaders particularly. In fact, I've often wondered what would have happened if all of the hundreds of Fellowship Churches that came into existence had become organizationally related. This kind of structure reveals that there are significant benefits.

On the other hand, there are also simple forms to maintain this accountability. For example, when we later laid the groundwork for one of our successful church plants, the lead pastor took the initiative to develop a means of accountability for himself as well as his prospective elders. He prepared a document in which he proposed that should he and his fellow elders ever reach an impasse in their relationship, they would all abide by recommendations from the home base elders. Lead pastors and elders on both sides signed this document.

To this pastor's credit, he had observed the two events in our Fellowship churches that I shared earlier, and he did not want to enter this new ministry without an agreed-upon plan for expanded accountability.

Fortunately, this has become one of our most successful church plants and we've never had to face problems he and his elders couldn't resolve.

However, I must close this lesson with a personal illustration. As I engaged in an in-depth study of biblical leadership in the church with my fellow elders, I was impressed with the principle of expanded accountability. And since we were an independent church, I felt I needed to take this biblical concept seriously. I proposed to my fellow elders that I approach three reputable lead pastors in the Dallas area to participate in practicing this principle of expanded accountability. The plan was to give them the authority in writing to arbitrate and solve any tensions that might come about between me and my fellow elders. In turn, I and my fellow elders would abide by their recommendations.

All of us agreed to this proposal. However, I never had the opportunity to implement the plan. Shortly thereafter I passed my baton of leadership to my pastoral successor, who has developed his own plan for expanded accountability.

A Question for Thought and Discussion

In terms of your own ministry experience,
what is one of the most practical lessons you've learned?

Section 4

THE LENS OF CULTURE

Video Intro from Gene

3lenses.org/sc4

To quote the late Dr. George Peters, "Culture is a stern reality."[1] It involves all of our thoughts, sentiments, values, social relationships, attitudes, and actions. As pastoral leaders, we must not ignore culture, since it is all-encompassing and pervades all aspects of human life.

As stated in the introduction to this rewrite, there are cultural issues today that were not even on the horizon in the 1970s. Moral issues have multiplied, involving premarital sex, abortion, and pornography. And more recently, one of the most challenging issues facing church leaders involves a new openness and acceptance of same-sex relationships and marriage. To be faithful to biblical teaching, pastors and leaders must address these issues with both truth and grace.

Another serious cultural issue is racism, favoritism, and prejudice. These issues have been a part of our culture for decades, but they have become more front and center as we entered the twenty-first century. Consequently, I've devoted an entire chapter to this social disease that still exists within church communities.

Whole books have been written that biblically address these cultural and spiritual issues facing the church today. In the following brief chapters, I've attempted to share a concise perspective that will assist all pastoral leaders particularly to be faithful in carrying out our biblical responsibilities.

29

A Culture in Turmoil

Video Intro from Gene

3lenses.org/c29

Matthew D. Kim and Paul A. Hoffman began their perceptive and practical book, *Preaching to a Divided Nation*, with these challenging words:

> Countless pastors, preachers, teachers, and ministry leaders are dismayed at the dysfunction engulfing the church and the wider culture. Every day, headlines reveal a world divided across ethnic, class, sex, and political lines. We are simultaneously a nation and a church with comparable cavernous disagreements. Make no mistake: these chasms are expanding and feel increasingly insurmountable. [1]

Focusing specifically on the state of the church, Michael Graham adds this disturbing comment in "The Six Way Fracturing of Evangelicalism":

> The tectonic plates are shifting underfoot. This fracturing will likely be irrevocable not because our Gospel essentials are not unifying enough but because the diversions of ethical priorities, cultural engagement, racial attitudes, political visions/illusions, and their implications for

[a] philosophy of ministry mean that unity is fundamentally no longer tenable.[2]

Though some of us as Bible-believing church leaders may disagree with some of the specifics in these comments and conclusions, most of us will agree that the American culture is in trouble and the church generally has lost a significant amount of respect from the world at large. What is most troubling, statistics demonstrate that many people who once only identified with Bible-believing Christianity no longer participate in Christian worship—at least in organized church life. The authors of *The Great Dechurching* state the following:

> In the United States, we are currently experiencing the largest and fastest religious shift in the history of our country, as tens of millions of formerly regular Christian worshippers nationwide have decided they no longer desire to attend church at all. These are what we now call the dechurched. About 40 million adults in America today used to go to church but no longer do, which accounts for around 16 percent of our adult population. For the first time in the eight decades that Gallup has tracked American religious membership, more adults in the United States do not attend church than attend church. This is not a gradual shift; it is a jolting one.[3]

Facing Cultural Realities

One of the most challenging dynamics we face today as pastors is to help our congregations respond biblically to what is happening within our culture generally and politically. Dramatic changes have taken place in our value system. Though our history reveals a significant element of hypocrisy in the lives of our political leaders, never have we seen so much awareness of these inconsistencies.

This does not mean all politicians are a bad lot. I'm thankful for dedicated believers who are devoting their vocational lives to leading the American people with integrity. For example, I have a close friend who serves as a senator in the state of Texas. He is a committed believer and arranged to put in the hands of every member of the House and Senate a copy of my *Life Essentials Study Bible*. I'm grateful! But I have no illusions that this will cause these politicians to make decisions that will change the direction of our culture.

These realities lead to a significant and practical question.

As a Culture, How Have We Gotten to Where We Are?

Perhaps the late Tim Keller has left us with some of the most insightful answers to this question. He has quoted significant and reliable sources, and then added his own perspectives. I've chosen to summarize some of his insights to help us understand what is happening in our society.[4]

Clearly, our American culture has been dramatically influenced by the process of secularization. This has happened over a period of time but has gained significant momentum in the American culture beginning in the mid-twentieth century. This movement is characterized by moral relativism, individual freedom, materialism, and human reason as the ultimate answer to the world's problems. These cultural values have more recently been promoted at the university level, speeding up the process of secularization.

One of the greatest conflicts with historic Christian beliefs relates to the sexual revolution. Keller concludes:

> Since the 1960's, the culture has been swept by the idea that we discover our own authentic self by looking inward and affirming what we see—and that expressing sexual desires is a crucial part of being authentic. . . . The Christian sex ethic is seen now as unrealistic and perverse. This is massively discrediting and makes biblical faith implausible to hundreds of millions both inside and outside the church.[5]

One of the most recent developments that has run counter to a biblical view on sexuality is what is happening on university campuses. "Sex Weekends" involve a series of events allegedly to serve as sexual education. What is presented not only seriously violates biblical teaching but is evaluated by some secularists as being unhealthy and exploitive. The movement is gaining in popularity from university students and adding momentum to the sexual revolution.

Impact on the Church

As one who has planted and pastored several local churches over the last fifty years, and who has been in touch with numerous churchgoers, it has become increasingly obvious to me that Paul's message to the Romans is just as relevant today as it was among believers in the first century. I'm confident I speak on behalf of a multitude of my fellow servants who take this exhortation seriously as we minister to our people:

> Therefore, brothers and sisters, in view of the mercies of God, I urge you to present your bodies as a living sacrifice, holy and pleasing to God; this is your true worship. **Do not be conformed to this age**, but be transformed by the renewing of your mind, so that you may discern what is the good, pleasing, and perfect will of God. (Rom. 12:1–2)

This biblical exhortation is necessary and applicable as it relates specifically to the sexual revolution. Being "conformed to this age" certainly includes premarital sexual activity, extramarital affairs, abortion, pornography, and engaging in same-sex relationships. This trend does not downplay the all-pervasive impact of materialism and relativism in other areas of life.

Again, I'm confident my experience represents many fellow pastors who are committed to living and promoting a biblical lifestyle in all of these areas. However, I must sadly add that our Christian message and witness as believers has been eroded by the revelations regarding sexual sins on the part of prominent leaders in both Protestant and Roman Catholic churches. Keller adds that "this includes the many high profile 'melt downs' of celebrity Evangelical pastors."[6]

After a lengthy evaluation of how all this happened in our American culture, and the impact it has had on churches, Keller went on to draw this significant conclusion:

> Since becoming the ascendent religion in the western world (a process completed almost 1,000 years ago), the Christian church has not faced the challenges that it's facing now. Though there remains "Bible

belts" of traditional conservatism in various part of society where the Christian church still commands significant forms of influence—these places are increasingly both cultural and geographic shrinking 'islands' in the larger society. . . . In other words, the Christian world view continues to retreat, and the Christian church continues to decline and weaken even when political conservatism does better.[7]

Challenging Questions

As pastors and spiritual leaders who are committed to the authority of Scripture and its values, what must we do to help all believers live in this world without becoming a part of the world? How can we renew our churches?

Though we have no specific promises in Scripture that we'll change the world culture we live in, we have many promises that with God's empowerment and obedience to His commands, we can be light in the darkness. Paul's words to the Ephesians certainly ring true for all of us. Referring to those who lived unbelievably sinful lives, he wrote:

> Therefore **do not become their partners**. For you were once darkness, but now you are light in the Lord. **Walk as children of light**—for the fruit of the light consists of all **goodness, righteousness**, and **truth**—testing what is pleasing to the Lord. Don't participate in the **fruitless works of darkness**, but instead expose them. (Eph. 4:7–11)

How can this happen? Though I hope I'm wrong, it's my opinion that we'll never change the values of the American culture through the "church at large"—or through what has been identified as the evangelical movement. Those opportunities have passed us by. Though we certainly need to learn from our mistakes, it does not help us carry out the Great Commission to focus on what we did wrong as a Christian movement.

Yes, perhaps God in His grace will indeed raise up a significant voice or a "community of voices" to reignite our corporate and authentic influence as "one church" in our current culture. I will indeed rejoice! But again, I do not see this happening.

I do, however, see great possibilities for every local Bible-believing church to make a significant impact within our culture. We see this modeled by communities of faith located throughout the New Testament world. If this was happening in this culture that was totally pagan, it can certainly happen in our culture that was initially based on the Hebrew/Christian ethic. I'm more convinced than ever that if we follow what the Bible teaches regarding becoming effective communities of faith, we'll discover that the darker the world culture becomes, the brighter our light can shine. We *can* renew our local churches—and plant dynamic new ones—if we as pastoral leaders engage in the following functions:

1. Teach clearly and accurately, applying the whole counsel of God as inspired by the Holy Spirit, always "speaking the truth" with grace and in love.
2. Provide all believers with opportunities to grow in love for one another and to have regular authentic worship experiences.
3. Lead all believers to be one unified body in Christ that becomes visible throughout their local communities.

This also means creating an environment that welcomes all people, regardless of race, ethnic, or economic backgrounds, so they can witness authentic love and unity and hear a clear message that Jesus Christ is indeed the incarnate Son of God and Savior of the world.

Note: In essence, with these three statements I have summarized what I've called the "three vital experiences" that were initially and so beautifully illustrated in the church in Jerusalem (see chapters 11–13). However, to become communities of faith that penetrate our surrounding culture, we must take the following additional steps:

1. We must equip all believers to function as members of the body of Christ (see chapters 14–15).
2. We must help all believers grow in faith, hope, and love, but especially in love (see chapters 16–17).
3. We must model Christlike characteristics of maturity and equip other Christian leaders to also be able to say with the

apostle Paul—"Imitate me, as I also imitate Christ" (1 Cor.
11:1; see chapters 18–20).

Please don't misunderstand. I thank God for Christ-centered parachurch ministries—such as Bible colleges and seminaries, mission organizations, Christian radio and television programs, publishing houses, etc.
I've been personally involved in all of these entities. In fact, this book would
not have been published apart from a ministry like Moody Publishers.

These ministries are accomplishing what local churches could never do.
But to be even more effective, these ministries must focus on helping local
churches become all that God intended them to be as communities of faith
that penetrate their neighborhoods with the gospel and, in turn, support
church planting ministries around the world.

Another Biblical Priority

One of the important questions all Christians face today in our American
culture relates to government. What is our responsibility? To answer this,
I'd like to address a clear biblical priority. Paul addressed this when he
was released from his first imprisonment and wrote a letter to Timothy
who was in Ephesus:

> First of all, then, I urge that **petitions, prayers, intercessions,** and
> **thanksgivings** be made for everyone, **for kings** and **all those who
> are in authority,** so that we may lead a tranquil and quiet life in all
> godliness and dignity. This is good, and it pleases God our Savior,
> who wants everyone to be saved and to come to the knowledge of the
> truth. (1 Tim. 2:1–4)

To understand and apply what Paul wrote, it's important to compare
his directives with what has often been a clarion call on the part of spiritual
leaders in our culture. I'm referring to God's direct message to Solomon:

> And my people, who bear my name, humble themselves, **pray** and
> **seek my face,** and turn from their evil ways, then I will hear from
> heaven, forgive their sin, and **heal their land.**" (2 Chron. 7:14)

Though this was a significant message to the children of Israel, the promise does not apply specifically to Americans—or to the people of any country. This promise was made specifically to God's people in the Old Testament. Clearly, the "land" is Canaan. And the promise related to opening the sky to literally bring "rain" so crops could grow with a promise to "keep the grasshopper" from eating the produce of the land and a promise to keep a "pestilence" or "fatal epidemic disease" from taking the lives of the children of Israel (7:13). Consequently, we must not spiritualize this promise. To do so violates an important principle of biblical interpretation.

There is, though, an important aspect of this Old Testament promise that has continuity in the New Testament. It's the importance and priority of prayer. As we've noted, when Paul wrote to Timothy he emphasized "**petitions, prayers, intercessions**, and **thanksgivings**" (1 Tim. 2:1). But note the objects of this communication with God. New Testament believers were to pray "for **kings** and **all those who are in authority**" (2:2a).

To interpret what was in Paul's mind, we must understand that he had just been released from prison, where he had been incarcerated under the authority of Nero, one of the most evil Roman emperors. Tradition indicates that he must have orchestrated Paul's second imprisonment and then sentenced him to death. Yet Paul requested prayer for this evil man.

When Paul referenced "kings and all those in authority" he was reflecting on his witness before King Agrippa who listened to Paul's testimony, but ultimately approved of his imprisonment in Rome (Acts 26:1–32). And when he referred to "all those in authority," he was reflecting on his encounter with the Roman governors, Felix and Festus, who also listened to Paul but eventually approved of his imprisonment (24:10–25:12).

It true that some of our US presidents and others in high political positions have fallen far short in measuring up to biblical values, particularly in terms of integrity and morality. However, all of them have fallen short of the evil behaviors that characterized those who served as Roman emperors and other high officials within the Empire. Since they were evil men, guilty of the worst atrocities against other human beings, you didn't even dare to disagree with them. But the point of application is this. Regardless of the character of those who occupy political positions, all churches are to make prayer for our political leaders a priority.

But notice *why* Paul encouraged believers to pray "for all those who are in authority." There are two basic reasons:

First, that as believers they might "lead a tranquil and quiet life in all godliness and dignity" (1 Tim. 2:2b). *Second*, that God "wants everyone to be saved and to come to the knowledge of the truth" (2:4).

These two reasons blend together. In essence, Paul's concern was that all communities of faith within the Roman Empire have a peaceful environment, free from persecution so that as believers they could demonstrate what Jesus commanded and prayed for—love and unity.

This prayer request was not only for a comfortable existence in a hostile environment. The ultimate purpose was that they might carry out the Great Commission, enabling their neighbors to "come to the knowledge of the truth" and to be saved.

I firmly believe that Paul's directives to Timothy should be a priority today for all churches and in all cultures of the world. We're to pray for government leaders—no matter who they are and how they live—that we might have an environment in which we can continue to be dynamic witnesses in this world. In short, to be "light in the darkness."

Direct Political Involvement

Prayer for *all* government leaders should be a priority for every local church. Yet beyond prayer, what should be our political concerns and involvement?

Since we live in a country that gives us the opportunity and privilege to vote for potential government officials, we must certainly participate. To not do so is to neglect our responsibility as citizens here on earth.

However, this poses a challenge. How should we be involved in the political process when key candidates fall short of practicing honesty, integrity, and morality? I believe we must vote for those who—in spite of their weaknesses—will do what is best for our country and hopefully what is best for those of us who are becoming a Christian minority. Increasingly, our freedom to worship and witness is at risk. When we fail to vote, we open the door to those who fall short in the worst ways. When we elect imperfect candidates, God will in turn judge those individuals.

One additional note. It's my conviction that, as pastors, we must avoid publicly endorsing any political candidates. Rather, our primary responsibility is to lead our congregations to pray for all those in authority—and for those who will occupy positions of authority in the future. The reasons Paul outlined in his letter to Timothy are forever relevant in all cultures of the world and in any moment in history.

Even though as a pastoral leader I did not publicly endorse political candidates, I encouraged all believers to become informed and to participate in the voting process, seeking to support those who are the most committed to values that are in harmony with Scripture. This also involves encouraging believers to be involved in the political process without becoming argumentative and divisive, both within the culture at large but particularly within the family of God. We must make "every effort to keep the unity of the Spirit through the bond of peace" (Eph. 4:3).

What of the Future?

Beyond specific biblical prophecies, we have no specific information on what the future holds for America. In fact, our nation seems to be totally missing from references in Scripture. Perhaps this is related to continued cultural deterioration, although that, too, is pure speculation.

As stated earlier, and barring a miracle of God's grace, our culture at large will continue to deteriorate when evaluated by biblical values. But also based on Scripture, there is no reason to succumb to a gloom-and-doom mentality. We must remember that as believers "our citizenship is in heaven" (Phil 3:20). When Paul wrote these words, he was chained to a Roman guard—not knowing what the future held—except that he may soon face martyrdom (1:20–21). Furthermore, while incarcerated, Paul "welcomed all who visited him, proclaiming the **kingdom of God** and teaching about the Lord Jesus Christ with all boldness and without hindrance" (Acts 28:30b–31). Luke reported Paul continued this ministry "from dawn to dusk" (28:23).

Note: To look more carefully at the **number** of references to proclaiming the "kingdom of God" in the book of Acts and the Epistles, see Appendix C.

For those of us who have had the privilege to be a part of the American dream, we can indeed be thankful. We've been able to live in a culture that has provided us with more blessings and resources in life than the majority of people who have ever lived on planet earth. But we have no guarantee this will continue indefinitely.

It's true that one of the reasons we've experienced unusual success is because our system of government was in many respects built on the Hebrew-Christian ethic. In fact, the Ten Commandments are still emblazoned on the door and walls of the Supreme Court. And in spite of our history as a country that is more and more ignoring these commandments, and though it has been filled with many injustices—including horrible racism—it has become one of the most successful countries on earth.

But the fact is, we were never a Christian nation per se. Rather, we've been a nation that has benefited from the values of Christianity. In his book *Rebranding Christianity*, my pastoral successor wrote these words:

> America is not a Christian nation now, and it never has been. This is not just my opinion; it's historical fact and good biblical theology. America is unique because many of its Founding Fathers were Christians, and many biblical values are included in the U.S. Constitution (values which certainly have benefited this country). However, America is and always has been a kingdom of this world. It's part of the worldly system, not part of God's above-the-world kingdom. Any biblical principles that have been applied in America has been done so imperfectly and incompletely. This country is not ours to reclaim as Christians because we never had it to begin with.[8]

A Positive Perspective

At this point, I'd like to return to an earlier statement: the darker the world becomes, the brighter our light can shine. In fact, some believe our greatest opportunities to carry out the Great Commission are ahead. For example, "The Great Opportunity" report published in 2017 proposes that if we respond faithfully to the trends and currents of our time, the next thirty years will present the greatest mission and outreach opportunities in our country's history.[9]

Tim Keller, whom I've referred to rather extensively in this chapter, spoke compassionately shortly before he entered heaven's gates about the need for renewal in the church:

> There's therefore a great need for a *new Christian church movement* that practices love and justice, that equips its members to do enormous good in society, YET, at the same time resists the forces seeking to make it a political instrument; that speaks to and answers the great questions of the human heart and of the human race—of purpose, meaning, hope, happiness, guilt and forgiveness, identity—questions to which the secular culture cannot speak as powerfully.[10]

Regardless of our various eschatological views regarding the "end of the age," we all must have a correct philosophy of history. Life on this earth will not continue indefinitely. Eternity for all of us will eventually begin. Time as we know it will cease to exist. As believers, we "know" this theologically, but it's easy to live as if it's not true—particularly in terms of the blessings that we have had within the American experience.

A correct view of history and culture gives all believers hope, no matter what happens in our society. It was a significant factor in sustaining believers in the New Testament world. They were looking for the return of Christ within their lifetime, to deliver them from their own oppressive cultural environment, and, in many instances, the terrible periods of persecution that continued into the first, second, and third centuries.

As American Christians, we must live out this philosophy of history, doing all we can to strengthen our local churches. We must keep this goal front and center, recognizing that when time runs out, our sojourn in space-time history will cease. We'll stand before Christ to give account of what we have done with the time He has allotted us to carry out His purposes on earth. As American Christians, we will certainly be evaluated in the light of the opportunities we've had to live in a culture that has provided us with more blessings and resources in life than the majority of people in other parts of the world. We need to remind ourselves of the words of the Lord Jesus Christ Himself, who said, "From everyone who has been given much, much will be required; and from the one who has been entrusted with much, even more will be expected" (Luke 12:48b).

And let's remember that it was the Lord Jesus Christ who said, "I will build my church, and the gates of Hades will not overpower it" (Matt. 16:18). And when the church of Laodicea was so "lukewarm, and neither hot nor cold," so much so that Jesus said, "I am going to vomit you out of my mouth," yet He also said with compassion, "As many as I love, I rebuke and discipline. So be zealous and repent. See! I stand at the door and knock. If anyone hears my voice and opens the door, I will come in to him and eat with him, and he with me" (Rev. 3:16, 19–20).

This message from Jesus has often been interpreted as referring to the "door" of our individual hearts. However, Jesus was clearly using this metaphor to refer to the local community of believers in Laodicea. If they repented of their sins, Jesus was willing to occupy His rightful position in the lives of these carnal believers. Based on His promise to "build the church," He is willing to take His rightful place in every local church in the world today. In conclusion, let's remember that Paul's prayer for the Ephesians is forever true:

> Now to him who is able to do above and beyond all that we ask or think according to the power that works in us—to him be glory **in the church** and **in Christ Jesus** to all generations, forever and ever. Amen. (Eph. 3:20–21)

A Question for Thought and Discussion

As you reflect on the changing culture in America,
how has it impacted your personal life as a Christian?

30

The Sexual Revolution

Video Intro from Gene

3lenses.org/c30

There was a time in the American culture when biblical values considerably overlapped cultural values. Some of us remember that this was true in our early years of ministry. We also remember when this overlap began to separate.

Tim Keller succinctly summarized this reality. Referencing what followed the Great Depression and the two World Wars, he wrote:

> There was still great agreement across the political spectrum on what a good, moral life looked like. Love of country, sexual chastity, faithfulness, thrift and generosity, modesty and respect for authority, sacrificial loyalty to one's family and relationships—nearly everyone believed in all of these even if there were plenty of deviations in actual behavior. But by the late 1960s such survival challenges were just memories, and as people followed the culture's direction to discover truth within themselves, they began to come to radically different conclusions about what was right and wrong. American society began to splinter and has been doing so ever since.[1]

As we've seen in the previous chapter, these dramatic changes have definitely spilled over into the believing community. But clearly, one of the greatest changes that is affecting Christians is the sexual revolution. In this chapter, I want to address four significant areas where all pastors need to "speak the truth in love" and address the problem with a clear, biblical perspective.

Premarital Sex

Unfortunately, there are people who confess to be Christ followers who have no convictions regarding engaging in sexual activity prior to marriage. Without question, this is being "conformed to this age" and violates God's "good, pleasing, and perfect will" (Rom. 12:2). And as pastors, to avoid this subject in our teaching means we'll bypass significant sections of Scripture.

The "One Flesh" Relationship

God's plan for sexual intimacy began when He created Eve and brought her to Adam—an illustration and model for all men and women thereafter. Thus, we read: "This is why a man leaves his father and mother and **bonds with his wife**, and **they become one flesh**" (Gen. 2:24).

Clearly, God was not referring to bonding with a "girlfriend," a "significant other," or even a woman a man plans to marry. God says the "one flesh" relationship is for a husband and his wife.

When Jesus began His teaching ministry, He quoted this Old Testament reference, affirming God's plan for a marital union that began with Adam and Eve (Matt. 19:5–6). Later, Paul made the same point when he quoted both Moses and Jesus in his letter to the Ephesians (Eph. 5:31). The "one flesh" relationship is for married men and women.

Redefining the Sexual Relationship

This biblical perspective is generally rejected in the current American culture. For many, it's considered old-fashioned and out of touch with reality. Many Christians also have either ignored this biblical absolute, misunderstood it, or have reinterpreted the teachings of Scripture. To do so is to conform to the world's system.

Unfortunately, there's another trend in the American culture that has gained momentum, particularly among college students. They have redefined what is a sexual relationship and remaining a virgin. However, any relationship that involves physical intimacy is a sexual relationship and is certainly a violation of the will of God. To interpret otherwise is to again ignore the clear teachings of Scripture. For example, consider Paul's words to the Ephesians:

> Therefore, be imitators of God, as dearly loved children, and walk in love, as Christ also loved us and gave himself for us, a sacrificial and fragrant offering to God. But **sexual immorality** and **any impurity** or greed should not even be heard of among you, as is proper for saints. (Eph. 5:1–3)

Consider also Paul's words to the Thessalonians:

> For this is God's will, your sanctification: that you keep away from **sexual immorality**, that each of you knows how to control his own body in holiness and honor, not with lustful passions, like the Gentiles, who don't know God. This means one must not transgress against and take advantage of a brother or sister in this manner, because the Lord is an avenger of all these offenses, as we also previously told and warned you. For God has not called us to **impurity** but to live in holiness. Consequently, anyone who rejects this does not reject man, but God, who gives you his Holy Spirit. (1 Thess. 4:3–8)

It's possible to interpret these verses as referring to promiscuous and casual sexual activity and conclude it does not apply to loving, consensual sex outside of marriage. But the whole of Scripture does not align with this interpretation.

Our Pastoral Responsibility

As pastors, we have a responsibility to address this moral issue directly. In some respects, it's easier today since these non-biblical values have become commonplace and accepted in our culture at large. This distinction is clear. Predictably, the challenge we will often face is resistance.

Those most vulnerable to this false trend in our culture are young people who are bombarded with false messages regarding God's plan for sexual activity. Movies, TV programs, magazines, and other media present premarital sexual relationships as the norm. Many college campuses have set aside a period of time known as "sex week," when every form of sexual activity is discussed and illustrated with pornographic presentations—both live and on video. Many liberal professors approve and promote these so-called educational experiences.

As our churches reach out in our present-day culture inviting new people to attend—which we should—numerous people are now attending who have not been taught a biblical perspective on this God-created gift. As pastors, we must address God's perfect will in this area of human relationships.

In doing so, we must remind ourselves of the power of the Word of God. The Holy Spirit speaks through Scripture that is taught directly, clearly, and sensitively. Though it may take time for people to respond, those who are open to God's voice and His Word will eventually respond positively.

A Personal Pastoral Experience

I'm reminded of a couple my wife and I met at a luncheon we sponsored, particularly for new visitors to our church. As those attending introduced themselves, one couple somewhat sheepishly stated they were not married but were living together. They also expressed thankfulness for discovering our church. The couple continued attending the church, listening to my messages.

Then one Sunday, several months later, I vividly remember walking toward the front of the church, getting ready to start the service. Out of the corner of my eye I noticed this couple, seated on the aisle. The woman signaled me, obviously wanting to say something. With a smile on her face, she whispered, "We're married." In essence, she was saying, "We are now living in God's perfect will."

I was encouraged, and thankful that this couple continued attending our church following their confession at our luncheon. If we are carrying out the Great Commission in the American culture, this story should be repeating itself many times over. We are indeed ministering to people who have been living in and greatly influenced by a post-Christian culture.

The New Testament World

Imagine the challenge the apostle Paul faced in planting churches throughout the Roman world. The Corinthian church was a classic illustration of what happened when people are converted out of a pagan culture. Even after Paul had continued to minister to believers in this church at least for a year and a half, many were still living sinful lives involving sexual immorality. And even after another significant period of time passed, Paul wrote his first letter addressing the immorality that continued to exist among some of those whom he called "saints." Some were continuing the behavior they engaged in as unbelievers, participating in temple prostitution. Consequently, Paul wrote:

> Don't you know that your bodies are a part of Christ's body? So should I take a part of Christ's body and make it **part of a prostitute**? Absolutely not! Don't you know that anyone joined to a prostitute is one body with her? For Scripture says, The two will become one flesh. But anyone joined to the Lord is one spirit with him. Flee sexual **immorality**! Every other sin a person commits is outside the body, but the person who is **sexually immoral sins** against his own body. Don't you know that your body is a temple of the Holy Spirit who is in you, whom you have from God? You are not your own, for you were bought at a price. So glorify God with your body. (1 Cor. 6:15–20)

Though immoral sexual behavior in our culture has certainly not deteriorated to the same extent as that which existed in the Roman world, we're definitely moving in a wrong direction. This non-biblical approach to sexual values is impacting not only those who are unbelievers in our culture but believers as well. We must address these issues from a biblical perspective, but always "speaking the truth in love." To do less is to avoid what Paul outlined in his letter to Titus as a qualification for eldership.

The island of Crete was one of the most pagan cultures in the Roman world. Paul wrote that a spiritual leader must hold "to the **faithful message** as taught, so that he will be able both to encourage with **sound teaching** and to refute those who contradict it" (Titus 1:9). Clearly, "sound teaching" includes what the Bible teaches about premarital sex.

Abortion: Taking Human Life

One of the great tragedies in the American culture happened in 1973 when the US Supreme Court ruled that the Constitution gives the right to have an abortion. This landmark decision expanded exponentially a serious violation of the Word of God. Multiple millions of unborn babies have lost their lives because of this cruel and heartless decision. And though we can be encouraged by the Court's decision to overturn *Roe v. Wade* and return this issue to be decided by each state, we're told that abortions have continued to increase. This is a national tragedy that continues to rear its ugly head.

When Life Begins

Though references are few, the Scriptures indicate that life begins at conception, and to take life in the womb at any stage is a violation of one of the Ten Commandments (Ex. 20:13). Though it may sound insensitive to our twenty-first-century ears, God has called it murder.

In his prayer, Job clearly implied that life begins at conception. As he was communicating directly with the Creator, he wrote:

> "Your hands shaped me and formed me. . . . Please remember that you formed me like clay. . . . You clothed me with skin and flesh, and wove me together with bones and tendons. You gave me life and faithful love, and your care has guarded my life." (Job 10:8–12)

Job then clarified that he was referring to his prenatal existence: "Why did you bring **me** out of the **womb**? **I** should have **died** [in the womb] and never been seen. **I** wish **I** had never **existed** but had been carried from the **womb** to the grave" (10:18–19). In other words, Job stated he was

alive in the womb and "existed" as a human being.

What this Old Testament saint recorded is certainly in harmony with King David's testimony:

> For it was you who created **my** inward parts; you knit **me** together in my mother's **womb**. **I** will praise you because **I** have been remarkably and wondrously made. Your works are wondrous, and **I** know this very well. (Ps. 139:13–14)

David's pronouns ("my," "me," and "I") indicate he was fully alive in his prenatal state. Like Job, he was a human being created in the image of God.

In the New Testament we have a beautiful illustration of conscious life in the womb involving John the Baptist and Jesus. When Elizabeth, John's mother, was only six months pregnant, her cousin Mary paid her a visit. Luke has recorded that John as a "baby leaped inside" Elizabeth's womb and she immediately sensed there was supernatural communication between John and Jesus who had just been conceived (Luke 1:39–41).

It's true that both of these pregnancies had a supernatural element. Elizabeth became pregnant through normal means even though she was barren (Luke 1:5–14). Mary, of course, experienced an incomparable miracle. Apart from normal means, she conceived Jesus by the Holy Spirit (Luke 1:26–37). Both of these mothers responded in a very human sense, and once conceived, the babies both went through the same natural processes of prenatal development. Jesus, though divine, was also fully human. We see this same dynamic after He was born, since Luke again recorded that He "increased in wisdom and stature, and in favor with God and with people" (Luke 2:52). This is a divine mystery and antinomy—but it's true!

A Personal Pastoral Experience

Over the years as a pastor, I've had a deep sense of responsibility to periodically address this corporate and personal sin with the total congregation. Both believers and unbelievers need to hear a clear and definitive—but sensitive—message from the Word of God that life begins at conception and that to abort a baby is to take human life. Without question, people have been brainwashed by the mainstream media that life doesn't even begin until birth—a direct violation of what we know from Scripture. This reality is being more and more validated by scientific discoveries. We can now look into the womb and see prenatal human activities almost from conception, verifying what the Bible teaches.

To illustrate the power of both biblical truth and what is being discovered from science, I'd like to share a personal experience. On one occasion, following my Bible exposition based on the Scriptures I've just shared, I illustrated my message with a video featuring a sonogram showing an eleven-week-old fetus in the womb. In addition to being able to see all the features and prenatal activity on our huge screens, we could also hear the beating heart. To help capture and illustrate both the miraculous and human elements of this experience, we were able to literally fill the church sanctuary with the sounds of this baby's pulsating heartbeat!

Needless to say, people were deeply moved. For most of us it was both an insightful and worshipful experience. For me, this was a dramatic and emotional experience. The little eleven-week-old baby was my granddaughter. She was literally doing somersaults in the womb and conveying her humanness with a pulsating and beating heart.

However, there's more to this story. A middle-aged mother attended our service with her whole family. Previously, she had made it clear that she did not agree with my position on abortion. Thankfully she still respected me and generally enjoyed my Bible teaching, but when some of her friends discovered I was going to preach on the subject, they gave her a "heads up" so, if she wished, she could miss the service. But she immediately responded by saying, "I can handle it!" In fact, she seemed to be a bit offended that they thought she would not want to hear what I was going to say.

But here's how God miraculously used both the biblical illustrations and the sonogram. After the service, her whole family went out to one of her favorite restaurants. As they sat together, this mother made a startling confession. "I want all of you to know," she said, "that I've been terribly wrong. That was a living baby in the womb. I now understand and believe that abortion is taking human life." Hearing this humble and contrite admission, her teenage son graciously responded: "Mom, that's what we've been trying to tell you."

When I heard this story I was grateful. Subsequently, I invited this mother to join me on my daily radio program to tell her story. She agreed and gave a firsthand account of her thinking and convictions before, during, and after this life-changing experience.

Along with this mother I also interviewed a woman who had a remarkable conversion experience. She had operated several abortion clinics in the Dallas area before she became a believer. As these two women sat together, the one who had been in the abortion business shared this startling statistic. Prior to her conversion, she was scheduled to make a million dollars during just the coming year—and then she said, "I would have made $25 on each abortion."

The middle-aged mother was aghast when she heard these words. She actually confessed at that moment—on radio—that she didn't know that this woman was paid for the abortions that were conducted in her clinics! And to add to this revelation, if this woman made $25 per abortion, imagine how much money the doctors would have made during that same year.

What Can We Learn?

I'm sharing this story for several reasons. *First,* as pastors and leaders, we have a biblical responsibility to address this issue. It involves a serious sin—a violation of the will of God personally and corporately.

Second, we must understand that intelligent, sincere people are being brainwashed into thinking that life doesn't begin until birth—or at some other point between conception and delivery. And, like this mother, many have little awareness regarding the materialistic motives that drive participation in this industry!

Third, our younger generation is greatly at risk. Social media and teachers in both schools and colleges are promoting a false view regarding pregnancy—that what is in the womb only involves a blob of human flesh without life. Christian parents definitely need pastoral assistance in addressing this inhumane blight that exists within our culture.

Again, we must always address this issue with grace, compassion, and sensitivity. We must always speak the truth in love. I have never spoken on this subject without culminating my message with the subject of God's gracious forgiveness. John's powerful and redemptive words in his first epistle definitely includes the sin of abortion:

> If we confess our sins, he is faithful and righteous to **forgive us our sins** and to **cleanse us from all unrighteousness**. (1 John 1:9)

Pornography

The availability of pornographic images and literature in films and video has multiplied exponentially since the 1960s. And since the internet has opened the door to all forms of porn, there are basically no restrictions on private viewing. This has become a worldwide phenomenon.

This mind-boggling development has created a negative impact on all human beings (I encourage you to study books that are written specifically to address this problem and its harmful results).

From a biblical point of view, there is no justification for indulging in this sinful behavior. Jesus' statement regarding mental adultery certainly relates to pornography, even though the images are pictorial in nature:

> You have heard that it was said, Do not commit adultery. But I tell you, everyone who looks at a woman lustfully has already committed adultery with her in his heart. (Matt. 5:27–28)

With this pronouncement, Jesus established a universal principle: to think about and look upon other human beings engaging in sexual behavior and then responding in lustful ways is immoral.

As pastors who believe the Bible and all that it teaches about moral purity, we must take our responsibility seriously to teach the whole counsel of God. More importantly, we must flee from any participation in our own lives. Statistics are alarming regarding spiritual leaders who access pornographic images on the internet. We will not be able to address this issue for others with a clear conscience. To attempt to do so can only be defined as hypocritical behavior.

It's important to note that the negative impact of pornography is not only a concern among Christians. Many of the most significant books that deal with the negative impact on human relationships, particularly in marriage, are secular. It not only impacts the mind but our physiology as well, causing serious addictive behavior. Indulging in this activity is not only forbidden in Scripture but scientific studies verify how this industry impacts an individual's physical and emotional well-being and dehumanizes women. It impacts all human relationships in a negative way.

One of the most significant verses in Scripture that impacts my own thinking in this area is from Paul's letter to the Philippians:

Finally brothers and sisters, whatever is true, whatever is honorable, whatever is just, whatever is pure, whatever is lovely, whatever is commendable—if there is any moral excellence and if there is anything praiseworthy—dwell on these things. (Phil. 4:8)

When pornography is measured and evaluated with this biblical criteria, its use violates almost every point. It is certainly not "honorable," "pure," "commendable," and is certainly not considered "moral excellence." In most instances, it is not "true" since it projects pure fantasy rather than reality.

Since pornography has become such a prominent part of the current culture—literally worldwide—as pastors we need to discretionately and sensitively address this problem in our congregational messages—particularly as it comes up naturally in biblical expositions. However, in my own pastoral ministry, I've addressed this issue with men—personally, in small groups, and men's retreats. It's true this is increasingly becoming a problem among women, but it's still a major problem among men based on our visual, psychological, and physical nature—an issue Jesus certainly addresses in His pronouncement—"Everyone who **looks at a woman lustfully** has already committed adultery with her in his heart" (Matt. 5:28).

Without question, pornography is also addictive. To see for yourself, check out the numerous books that address this issue. Since it is addictive, recovery often involves accountability—participating in a recovery group—the same process for dealing with alcoholism or drug abuse.

As pastors particularly, we have a biblical responsibility to address this issue—in our own lives, in the lives of the men in our churches and in the lives of the total congregation. This includes the younger generation. We must help parents to take steps to protect their children who are exceptionally vulnerable because of the availability of mobile phones, tablets, and computers.

Same-Sex Relationships and Marriage

Following the Supreme Court decision on gay marriage in June of 2015, Mark Galli responded with these thoughtful and challenging words:

> We lost this one. We and many others made the case to our culture that traditional marriage is God's good design, that this institution embodied by a man and a woman joining together leads to social flourishing. But our culture is not convinced. Much to our disappointment, it is now the law of the land to permit other forms of marriage.[2]

In view of the direction of our culture generally, this decision came as no surprise to the majority of Americans. In fact, Pew Forum Research indicated that in 2004, 31 percent of Americans already supported same-sex marriage and by 2016, the numbers had already increased to 55 percent.[3]

What is surprising is that even prior to the Supreme Court decision, "The percentage of those who identify as Christian (whether Evangelical, mainline Protestant, or Catholic) who have also come to accept same-sex marriage had increased at nearly identical rates as the general population."[4]

Statistical studies, of course, are subject to serious error. However, this trend is verified by the number of leaders who claim to be conservative Christians who are reinterpreting all the scriptural passages that forbid same-sex relationships (Lev. 18:22; 20:13; Rom. 1:26–27; 1 Cor. 6:9; 1 Tim. 1:9–10). In essence, they claim that most of these passages in both the Old and New Testaments refer to sexual abuse and do not apply to same-sex couples who are married and committed to a loving, sensitive, monogamous relationship.

Beyond this reinterpretation of Scripture, they give a number of other reasons to justify same-sex marriage among believers. Preston Sprinkle presents a number of these reasons in his biblical and insightful book,

Does the Bible Support Same-Sex Marriage? 21 Conversations from a Historically Christian View.[5] The following are several conversations:

- Sex difference is described, not prescribed, in Scripture
- "One flesh" does not imply sex difference
- Paul was not talking about consensual same-sex relationships
- Romans 1 is condemning excessive lust, not same-sex love
- The biblical writers didn't know about sexual orientation
- Romans 1:26 isn't referring to female same-sex sexual relationships
- The word "homosexual" was added to the Bible in 1946
- The biblical writers were products of their homophobic and patriarchal culture[6]

Sprinkle goes on to address these reasons, acknowledging that we need to evaluate these perspectives directly but sensitively, and then presents a biblical response. His second chapter, "The Historically Christian View of Marriage," sets the stage theologically and historically in order to address the above arguments—and others.

Following are his foundational and biblical reasons with significant quotes:

1. Sex difference is an intrinsic part of what marriage is.

   The creation of humanity as sexually different persons, "male and female," is woven into the fabric of God's diverse creation account. "Male and female" describes our biological sex, and our different sexes are defined by the respective roles that humans play in reproduction. This is why God commands the male and female to "be fruitful and multiply and fill the earth" ([Gen. 1:28]ESV).[7]

2. Same-sex sexual relationships are always prohibited.

   When it comes to same-sex sexual relations. There are no tensions, developments, or differences between the Old and New Testaments. Whenever Scripture mentions them, they are always prohibited.[8]

3. The multiethnic global church affirms the historically Christian view.

The global, multiethnic, multi-denominational church has, for the last two thousand years, believed that sex difference is an intrinsic part of what marriage is and that same-sex sexual relationships are always sinful.[9]

4. Marriage and sex are not essential to human flourishing.

Christians throughout history have taken the New Testament's emphasis on singleness seriously. Both Western and Eastern Christianity had a high view of singleness and applauded those who pursued it.[10]

5. Marriage has a purpose.

Marriage is the foundation stone upon which family and therefore society is built. . . . And throughout Scripture, marriage is also used as an image to describe God's relationship with Israel (Isa. 50:1; 54:1–10; 62:4; Jer. 2–4; Ezek. 16; 23; Hos. 1–3) and Christ's relationship with the church (Matt. 22:1–14; 25:1–13; 2 Cor. 11:2; Eph. 5:22–33; Rev. 19–21). Paul goes so far as to say that human marriages are ultimately about Christ and the church.[11]

Facing Reality

We're facing a whole new trend within the culture at large and within the Christian community. Unfortunately, it is becoming a divisive issue among Bible-believing Christians. More and more, we're encountering same-sex individuals and couples who are convinced they were born with same-sex tendencies. Many testify that they have sincerely attempted to change their orientation, actually pleading with God to remove these same-sex feelings—but without success.[12]

This trend and reality raises some basic questions. How should local communities of faith relate to this reality? How would Jesus and even Paul handle these situations today? And more specifically, how should pastors give direction to this trend?

Once again, space prohibits addressing these questions in a comprehensive fashion. Thankfully, there are books to help answer these questions from a biblical, historical, and cultural point of view. For example, I would like to refer to *Leading a Church in a Time of Sexual Questioning* by Bruce Miller,[13] who pastors one of our dynamic church plants. In three chapters, Bruce addresses same-sex sexuality respectfully, sensitively, and biblically.

- Leading people to read the Bible humbly
- Leading people to understand being "gay"
- Leading people to holy ways of living

Bruce also introduces the subject with these convicting words:

> Christians have a bad reputation in this arena, and sadly, in many cases it is well deserved. We do not have a good track record of showing love and pursuing justice for LGBT+ people who have commonly suffered ridicule, condemnation, rejection, exclusion, discrimination, and even violence.[14]

Unfortunately, Bruce is correct. I agree with him that we need to take a lesson from Jesus as He communicated with sexual sinners. Though we have no examples of His interaction with individuals who were in same-sex relationships, the way He treated the woman at the well, the woman taken in adultery, and a prostitute provides us examples and a model that comes directly from God Himself. Before we say, "Go and sin no more," we must always convey Christ's love, compassion, and acceptance.

In conclusion, I want to once again quote Mark Galli, who addressed these questions immediately following the Supreme Court decision. Speaking almost prophetically, he wrote:

> Now that the issue of gay marriage is decided, we may find that we have a greater opportunity than ever to build fruitful relationships with those in the LGBT community who have been hostile to all things Christian.[15]

To take advantage of this opportunity, as believers and pastors, we must "rethink" old patterns and thoughts and behavior in the light of true Christlike love for all people who are walking outside of the will of God. Without compromising what the Bible teaches about same-sex relationships, we must create an environment that accepts all people regardless of their lifestyles and at the same time, we must speak the truth in love regarding God's "good, pleasing, and perfect will" (Rom. 12:2).

A Question for Thought and Discussion

How can our churches create an environment where people who have same-sex attraction feel welcome and at the same time present the one-man and one-woman relationship in marriage as God's will?

31

Racism, Favoritism, and Prejudice

Video Intro from Gene

3lenses.org/c31

Every professor, pastor, and author who seriously addresses the problem of ethnocentrism and racism in the church invariably cites Peter's experience with Cornelius. Although Jesus had chosen Peter to be the primary leader of the apostles and a significant foundation stone in the church (Matt. 16:18), he had a serious blind spot. For a number of years after Pentecost, he did not believe Gentiles could be saved. Jewish tradition continued to impact his understanding of what Jesus meant when He stated in the Great Commission: "Go, therefore, and make disciples of **all nations**" (Matt. 28:19).

Peter's prejudice was so deeply ingrained in his mind and heart that it took a dramatic experience with the Lord and a direct encounter with Cornelius to open his prejudicial eyes. Up to that point he had no idea he was walking directly outside of the will of God.

When Peter finally made his journey to Caesarea, his public confession before Cornelius, his household, and other invited guests (Gentiles) revealed the depth of his racist perspective:

You know it's forbidden for a Jewish man to associate with or visit a **foreigner**, but God has shown me that I must not call any person impure or unclean. . . . **Now** I truly understand that **God doesn't show favoritism**, but in **every nation** the person who fears him and does what is right is acceptable to him. He sent the message to the Israelites, proclaiming the good news of peace through Jesus Christ—he is **Lord of all**. (Acts 10:28, 34–36)

In this confession, Peter's reference to "every **nation**," indicates that through this experience he then **understood** what Jesus meant when He said, "make disciples of **all nations**." His eyes were opened to his prejudiced and racial perspectives. Jesus died for the sins of the whole world—all people, everywhere.

Personal Identification

In this chapter, I want to share some personal experiences regarding my own religious background and deep-rooted prejudice. I can definitely identify with some elements in Peter's experience that were also blind spots in my own life. I, too, was reared in a cultural environment that was particularistic, legalistic, and ethnocentric.

Fortunately, when I decided to become a member of this religious group, I already understood from listening to Christian radio that we're saved by believing in Jesus Christ—not by joining a church and keeping the rules. Though I was confused theologically regarding my security in Christ, thankfully I was already born again. However, since I had been taught from childhood—especially by example—that we were the only religious group that had the truth, I developed a deep sense that I was better and more enlightened than Christians outside this group. If anyone had called this to my attention, I would have denied it was true. I was unaware of my prejudicial attitudes—until I experienced an emotional crisis which changed my life dramatically. It was then I became conscious of my ethnocentric pride. In some respects, my response was indeed like Peter's. I discovered "that God doesn't show favoritism" (Acts 10:34).

To make a rather involved story short, I went into a deep period of disillusionment and depression. As a result of a painful series of circumstances, I developed serious spiritual doubts about the Christian faith and even experienced some emotional despair. However, God used it to unveil my prejudice and spiritual pride.

Once I began to understand and deal with my prejudices, I also began to understand the larger cultural influences in my life. In actuality, the group I grew up in was more than just a religious community; it was basically German. These two "cultural environments" blended so tightly that much of the prejudice that I felt was both religious and secular. In fact, a small contingency within this movement conducted only German services—believing that Luther's German translation of the Bible was God's original communication with humanity. A few within these churches were so uninformed they believed Jesus actually spoke German.

Note: I must add that over the years, this religious group has experienced dramatic changes in understanding salvation through grace by faith as well as experiencing a growing appreciation for the multitudes of fellow Christians and ministries beyond this particular religious community.

Following this crisis experience that enabled me to see more clearly into the depths of my soul, I began to more honestly and openly see people from all walks of life and from all races as fellow human beings who are made in God's image, equally loved—regardless of our languages, values, belief systems, external appearances, geographic locations, etc. I began to believe in my heart that we are all created by God and as believers we need to become members of one unified body in Christ. Most importantly, I saw I needed all members of the body of Christ to help me personally to become a mature believer.

A New Beginning

Following this difficult but enlightening and freeing experience, a door unexpectedly opened for me to join the faculty at Moody Bible Institute. As I look through the rear-view mirror, I have difficulty believing this actually happened. I was only twenty-three years old and teaching college-level students. But in retrospect, I began to understand that God in His "severe grace" had been preparing me for this opportunity—but letting me know in no uncertain terms that I wasn't ready for this position until I faced my prejudice and responded with true humility.

Eventually I was appointed as Director of the Moody Evening School, enabling me to help the Moody faculty minister to nearly a thousand students from all over the Chicago area. The majority were dedicated laypeople who worked long hours to make a living but who attended our classes for biblical and practical training. About one-third of these students were African Americans, godly men and women who were committed to becoming equipped to minister to others in their churches. As I spent time interacting with these students and getting to know them at a personal level, I was deeply moved by their commitment to Jesus Christ and to the body of Christ.

This was just the beginning of a new adventure that continued in my doctoral studies at New York University. The majority of my fellow students were socially and racially diverse, coming from a number of different countries. I spent many hours studying together with both African Americans and Latinos. One of my closest student friends was from Persia (from Iran) and a Muslim. On several occasions, he accompanied me to weekend services where I preached and spoke on the gospel of John, demonstrating that Jesus Christ is God who came in human flesh. Unfortunately, after our summer studies ended, our paths separated, but we had developed a special friendship. Though at that point he did not profess faith in Jesus Christ, hopefully it happened, and I'll spend eternity with him in heaven.

Another Unexpected Opportunity

All of these experiences prepared me to leave my position at Moody Bible Institute and accept an invitation to join the faculty at Dallas Theological Seminary. Since the school was located in the South, the doors were just beginning to crack open for African Americans to matriculate. One of those students, Tony Evans, had come to Dallas with a vision to become an evangelist, particularly within the African American community. However, after our paths crossed in the very class that led to the original edition of this book, he developed a deep passion for the local church.

On one occasion, following his graduation from seminary, Tony was attending one of our services at the original Fellowship Bible Church. We began to discuss his vision to start a church. I immediately knew that for him to devote time to this effort, he needed financial support to care for his growing family. Consequently, I introduced him to our elders. He shared his vision—to start a church in the predominantly African American community in Oak Cliff—a thriving southern suburb of Dallas.

In a quick moment of deliberation and without reservation, we made a unified decision for our first Fellowship Bible Church to support Tony, his wife, Lois, and their family, caring for their salary for a period of three years. This enabled him to launch a dynamic sister church.

A Significant Corollary Experience

While teaching a class in journalism at the Seminary, I met an older black gentleman named Ruben Conner. Having asked the members of the class to write their personal stories, I was absolutely amazed at this man's personal journey.

Ruben was born in 1930—just two years before I entered this world. He grew up in an African American farming community. His mother died shortly after he was born, and his father remarried seven times. He dropped out of school in seventh grade and joined the military at age sixteen. He eventually moved to Dallas—a disillusioned and angry young man.

However, his life changed dramatically when he reluctantly attended a Bible study and became a new person in Jesus Christ. Eventually, Ruben's wife, Geneva, joined him on his spiritual journey and together they started a church called Community Bible Church—which was the first African American Bible Church in the South. Ruben served as the pastor but felt a need for more education. Eventually he entered Dallas Seminary.

As I read Ruben's story, I was more than amazed at his spiritual commitment and tenacity. Because he had dropped out of high school, he went on to earn his GED, attended a Bible institute, graduated from college and seminary, earning two master's degrees plus a doctorate—all the while mentoring his five children and pastoring a growing church.

I then discovered something else. Ruben had a vision to plant Bible churches in African American communities in various cities throughout the United States. To do so, he started an expanded ministry called Black Evangelistic Enterprise—later called the Urban Evangelical Mission. In actuality, before our elders decided to support Tony Evans and his family, Ruben had been encouraging him to start a church. Our partnership merged, and with our support, Tony and his wife started Oak Cliff Bible Fellowship under the auspices of this mission.

In my subsequent communication with Ruben, I discovered that he was not only raising financial support for these African American church planting pastors, but he also needed to raise his own support so he could be devoted full-time to this church planting ministry. So I again approached our elders and shared his story. I suggested that we support Ruben, freeing him up from having to raise his own salary so he could devote his time to raising support for these church planting pastors.

The elders then invited Ruben to meet with us personally to share his vision, and all of us enthusiastically agreed to provide Ruben with his full salary—which we did for twenty-five years. When able, he and Geneva worshiped with us and periodically shared with our congregation what was happening in his church planting ministry.

Thankfully, our total church family considered this as a wonderful opportunity to build God's kingdom, which was essentially an extension of our church planting ministry. I simply share these stories to illustrate an important cultural insight. As pastors and leaders, we cannot lead people to overcome their own racial attitudes and actions without facing our own prejudicial problems—both conscious and unconscious.

God in His grace and loving discipline helped me to understand this need in my own life. I discovered that one of the true tests for discovering if we've faced racial issues both subjectively and objectively will be the way we relate to all human beings who have been created in the image of God. We'll be able to legitimately expand on and practice Paul's words to the Galatians: "There is no Jew or Greek, slave or free, male and female [black or white, Asian or Caucasian, American or Latin, rich or poor, etc.]; **since you are all one in Christ Jesus**" (Gal. 3:28).

Practical Steps for Solving Racial Tensions

In order to address the subject of racism, there are a number of helpful books from both a sociological and biblical perspective. Regardless of each author's presuppositions, perspectives, and conclusions, they all provide helpful insights for unraveling the dynamics associated with slavery and the results that are still impacting segments of the American culture. Because of space limitations, I've chosen to include insights from Tony Evans's concise and significant book *Kingdom Race Theology: God's Answer to Our Racial Crisis.*[1] And in choosing this book, I readily acknowledge my bias based on our professor-student relationship, our theological perspectives, our church planting experiences, and our mutual pastoral ministries and friendship.

From a theological perspective, I deeply appreciate this approach in bringing God's directives and principles to bear on the present racial crisis that is still ongoing in our American culture and still impacting a number of Bible-believing churches. He states:

> There exists great legitimacy in looking at research and identifying problems from a sociological or sociopolitical standpoint in order to gain better awareness of the realities of life such as systemic racism, microaggressions, implicit biases, and the like. But for believers in Christ, **the Bible must sit on top of all problems to serve as the defining reference point**. If not, our methods, messages, and approaches to rectify racism and its schisms and stains in our land may be not only inept, but may even lead to greater division and furtherance of racism (from both sides).[2]

Based on his commitment to the authority and primacy of Scripture, Tony describes and evaluates "Black Lives Matter," "Critical Race Theory," "The 1619 Project," and "1776 Unites." In view of the presuppositions that undergird these movements and their actions, he not only evaluates the goals and activities that are out of harmony with biblical and ethical principles, but he also points out what we can learn that are positive lessons. He cites the terrible tragedies involving the deaths of

Michael Brown and George Floyd, which resulted in serious crises in our current culture.[3]

Though most of us do not want to be called racists—including yours truly—we must acknowledge that the negative results of racism continue to plague the American culture. As Tony states:

> It is my belief that racism has embedded itself not only in many individual hearts throughout our history, but also, to varying degrees, in the many structures of our society. Whether those structures are political, economical, legal, or many others, they impact how entire groups of people think and live.[4]

We've made positive strides in combating the lingering effects of this social disease. Having lived in Dallas since 1968, I've seen dramatic progress. But it's still true that our particular culture and overall society has a long way to go in bridging the chasm that still exists in many places in our country and, more specifically, in a number of our communities of faith.

What then can we do as Bible-believing Christians to help remove this insidious cancer that is still eating away in what we call the "land of the free" as well as within our churches that are committed to the authority of Scripture? In answering this question, I want to share some biblical and practical suggestions from Tony himself, who I believe has earned the right and credibility to respond to this question. He speaks and writes not as a theorist but as a black man who has spent virtually a lifetime in ministry cutting a deep swath through the complicated racial maze that still impacts many of us. Following are his suggestions for both black and white believers.[5]

What Black Churches Should Do

- Appreciate, celebrate, and affirm the uniqueness of our divinely created racial identity while simultaneously guarding against an unbiblical pride that resists or deters us from biblical truth.
- Make the restoration and preservation of the nuclear heterosexual family our highest priority since it is God's foundational institution for a stable, productive, and peaceful community.

Fatherlessness and the demise of the nuclear black family is the greatest crisis we face as a people.

- Resist the temptation to automatically view every questionable action by those of another race as racism. Reject the tendency to stereotype people based on their racial identity, including all whites. Take the time to evaluate the motivation, knowledge, and intent of that person and the deed. Ask questions and seek clarification before making a final judgment. Also, accusations of racism should never be used as a tool to hold white people hostage to white guilt, thus creating the need for them to prove their innocence as a means of exercising and legitimatizing black power.

- Reject the victim mentality. Victimology nurtures an unfocused strain of resentment rooted in a defeatist identity through which all realities are filtered. Instead, view ourselves as God sees us and with the intrinsic value which He created in us. Even if we have been victimized, we are not victims. We must see ourselves as overcomers. This mindset empowers us with the appropriate mentality to properly address injustices. Where racism is real, however, it must be resisted and corrected. It must no longer be viewed as a substantive impediment to block progress. If our ancestors persevered and made great progress in the worst of times, we have no excuse today for not maximizing the opportunities of freedom that are at our disposal. Victimhood must be replaced with a **victor hood** mentality.

- Become an active part of a solid, biblically centered, disciple-making church where you use your time and talents and treasures to advance God's kingdom agenda in the areas of both righteousness and justice.

- Do not look to civil government to do for us what God holds us responsible for addressing ourselves, either personally, in our families, in our churches, or in our communities. We must accept, promote, and operate on God's definition regarding responsibility and limitations as civil government.

- Do not become guilty of the sin of racism or black privilege based on class that we condemn in others. We must pursue God's goal of reconciliation. Perpetual unaddressed anger about racism will drive us to sin and prohibit us from finding a godly solution to the problem.

What White Christians Should Do

- Accept the fact that racism is a genuine, historical, and contemporary problem that needs to be addressed personally and corporately. Learn and grow in your understanding of the history of racism and the accompanying pain many African American and other racial groups have experienced at the hands of white people in general and evangelical Christians in particular. Many have created scars that still need healing. Such exposure will increase sympathy while simultaneously decreasing micro aggressive behavior.

- Recognize how the Bible has been misused and even weaponized as a tool of oppression throughout history. Correct this errant use of Scripture. Bring people into a unified comprehensive kingdom understanding and application of God's revelation on the subjects of racism, injustice, and equity.

- Support and partner with opportunities for responsible, non-paternalistic black progress, especially for the poor, oppressed, and undeserved communities (allyship). This is needed since color alone has never been an impediment for white people in their personal, generational, social, medical, educational, and economic progress—though this has been the case with black people.

- Expose yourself, family, and friends to diverse racial environments and people who share God's kingdom values as outlined in His Word. Begin dismantling all forms of racism while simultaneously building authentic cross-racial bridges as God's agents and models of reconciliation.

- Become an active part of a kingdom-minded discipling church that partners with minority churches to work together on social service and justice issues, especially those issues that can be connected to evangelism and discipleship. Consider becoming an active part of a kingdom-minded minority led church.

- Recognize that it isn't enough to not be racist. In order to bring about positive changes in our country, you must be verbally and visibly against all forms of racism (anti-racist), whenever you encounter it on a personal and structural level.
- Reject the tendency to stereotype people based on their racial identity. Such stereotyping tends to elevate white pride and privilege while simultaneously reducing the dignity and significance of others.

Tony goes on to make more practical suggestions, not just for black and white believers, but for the churches we are a part of. Please consider using this power-packed book as a basis for group discussion and application. It will help all of us to carry out the Great Commission and to reveal to the world a dynamic and miraculous answer to Jesus' prayer:

> I pray not only for these, but also for those who believe in me through their word. May they all be one, as you, Father, are in me and I am in you. May they also be in us, so that the world may believe you sent me. I have given them the glory you have given me, so that they may be one as we are one. I am in them and you are in me, so that they may be made completely one, that the world may know you have sent me and have loved them as you have loved me. (John 17:20–23)

A Personal Past and Present Perspective

From the beginning of the first Fellowship Church nearly half a century ago, I was absolutely convinced that our doors—and arms—should be open to all people who wish to attend, either to worship or to explore and investigate the claims of biblical Christianity. In fact, we were in the midst of hippiedom and the subsequent "Jesus Revolution." Young people who had been in the drug culture came in droves, representing a number of ethnic backgrounds and lifestyles.

I was also greatly encouraged that all of our leaders who became elders were totally committed to welcoming people from all races, economic backgrounds, and other walks of life. Though it was not a stated requirement to become a spiritual leader in the church, it was simply assumed. It became a significant part of our DNA. This is important, since modeling at the leadership level is absolutely essential in creating an attitude and atmosphere of acceptance on the part of the total church body.

At this point I'd like to share some personal thoughts and feelings about the ongoing ministry of the last Fellowship Bible Church I helped launch and where I served as lead pastor. It has been over twenty years since I passed my leadership baton to my successor, Jeff Jones.

Jeff would be quick to say that he and the elders as well as the pastoral staff built on the foundation that was laid from the time we launched the first Fellowship Church. However, he has led Fellowship Bible Church North (now called Chase Oaks Church) to an even greater outreach to all classes of people representing a variety of backgrounds. The focus for all who visit is, "Come as you are, be transformed, and make a difference." Consequently, the cultural makeup of the congregation today is far more integrated.

I'm also encouraged that our pastoral church staff includes people from a variety of ethnic backgrounds. Our current campus pastor is Korean, and our small group leader is Chinese. And early on following the transition, an African American became our primary worship leader. As the weeks and months went by, the worship team included not only African Americans, but also Asians, Latinos, and Caucasians.

As I was putting the finishing touches on this chapter, Jeff invited me to speak once again. As I looked out at the total congregation, I was deeply moved by the number of people who were from a variety of ethnic backgrounds. I was even more deeply moved at the end of the service as people shook my hand, hugged my neck—and sincerely thanked me for my message—and for starting this church—where my wife and children have worshiped for the last twenty years.

This experience seemed to be a little foretaste of what it will be like in that great future revelatory scene described by John in the book of Revelation:

> After this I looked, and there was a vast multitude from **every nation, tribe, people**, and **language**, which no one could number, standing

before the throne and before the Lamb. . . . And they cried out in a loud voice: Salvation belongs to our God, who is seated on the throne, and to the Lamb! (Rev. 7:9–10)

There are certainly other steps I could have taken in my ministry experience to help overcome the racial sins in our American society generally and in our churches particularly. But I'm thankful for the opportunity the Lord gave me to at least take some redemptive steps to help bring more oneness and unity into the body of Jesus Christ. I'm thankful for the crisis I experienced early on in my ministry experience that enabled me to see the prejudice and ethnocentric attitudes that impacted my life. It's a wonderful experience to fellowship with fellow believers who represent a variety of people who reflect the beauty that God created and desires within the body of Jesus Christ.

As I reflect further on these experiences, I'm reminded of the two great banners that hung in the Worship Center at Fellowship Bible Church North, featuring the apostle Paul's words of thankfulness and praise:

Now to him who is able to do above and beyond all that we ask or think according to the power that works in us—to him be glory in the church and in Christ Jesus to all generations, forever and ever. Amen. (Eph. 3:20–21)

As I close out this chapter, I want to share some insightful and sensitive words from a fellow pastor. I agree with what he's written in a helpful book, *Ministers of Reconciliation: Preaching on Race and the Gospel.* In fact, his comments describe our own church and the community at large:

I recognize that some churches have greater opportunities here than others. At the Summit Church, where I pastor, we have the benefit of being in the heart of a large, ethnically diverse city. Many churches throughout the United States are more ethnically monochromatic areas, and they shouldn't be judged too harshly for that. They too must reflect the diversity of their communities, and if their communities are more monocultural, then their churches likely will be also. Furthermore, language barriers might make it more prudent, at least for a time, to conduct services tailored to specific communities. (For example, we have Mandarin services and Spanish services [as we do] for first generation immigrants who cannot speak English well enough to participate meaningfully in our English services.) **But regardless of our surrounding content, the core principle remains the same: churches that care about the Great Commission must promote multi-ethnic unity wherever they can. The Gospel's aim is to bring together what sin has separated.**[6]

A Question for Thought and Discussion

From your own perspective and experience, why do you think racism is such a difficult social disease to discover and understand?

Section 5

AN OPPORTUNITY FOR ACTION

Video Intro from Gene

3lenses.org/sc5

This final section includes a single chapter designed to evaluate the extent a local church is practicing the supracultural principles that emerge from the biblical story. There are also evaluation statements that relate to learning lessons from church history and gaining insights from contemporary culture.

What I've written in this book certainly relates to all believers. We are the "body of Christ" and to continue "growing into maturity with a stature measured by Christ's fullness," each one of us must do our part (Eph 4:13). However, to put these principles into practice effectively, pastoral leaders in each local church must authorize and guide this process of evaluation.

As you proceed to the following chapter, please watch the introductory video in which I give some additional cautions and suggestions.

32

Measuring Up to Christ's Fullness: Ephesians 4:13

Video Intro from Gene

3lenses.org/c32

Up to this point in this study, we've looked carefully at the biblical story of the church and particularly at the supracultural principles that emerge from this dynamic, exciting, and unfolding adventure recorded in the Scriptures. We've also considered some key lessons from the history of the church, particularly as it functioned immediately following the New Testament era. And finally, we've looked at our current culture, and how the church should address trends and changes that are out of harmony with enduring biblical values.

We would be remiss, however, if we did not take a final step in "sharpening the focus" of our individual churches. We need to address the following questions:

- To what extent are we practicing the supracultural principles that come from the biblical story?
- To what extent are we taking seriously the lessons we can learn from church history—as well as our own personal histories in church ministry?

- To what extent do we understand our current culture and the dramatic changes that are taking place and how well are we addressing these issues in a way that is in harmony with the supracultural principles that come from the biblical story?

The following evaluation scale is designed to help all pastors and spiritual leaders and other members of the body of Christ answer these questions realistically and practically.

You'll note that I've once again used the maturity goal for every local church stated by the apostle Paul in his letter to the Ephesians. We're indeed to continue "growing into maturity with a stature measured by Christ's fullness."

This evaluation process is designed to help all of us to become this kind of church. In fact, before engaging in this evaluation process, please reread Ephesians 4:11–16. This is a foundational passage for understanding and becoming the church God intended us to be.

Supracultural Principles from the Lens of Scripture

As you read the following statements that are based on supracultural principles, use the five-point evaluation scale to help you determine the extent your church is practicing these enduring truths.

Note: For review purposes, the chapter titles are listed that discuss each category of principles.

Principle of Evangelism (chapters 5–8)

Very Little   **To a Great Extent**

1 - - - - - - - - - - 2 - - - - - - - - - - 3 - - - - - - - - - - 4 - - - - - - - - - - 5

1. We are making every effort to demonstrate love and unity so that "the world may know" and "believe" that the Lord Jesus Christ is one with the Father and came from the Father to be the Savior of all who believe.

1 - - - - - - - - - - - 2 - - - - - - - - - - - 3 - - - - - - - - - - - 4 - - - - - - - - - - - 5

2. Our pastoral leaders are following the example of the apostles and other New Testament leaders by clearly teaching God's total redemptive truth from the Word of God: namely, how to be saved.

1 - - - - - - - - - - - 2 - - - - - - - - - - - 3 - - - - - - - - - - - 4 - - - - - - - - - - - 5

3. In order to reach unbelievers, we are targeting whole households, realizing that fathers and mothers particularly will naturally communicate the gospel to their children and whole families will become a part of the church.

1 - - - - - - - - - - - 2 - - - - - - - - - - - 3 - - - - - - - - - - - 4 - - - - - - - - - - - 5

4. When people put their faith in Christ for salvation, we have a definite plan to integrate them into the life of the church so that they will grow spiritually.

1 - - - - - - - - - - - 2 - - - - - - - - - - - 3 - - - - - - - - - - - 4 - - - - - - - - - - - 5

5. We are encouraging and supporting those who have a special burden and desire to be directly involved in sharing the gospel with the unsaved, locally as well as in other parts of the world.

1 - - - - - - - - - - - 2 - - - - - - - - - - - 3 - - - - - - - - - - - 4 - - - - - - - - - - - 5

6. We are regularly evaluating our evangelism forms and methods to make sure we are applying these supracultural principles for reaching unbelievers with the gospel.

1 - - - - - - - - - - - 2 - - - - - - - - - - - 3 - - - - - - - - - - - 4 - - - - - - - - - - - 5

Principles for Baptizing Believers (chapters 9–10)

1. We consistently encourage believers in Jesus Christ to be baptized, demonstrating and illustrating they have been, by faith, "buried with him" and are raised to "walk in newness of life."

1 - - - - - - - - - - - 2 - - - - - - - - - - - 3 - - - - - - - - - - - 4 - - - - - - - - - - - 5

2. We use a form of baptism that demonstrates that believers have, by faith, been "buried with Christ" and raised to "walk in the newness of life."

1 - - - - - - - - - - - 2 - - - - - - - - - - - 3 - - - - - - - - - - - 4 - - - - - - - - - - - 5

3. We make sure believers understand that baptism is to be a personal worship experience, but also an opportunity to be a witness and blessing to others, both believers and unbelievers.

1 - - - - - - - - - - - 2 - - - - - - - - - - - 3 - - - - - - - - - - - 4 - - - - - - - - - - - 5

Principles of Edification

Providing the Three Vital Experiences (chapters 11–13)

1. **The first vital experience:** Our pastor and teachers consistently and clearly teach the whole counsel of God which enables us to understand, internalize, and apply God's truth in our personal lives as well as in our corporate lives as a church.

1 - - - - - - - - - - - 2 - - - - - - - - - - - 3 - - - - - - - - - - - 4 - - - - - - - - - - - 5

2. **The second vital experience:** We regularly have meaningful relational experiences with one another that are blended with meaningful worship experiences with God.

1 - - - - - - - - - - - 2 - - - - - - - - - - - 3 - - - - - - - - - - - 4 - - - - - - - - - - - 5

3. **The third vital experience:** As a local body of believers, we are being equipped to love one another as Christ loved us in order to demonstrate oneness and unity to unbelievers. In addition, each one of us is being equipped to explain the gospel to our unsaved friends and neighbors.

1 - - - - - - - - - - - 2 - - - - - - - - - - - 3 - - - - - - - - - - - 4 - - - - - - - - - - - 5

4. Our church has an effective educational ministry that helps parents to rear their children "in the training and instruction of the Lord" by appropriately providing all age levels with the three vital experiences.

1 - - - - - - - - - - - - 2 - - - - - - - - - - - - 3 - - - - - - - - - - - - 4 - - - - - - - - - - - 5

5. Our church periodically evaluates our forms, structures and methodology to make sure we are providing all believers with the three vital experiences referred to in the previous questions.

1 - - - - - - - - - - - - 2 - - - - - - - - - - - - 3 - - - - - - - - - - - - 4 - - - - - - - - - - - 5

Principles of Edification

Building Up the Body of Christ (chapters 14–15)

1. As a community of faith, we believe and accept the fact that we need one another.

1 - - - - - - - - - - - - 2 - - - - - - - - - - - - 3 - - - - - - - - - - - - 4 - - - - - - - - - - - 5

2. As a community of faith, we love one another with deep affection.

1 - - - - - - - - - - - - 2 - - - - - - - - - - - - 3 - - - - - - - - - - - - 4 - - - - - - - - - - - 5

3. As a community of faith, we honor one another above ourselves.

1 - - - - - - - - - - - - 2 - - - - - - - - - - - - 3 - - - - - - - - - - - - 4 - - - - - - - - - - - 5

4. As a community of faith, we are experiencing oneness in our relationships with one another.

1 - - - - - - - - - - - - 2 - - - - - - - - - - - - 3 - - - - - - - - - - - - 4 - - - - - - - - - - - 5

5. As a community of faith, we are loving one another as Christ loved us.

1 - - - - - - - - - - - - 2 - - - - - - - - - - - - 3 - - - - - - - - - - - - 4 - - - - - - - - - - - 5

6. As a community of faith, we are peacemakers, making every effort to build up one another.

1 - - - - - - - - - - - - 2 - - - - - - - - - - - - 3 - - - - - - - - - - - - 4 - - - - - - - - - - - - 5

7. As a community of faith, we are living in unity with one another in order to honor God and be a witness in the world.

1 - - - - - - - - - - - - 2 - - - - - - - - - - - - 3 - - - - - - - - - - - - 4 - - - - - - - - - - - - 5

8. As a community of faith, we are overcoming areas of prejudice.

1 - - - - - - - - - - - - 2 - - - - - - - - - - - - 3 - - - - - - - - - - - - 4 - - - - - - - - - - - - 5

9. As a community of faith, we are teaching and admonishing one another.

1 - - - - - - - - - - - - 2 - - - - - - - - - - - - 3 - - - - - - - - - - - - 4 - - - - - - - - - - - - 5

10. As a community of faith, we are expressing appropriate godly physical affection to one another.

1 - - - - - - - - - - - - 2 - - - - - - - - - - - - 3 - - - - - - - - - - - - 4 - - - - - - - - - - - - 5

Principles of Edification

The Measure of a Healthy Church (chapters 16–17)

1. As a community of faith, we are more and more measuring up to Christ's fullness, demonstrating that we are God's "workmanship, created in Christ Jesus for good works."

1 - - - - - - - - - - - - 2 - - - - - - - - - - - - 3 - - - - - - - - - - - - 4 - - - - - - - - - - - - 5

2. As a community of faith, we are measuring up to Christ's fullness by understanding the "blessed hope" regarding Christ's return and knowing with certainty our eternal destiny is secure.

1 - - - - - - - - - - - - 2 - - - - - - - - - - - - 3 - - - - - - - - - - - - 4 - - - - - - - - - - - - 5

3. As a community of faith, we are more and more measuring up to Christ's fullness, and continuing to grow in our love for one another.

1 - - - - - - - - - - - - 2 - - - - - - - - - - - 3 - - - - - - - - - - - 4 - - - - - - - - - - - 5

Principles of Leadership (chapters 18–20)

1. We use titles for our spiritual leaders that are both biblically and culturally relevant.

   Note: In our churches, we've chosen to use the title "elder," which is a well-known term in our particular cultural environment.

   1 - - - - - - - - - - - - 2 - - - - - - - - - - - 3 - - - - - - - - - - - 4 - - - - - - - - - - - 5

2. Our elders or pastoral leaders and their wives (if married) are always selected and appointed based on the maturity profile outlined by Paul in the pastoral epistles.

   1 - - - - - - - - - - - - 2 - - - - - - - - - - - 3 - - - - - - - - - - - 4 - - - - - - - - - - - 5

3. Our elders or pastoral leaders, along with their wives, are managing and shepherding all of us just as fathers and mothers care for their families.

   1 - - - - - - - - - - - - 2 - - - - - - - - - - - 3 - - - - - - - - - - - 4 - - - - - - - - - - - 5

4. Our elders or pastoral leaders are managing and shepherding our church well by maintaining six important functions: 1) praying for the sick, 2) teaching the Word of God, 3) disciplining unruly believers, 4) overseeing the material needs of the church, 5) maintaining doctrinal purity, and 6) modeling Christlike behavior.

   1 - - - - - - - - - - - - 2 - - - - - - - - - - - 3 - - - - - - - - - - - 4 - - - - - - - - - - - 5

5. Our elders or pastoral leaders are led by a primary fellow pastoral elder who both leads and serves and who is also accountable to the other elders.

   1 - - - - - - - - - - - - 2 - - - - - - - - - - - 3 - - - - - - - - - - - 4 - - - - - - - - - - - 5

6. Our elders or pastoral leaders are committed to carrying out the Great Commission of our Lord Jesus Christ, locally and worldwide.

1 - - - - - - - - - - - - 2 - - - - - - - - - - - - 3 - - - - - - - - - - - - 4 - - - - - - - - - - - - 5

7. Our elders or pastoral leaders take the lead to make sure that adequate forms and structures are developed and refined to carry out the biblical functions outlined in the previous questions.

1 - - - - - - - - - - - - 2 - - - - - - - - - - - - 3 - - - - - - - - - - - - 4 - - - - - - - - - - - - 5

Principles of Administration and Organization (chapters 21–22)

1. The pastoral leaders in our church do not ignore people problems; rather they face reality.

1 - - - - - - - - - - - - 2 - - - - - - - - - - - - 3 - - - - - - - - - - - - 4 - - - - - - - - - - - - 5

2. The pastoral leaders in our church develop a proper perspective on problems before they propose concrete solutions.

1 - - - - - - - - - - - - 2 - - - - - - - - - - - - 3 - - - - - - - - - - - - 4 - - - - - - - - - - - - 5

3. The pastoral leaders in our church clearly establish priorities in solving problems and maintaining unity.

1 - - - - - - - - - - - - 2 - - - - - - - - - - - - 3 - - - - - - - - - - - - 4 - - - - - - - - - - - - 5

4. The pastoral leaders in our church delegate responsibility to other qualified people.

1 - - - - - - - - - - - - 2 - - - - - - - - - - - - 3 - - - - - - - - - - - - 4 - - - - - - - - - - - - 5

5. The pastoral leaders in our church maintain a proper balance between divine and human factors in their leadership style.

1 - - - - - - - - - - - - 2 - - - - - - - - - - - - 3 - - - - - - - - - - - - 4 - - - - - - - - - - - - 5

6. The pastoral leaders in our church take an approach to problem solving and decision-making that takes into consideration the attitudes and feelings of all of us who are directly involved.

1 - - - - - - - - - - - 2 - - - - - - - - - - - 3 - - - - - - - - - - - 4 - - - - - - - - - - - 5

7. The pastoral leaders in our church make an effort to solve every problem creatively under the leadership of the Holy Spirit.

1 - - - - - - - - - - - 2 - - - - - - - - - - - 3 - - - - - - - - - - - 4 - - - - - - - - - - - 5

8. The pastoral leaders in our church make decisions based on supracultural biblical principles and do not allow forms and structures to become ends in themselves.

1 - - - - - - - - - - - 2 - - - - - - - - - - - 3 - - - - - - - - - - - 4 - - - - - - - - - - - 5

9. The pastoral leaders in our church organize to meet the needs of people.

1 - - - - - - - - - - - 2 - - - - - - - - - - - 3 - - - - - - - - - - - 4 - - - - - - - - - - - 5

10. The pastoral leaders in our church make an effort to keep organization simple.

1 - - - - - - - - - - - 2 - - - - - - - - - - - 3 - - - - - - - - - - - 4 - - - - - - - - - - - 5

11. The pastoral leaders in our church make an effort to keep organizational structures flexible.

1 - - - - - - - - - - - 2 - - - - - - - - - - - 3 - - - - - - - - - - - 4 - - - - - - - - - - - 5

Principles of Communication (chapters 23–24)

1. As a community of believers, we're doing all we can to communicate with as many different people as possible, regardless of race, cultural backgrounds, economic levels, etc.

1 - - - - - - - - - - - 2 - - - - - - - - - - - 3 - - - - - - - - - - - 4 - - - - - - - - - - - 5

2. As a community of believers, we are committed to verifying that Jesus Christ is the incarnate Son of God by loving one another and demonstrating oneness and unity that reflects oneness and unity in the Trinity.

1 - - - - - - - - - - - - 2 - - - - - - - - - - - - 3 - - - - - - - - - - - - 4 - - - - - - - - - - - 5

3. Our pastoral leaders are using Jesus' model of communication.

1 - - - - - - - - - - - - 2 - - - - - - - - - - - - 3 - - - - - - - - - - - - 4 - - - - - - - - - - - 5

4. Our pastoral leaders are following the example of the apostles and other New Testament leaders in developing communication skills that involve significant human effort.

1 - - - - - - - - - - - - 2 - - - - - - - - - - - - 3 - - - - - - - - - - - - 4 - - - - - - - - - - - 5

5. Though our pastoral leaders engage in significant human effort to communicate effectively, they also first and foremost rely on God's supernatural power.

1 - - - - - - - - - - - - 2 - - - - - - - - - - - - 3 - - - - - - - - - - - - 4 - - - - - - - - - - - 5

6. Our pastoral leaders communicate first and foremost by exemplifying the life and ministry of Jesus Christ.

1 - - - - - - - - - - - - 2 - - - - - - - - - - - - 3 - - - - - - - - - - - - 4 - - - - - - - - - - - 5

7. Our pastoral leaders are free and flexible in their communication style and methodology.

1 - - - - - - - - - - - - 2 - - - - - - - - - - - - 3 - - - - - - - - - - - - 4 - - - - - - - - - - - 5

Lessons from the Lens of History (chapters 25–28)

1. Our pastoral leaders cite lessons from church history that help us avoid the mistakes spiritual leaders have made in the past.

1 - - - - - - - - - - - - 2 - - - - - - - - - - - - 3 - - - - - - - - - - - - 4 - - - - - - - - - - - 5

2. Our pastoral leaders cite lessons from church history that help us practice what were positive biblical and cultural examples.

1 - - - - - - - - - - - 2 - - - - - - - - - - - 3 - - - - - - - - - - - 4 - - - - - - - - - - - 5

3. Our pastoral leaders actively use our own local church and denominational history to learn lessons from our successes and failures.

1 - - - - - - - - - - - 2 - - - - - - - - - - - 3 - - - - - - - - - - - 4 - - - - - - - - - - - 5

Insights from the Lens of Culture (chapters 29–31)

1. Our pastoral leaders directly but sensitively address the trends and changes in culture that are out of harmony with biblical values.

1 - - - - - - - - - - - 2 - - - - - - - - - - - 3 - - - - - - - - - - - 4 - - - - - - - - - - - 5

2. Our pastoral leaders help create a climate in our church where all unsaved people, regardless of their lifestyles, feel welcome to attend.

1 - - - - - - - - - - - 2 - - - - - - - - - - - 3 - - - - - - - - - - - 4 - - - - - - - - - - - 5

3. Our pastoral leaders address publicly and privately all lifestyle issues that are out of harmony with biblical values but they always "speak the truth in love."

1 - - - - - - - - - - - 2 - - - - - - - - - - - 3 - - - - - - - - - - - 4 - - - - - - - - - - - 5

4. Our pastoral leaders practice the intervention process explained in Galatians 6:1–2 in the lives of professing Christians whose sinful lifestyles are out of harmony with biblical values.

1 - - - - - - - - - - - 2 - - - - - - - - - - - 3 - - - - - - - - - - - 4 - - - - - - - - - - - 5

5. Our pastoral leaders have a definite plan to avoid appointing anyone to serve in leadership positions in the church whose lifestyle reflects the "works of the flesh" rather than the "fruit of the Spirit" as outlined by Paul in Galatians 5:19–23.

1 - - - - - - - - - - - 2 - - - - - - - - - - - 3 - - - - - - - - - - - 4 - - - - - - - - - - - 5

Appendix A, B, and C

Appendix A
A Research Design: The Great Commission

Appendix A PDF

3lenses.org/apa

Use the QR code to access the complete biblical texts referenced in chapter 2.

Appendix B
Terms Used to Describe Believers in the Lord Jesus Christ

Appendix B PDF

3lenses.org/apb

Use the QR code to access the terms used to describe believers in the Lord Jesus Christ referenced in chapter 4.

Appendix C
The Kingdom of God

Appendix C PDF

3lenses.org/apc

Use the QR code to access a perspective on the kingdom of God.

Notes

1. From Professor to Pastor

1. Regarding church functions and forms, I was first introduced to the terms *absolutes* and *non-absolutes* by the late Dr. Francis Schaeffer in his book *The Church at the End of the 20th Century* (Downers Grove, IL: InterVarsity Press, 1970). I was impressed with these terms and have used them ever since. In essence, they represent what this book is all about.

2. The late Dr. Stanley J. Grenz effectively used **biblical**, **historical**, and **cultural** perspectives in *Renewing the Center: Evangelical Theology in a Post-Theological Era* (Nashville, TN: Broadman and Holman, 1994). Grenz defined these three perspectives as follows:

   First, the Bible must be the "primary voice" in any "theological conversation."

   Second, we must consult our historical heritage, since "we are not the first generation since the early church to seek to be formed into the community of Christ in the world."

   Third, we must consider what may be the "Spirit's voice in culture," but it must never contradict Scripture.

   I appreciate Grenz's serious work, which certainly reinforces my own experience in doing ecclesiological research. However, I prefer referring to the Word of God as "the ultimate voice" in doing theological research, not simply "the primary voice." I am also cautious in his reference to the "Spirit's voice in culture." On the one hand, we must certainly consider cultural insights in teaching and applying Scripture, but we must never equate any of these on the same level as insights from biblical revelation. I have deep respect for Grenz's love for the Bible and his compassion for the church and I told him so before he entered heaven's gates. I've also benefited greatly from his serious work *Theology for the Community of God* (Grand Rapids, MI: Eerdmans, 2000).

3. During my years as a lead pastor, I have used the three-lens approach in understanding and teaching a number of subjects in Scripture. I've also had the opportunity to do two more in-depth studies, using the three-lens research design. The first is *A Biblical Theology of Material Possessions* (Eugene, OR: Wipf and Stock, 2012), later released as *Rich in Every Way* (New York: Howard Books, 2004). The second book is *Elders and Leaders: God's Plan for Leading the Church* (Chicago: Moody Publishers, 2003). As with the original edition of *Sharpening the Focus of the Church*, both of these books were written in the context of community, but this time using my fellow elders from Fellowship Bible Church North.

2. Challenging Questions and a New Direction

1. John W. Gardner, "How to Prevent Organizational Dry Rot," *Harper's Magazine*, October 1965, 20.
2. Ibid.
3. Elton Trueblood, *The Company of the Committed* (New York: Harper Brothers, 1961); Findley B. Edge, *A Quest for Vitality in Religion* (Nashville, TN: Broadman, 1963); Larry Richards, *A New Face for the Church* (Grand Rapids, MI: Zondervan, 1970); Howard Snyder, *The Problem of Wineskins* (Downers Grove, IL: InterVarsity Press, 1975); David Mains, *Full Circle: The Creative Church for Today's Society* (Waco, TX: Word Books, 1971); and Robert Girard, *Brethren Hang Loose* (Grand Rapids, MI: Zondervan, 1972).
4. Schaeffer, *The Church at the End of the 20th Century*, 67.
5. "Functions" in the book of Acts in the most part become "directives" in the New Testament letters. "Results" in the book of Acts in the most part become "objectives" in the New Testament letters.
6. Based on the Great Commission, this second column could be initially titled "Teaching Disciples." However, as the New Testament story unfolds, it becomes clear early on that "teaching" was simply foundational in helping these "disciples" mature in their Christian faith. I used the phrase "Building Disciples" in the edification column. However, I now prefer "Equipping Disciples," which is based on Paul's statement in Ephesians: "And he himself gave some to be apostles, some prophets, some evangelists, some pastors and teachers, to equip the saints for the work of ministry, to build up the body of Christ" (Eph. 4:11–12).
7. In this study, I used the general chronology of the New Testament letters from Merrill C. Tenney's *New Testament Survey*, rev. ed. (Grand Rapids, MI: Eerdmans, 1961).
8. References that include both "making disciples" and "equipping disciples" are included in both columns.

4. Authentic Disciples

1. New Testament authors used the term *universal church* in two ways: (1) all first-century believers scattered throughout the Roman world, (2) all believers of all time who are members of the body of Christ.
2. In addition to the times *adelphoi* refers to "brothers and sisters" in the book of Acts, it is used ten times to refer to "brothers" in Christ, and the single term *adelphos* is used three times to refer to a single "brother" in Christ. (See Appendix B for a complete listing of *adelphoi* and *adelphos* in Acts and the rest of the New Testament.)
3. Here the term *adelphoi* may refer to the elders Paul and Barnabas appointed in the churches in Lystra and Iconium on the first missionary journey. It could be just "brothers"—a masculine term (Acts 14:21–23).
4. To see the depth of carnality and immaturity in the Corinthian church, see pages 365–66. In fact, Paul stated that they were living such sinful lives they appeared to be unbelievers. Yet, Luke identified them as authentic disciples.

Though the city of Corinth is not mentioned in Acts 18:27, Luke referred to the "disciples" in Achia, which included believers in Corinth. Furthermore, Apollos is mentioned, who ministered in the Corinthian church (1 Cor. 1:12).

5. Note that Paul identified the Corinthians as knowing Christ as Lord, even though He was not "Lord" of their lives. In other words, our salvation is based on the fact that we know the Lord Jesus Christ as Savior even though we may not be living in His will. Throughout the book of Acts and the Epistles, the term *Lord* is used almost always to refer to Christ's deity.

5. Making Disciples in Acts

1. The apostles began this process as revealed in the book of Acts. Paul's ministry throughout the Roman empire is, of course, detailed in Scripture. However, tradition tells us that a number of the apostles, chosen by Jesus, traveled to other parts of the world. It's difficult to substantiate what is accurate. Since Jesus told them they would be witnesses "to the ends of the earth," we can conclude with confidence that this included various parts of the world beyond the geographical locations mentioned in the book of Acts.

2. When Luke referred to "those who had been scattered," he may have been thinking primarily of those Grecian Jews who were among the seven men appointed to serve the widows. Stephen, of course, was martyred as a result of his evangelistic activity. Philip went to Samaria, also "making disciples." The others may have gone to Antioch. In fact, Nicholas was a convert to Judaism and from Antioch.

3. Here the term "teaching" is *didache*, which refers to the content or doctrine involved in the apostles' teaching process.

6. Making Disciples in the New Testament Letters

1. Schaeffer, *The Church at the End of the 20th Century*, 138.

2. In interpreting biblical passages on slavery, we must not equate this social disease with what existed in the early decades of America. Slaves in the Roman world had been acquired through the war with Greece and many were doctors, nurses, musicians, and skilled artisans. Though there were laws governing the way these slaves should be treated, they were often mistreated by their masters who ignored their legal rights. Their only recourse was to endure the suffering. On the other hand, slaves in America were the underprivileged and marginalized people who were brought from Africa in chains and sold to slave owners. Unfortunately, there were Bible-believing Christians who used these biblical passages on slavery to justify this evil practice. Sadly, it took a war to break this stronghold on human beings. We are still seeing the results of this racial and social sin in certain sections of the American society, and the greatest challenge for churches today is to address the remnants of racism, which we'll attempt to address in a section of this book titled "The Lens of Culture."

3. Tenney, *New Testament Survey*, 50.

4. This does not mean that Christian women should submit to spousal abuse. Fortunately, in many cultures there are laws that protect both men and women

from this kind of evil behavior. However, in the New Testament Roman world, many women had no such protection. To rebel could drive them into poverty and often prostitution, or could have also cost them their lives. Sadly, this is true in some cultures today.

5. When Peter referred to a wife as a "weaker partner," he was not saying women were inferior mentally, emotionally, and spiritually. In fact, women are often remarkably stronger than men in these aspects of their personalities. Rather, Peter was referring to a man's overall physical characteristics that were often used in insensitive ways toward his wife, particularly in intimate relationships. Spousal abuse and even rape was common among husbands in the pagan culture. Peter was saying that this kind of behavior should never exist among husbands who are Christ followers.

7. Household Conversions

1. George W. Peters, *Saturation Evangelism* (Grand Rapids, MI: Zondervan, 1970), 147. See also George W. Peters, *A Biblical Theology of Missions* (Chicago: Moody Publishers, 1984).

2. Peter addressed an exception in household conversions. He gives instructions to wives who have become believers but whose husbands had not. If these women followed these instructions, hopefully their husbands would also become believers (1 Peter 3:1–7).

3. Harry Boer, *Pentecost and Missions* (Grand Rapids, MI: Eerdmans, 1961), 165, 176.

4. Peters, *Saturation Evangelism*, 152–53.

8. Principles of Evangelism

1. For a definitive understanding of what Mormons believe about Jesus Christ, see excerpts from an address to the Harvard Divinity School in March 2001 by Robert L. Millet, former Dean of Religious Education at Brigham Young University. Representing Mormonism, Millet clearly denies the Trinity—that the Father, the Son, and the Holy Spirit are one God. This lecture also denies that salvation is by grace through faith alone as stated by Paul in Ephesians 2:8–9.

2. This in-depth approach to sharing the gospel does not mean we should not use a simple presentation of the gospel, outlining how to become a believer. This is a very effective approach when sharing the gospel with those unbelievers who already have a substantial understanding of the biblical story, such as the 3,000 who responded to Peter's message on the day of Pentecost.

3. Norm Wretlind, Becky Wretlind, and Jim Killam, *When God is the Life of the Party: Reaching Neighbors Through Creative Hospitality* (Colorado Springs, CO: NavPress, 2003), 128.

4. Ibid., 133.

5. *Why Die Before Your Time? God's Story in the Life of E. A. Abraham* (Kollam: Krithi Books, 2010), 139.

6. Peters, *Saturation Evangelism*, 147.

9. Baptizing Authentic Disciples

1. Merrill C. Tenney, *John: The Gospel of Belief* (Grand Rapids, MI: Eerdmans, 1976), 31–32.
2. Luke identified these Judaizers as "believers." However, only God knows if they were "authentic disciples." The same would have been true of those who claimed to have believed when Paul returned to Jerusalem years later (see Acts 21:20).
3. It's true that Jesus did not refer to a "baptism of fire" as John did. However, note that Jesus had spoken to the apostles about the coming of the Holy Spirit and perhaps He reviewed John's reference to the "tongues of fire" that would accompany this event.
4. It's true that Luke's statement that these believers "were baptized" implies that someone performed this act other than the persons who "were baptized." However, Luke may have used this terminology in a collective sense, not specifying how every baptismal event took place that day. In fact, as you follow Luke's account in the book of Acts, you'll note he often generalized when reporting on specific events. In fact, it's possible the apostles led the way that day by being baptized, perhaps immersing themselves in one of these immersion pools. Again, this is pure speculation.
5. This variation is significant. In the early church, believers visibly received the Holy Spirit at times prior to baptism and in other instances following baptism. There was no set pattern.
6. According to Alan Millard, "A copy of a lengthy book like Isaiah might take a professional scribe three days or so to make, so the price would be his wages and the cost of the materials." Alan Millard, "Reading and Writing in the Time of Jesus," *The Bible and Interpretation*, January 2000, https://bibleinterp.arizona.edu/articles/2000/Millard_Jesus.
7. Luke actually may have simply omitted any reference to the coming of the Holy Spirit on the Ethiopian. However, this would have been an unusual omission in view of other references to this visible event.
8. Though plural pronouns are used in these references, it's clear from the overall context in Scripture that each individual person received forgiveness of sins as a result of personal faith in Jesus Christ (see Heb. 10:43).
9. Various stanzas from "Nothing but the Blood of Jesus," words and music by Robert Lowry (1876).
10. Note again the variance, this time in a Gentile setting. In contrast to what happened when Philip preached the gospel in Samaria, the Holy Spirit came on Cornelius, his household, and his guests before—not after—they were baptized with water.
11. We're not told who baptized the majority of the Corinthian believers. As noted in 1 Corinthians, it was not Paul (1 Cor. 1:14–16).
12. It's interesting to note in the biblical story that we see variance in carrying out Jesus' command to baptize disciples "in the name of the Father and of the Son and of the Holy Spirit" (Matt. 28:19). Sometimes they were baptized in

Jesus' name—who is one with the Father and who is One with the Holy Spirit who is also Christ in all true believers (Col. 1:27; Eph. 3:16–17a). This is the miracle of the Trinity.

13. There is a difference of opinion among serious Bible interpreters regarding being baptized by the Holy Spirit. It's my opinion that there is a two-fold meaning. Some spiritual leaders particularly were "baptized by the Holy Spirit," resulting in supernatural power to verify the gospel—such as the apostles and men like Stephen and Philip (Acts 1:4–5, 8; 6:5; 8:6). Furthermore, believers generally were visibly "baptized by the Holy Spirit," first in Jerusalem and Judea, and then in Samaria and beyond. However, Paul's reference to being "baptized by one Spirit into one body" refers to the supernatural work of the Holy Spirit in the lives of all believers when, by faith, we are "born again" (1 Cor. 12:13; John 3:3).

14. In this letter some believe Paul was referring to "Spirit baptism." This may be true, but it's my opinion he is referring to "water baptism" since he referred to "being baptized into Christ Jesus" whereas in the Corinthian letter he referred to being "baptized by one Spirit into one body" (1 Cor. 12:13).

10. Principles for Baptizing Believers

1. Stanley J. Grenz, *Theology of the Community of God* (Grand Rapids, MI: Eerdmans, 2000), 689. See also G. R. Beasley-Murray, *Baptism in the New Testament* (Eugene, OR: Wipf & Stock, 1972), 306–86.

2. Mikhail Gorbachev introduced perestroika to the Soviet Union, which proposed returning to what he believed were foundational principles of democratic socialism. See Mikhail Gorbachev, *Perestroika: New Thinking for Our Country and the World* (New York: HarperCollins, 1987).

11. Teaching Authentic Disciples

1. In addition to the apostles Matthew, John, Peter, and Paul, those who gave us the New Testament are Mark and Luke as well as James and Jude, Jesus' half-brothers. They too became recipients of the promise Jesus made regarding the "Spirit of truth" who would reveal the written Word of God.

2. The Greek verb *oikodomeo* means to edify, to build up, confirm. The meaning is closely related to *episterizo*.

3. This may refer to several of the seven men who were appointed to serve the widows in Jerusalem. They were all especially anointed the Holy Spirit (6:3, 5). Stephen, of course, was martyred. Philip went to Samaria and other similar areas, especially since his home was in Caesarea (21:8). Those who went to Antioch may have been from the other five (6:5). Nicolaus was actually from Antioch and a convert to Judaism (6:5).

4. After Judas and Silas spent time in Antioch, Luke recorded that "they were sent back in peace by the brothers and sisters to those who had sent them"— namely, the "apostles and elders" in Jerusalem (Acts 15:22, 32–33). However, in the same context we read that Paul chose Silas to join him on his second journey. To reconcile these statements, it appears that Paul made this choice

before Silas returned to Jerusalem; Silas then joined Paul later in Lystra. This also correlates with Luke's report that Paul, after separating from Barnabas, "traveled through Syria and Cilicia, strengthening the churches." This happened before he traveled on to Lystra. Here he evidently met Silas, chose Timothy as his missionary companion, and the three of them continued together on the second journey.

5. The Greek word *parakaleo* means to exhort, comfort, encourage.

6. The Greek word *paramutheomai* means to "comfort" and "encourage."

7. The Greek word *martus* means to "witness," here translated "implore."

8. The English text states "each one of you." The Greek text is redundant— namely, ministering "to each one of you one by one." We cannot miss the personalized nature of teaching these disciples what it means to grow "into maturity with a stature measured by the fullness of Christ" (Eph. 4:13).

9. Paul actually wrote four letters to these believers. Two are lost and two are in the New Testament.

10. The Greek term *aspazomai* means to "embrace" which certainly correlates with his repeated directive to "greet one another with a holy kiss" (Rom. 16:16; 1 Cor. 16:20; 2 Cor. 13:12; 1 Thess. 5:26).

12. The Jerusalem Model

1. Some believe this was actually the fourth cup of wine that was used at the Passover meal. In fact, Luke states that Jesus shared the first cup of wine prior to breaking bread (Luke 22:17).

2. It should be remembered that these three thousand believers in Jerusalem and the multiplied thousands to follow came from all over the Roman world to worship in the temple in Jerusalem. While there they experienced personal salvation and the birth of the church. When they returned to their local areas, they would have shared their experiences with those who became believers in their own communities and continued to devote themselves to prayer.

3. Some translators believe that Paul's reference to the "Spirit" is actually a reference to the human "spirit." The reasoning relates to the context where Paul exhorted, "Don't get drunk with wine"—which often leads to singing that is anything but edifying. Rather than engaging in boisterous, coarse, and worldly singing that often accompanied drunkenness and their inner being out of control, believers were to be in control of their human spirit and use their voices to engage in spiritual singing. This interpretation is also supported by the fact that this is the only reference in the New Testament where believers are exhorted "to be filled with the Spirit." In all other references, believers were "filled with the Holy Spirit" as a sovereign act of God's grace apart from any noticeable human effort.

4. For a more complete development of these three concepts and their relationship to "making disciples," see chapter 6.

13. Biblical Principles of Edification—Part 1

1. Over the years as a pastor and as a result of messages on Old Testament personalities, I subsequently published ten books on the following Old Testament personalities, now available from Entrust Source.com. Based on this series, I was later asked by Broadman and Holman to do a Men of Character Study Bible. This study Bible includes 125-character profiles in both the Old and New Testaments. Hopefully these profiles will generate additional ideas for character-based messages.

2. Gene A. Getz, *A Biblical Theology of Material Possessions* (Chicago: Moody Publishers, 1990), Gene A. Getz, *Rich in Every Way* (West Monroe, LA: Howard Publishing, 2004).

3. These messages were subsequently published under the title *The Measure of a Family* (Glendale, CA: Gospel Light, 1976).

4. Carl F. Keil and Franz Delitzsch, *Commentary on the Old Testament: Proverbs, Ecclesiastes, and Song of Solomon*, vol. 6 (Grand Rapids, MI: Eerdmans, 1971), 86–87.

14. The Functioning Body

1. Wayne Grudem, *Are Miraculous Gifts for Today? Four Views* (Grand Rapids, MI: Zondervan, 1996). This book features four prominent spokesmen who represent four significant general positions: 1) the cessation position, 2) the open, but cautious, position, 3), the third wave position (the Vineyard Movement), and 4) the Pentecostal/Charismatic position.

2. In Peter's first letter, he simply generalized regarding spiritual gifts. The gift of "speaking" no doubt involved the gifts of teaching, prophesy, exhorting, a message of wisdom, a message of knowledge, tongues, interpretation of tongues, distinguishing between spirits. The gift of "serving" may have included faith, healing, miracles, helping, leading, giving, and mercy.

3. As stated in chapter 18, the "greater gifts" to the church have a dual meaning. They referred to individuals such as the apostles, prophets, evangelists, pastors, and teachers as well as to their special abilities such as prophesying, evangelizing, teaching, and pastoring.

4. In Paul's first letter to Timothy, he stated—"Don't neglect the gift that is in you; it was given to you through prophecy, with the laying on of hands by the council of elders" (1 Tim. 4:14). This may appear to contradict Paul's statement in 2 Timothy that the gift was given through the laying on of his hands. However, Paul was evidently saying that the elders were present and laid their hands on Timothy as well when he received his spiritual gift. However, it was Paul's apostolic authority and spiritual power that caused it to happen.

5. W. Harold Mare reminds us that "to walk *kata anthrōpon* [acting like mere men]…means to live only the way the ordinary sinful man lives—in selfishness, pride, and envy." W. Harold Mare, "1 Corinthians" in *The Expositor's Bible Commentary*, vol. 10, ed. Frank E. Gaebelein (Grand Rapids, MI: Zondervan, 1976), 205.

6. Paul also used the "one another" concept in a negative sense—what we should not do in relationship with "one another." Believers are not to "lust

for one another" and "judge one another" (Rom. 1:27; 14:13). They are not to "deprive one another" (1 Cor. 7:3) or to "bite and devour one another"; to "be consumed by one another"; "provoking one another" and "envying one another" (Gal. 5:15a, b, c; 5:26a, b), they are not to "lie to one another" (Col. 3:9), "detesting one another" (Titus 3:3).

15. Biblical Principles of Edification—Part 2

1. Subsequently, I published five books on these "one another" messages: *Building Up One Another, Loving One Another, Encouraging One Another, Serving One Another,* and *Praying for One Another* (Colorado Springs, CO: David C. Cook, 2002).

16. Measuring Local Church Maturity

1. Luke apparently made reference to these "grace gifts" when he recorded the following: "With great power the apostles were giving testimony to the resurrection of the Lord Jesus, and great grace was on all of them" (Acts 4:33).
2. W. Harold Mare, "1 Corinthians," 205. The term *man* in this case is no doubt generic and means "mere humans."
3. In 2 Corinthians 13:13, the term *grace* means a divine source of strength. For example, when Paul prayed that his "thorn in the flesh" be removed, God responded with these reassuring words, "My grace is sufficient for you, for my power is perfected in weakness" (2 Cor. 12:9). When Paul wrote to Timothy, he encouraged him to "be strong in the grace that is in Christ Jesus" (2 Cor. 2:1). The author of Hebrews wrote: "Therefore, let us approach the throne of grace with boldness, so that we may receive mercy and find grace to help us in time of need" (Heb. 4:16).
4. Some believe Paul also wrote Hebrews. However, internal evidence seems to point to another author. Personally, I favor Apollos. As some scholars point out, the exquisiteness of his Greek points to that possibility.
5. For an even more in-depth look at the concepts of faith, hope, and love, see Gene A. Getz, *The Measure of a Healthy Church* (Chicago: Moody Publishers, 2007) (available online).

17. Biblical Principles of Edification—Part 3

1. Peter Oakes, *Philippians: From People to Letter* (Cambridge University Press, 2001), 46, 62.
2. "Blessed Assurance," words by Fanny Crosby (1873), music by Phoebe Palmer Knapp.
3. F. Kefa Sempangi with Barbara R. Thompson, *A Distant Grief* (Glendale, CA: Regal, 1979).
4. See Getz, *The Measure of a Healthy Church.*

18. New Testament Church Leadership—Phase 1

1. George W. Peters, *A Theology of Church Growth* (Grand Rapids, MI: Zondervan, 1981), 17.

2. See Ken Curtis, "What Happened to the 12 Disciples and Apostles of Jesus," April 2, 2024, www.christianity.com/church/church-history/timeline/1-300/ whatever-happened-to-the-twelve-apostles-11629558.html.

3. Merrill F. Unger, *Unger's Bible Dictionary* (Chicago: Moody, 1957), 892.

4. For examples of Old Testament prophecies, see Acts 2:29–31; 7:37; 8:34–35; 13:27.

5. It appears there may have been two variations in prophetic gifts. There were those closely aligned with the "apostles" and called "prophets" (Acts 11:28; 13:11; 15:32; Eph 2:19–20; 3:5; 4:12). The second reference to prophetic gifts are similar to other gifts possessed by individual believers in local churches (Rom. 12:6; 1 Cor. 12:7–11; 13:2; 14:1–5).

6. For example, see Revelation 11:3, 10; 16:6; 18:21–24.

7. See chapter 5 for additional references where the Greek word *euangelidzo* is used to describe the evangelistic ministry of key individuals such as Philip in Samaria, Peter and John in Samaritan villages, Paul and Barnabas in Lystra and Derbe and in his vision to go to Macedonia.

8. You'll note I often use the phrases "may have been" or "it seems." Though the Scriptures imply these conclusions, they were not totally definitive.

9. The terms *strengthen* and *encourage* are used throughout the book of Acts to describe Paul's teaching ministry (see chapter 11).

10. In Paul's second letter he referenced his own spiritual gift that enabled him to bestow a spiritual gift to Timothy: "Therefore, I remind you to rekindle the gift of God that is in you through the laying on of my hands" (2 Tim. 1:6). Here Paul made it clear that it was his apostolic and prophetic gifts that bestowed these gifts to Timothy. The elders, however, were present also and laid hands on Timothy.

11. Having referenced those who may have had the pastoral and teaching gifts, there is one other possibility. These gifts may have been revelatory in nature, enabling the apostles particularly to author the New Testament. If so, Timothy and Titus and the others I've just listed were able to "teach others" because of what they had learned from men like Paul who had the "gift of pastor and teacher." If this is accurate, the reference to Timothy's gift is not specifically described (2 Tim. 1:6).

19. New Testament Church Leadership—Phase 2

1. Gene A. Getz, *Elders and Leaders: God's Plan for Leading the Church* (Chicago: Moody Publishers, 2003).

2. We can only speculate what was involved in distributing these financial gifts. Luke simply stated the relief was for "the brothers and sisters who lived in Judea" and the gift was sent to "the elders." As stated, it's logical that this reference to "the elders" referred to those spiritual leaders in the Jerusalem church who were then responsible to distribute this money to believers throughout Judea. By this time there were probably many churches outside of Jerusalem with their own elders. These men would have helped in this distribution, but

it still would have been a huge task calling for a lot of effort and significant responsibility and accountability.

3. Barnabas clearly illustrates how spiritual growth could take place quickly in the lives of devoted Jews even prior to their salvation experience. Following his conversion in Jerusalem, he quickly became a great example of generosity (Acts 4:36–37). And when the spiritual leaders in Jerusalem heard about the birth of the church in Antioch, "they sent out Barnabas" to encourage these believers. He was chosen because "he was a good man, full of the Holy Spirit and of faith" (11:23–24).

4. In most instances the term *adelphoi* in the Christian Standard Bible is translated "brothers and sisters" in the book of Acts. However, in Acts 16:2 it's my opinion it refers to the "brothers" or elders in both Lystra and Iconium who were appointed on the first missionary journey. Their evaluation of the spiritual growth would have been very meaningful to Paul.

5. Paul made reference to Timothy's spiritual gift (2 Tim. 1:6). However, it seems clear that Paul used his apostolic authority to bestow this gift after he selected Timothy to be a missionary companion based on his reputation and character.

6. The word translated "to lead" comes from the Greek word *proistamenous*. This Greek participle is the same basic word Paul used later when writing to Timothy, stating that a basic requirement for serving as an elder is that a man be competent in managing his own family (see 1 Tim 3:5; 5:17).

7. Note that Paul identified that the Holy Spirit had appointed these men as overseers. Does this mean they were appointed to this position just as Paul and Barnabas had been, as communicated by direct revelation from the Holy Spirit as recorded in Acts 13:1-3? If so, this may relate to what happened when Paul returned to Ephesus and encountered the "twelve men" who were disciples. In the process, they had a similar experience as the apostles on the day of Pentecost. We read—"And when Paul had laid his hands on them, the Holy Spirit came on them, and they began to speak in tongues" (Acts 19:6). Conceivably, these men became the first elders in Ephesus, which leads to Paul's reference to the Holy Spirit's direct involvement in their appointment (Acts 20:28). However, this doesn't seem to be the norm as the biblical story continues to unfold. Local church leaders were chosen based on character qualifications—not direct revelation.

8. Paul implied that any man who reflected Christlike maturity could desire to be an elder. It's true that "anyone" is a correct translation. However, from the overall context in Scripture, it's clear that Paul was referring to men. In fact, this is clear from Paul's immediate reference to the qualification—"the husband of one wife"—and later that "he must manage his own household competently and have his children under control with all dignity" (1 Tim. 3:2, 4).

9. For various interpretations of what Paul meant with the phrase "husband of one wife," see Getz, *Elders and Leaders*, 164–68.

10. In my book *The Measure of a Man*, I combined these two lists to give a more comprehensive profile for measuring maturity. Gene A. Getz, *The Measure of a Man* (Grand Rapids, MI: Revell, 2016), 21.

11. Some believe that the first reference to deacons happened when the seven men were appointed to care for the widows in Jerusalem. It's true these men were to be servants to these women, the very meaning of the word *deacon*. However, the term *deacon* is not used as it is when Paul used the term in his letters to the Philippians and to Timothy. It appears that these are the first official references to this leadership role in the church. However, the seven men appointed in Jerusalem certainly illustrate the same kind of function for official deacons. It was a cultural need.

12. "Not hypocritical" comes from the Greek *dilogos*, which describes honesty and integrity in communications.

13. There were leaders emerging in the New Testament churches who used biblical truth to "pursue dishonest gain"—to manipulate people to give money that was used selfishly.

14. "Blameless" (*anegkletos*) is the same qualification Paul used for elders in his letter to Titus (Titus 1:6).

15. The basic Greek word *semnos*, translated "worthy of respect," describes an overarching quality for both men and women (1 Tim. 3:8a, 11a).

16. "Self-controlled" is the same characteristic Paul had already outlined for elders/overseers (1 Tim. 3:2).

17. Obviously "faithful in everything" applies to men as well, but for some unstated reason, Paul believed he should emphasize this character trait for women who are being considered as deacons.

18. The qualifications for deacons raise a very interesting question. Did the elders in Jerusalem during the famine appoint men and women to help them distribute the funds to people throughout Judea? This would be a special need related to a cultural situation. If they did, were they called deacons? Perhaps this happened but Luke did not feel it necessary to include it in his narrative. Regardless, the first official reference to deacons is in Paul's letter to the Philippians (Phil. 1:1).

19. Since the author of Hebrews used the generic term for *leaders* to refer to those who had an "apostolic ministry," it would be logical for him to use the same nomenclature in describing spiritual leaders in the local church. This may reflect the author's unique ability as a writer—which is clear through this letter. Greek scholars comment on his elegant use of the Greek language—which may indicate that he was concerned about maintaining consistency in language forms.

20. Principles of Leadership

1. Much of what I've included in this chapter on supracultural principles of leadership is condensed and adapted from my publication *Elders and Leaders: God's Plan for Leading the Church* (Chicago: Moody Publishers, 2003).

2. Though each set of qualities in 1 Timothy and Titus are self-contained in describing aspects of maturity, we eliminated the overlap and combined the two lists for more comprehensive criteria.

3. Selecting couples did not mean that mature single men are disqualified from serving as elders. If it did, how do we explain that both Paul and Timothy were no doubt single with even more pastoral responsibility than elders?

4. All except two qualities outlined in 1 Timothy 3 and Titus 1 are repeated for women elsewhere in the New Testament. The first is being "the husband of one wife" and the second is "managing well his household." However, these qualities are also stated for women in leadership roles—to be a "wife of one husband" and a good household manager (1 Tim. 5:9).

5. We called all of our small group leaders pastors, even though they were not elders. Their primary responsibility was to shepherd these small groups of people. Some churches use the term *pastor* only for "ordained" leaders. However, ordination as it has been traditionally practiced is a "cultural form" issue. We chose to use the term *pastor* more generally since we consider any person who is "shepherding" people as a "pastor"—which has the same meaning.

6. Since we didn't have the traditional form for church membership, we invited feedback from anyone who attended the church. This obviously included unbelievers, which is in harmony with the qualification outlined by Paul in 1 Timothy that an elder "must have a good reputation among outsiders" (1 Tim. 5:7).

7. The terms *manage* (*proistemi*) and *shepherd* (*poimaino*) are used interchangeably in the New Testament story to describe the overall responsibilities and functions of these local church leaders. (See 1 Thess. 5:12; 1 Tim. 3:4–5; Acts 20:28; 1 Peter 5:2.)

8. Some people have serious misunderstandings regarding the elder qualification to "manage his own household competently." When this requirement is misinterpreted it can lead to a standard that Paul did not have in mind. He was referring to grown children, many who may have been married and who were living in the same family compound. He was not referring to small children and youth as defined in our current culture. He made this clear in his letter to Titus when he used the Greek term *asotia*, which refers to riotous living such as characterized in the prodigal son (Titus 1:6). In context Peter used this word to summarize "debauchery, lust, drunkenness, orgies, carousing and detestable idolatry" (1 Peter 4:3–4 NIV). The most important application of this requirement in our current culture relates to a father's reputation. Grown children often live in other parts of the country. Unfortunately, some choose to depart from the faith and values of their parents even though they have been reared in God-fearing homes. Since they are not living in the same community, this does not affect the father's reputation.

9. Any group of believers who meet together regularly can be identified as a local church. This is the only specific description in the biblical story. However, the more all social units (singles, couples, and families) are involved, the more each "family of God" will "[grow] into maturity with a stature measured by Christ's fullness" (Eph. 4:13). For example, when Paul and Barnabas returned to Lystra, Iconium, and Pisidia Antioch, Luke identified these believers as churches before they had elders (Acts 14:23).

10. Within the biblical story, an elder/overseer was male. Within the churches I served as lead pastor, we maintained this requirement, believing this is a supracultural principle and a biblical ideal. However, we have respected other leaders who have concluded that the Scriptures allow for freedom in this requirement.

11. There are some evangelical leaders who interpret the concept of "headship" as meaning "source." However, as elders, we interpreted Paul's exhortation as referring to a loving servant-leader who is teachable and willing to submit to his wife when her opinions are valid and more appropriate than his. We believe that this mutually "submissive" attitude applies to any leader, including elders.

12. Unfortunately, God's ideal for marriage is often interrupted due to divorce. Furthermore, some marital partners pass away, leaving a widow or widower. We're not sure of Lydia's marital circumstances, but her conversion in Philippi demonstrates that a family can become mature in Christ in situations that are less than ideal. She obviously served as a single, godly woman in leading her family and in serving within the church.

13. For a more in-depth perspective regarding an elder's prayer responsibility, see Appendix B in Getz, *Elders and Leaders,* 331–40.

14. There are some who believe Paul was referring to elders/overseers in his reference to "pastoral leaders" in Ephesians 4:11. However, it's my opinion as described in chapter 18 that Paul was referring to those who had and were "the greater gifts" appointed by Jesus Christ and subsequently by the Holy Spirit. Paul made it clear that only "some" were divinely appointed to this role. Furthermore, he also made it clear that any believing man who "aspires to be an overseer [elder]...desires a noble work" (1 Tim. 3:1). In other words, this opportunity to serve in a "shepherding" and "teaching" role is open to any qualified individual. In addition, there is no reference to the gifts of "pastor and teacher" in the list of qualifications in 1 Timothy and Titus.

15. In our contemporary culture, the term *staff pastors* is frequently used to describe those spiritual leaders who are compensated for the time they devote to ministry. "Non-staff pastors/elders" are those who are employed in other situations but who volunteer their time to serve as ministry leaders in the church.

16. We can learn what was taking place in the biblical story by looking at what already existed toward the end of the first century and was beginning to take place in the second century. This is clear from the letters of Ignatius written at some point near the end of the first century. See chapter 26, "Leadership Lessons from Church History."

17. In the first two churches where I served as lead pastor, a lay elder was board chairman. However, this led to what we felt were unnecessary meetings between me and the board chairman. Furthermore, in our meetings, the lay chairman looked to me throughout the meetings to report on everyday operations in the church. Consequently, as elders we decided it would be more efficient if I simply led the meetings. However, with this arrangement I found it very important to involve the elders in all discussions and in making decisions and, as Peter exhorted, "not lording it over those entrusted" to me (1 Peter 5:3).

18. One of the unfortunate distortions in elder led churches relates to how the elders view the lead pastor. Unfortunately, his responsibility is defined as the elder who exclusively teaches and preaches. In these cases, the board is usually chaired by a lay leader who also assumes responsibility to be the primary leader

in the church. As a result, the staff pastor often has virtually no authority to guide the elders or the church. This frequently creates serious leadership dysfunction and intense discouragement for the lead pastor.

19. See chapter 6 for the way New Testament authors instructed local churches to model Christlike behavior in their communities.

21. Biblical Examples of Administration and Organization

1. It is interesting to note the references to numbers in the first part of the book of Acts. The church was launched with approximately 120 (Acts 1:15); in 2:41 about 3,000 were added to the original 100: in 4:4 we are told that "the number of men came to about 5,000." Some believe that the mention of "men" refers to 5,000 households. If so, the number of disciples would have been five to ten times this number, or maybe more, at the time the events in Acts 6 took place.

2. We're not told how many Grecians were involved in selecting these seven men. It certainly didn't involve all those who had become believers. They were scattered throughout Jerusalem and were meeting in homes. It would have been virtually impossible to have a traditional "congregational meeting." From a pragmatic perspective, those who came to the apostles with their complaints were representatives, probably those whose widows were being neglected. However, the observation still stands. Those affected by this problem helped in a direct way to solve it.

3. Here the term *church* no doubt refers to the assembled believers who were gathered, perhaps in Mary's home. It was certainly not possible to have a congregational meeting that involved the total church in Jerusalem.

22. Principles of Administration and Organization

1. Peter F. Drucker, *The Effective Executive*, (New York: Harper & Row, 1967), 71.
2. Schaeffer, *The Church at the End of the 20th Century*, 67.

23. Models of Communication

1. Darrell L. Bock and Benjamin I. Simpson, *Jesus According to Scripture: Restoring the Portrait from the Gospels* (Grand Rapids, MI: Baker Academic), xx.

2. A.T. Robertson's *A Harmony of the Gospels* was used to determine these 184 communication situations. This specific analysis began with "Christ's Public Ministry," Part VI, p. 19. It was terminated at Part XIII, p. 205, titled, "The Arrest, Trial, Crucifixion, and Burial of Jesus." Before Jesus' public ministry there are no references to specific communication situations, and following His arrest the references are very limited. Obviously, I've made certain judgments as to what were "specific" communication situations. Furthermore, I've excluded general references from this list, such as—"Jesus continued going around to all the towns and villages, teaching in their synagogues, preaching the good news of the kingdom, and healing every disease and every sickness" (Matt. 9:35; see also Mark 16:20).

3. Since gospel writers were obviously selective in the events that were recorded, we can assume that what is recorded represents Jesus' overall ministry during

the three plus years of His ministry to individuals and groups. Consequently, His ministry to individuals and groups can be multiplied substantially.

4. Though there is no specific reference to Paul performing miracles in Thessalonica to verify the message of the gospel, it appears this happened when he referenced "the power of the Holy Spirit." This reference correlates with Paul's ministry in Ephesus when he performed "extraordinary miracles" (Acts 19:11) and with his reference to the Holy Spirit and miracles in his letter to the Galatians (3:5). It also correlates with what happened in Iconium where the Lord enabled both Paul and Barnabas "to do signs and wonders" (Acts 14:3). The same thing happened in Lystra when Paul healed a man lame from birth (Acts 14:8-10). Also note Paul's ministry in Corinth. While there he performed "signs and wonders and miracles" (2 Cor. 12:12). He also referenced that his message was verified by "the Spirit's power" (1 Cor. 2:4).

24. Principles of Communication

1. Jeff Jones, Mike Hogan, and Dwight Jewson, *Rebranding Christianity: When the World's Most Important Brand Loses Its Way* (Austin, TX: Fedd Books, 2023).

2. Gene A. Getz, *The Measure of a Man* (Grand Rapids, MI: Revell, 1974).

3. My wife Elaine and I had the opportunity to do a Bible study with our elders' wives based on the qualities Paul outlined in Titus 2:3–5. We then published the results of this study as *The Measure of a Woman* (Grand Rapids, MI: Revell, 2004).

4. It may appear that there are two prayers in Ephesians. However, if you follow the grammatical development in this letter, I'm confident you'll conclude, as I have, that these two prayer segments in chapters 1 and 3 form one powerful and exemplary prayer.

5. My interest in creative communication happened early in my ministry career at Moody Bible Institute. I was asked to teach a course in audiovisual methods in the church. Challenged by the opportunity, I wrote my own textbook, the first in that field—also published by Moody. In terms of communication, this experience impacted the rest of my ministry life. I had the great privilege of helping develop the media centers at both Moody Bible Institute and Dallas Theological Seminary and authoring the first multi-media study Bible, *Life Essentials Study Bible*. I'm indeed thankful for these creative opportunities.

25. Lessons from the Seven Churches of Asia

1. When Jesus said to the church in Thyatira, "Unless they repent of her works, I will strike her children dead," this may be more literal than figurative. For example, some believers in Corinth were so carnal and sinful that they turned the *agape* meal into a time to be gluttonous and intoxicated. They had allowed elements of the idolatrous meals in the pagan temples to become a part of this sacred meal designed to remember the body and shed blood of Christ. Consequently, Paul wrote: "For at the meal, each one eats his own supper. So one person is hungry while another gets drunk!" (1 Cor. 11:21). Paul went on to explain the true meaning of the Lord's Supper and then shared these startling

words: "For whoever eats and drinks without recognizing the body [of Christ], eats and drinks judgment on himself. This is why many are sick and ill among you, and many have fallen asleep" (1 Cor. 11:29–30).

This is an unusual and extreme case of sinful and pagan behavior among some believers. But it illustrates the reason for Jesus' stern words to those in the church in Thyatira who were engaging in "sexual immorality" and eating "meat sacrificed to idols" (Rev. 2:20, 22b, 33a).

26. Leadership Lessons from Church History

1. Jon Payne, "Why Study Church History?" Ligonier.org, November 3, 2022, https://www.ligonier.org/learn/articles/why-study-church-history.
2. Andrew Davis, "Why Study Church History?" *Two Journeys*, September 29, 2020, https://twojourneys.org/articles/detail/1887579/why-study-church-history/.
3. For a quick, succinct, and helpful overview of the church through the ages, see John D. Hannah, *The Kregel Pictorial Guide to Church History*, vols. 1–6 (Grand Rapids, MI: Kregel, 2001).
4. "The Didache," Early Christian Writings, accessed June 4, 2024, https://early christianwritings.com/text/didache-roberts.html.
5. Ibid.
6. "The First Epistle of Clement to the Corinthians," in *The Ante-Nicene Fathers*, eds. A. Cleveland Coxe, James Donaldson, and Alexander Roberts (Peabody, MA: Hendrickson, 1994), 1:16.
7. Ibid., 1:17.
8. Ibid., 1:18. This quotation also indicates that the Corinthian church greatly matured spiritually following Paul's letters. Clement mentioned that these believers had become "steadfast" in the faith.
9. Ibid., Ignatius of Antioch.
10. Ignatius of Antioch, *Epistles of Ignatius,* trans. William Wake, (Sharp Ink Publishing, 2023), ebook.
11. Ibid., *The Epistle to the Magnesians*, Chapter I, 5.
12. Ibid., *The Epistle to the Smyrneans*, Chapter III, 7.
13. For a more detailed analysis on how Ignatius and his letters contributed to an unfortunate hierarchical structure, see G. W. Hansen, "Authority," in *Dictionary of the Later New Testament and Its Developments*, ed. Ralph P. Martin and Peter H. Davids (Downers Grove, IL: InterVarsity, 1997), 109–10.
14. John D. Hannah, *The Kregel Pictorial Guide to Church History, vol. 2, The Early Church, AD 33–500* (Grand Rapids, MI: Kregel, 2005), 25.
15. Ibid. Hannah adds this rather shocking quip from Augustine—"There's a great difference between an apostle and a drunkard; but there's no difference at all between a Christian baptism performed by a drunkard . . . There's no difference between a Christian baptism performed by an apostle than that performed by a heretic." Hannah then added this further explanation regarding Augustine's thinking: "The church, being a repository of grace from God, is the means of the distribution of grace to people. The church is the redeeming

community, and there is no salvation outside of it. A heretic or immoral person in the church authentically conveys grace through his official functions."

16. Recommended books: Thabiti M. Anyabwile, *Finding Faithful Elders and Deacons* (Wheaton, IL: Crossway, 2012); Greg Scharf and Arthur Kok, *The New Elder's Handbook* (Grand Rapids, MI: Baker Books, 2018); Benjamin L. Merkle, *Why Elders? A Biblical and Practical Guide for Church Members* (Grand Rapids, MI: Kregel 2009); Jeramie Rinne, *Church Elders* (Wheaton, IL: Crossway, 2014).

27. Forms and Institutionalism

1. Robert A. Nisbet, *Social Change and History* (New York: Oxford University Press, 1969), 270.
2. Ibid.
3. Ibid., 282.
4. Gardner, "Prevent Organizational Dry Rot," 20.

28. Lessons from My Personal History

1. For an excellent study on eldership in the New Testament, see Benjamin L. Merkle, *Why Elders? A Biblical and Practical Guide for Church Members* (Grand Rapids, MI: Kregel Academic, 2009). It's interesting that the author makes church membership a biblical absolute in terms of final accountability. He supports this conclusion with some biblical examples (Matt. 18:17; Acts 1:23; 6:2–3; 13:3; 14:27; 15:22). However, it's my opinion that he superimposes on Scripture a concept that is difficult to substantiate. As I've said, however, I do believe the Scriptures allow freedom to develop a plan for some form of church membership that has practical benefits.

Section 4: The Lens of Culture

1. Peters, *Saturation Evangelism*, 193.

29. A Culture in Turmoil

1. Matthew D. Kim and Paul A. Hoffman, *Preaching to a Divided Nation* (Grand Rapids, MI: Baker Academic, 2022), 1.
2. Michael Graham, "The Six Way Fracturing of Evangelicalism," MereOrthodoxy .org, June 7, 2021, https://mereorthodoxy.com/six-way-fracturing-evangelicalism.
3. Jim Davis, Michael Graham, and Ryan P. Burge, *The Great Dechurching* (Grand Rapids, MI: Zondervan, 2023), 3.
4. For Keller's comprehensive analysis of the current state of both the American culture and the church in America, and how we've arrived at this moment, see Tim Keller, "The Decline and Renewal of the American Church" (Extended Version), aggregation of four articles originally published in *Life in the Gospel* (2021–2022).
5. Ibid., 38.
6. Ibid., 39.
7. Ibid., 44.

8. Jones, Hogan, and Jewson, *Rebranding Christianity*, 60.

9. This report is available as a download at GreatOpportunity.org.

10. Keller, "Decline and Renewal," 48.

30. The Sexual Revolution

1. Keller, "Decline and Renewal," 13.

2. Mark Galli, "Six Things to Do After the Supreme Court Decision on Gay Marriage," *Christianity Today*, June 26, 2015, https://www.christianitytoday.com/ct/2015/june-web-only/6-things-to-do-after-supreme-court-gay-marriage-decision.html.

3. Bekah Mason, "Finding My 'True Self' as a Same-Sex Attracted Woman," *Christianity Today*, June 23, 2017, https://www.christianitytoday.com/ct/2017/june-web-only/finding-my-true-self-as-same-sex-attracted-woman-obergefell.html.

4. Ibid.

5. Preston Sprinkle, *People to Be Loved: Why Homosexuality Is Not Just an Issue* (Grand Rapids, MI: Zondervan, 2015).

6. Ibid., see table of contents.

7. Ibid., 20.

8. Ibid., 46.

9. Ibid., 47.

10. Ibid., 52.

11. Ibid.

12. For a more in-depth look at the causes for same-sex attraction, see Preston Sprinkle, *Embodied: Transgender Identities, the Church, and What the Bible Has to Say* (Colorado Springs, CO: David C. Cook, 2021).

13. Bruce B. Miller, *Leading a Church in a Time of Sexual Questioning: Grace-Filled Wisdom for Day-to-Day Ministry* (Nashville, TN: Thomas Nelson, 2019).

14. Ibid.

15. Galli, "Six Things to Do."

31. Racism, Favoritism, and Prejudice

1. For a more in-depth look at Dr. Tony Evans's Kingdom Race Theology, see the expanded volume *Oneness Embraced: A Kingdom Race Theology for Reconciliation, Unity, and Justice* (Chicago: Moody Publishers, 2022).

2. Tony Evans, *Kingdom Race Theology: God's Answer to Our Racial Crisis* (Chicago: Moody Publishers, 2022), 42–43, emphasis added.

3. Ibid., 14–19.

4. Ibid., 23.

5. Ibid., 90–98.

6. J. D. Greear, "Race and the Great Commission" in *Ministers of Reconciliation: Preaching on Race and the Gospel*, ed. Daniel Darling (Bellingham, WA: Lexham Press, 2021), 28.

Bibliography

Allison, Gregg R. *The Church: An Introduction*. Wheaton, IL: Crossway, 2021.

Avila, Charlie. *The Biblical Qualifications of Church Elders*. Fresno, CA: Clovis Christian Center, 2023.

Beasley-Murray, G. R. *Baptism in the New Testament*. Grand Rapids, MI: Eerdmans, 1973.

Bloesch, Donald G. *The Church: Sacraments, Worship, Ministry, Mission*. Westmont, IL: InterVarsity Press, 2005.

Bock, Darrell L. and Benjamin I. Simpson. *Jesus According to Scripture: Restoring the Portrait from the Gospels*. Grand Rapids, MI: Baker Academic, 2017.

Boer, Harry. *Pentecost in Missions*. Grand Rapids, MI: Eerdmans, 1961.

Bonhoeffer, Dietrich. *Life Together: The Classic Exploration of Christian Community*. San Francisco: HarperOne, 1978.

Bruggerman, Walter. *In Essentials Unity: Reflections on the Nature and Purpose of the Church*. Burnsville, MN: Kirk House, 2001.

Byrskog, Samuel. *Institutions of the Emerging Church*. Edinburgh, Scotland: T&T Clark, 2016.

Clowney, Edmund P. *The Church*. Westmont, IL: InterVarsity Press, 1995.

Connor, Kevin. *The Church in the New Testament*. Portland, OR: City Christian Publishing, 1998.

Cross, Terry L. *The People of God's Presence: An Introduction to Ecclesiology*. Grand Rapids, IL: Baker, 2019.

Darling, Daniel, ed. *Ministers of Reconciliation: Preaching on Race and the Gospel*. Bellingham, WA: Lexham Press, 2021.

Davis, Jim and Michael Graham. *The Great Dechurching*. Grand Rapids, MI: Zondervan, 2023.

Dever, Mark. *Discipling: How to Help Others Follow Jesus*. Wheaton, IL: Crossway, 2016.

_____. *The Church: The Gospel Made Visible*. Nashville, TN: B&H, 2012.

_____. *Twelve Challenges Churches Face*. Wheaton, IL: Crossway, 2008.

Dever, Mark et al. *Theology for the Church*. Nashville, TN: B&H Academic, 2014.

Dockery, David S. *Theology, Church, and Ministry: A Handbook for Theological Education*. Nashville, TN: B&H Academic, 2017.

Drucker, Peter F. *The Effective Executive*. New York: HarperCollins, 2006.

Elavatta, Abraham. *Why Die Before Your Time? God's Story in the Life of E.A. Abraham*. Kollam, India: Krithi Books, 2010.

Evans, Tony. *Oneness Embraced*. Chicago: Moody Publishers, 2022.

_____. *Kingdom Race Theology*. Chicago: Moody Publishers, 2022.

Ferreira, Johan. *Johannine Ecclesiology*. London, England: A&C Black, 1998.

Fitch, David E. *The Church of Us v. Them*. Grand Rapids, MI: Brazos Press, 2019.

Gaebelein, Frank E. et al. *The Expositors Bible Commentary*. Vol. 10, *Romans through Galatians*. Grand Rapids, MI: Zondervan, 1977.

Galli, Mark. "Six Things to Do After the Supreme Court Decision on Gay Marriage." *Christianity Today*. June 26, 2015.

Gardner, John W. "How to Prevent Organizational Dry Rot." *Harper's Magazine,* 1965.

Geisler, Norman L. *Systematic Theology*. Vol. 4, *Church/Last Things*. Bloomington, MN: Bethany House, 2005.

Getz, Gene A. *A Biblical Theology of Material Possessions*. Chicago: Moody Publishers, 1990.

_____. *Elders and Leaders: God's Plan for Leading the Church*. Chicago: Moody Publishers, 2003.

_____. *Rich in Every Way*. West Monroe, LA: Howard, 2004.

_____. *The Measure of a Man: Twenty Attributes of a Godly Man*. Grand Rapids, MI: Revell. 2016.

_____. *CSB Life Essentials Study Bible*. David K. Stabnow, ed. Nashville, TN: Holman, 2020.

Graham, Michael. "The Six Way Fracturing of Evangelicalism." *Mere Orthodoxy*. July 7, 2021.

Green, Christopher C. *The Message of the Church*. Westmont, IL: InterVarsity Press, 2014.

Grenz, Stanley J. *Renewing the Center: Evangelical Theology in a Post-Theological Era*. Grand Rapids, MI: Baker Academic, 2000.

_____. *Theology of the Community of God*. Grand Rapids, MI: Eerdmans, 2000.

Grudem, Wayne, et al. *Are Miraculous Gifts for Today? 4 Views*. Grand Rapids, MI: Zondervan Academic, 1996.

Hall, Darrell E. *Speaking Across Generations*. Westmont, IL: InterVarsity Press, 2022.

Hammet, John. *Biblical Foundations for Baptist Churches: A Contemporary Ecclesiology*. 2nd ed. Grand Rapids, MI: Kregel Academic, 2019.

Harris, Rev. Frank Henry. *Jesus' Method of Training the 12 Disciples*. Independently Published, 2018.

Horton, Michael S. *People and Place: A Covenant Ecclesiology*. Louisville, KY: Westminster John Knox Press, 2008.

Hull, Bill. *Jesus Christ, Disciplemaker*. Grand Rapids, MI: Baker Books, 2004.

Humphey, Edith M. "One Marriage Was Designed for Male and Female." *Christianity Today*. September 1, 2004.

Ignatius of Antioch, William Wake, trans. *Epistles of St. Ignatius: Seven Letters: Ephesians, Magnesians, Trallians, Romans, Philadelphians, Smyrnaneans & Polycarp*. DigiCat, ebook.

Jethani, Skye. *What If Jesus Was Serious about the Church? A Visual Guide to Becoming the Community Jesus Intended*. Chicago: Moody Publishers, 2022.

Jones, Jeff, Mike Hogan, and Dwight Jewson. *Rebranding Christianity: When the World's Most Important Brand Loses Its Way*. Austin, TX: The Fedd Agency, 2023.

Keller, Tim. "The Decline and Renewal of the American Church." *Gospel in Life*. New York, NY, 2022.

Kim, Matthew D. and Paul A. Hoffman. *Preaching to a Divided Nation*. Grand Rapids, MI: Baker Academic, 2022.

Kreider, Larry, Ron Myer, Steve Prokopchak, and Brian Sauder. *The Biblical Role of Elders for Today's Church*. Lititz, PA: DOVE International, 2003.

Leeman, Jonathan. *One Assembly: Rethinking the Multisite and Multiservice Church Models*. Wheaton, IL: Crossway, 2020.

_____. *Understanding the Congregation's Authority*. Nashville, TN: B&H Books, 2016.

Longenecker, Richard N., ed., and Howard Marshall. *Community Formation: In the Early Church and in the Church Today*. Carol Stream, IL: Hendrickson, 2002.

Loritts, Bryan. *Insider Outsider: My Journey as a Stranger in White Evangelicalism and My Hope for Us All*. Grand Rapids, MI: Zondervan, 2018.

Mason, Bekah. "Finding My 'True Self' as a Same-Sex Attracted Woman." *Christianity Today*. June 23, 2017.

Merkle, Benjamin L. *40 Questions About Elders and Deacons*. Grand Rapids, MI: Kregel, 2008.

Miller, Bruce B. *Leading a Church in a Time of Sexual Questioning*. Nashville, TN: Thomas Nelson, 2019.

Minear, Paul S. *Images of the Church in the New Testament*. Louisville, KY: Westminster John Knox Press, 2004.

Moore, Russell D. *Losing Our Religion: An Altar Call for Evangelical America*. New York: Sentinel, 2023.

Oakes, Peter. *Philippians: From People to Letter*. Cambridge University Press, 2001.

Ortlund, Raymond C. *The Gospel: How the Church Portrays the Beauty of Christ*. Wheaton, IL: Crossway, 2014.

Owles, R. Joseph. *The Didache: The Teaching of the Twelve Apostles*. Scotts Valley, CA: CreateSpace Independent Publishing Platform, 2014.

Peters, George W. *A Biblical Theology of Missions*. Chicago: Moody Publishers, 1984.

_____. *A Theology of Church Growth*. Grand Rapids, MI: Zondervan, 1981.

_____. *Saturation Evangelism*. Grand Rapids, MI: Zondervan, 1970.

Rinne, Jeramie. *Church Elders*. Wheaton, IL: Crossway, 2014.

Roberts, Alexander, trans., James Donaldson, ed. *Early Christian Writings: Apostolic Fathers and Related Texts*. Bengal Press, 2022.

Robertson, A.T. *A Harmony of the Gospels*. New York: HarperCollins, 1950.

Sayers, Mark. *A Non-Anxious Presence: How a Changing and Complex World will Create a Remnant of Renewed Christian Leaders*. Chicago: Moody Publishers, 2022.

_____. *Disappearing Church*. Chicago: Moody Publishers, 2016.

_____. *Reappearing Church*. Chicago: Moody Publishers, 2019.

Schaeffer, Francis A. *The Church Before the Watching World: A Practical Ecclesiology*. Westmont, IL: InterVarsity Press, 1971.

_____. *The Church at the End of the 20th Century*. Westmont, IL: InterVarsity Press, 1970.

Sempangi, F. Kefa and Barbara R. Thompson. *A Distant Grief.* Glendale, CA: Regal Books, 1979.

Simson, Wolfgang and George Barna. *The House Church Book: Rediscovering the Dynamic, Organic, Relational, Viral Community Jesus Started.* Carol Stream, IL: BarnaBooks, 2009.

Smethurst, Matt. *Deacons: How They Serve and Strengthen the Church.* Wheaton, IL: Crossway, 2021.

Sprinkle, Preston. *Does the Bible Support Same-Sex Marriage? 21 Conversations from a Historically Christian View*, Colorado Springs, CO: David C. Cook, 2023.

_____. *Embodied: Transgender Identities, the Church, and What the Bible Has to Say.* Colorado Springs, CO: David C. Cook, 2021.

Sproul, R. C. *Why Should I Join a Church?* Sanford, FL: Ligonier Ministries, 2019.

Strauch, Alexander. *Biblical Eldership.* Littleton, CO: Lewis & Roth, 1995.

Suderman, Robert J. *Re-Imagining the Church: Implications of Being a People in the World.* Eugene, OR: Wipf & Stock, 2016.

Tenney, Merrill C. *John: The Gospel of Belief.* Rev. ed. Grand Rapids, MI: Eerdmans, 1976.

_____. *New Testament Survey,* Grand Rapids, MI: Eerdmans, 1961.

Thompson, James W. *The Church According to Paul: Rediscovering the Community Conformed to Christ.* Grand Rapids, MI: Baker Academic, 2014.

Thorn, John. *The Life of the Church: The Table, Pulpit, and Square.* Chicago: Moody Publishers, 2017.

Tisby, Jemar. *How to Fight Racism.* Grand Rapids, MI: Zondervan, 2021.

Viola, Frank. *Pagan Christianity: Exploring the Roots of our Church Practices.* Carol Stream, IL: Tyndale, 2008.

Webster, John. "On Evangelical Ecclesiology" in *Confessing God: Essays in Christian Dogmatics II.* London, England: T&T Clark International, 2005.

Wretlind, Norm, Becky Wretlind, and Jim Killam. *When God Is the Life of the Party: Reaching Neighbors through Creative Hospitality.* Carol Stream, IL: NavPress, 2003.

Wright, N.T. *Surprised by Hope: Rethinking Heaven, the Resurrection, and the Mission of the Church.* San Francisco, CA: HarperOne, 2012.

Yarhouse, Mark and Julia Sadusky. *Emerging Gender Identities.* Grand Rapids, MI: Brazos Press, 2020.

Subject Index

A

abortion, 421–425
above reproach, 267
Abraham, 65, 92
Abraham, E. A., 107–108
abuse, 461–462nn4–5
accountability, 258–259, 293–295, 397–401
Adam, 91, 376, 417
addiction, 426
adelphoi (brothers), 54–55, 460nn2–3, 469n4
administration
  of apostles and elders in Jerusalem, 308–310
  appropriate constituency in, 319–321
  biblical examples of, 311–312, 313–314, 315, 319–320
  comparative study regarding, 301–304
  contemporary situations regarding, 312, 314, 315–316, 320–321
  creative resolutions in, 321
  delegation in, 316–317
  divine and human factors in, 317–319
  facing reality in, 311–313
  gaining perspective regarding, 313–314
  of Nehemiah, 304–308
  principles of, 311–324
  prioritizing in, 315–316
  problem solving in, 303
  survey regarding, 454–455
  unsolvable problems regarding, 313
admonishing, 208–209
adultery, 425
affection, 210–211
affective movement, 385
Agabus, 248, 257
agape, defined, 200
agape meal, 150–151, 165–167, 390–393. See also Lord's Supper
Agrippa (King), 117, 410
America, culture and Christianity in, 413
Amin, Idi, 237–238
Amsterdam 2000, 107–108
Ananias, 73

Andrew, 365
announcing, in making disciples (evangelism) command, 68
Antioch. See also Pisidia Antioch
  believers in, 115–116
  church growth in, 228
  church in, 74
  elders in, 257
  equipping disciples (edification) command in, 139–141
  evangelizing in, 64
  Ignatius in, 367–369
Apollos, 251
apostles. See also specific persons
  administration of, in Jerusalem, 308–310, 319
  baptism of, 117–118, 463n4
  commissioning of, 47, 49–50
  communication of, 66, 325, 342
  favor to, 157–158
  Jesus' commissioning of, 47
  Jesus' communication with, 327–328
  Luke's focus on, 247
  ministry of, 93, 247
  overview of, 245–248
  primary, 246
  secondary, 246
  teachings of, 148–149
Aquila, 87, 95–96
Archippus, 253
Aristarchus, 253
Aristobulus, 87
Artaxerxes, 318
Artemis, 252
Asyncritus, 87
Athens, 70–71, 116
Augustine, 373–374, 475–476n15
automotive industry, 376

B

baptism/baptizing command
  in Acts, 119–124
  apostles and, 117–118, 463n4
  biblical directive for, 129–131

You finished reading!

Did this book help you in some way? If so, please consider writing an honest review wherever you purchase your books. Your review gets this book into the hands of more readers and helps us continue to create biblically faithful resources.

Moody Publishers books help fund the training of students for ministry around the world.

The **Moody Bible Institute** is one of the most well-known Christian institutions in the world, training thousands of young people to faithfully serve Christ wherever He calls them. And when you buy and read a book from Moody Publishers, you're helping make that vital ministry training possible.

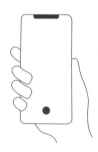

Continue to dive into the Word, *anytime, anywhere.*

Find what you need to take your next step in your walk with Christ: from uplifting music to sound preaching, our programs are designed to help you right when you need it.

Download the **Moody Radio App** and start listening today!